Java™

By

EXAMPLE

que®

Clayton Walnum

Java By Example

Copyright© 1996 by Que® Corporation

Library of Congress Catalog No.: 96-68581

ISBN: 0-7897-0814-0

98   97   96   6   5   4   3   2   1

Interpretation of the printing code: the rightmost double-digit number is the year of the book's printing; the rightmost single-digit number, the number of the book's printing. For example, a printing code of 96-1 shows that the first printing of the book occurred in 1996.

President and Publisher: *Roland Elgey*

Associate Publisher: *Joseph B. Wikert*

Director of Marketing: *Lynn E. Zingraf*

Editorial Services Director
Elizabeth Keaffaber

Managing Editor
Sandy Doell

Title Manager
Bryan Gambrel

Acquisitions Editor
Fred Stone

Product Director
Ben Milstead

Production Editor
Mitzi Foster Gianakos

Editors
Anne Owen
Joe Williams

Assistant Product Marketing Manager
Kim Margolius

Technical Editors
David Medinets

Acquisitions Coordinator
Jane Brownlow

Operations Coordinator
Patty Brooks

Editorial Assistant
Andrea Duvall

Book Designer
Kim Scott

Cover Designer
Ruth Harvey

Production Team
Steve Adams
Marcia Brizendine
Jason Carr
Jenny Earhart
Joan Evan
Jessica Ford
Trey Frank
Amy Gornik
Jason Hand
Daniel Harris
Damon Jordan
Daryl Kessler
Clint Lahnen
Bob LaRoche
Kaylene Riemen
Laura Robbins
Bobbi Satterfield
Kelly Warner
Jeff Yesh
Jody York

Indexer
John Hulse

Composed in *Palatino* and *MCPdigital* by Que Corporation.
Screen reproductions in this book were created using Collage Plus from Inner Media, Inc., Hollis, NH.

Dedication

To my brothers, Arthur, Jared, and Glenn.

About the Author

Clayton Walnum, who has a degree in computer science, has been writing about computers for almost 15 years and has published hundreds of articles in major computer publications. He is also the author of over 25 books, which cover such diverse topics as programming, computer gaming, and application programs. His most recent book is *Windows 95 Game SDK Strategy Guide*, also published by Que. His other titles include the award-winning *Building Windows 95 Applications with Visual Basic* (Que), *3-D Graphics Programming with OpenGL* (Que), *Borland C++ 4.x Tips, Tricks, and Traps* (Que), *Turbo C++ for Rookies* (Que), *Dungeons of Discovery* (Que), *PC Picasso: A Child's Computer Drawing Kit* (Sams), *Powermonger: The Official Strategy Guide* (Prima), *DataMania: A Child's Computer Organizer* (Alpha Kids), *Adventures in Artificial Life* (Que), and *C-manship Complete* (Taylor Ridge Books). Mr. Walnum lives in Connecticut with his wife Lynn and their four children, Christopher, Justin, Stephen, and Caitlynn.

Acknowledgments

I would like to thank the following people for their contribution to this book: Joe Wikert for his confidence in my writing; Fred Slone for keeping everything running smoothly; Mitzi Gianakos, Anne Owen, and Joe Williams for keeping my abuse of the English language to a minimum; David Medinets for checking the facts; and all the other fine folks at Que. And, as always, thanks to my family—Lynn, Christopher, Justin, Stephen, and Caitlynn.

We'd Like to Hear from You!

As part of our continuing effort to produce books of the highest possible quality, Que would like to hear your comments. To stay competitive, we *really* want you, as a computer book reader and user, to let us know what you like or dislike most about this book or other Que products.

You can mail comments, ideas, or suggestions for improving future editions to the address below, or send us a fax at (317) 581-4663. Our staff and authors are available for questions and comments through our Internet site at `http://www.mcp.com/que`, and Macmillan Computer Publishing also has a forum on CompuServe (type **GO QUEBOOKS** at any prompt).

In addition to exploring our forum, please feel free to contact me personally to discuss your opinions of this book: I'm **bmilstead@que.mcp.com** on the Internet, and **102121,1324** on CompuServe.

Thanks in advance—your comments will help us to continue publishing the best books available on computer topics in today's market.

Ben Milstead
Product Director
Que Corporation
201 W. 103rd Street
Indianapolis, Indiana 46290
USA

Overview

Contents

Contents

Contents

Contents

Part III: Putting Java to Work

Contents

Contents

Contents

Contents

Part VI: Appendixes

A Answers to Review Questions   487

Introduction

The Internet is growing by leaps and bounds. It won't be too long before you'll be able to contact just about anyone online, not only your friends and acquaintances, but also every major company in the country. This incredible growth is the pathway to opportunity. Everybody who's anybody in the world of telecommunications is looking for ways to enhance the Internet's online experience. One company that has scored a big hit on the Internet is Sun Microsystems, who recently released an unusual programming language called *Java*. Once people got their hands on Java, the Internet was guaranteed to never be the same again.

What's so special about Java? Java enables programmers to create something called *applets*. Applets are special computer programs that can be included as an element of a Web page. When the user views a Web page containing one of these applets, the machine he's connected to automatically sends the applet to the user and the user's own Java-compatible browser runs the applet. Because applets are transferred in a non-machine-specific form, they can run on any machine that has a Java interpreter.

Using Java, you can do everything from adding simple animation to your Web pages to writing sophisticated computer programs that your Web page's users can use online. Applets that have already been released include games, spreadsheets, graphing programs, animation controllers, simulators, and much, much more. Java is so intriguing and so successful that even major players in the industry, including Netscape and Microsoft, have jumped aboard, providing Java-compatible software for the Internet.

In this book, you'll learn not only how Java applets work on the Internet, but also how to include Java applets in your Web pages. More importantly, you'll learn step-by-step how to write your own applets. You can write these applets for your own personal use, or write them for general release on the Internet. Imagine the thrill of seeing one of your own Java creations being used on Web pages all over the world!

Who This Book Is For

This book is the perfect starting point for anyone wanting to learn from scratch about Java. Although it's helpful to have previous programming experience (especially with C or C++), this book includes a complete tutorial on the Java language and how to build applets with it. The Java tools, such as the compiler and interpreter, that you'll need to create your own applets are described in detail. Moreover, you'll learn the Java language starting from the very basics and working your way toward writing full-featured applets and applications.

Although this book is suitable for programming novices, more experienced programmers will find a great deal of interest here, as well. If you're already familiar with languages such as C and C++, you'll be able to skim over the Java language introduction and dive right into the business of creating applets. Although the Java language is very much like C++, the way it's used is unique. Up until Java, you've never seen anything quite like applets.

To summarize, this book is for both novice and intermediate programmers. Novice programmers will get a gentle introduction to the Java language, whereas more experienced programmers can concentrate on getting the most from the language by quickly learning how to build powerful applets for the Internet. Even expert programmers may find this book to be a useful introduction to the world of Java.

Hardware and Software Requirements

The Java language is currently supported on Windows 95, Windows NT, Sun Solaris, Macintosh, and UNIX machines. Most of this book's content is applicable to any type of computer that can run the Java Developers Kit. However, because Windows 95 will undoubtedly be the operating system under which the greatest majority of Java applets are created, the programs and examples in this book were written for the Windows 95 version of Java. Still, as long as you're familiar with your computer's operating system, you should have little difficulty following the examples in this book no matter what machine you use.

The minimum system requirements for Windows 95 or NT users are as follows:

♦ An IBM-compatible 80486 with at least 8M of memory

♦ Windows 95 or Windows NT

♦ A hard drive

♦ A CD-ROM drive

♦ A Microsoft-compatible mouse

♦ 256-color graphics

♦ A Windows-compatible sound card*

* If you don't care about hearing sound files with Java's applets, you don't need a sound card.

The CD-ROM included with this book runs on Windows machines and includes the Windows versions of the Java Developers Kit and the HotJava Web browser. Users of other systems can get a copy of the Java Developers Kit for their machine from Sun Microsystems' Web site at `http://www.sun.com`.

Compiling the Programs in This Book

As you work through the examples in this book, you'll learn to install the Java Developers Kit and to compile the example programs that are presented in each chapter. In general, though, you can compile the programs in this book by following the procedures given here.

First, you must have the Java Development Kit installed on your system, using the default root directory of `C:\JAVA`. It would also be useful to have a copy of Netscape Navigator 2.0 installed. You can get a copy of this Java-compatible browser from Netscape's Web site at `http://www.netscape.com`.

After installing the Java Development Kit, you must include the kit's path in your system's PATH statement. To do this, load your system files with SYSEDIT.EXE (you can find SYSEDIT.EXE in your WINDOWS\SYSTEM directory). When you start SYSEDIT, go to the AUTOEXEC.BAT window and find the PATH statement. At the end of the PATH statement, add a semicolon followed by the path C:\JAVA\BIN. Then, save the changes and restart your machine so the changes take effect. Adding the path to your PATH statement ensures that the system can find Java's tools.

Finally, you should create a directory called C:\CLASSES in which you will place the Java files you create throughout this book. To compile and run an applet's Java source-code file, follow these steps:

1. Select the Start/Programs/MS-DOS Prompt command from the Start menu. A DOS window appears.

2. Change to the C:\CLASSES directory by typing `cd c:\classes` at the DOS prompt.

3. Type `javac filename.java`, where `filename.java` is the name of the Java source-code file you want to compile. After compilation is complete, you should have a file called filename.class in the directory, where `filename` is the same program name you used for the `.java` source-code file. The `.class` file is the compiled Java program.

4. Create an HTML document containing the `<applet>` tag for the applet you want to run (see the following example). Save this HTML document in the C:\CLASSES directory.

5. To run the applet, type `appletviewer filename.html`, where `filename.html` is the name of the HTML document containing your applet's `<applet>` tag.

You can usually use the same HTML document for each applet just by changing the name of the applet in the document. Here is an example of a simple HTML document that will load and run an applet:

```
<applet
    code="filename.class"
    width=250
    height=250>
</applet>
```

In this HTML document, `filename.class` is the name of the compiled applet you want to run. Just change this file name for a new applet, and you're ready to go. You can also set the size of the applet when it runs by changing the values following the `width` and `height` parameters.

Running a Java stand-alone application is a little different. To compile the application, follow steps 1 through 3 above. To run the application type the command `java filename`, where `filename` is the name of the compiled Java application minus the `.class` file extension. This command line invokes the Java interpreter rather than the Appletviewer application.

A Word to the Wise

As every programmer knows, a good program is virtually crash-proof. Error checking must be done for every action that may fail, and appropriate error messages must be given to the user. Unfortunately, good error checking requires a lot of extra program code. For the programmer working on his next magnum opus, this is all just part of the game. But for an author writing a programming book, this extra code has different implications.

A programming book should present its topics in as clear a manner as possible. This means featuring programs whose source code is not obscured by a lot of details that don't apply directly to the topic at hand. For this reason, the programs in this book do not always employ proper error checking. For example, user input often goes unverified and dynamic construction of objects is assumed to be successful.

In short, if you use any of the code in this book in your own programs, it's up to you to add whatever error checking may have been left out. Never assume anything in your programs. Any place in your code that you can't be 100 percent sure of your program's state, you must add error checking to ensure that the program doesn't come crashing down on your user. Just because this book's author may have been lax in his error checking (for good reasons), does not let you off the hook.

On to the Wonderful World of Java

If you're still reading this introduction, you're probably convinced that Java is something you really want to learn about. If you're interested in the Internet, that decision is a wise one. (If, on the other hand, you thought this was a book of coffee recipes, return this book to the shelf and leave the store.) At this point, Java is virtually guaranteed its place in Internet history. Want to know why? Turn the page and keep reading.

Clayton Walnum
May 1996

Part I

Java, Applets, and the Internet

CHAPTER 1

Java Overview

Anyone who's had anything to do with computers in the '90s knows that the Internet is all the rage. The immense growth of this global computer network has not only created a handy way to download files and information but has also sparked major controversies over freedom of speech, copyright law, and computer security. Hardly a day goes by without the Internet making the news.

But not all Internet activity is steeped in controversy. One of the more positive Internet newsmakers has been the release of Java, a computer programming language that enables folks like you and me to easily create applications that can be used across the Internet without worrying about platform compatibility or network security. The two types of Java applications—applets for use within World Wide Web pages and stand-alone Java applications—are guaranteed to do more to liven up the World Wide Web than even the most heated controversy.

Java, however, was conceived long before its suitability for the Internet was noted and taken advantage of. You may be surprised to learn that Java was developed for a very different use. In fact, "Java" isn't even the language's original name. In this chapter, you'll get a quick look at Java's history, as well as learn why Java is an excellent tool for creating Internet applications.

The Java Story

Back in 1990, a gentleman by the name of James Gosling was given the task of creating programs to control consumer electronics. Gosling and his team of people at Sun Microsystems started designing their software using C++, the language that most programmers were praising as the next big thing because of its object-oriented nature. Gosling, however, quickly found that C++ was not suitable for the projects he and his team had in mind. They ran into trouble with complicated aspects of C++

such as multiple inheritance of classes and with program bugs such as memory leaks. Gosling soon decided that he was going to have to come up with his own, simplified computer language that would avoid all the problems he had with C++.

Although Gosling didn't care for the complexity of languages such as C++, he did like the basic syntax and object-oriented features of the language. So when he sat down to design his new language, he used C++ as its model, stripping away all the features of C++ that made that language difficult to use with his consumer-electronics projects. When Gosling completed his language-design project, he had a new programming language that he named Oak. (The story goes that the name Oak came to Gosling as he gazed out his office window at an oak tree.)

Oak was first used in something called the Green project, wherein the development team attempted to design a control system for use in the home. This control system would enable the user to manipulate a list of devices, including TVs, VCRs, lights, and telephones, all from a hand-held computer called *7 (Star Seven). The *7 system featured a touch-sensitive screen that the owner used to select and control the devices supported by the control.

> **Note:** The *7 screen display featured a number of animated figures, of which Duke (now the little guy considered to be the Java mascot) was one. Once you get involved with Java, you're liable to see a lot of Duke, who pops up on the Sun Microsystems Web site (Figure 1.1), and who is featured in some of Sun's sample Java applets.

Figure 1.1

Duke has become the Java mascot.

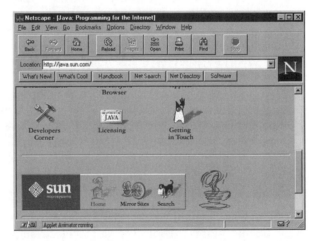

The next step for Oak was the video-on-demand (VOD) project, in which the language was used as the basis for software that controlled an interactive television system. Although neither *7 nor the VOD project led to actual products, they gave

Oak a chance to develop and mature. By the time Sun discovered that the name "Oak" was already claimed and they changed the name to Java, they had a powerful, yet simple, language on their hands.

More importantly, Java was a *platform-neutral language*, which meant that programs developed with Java could run on any computer system with no changes. This platform independence was attained by using a special format for compiled Java programs. This file format, called *byte-code*, could be read and executed by any computer system that has a Java interpreter. The Java interpreter, of course, must be written specially for the system on which it will run.

In 1993, after the World Wide Web had transformed the text-based Internet into a graphics-rich environment, the Java team realized that the language they had developed would be perfect for Web programming. The team came up with the concept of Web *applets*, small programs that could be included in Web pages, and even went so far as to create a complete Web browser (now called HotJava) that demonstrated the language's power.

In the second quarter of 1995, Sun Microsystems officially announced Java. The "new" language was quickly embraced as a powerful tool for developing Internet applications. Netscape Communications, the developer of the popular Netscape Navigator Web browser (Figure 1.2), added support for Java to its new Netscape Navigator 2.0. Other Internet software developers are sure to follow suit, including Microsoft, whose Internet Explorer 3 (currently in beta) offers Java support. After more than five years of development, Java has found its home.

Figure 1.2

The new Netscape Navigator 2.0 Web browser is Java capable.

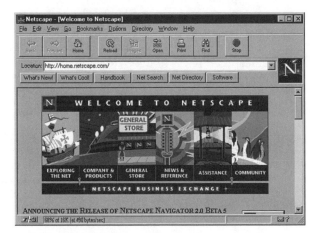

Introducing Java

By now, you may be curious why Java is considered such a powerful tool for Internet development projects. You already know that Java is a simplified version of C++. Anyone who has struggled with learning C++ knows that the key word in the previous sentence is "simplified." C++ added so much to the C language that even professional programmers often have difficulty making the transition.

According to Sun Microsystems, Java is "simple, object-oriented, statically typed, compiled, architecture neutral, multi-threaded, garbage collected, robust, secure, and extensible." That's a mouthful, but this description of Java probably doesn't help you understand the language much. The following list of Java's attributes, however, should clear out some of the cobwebs:

◆ **Simple**. Java's developers deliberately left out many of the unnecessary features of other high-level programming languages. For example, Java does not support pointer math, implicit type casting, structures or unions, operator overloading, templates, header files, or multiple inheritance.

◆ **Object-oriented**. Just like C++, Java uses classes to organize code into logical modules. At runtime, a program creates objects from the classes. Java classes can inherit from other classes, but multiple inheritance, wherein a class inherits methods and fields from more than one class, is not allowed.

◆ **Statically typed**. All objects used in a program must be declared before they are used. This enables the Java compiler to locate and report type conflicts.

◆ **Compiled**. Before you can run a program written in the Java language, the program must be compiled by the Java compiler. The compilation results in a "byte-code" file that, while similar to a machine-code file, can be executed under any operating system that has a Java interpreter. This interpreter reads in the byte-code file and translates the byte-code commands into machine-language commands that can be directly executed by the machine that's running the Java program. You could say, then, that Java is both a compiled *and* interpreted language.

◆ **Multi-threaded**. Java programs can contain multiple threads of execution, which enables programs to handle several tasks concurrently. For example, a multi-threaded program can render an image on the screen in one thread while continuing to accept keyboard input from the user in the main thread. All applications have at least one thread, which represents the program's main path of execution.

◆ **Garbage collected**. Java programs do their own garbage collection, which means that programs are not required to delete objects that they allocate in memory. This relieves programmers of virtually all memory-management problems.

◆ **Robust**. Because the Java interpreter checks all system access performed within a program, Java programs cannot crash the system. Instead, when a serious error is discovered, Java programs create an exception. This exception can be captured and managed by the program without any risk of bringing down the system.

♦ **Secure**. The Java system not only verifies all memory access but also ensures that no viruses are hitching a ride with a running applet. Because pointers are not supported by the Java language, programs cannot gain access to areas of the system for which they have no authorization.

♦ **Extensible**. Java programs support *native methods*, which are functions written in another language, usually C++. Support for native methods enables programmers to write functions that may execute faster than the equivalent functions written in Java. Native methods are dynamically linked to the Java program; that is, they are associated with the program at runtime. As the Java language is further refined for speed, native methods will probably be unnecessary.

♦ **Well-understood**. The Java language is based upon technology that's been developed over many years. For this reason, Java can be quickly and easily understood by anyone with experience with modern programming languages such as C++.

As you can tell from the preceding list of features, a great deal of thought went into creating a language that would be fairly easy to use but still provide the most powerful features of a modern language like C++. Thanks to features such as automatic garbage collection, programmers can spend more time developing their programs rather than wasting valuable man-hours hunting for hard-to-find memory-allocation bugs. However, features such as Java's object-oriented nature, as well as its ability to handle multiple threads of execution, ensure that the language is both up-to-date and powerful.

Java Programs

As I mentioned previously. Java can be used to create two types of programs: applets and stand-alone applications. An Applet is simply a part of a Web page, just as an image or a line of text can be. Just as a browser takes care of displaying an image referenced in an HTML document, a Java-enabled browser locates and runs an Applet . When your Java-capable Web browser loads the HTML document, the Java applet is also loaded and executed.

Using applets, you can do everything from adding animated graphics to your Web pages to creating complete games and utilities that can be executed over the Internet. Some applets that have already been created with Java include Bar Chart, which embeds a configurable bar chart in an HTML document; Crossword Puzzle, which enables users to solve a crossword puzzle on the Web; and LED Sign, which presents a scrolling, computerized message to viewers of the Web page within which the applet is embedded. Figure 1.3 shows a spreadsheet applet running in Netscape Navigator 2.0.

Figure 1.3

Applets are small programs that are run from within an HTML document.

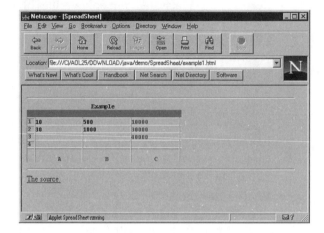

Although most Java programmers are excited by the ability to create applets, Java can also be used to create stand-alone applications—that is, applications that don't need to be embedded in an HTML document. The most well-known application is the HotJava Web browser itself, shown in Figure 1.4. This basic browser is completely written in the Java language, showing how Java handles not only normal programming tasks such as looping and evaluating mathematical expressions, but also how it can handle the complexities of telecommunications programming.

Figure 1.4

The HotJava Web browser is written entirely in the Java programming language.

The Java Developer's Kit

Java is actually more than a computer language; it's also a programming environment that includes a complete set of programming tools. These tools include a compiler, an interpreter, a debugger, a disassembler, a profiler, and more. To create a Java program, you first use a text editor to create the source-code file. You write the source code, of course, in the Java language. After completing the source code, which is always saved with a .java file extension, you compile the program into its byte-code format, the file for which has the .class file extension. It is the .class file that the interpreter loads and executes. Because the byte-code files are fully portable between operating systems, they can be executed on any system that has a Java interpreter.

> **Note:** Note that many of Java's tools require long file names, especially the long extensions .java and .class. Both Windows 95 and Windows NT allow these long file names, even under DOS sessions.

After compiling and running a Java program, you may discover that the source code needs modification. The Java debugger can help you find your errors, whereas the Java profiler provides handy information about your program. If you run into a compiled Java program that you'd like to see in source-code form, the Java disassembler will do the translation for you. Java also includes a program that creates the files you need to take advantage of native methods (functions written in another language, such as C++). There's even a program that can create HTML documents from Java source-code files. Although all the development tools are DOS applications—that is, they don't run under Windows—they provide a complete environment for creating and managing Java projects.

If you're a little confused about how the many Java programs work together, don't worry about it. You'll get a chance to learn more about the Java tools as you work through this book. At this point, just be aware that Java provides everything you need to create your own applets and stand-alone applications. In the second part of this book, you'll start learning the Java language, and in the third part, you'll start using Java's tools to create your own applets.

Where Is Java?

All this talk about Java doesn't do you much good until you get your own copy of the Java Development Kit (JDK). You'll probably also want a copy of HotJava and Netscape Navigator 2.0, so that you can try out the Web pages you create with your Java applets. Two versions of the JDK are included on this book's CD-ROM. While version 1.0.1 has been used for many of the test applets, version 1.0.2 represents

Sun's latest installment of the JDK at the time of this book's completion. However, because the language is constantly being refined (and was only recently released for Windows), there may have been a newer version released since this book was written.

If you'd like to be sure you have the latest version, you can find HotJava and the JDK on the Sun Microsystems site, located at http://www.sun.com. Once you connect up to Sun Microsystems' home page, navigate to the page shown in Figure 1.5, which provides access to tons of information about Java and enables you to download the files you need. (Of course, Web pages constantly change. Sun Microsystem's site may have changed significantly by the time you read this.)

Figure 1.5

You can download HotJava and the Java Development Kit from Sun Microsystems' Web pages.

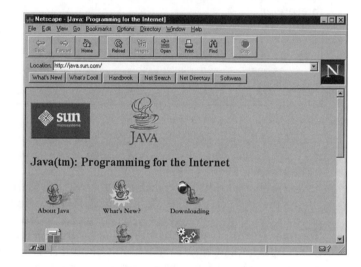

If you want to try out a copy of Netscape Navigator 2.0, hop onto the ol' WWW and go to http://www.netscape.com, which is Netscape's home page. From there, you can find your way to the page shown in Figure 1.6. From this page, you can download any of the software that Netscape has up on the Web.

> **Note:** You might also want to find your way to http://www.microsoft.com, where you can find information about Microsoft's new Web browser, Internet Explorer 3, which features Java support.

Figure 1.6

You can get
Netscape
Navigator 2.0
from Netscape's
WWW site.

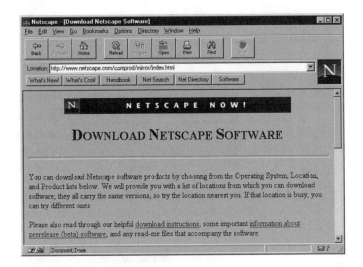

Example: Installing HotJava

The HotJava browser is contained in a self-extracting compressed file, which you may download from Sun's Web site at http://java.sun.com. After you extract HotJava's many files (there's a ton of them!) by double-clicking the file, the extraction program uncompresses the files and stores them in a folder named HOTJAVA. Once the files are extracted, you can copy the folder anywhere you like on your hard disk.

When you examine the HOTJAVA folder, you'll see the directory structure shown in Figure 1.7. The BIN folder contains the main HotJava application (HOTJAVA.EXE), as well as many of the Java environment's tools, including the compiler, interpreter, and profiler. The LIB folder contains a number of other files needed for HotJava:

lib / classes.zip.	This file is needed by the compiler and interpreter, so do not unzip it.
lib / properties / .	This is the template and system defaults for the HotJava properties file.
lib / hotjava / and lib / templates / .	These are customizable textual elements and HTML.

> **Note:** Documentation for HotJava must be accessed online from the program's Help menu.

Figure 1.7

After extraction, the HOTJAVA directory will contain all of HotJava's files.

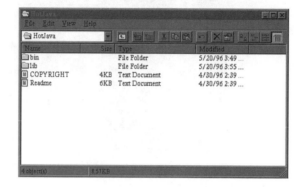

Example: Installing the JDK

Although the compressed HotJava file contains many of the Java environment's programs such as the compiler and the interpreter, the Java Developer's Kit contains the complete development suite, including some files not packaged with HotJava. For example, the HotJava compressed file doesn't include the Java debugger or the Appletviewer application, which enables you to view applets without having to load them into a Web browser. The JDK also comes packaged with over 20 sample applets. More importantly, the JDK contains the most up-to-date documentation and tools.

You can find the JDK on this book's CD-ROM, in the JDK folder, or you can download the latest version of the JDK from the Sun Microsystems Web site. On the CD-ROM, the compressed file that contains the JDK is called JDK.EXE. After copying the file to your hard disk (or after downloading the JDK from Sun), you install it in exactly the same way you installed the HotJava browser. That is, you double-click the self-extracting compressed file.

When the files have been extracted (it might take a while), you can move the resultant JAVA folder anywhere you like on your hard disk, although you'll probably want it on the disk's root directory, which is where this book's forthcoming examples will assume it's located. Figure 1.8 shows the contents of the JAVA folder (at least, the contents at the time of this writing; the development kit may have been revised by the time you read this).

Figure 1.8

The Java Developer's Kit will be in the JAVA folder after you extract its compressed files.

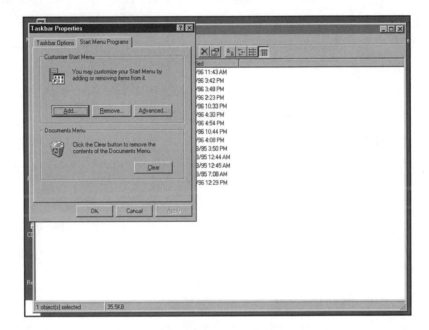

If you examine the folders that make up the JDK, you'll see that the BIN folder holds the developer tools, such as the compiler, the interpreter, the debugger, and the profiler. The DEMO folder contains the many example applets that you can examine to learn more about the Java language and how it's used. In your JAVA folder, you'll also find a file called SRC.ZIP. This compressed file contains the source code for the classes included with the JDK.

Summary

Java just may be the biggest thing to hit the World Wide Web since, well, the Web itself. As you'll see in the forthcoming chapters, Java not only provides a way to create secure applications that can be used safely on the Internet, but the language also represents a complete shift in the way people may think about their computers in the future. Because a Java applet can be located anywhere on the Web yet still be executable on your computer, your computer's storage may well expand from its tiny hard drive to include all of the Internet. As Java becomes more refined, and as more people like yourself start writing Java applets and applications, the cyber world that is the Internet may never be the same.

Review Questions

1. Give three reasons why Java is so suitable for Web applications.

2. What's the difference between a Java applet and a Java stand-alone application?

3. Why are Java applets considered to be platform neutral?

4. How does an Applet work within an HTML document?

5. What are the two benefits of Java that make it an Internet-saavy language?

Review Exercises

1. Explore the many resources available to Java programmers on the Java WWW pages, located at `http://www.netscape.com`. (Remember that some commerical online services, such as America Online, give you access to the World Wide Web.)

2. Explore Netscape's Web pages, located at `http://www.netscape.com`.

3. If you've downloaded a copy of Netscape Navigator 2.0, install it on your system.

4. Using the HotJava or Netscape browser, do a Webcrawler search (`www.webcrawler.com`) using the keywords "java" or "java applet." Locate Applets others have written, follow the links and load them into your browser

CHAPTER 2

Running Java Applets

Because you're interested in writing Java applets (you bought this book, after all), you're probably already pretty familiar with using HTML (Hypertext Markup Language) to create Web pages. If not, you should pick up a book on HTML and get some idea of how that markup language works. Even if you're an HTML expert, though, you may not have seen the HTML extension that Sun Microsystems created to support Java applets in Web pages. In this chapter, then, you not only get a chance to see Java applets up and running, but you also learn how to add them to your Web pages.

The Sample Java Applets

As you learned in Chapter 1, "Java Overview," the Java Developer's Kit (JDK) includes many sample applets that you can test in your Web pages. (The HotJava browser, too, comes with a few of these sample applets.) If you installed the JDK as described in Chapter 1, you're ready to start experimenting with Java applets. In this section, you will use the Appletviewer tool—which comes with the JDK—to get a quick look at some applets. A following section, "Adding Applets to an HTML Document," will show you how to add an applet to a Web page.

The Appletviewer Tool

The truth is that you can write and run applets without even having a Java-compatible browser. This is thanks to the Appletviewer tool that comes as part of the JDK. Appletviewer is a Windows application (unless you're using a non-Windows version of the JDK) that you run from a DOS command line. Part of the command line is the applet that you want to run. When Appletviewer appears, the applet appears in the viewer's main window.

To run the Appletviewer application, first bring up an MS-DOS window by selecting the MS-DOS Prompt command from Programs on the Start menu. Then, switch to the folder containing the applet you want to run and type the command line `C:\JAVA\BIN\APPLETVIEWER DOC.HTML`.

In the preceding command line, DOC.HTML is the name of an HTML document that contains the tag for the applet you want to see.

Example: Running TicTacToe

Suppose you want to run the TicTacToe demo applet that comes with the JDK. To do this, just follow these steps:

1. Select the Start/Programs/MS-DOS Prompt command. The DOS window appears, as shown in Figure 2.1.

Figure 2.1

The first step in running Appletviewer is to bring up the MS-DOS window.

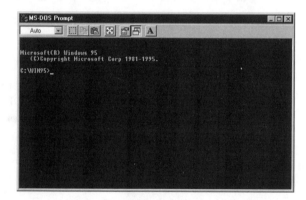

2. Change to the directory containing the TicTacToe applet (Figure 2.2).

Figure 2.2

The second step is to change to the applet's directory.

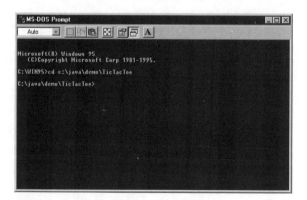

3. Type the command line `C:\JAVA\BIN\APPLETVIEWER EXAMPLE1.HTML`. The Appletviewer runs, loading and displaying the TicTacToe applet (Figure 2.3).

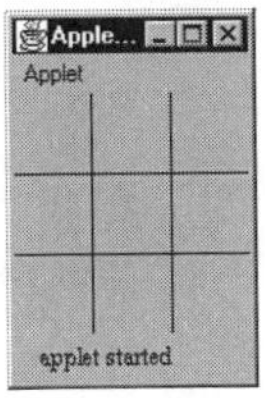

Figure 2.3

The requested applet appears in Appletviewer's main window.

Now that you have the applet started, try a few games of TicTacToe against the computer. To place an X, click the square you want. You'll quickly discover that the computer player is as dumb as yogurt. Let's just say that you don't have to be a rocket scientist to win (Figure 2.4).

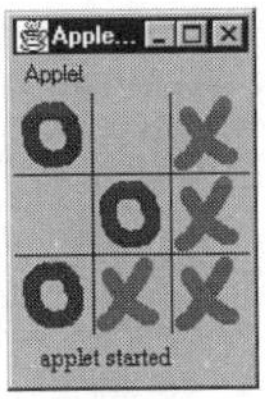

Figure 2.4

Beating this version of TicTacToe doesn't require a degree in computer science.

Tip: If you want to avoid typing the full path name for Appletviewer every time you run it, type the command `PATH=C:\JAVA\BIN` at the MS-DOS prompt to add Appletviewer's directory to your path. (Of course, if you've installed the JDK somewhere else on your hard drive, you'll have to use a different path in the command.) After you type this command, MS-DOS will be able to find Appletviewer without your having to type the full path. For example, you'll be able to run TicTacToe by switching to the TicTacToe directory and simply typing `APPLETVIEWER EXAMPLE1.HTML`. You can also add Appletviewer's path to the PATH statement in your AUTOEXEC.BAT file and thus avoid having to type it in by hand every time you start your system and want to use Appletviewer.

The Animator Applet

Another applet that demonstrates some interesting facets of Java programming is the Animator applet, which not only displays various animation sequences, but also plays sound effects simultaneously. To run the Animator applet, switch to the

C:\JAVA\DEMO\ANIMATOR folder and type the command line **APPLETVIEWER EXAMPLE1.HTML**. (The previous command line assumes that you've set your path to the JAVA\BIN directory.) When you do, you see the display shown in Figure 2.5. (Yep, it's the ubiquitous Duke, waving at you from his very own applet.)

Figure 2.5

The Animator applet includes several animation and sound examples, including this one featuring Duke, the Java mascot.

Animator is an example of a configurable applet. That is, by modifying the HTML tag that loads and runs the applet, the user can display his or her own custom animation sequence and sound effects. You'll learn about configurable applets in Chapter 26, "Configurable Applets." For now, though, it's enough for you to know that Java is capable of adding both animation sequences and sound effects to your Web pages.

> **Note:** If you'd like to see what the applet's HTML tag looks like, select Appletviewer's Applet,Tag command.

The BarChart Applet

BarChart, another configurable applet, is especially useful when you need to graphically display data values in a Web page. To check out BarChart, switch to the JAVA\DEMO\BARCHART folder and type the command line **APPLETVIEWER EXAMPLE1.HTML**. When you do, you see the window shown in Figure 2.6.

Figure 2.6

The BarChart applet enables you to create graphs in your Web pages.

Because BarChart is configurable, you can create all sorts of different bar charts in your Web pages just by specifying different parameters in the applet's HTML tag. As you can see, applets can be powerful tools for creating dynamic and useful Web pages. (Try out Appletviewer's Applet,Tag command to see the code that specifies how the bar chart appears.)

Other Demo Applets

The DEMO folder contains many sample applets that you can experiment with using Appletviewer. All of the demo applets are run from HTML documents with names such as EXAMPLE1.HTML, EXAMPLE2.HTML, and so on. All demo applets have at least the EXAMPLE1.HTML document, while others have additional examples. To run any demo applet, change to the applet's folder and type `APPLETVIEWER EXAMPLE1.HTML` (assuming that you've set your path to the Appletviewer application). Use the `DIR` command to display the contents of an applet's directory in order to discover whether the applet features additional example HTML files.

> **Note:** Remember that the HotJava browser cannot load and run newer applets like those that come with the latest version of the JDK.

Adding Applets to an HTML Document

If you've created Web pages before, you know that you use HTML to create a template for the page. The commands in the template tell a Web browser how to display the Web page. When Sun Microsystems developed Java, they also had to come up with an extension to HTML that would enable Web pages to contain Java applets. That extension is the `<applet>` tag, which Sun Microsystems defines as shown in Listing 2.1.

Listing 2.1 LST2_1.TXT: The *<applet>* Tag Definition.

```
<applet attributes>
parameters
alternate-content
</applet>
```

In the preceding tag, the text in normal characters is typed literally; the text shown in italics is replaced by whatever is appropriate for the applet you're including in the document. As you can see, the `<applet>` tag is similar to other HTML tags with which you may be familiar. For example, the tag starts with `<applet attributes>` and ends with `</applet>`, which is not unlike the format of other HTML tags. The first and last lines are required. Other lines in the tag are optional.

The attributes section of the `<applet>` tag contains important information about the tag, including the associated .CLASS file and the applet's width and height. The last line tells the browser that it has reached the end of the tag. You can load and run the TicTacToe applet, for example, with the `<applet>` tag shown in Listing 2.2.

Listing 2.2   LST2_2.TXT: A Tag for Loading and Running TicTacToe.

```
<applet
    code=TicTacToe.class
    width=120
    height=120>
</applet>
```

In the preceding example, the code attribute is the name of the .CLASS file for the applet. If you remember, the .CLASS file holds the applet's byte-code representation, which can be run by the Java interpreter. The width and height attributes control the size of the applet.

The TicTacToe tag above is the simplest <applet> tag you can write. That is, the code, width, and height attributes are all required, as is the final </applet> line.

Optional Attributes for Applets

There are several optional attributes you can use with the <applet> tag. The first is codebase, which specifies the applet's base folder or URL (Uniform Resource Locator). This folder or URL is used in combination with the file specified in the code attribute to find the applet's code. In the case of a folder, the codebase attribute is relative to the location of the HTML document containing the applet's tag. In Listing 2.2, because the codebase attribute is missing, the Web browser will look for the applet's files in the same folder as the HTML document. The <applet> tag in Listing 2.2 looks like Listing 2.3 when using the codebase attribute. (Don't try to use run this HTML code, as it's only an example of the attribute's format and may not run.)

Listing 2.3   LST2_3.TXT: Using the *codebase* Attribute.

```
<applet
    codebase=tictactoe
    code=TicTacToe.class
    width=120
    height=120>
</applet>
```

The preceding tag tells the browser that the TicTacToe.class file is located in a folder called TICTACTOE. This folder must be on the same level in the directory tree as the HTML file. That is, if the HTML file is in the folder JAVA\DEMO, then the path for the .CLASS file should be JAVA\DEMO\TICTACTOE\TicTacToe.class. You can also use an URL, such as http://www.provider.com/my_pages/tictactoe, for the codebase attribute. This causes the applet to be loaded from the specified site.

Other optional attributes you can use with the <applet> tag are alt, align, name, hspace, and vspace. The alt attribute enables you to specify text that will be displayed by text-only browsers, whereas the name attribute gives the applet a symbolic name that's used to reference the applet (used when you need to communicate between applets).

The `align`, `hspace`, and `vspace` attributes all work together to position the applet within the text flow of the HTML document. These attributes work exactly as they do with the `<img>` tag that's used to display images in Web pages. The `align` attribute can be one of these values: `left`, `right`, `middle`, `absmiddle`, `bottom`, `absbottom`, `baseline`, `top`, or `texttop`. The `hspace` and `vspace` attributes control the amount of white space around the applet when `align` is set to `left` or `right`.

Listing 2.4 shows the script for a simple Web page using the `<applet>` tag. Figure 2.7 shows Netscape Navigator 2.0 displaying the page.

Listing 2.4   LST2_4.TXT: A Simple HTML Document Using the *<applet>* Tag.

```
<title>TicTacToe</title>
<hr>
This is a bunch of text whose sole purpose is to demonstrate
the placement
<applet
    codebase=TicTacToe
    code=TicTacToe.class
    width=120
    height=120
    alt="This is the TicTacToe applet."
    name=TicTacToe
    align=middle>
</applet>
of the TicTacToe applet within the text flow of an HTML document.
<hr>
```

Figure 2.7

This is the Web page created by Listing 2.4.

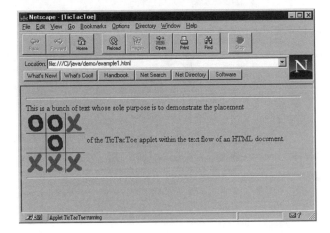

> **Tip:** To load an HTML document into Netscape Navigator 2.0, select the File, Open File command or press Ctrl+O. Then select the file in the dialog box that appears.

Applet Parameters

As you know, many Java applets are configurable, meaning that the applet user can specify certain values that the applet will use when it starts. A good example is the BarChart applet you saw earlier in this chapter. When you need to specify parameters for an applet, you use the <param> tag. The <param> tags, one for each parameter you want to set, are placed after the starting <applet> tag and before the ending </applet> tag. For example, Listing 2.5 shows parameters being set for the BarChart applet. Figure 2.8 shows the resultant bar chart. As you can see from the listing, each parameter has two parts, the parameter name and the value to which it should be set. You'll learn more about applet parameters in Chapter 26, "Configurable Applets."

Listing 2.5   LST2_5.TXT: Using Parameters with Applets.

```
<applet
    code="Chart.class"
    width=251
    height=125>
<param name=title value="Sales">
<param name=orientation value="vertical">
<param name=scale value="5">
<param name=columns value="3">
<param name=c1_style value="solid">
<param name=c1 value="10">
<param name=c1_color value="blue">
<param name=c1_label value="Jan">
<param name=c2_style value="solid">
<param name=c2 value="12">
<param name=c2_color value="green">
<param name=c2_label value="Feb">
<param name=c3_style value="solid">
<param name=c3 value="15">
<param name=c3_color value="red">
<param name=c3_label value="Mar">
</applet>
```

Figure 2.8

This is the bar chart created by the parameters in Listing 2.5.

Non-Java Browsers

You may wonder what happens when a browser that's not Java-compatible finds an applet in an HTML document. In this case, as is standard behavior for browsers, the non-Java browser simply ignores the tags it doesn't recognize. However, you may want to provide a more user-friendly response to users who are trying to view your applets with non-Java browsers. You can do this easily by placing alternate content right before the ending </applet> tag. Listing 2.6, for example, shows the HTML script for running the TicTacToe applet with alternate content for browsers that don't support Java.

Listing 2.6   LST2_6.TXT: Supplying Alternate Content for TicTacToe.

```
<applet
    code=TicTacToe.class
    width=120
    height=120>
<b>If you had a Java-compatible browser,
you'd be playing TicTacToe right now!</b>
</applet>
```

The alternate content you provide can comprise any standard HTML commands and is ignored by Java-compatible browsers. That is, the alternate content appears only in non-Java browsers.

Example: A Java-Powered Home Page

In the previous section, you saw a sample HTML document that contains an applet. You also saw what this document looks like when loaded into Netscape Navigator 2.0. Now you'll use what you've learned to create your own "appletized" home page for Netscape Navigator. To do this, you must first write your home page's HTML file. Then you must set Netscape Navigator's home-page property, which determines the document the browser displays at startup. Just follow the steps below to accomplish these tasks:

1. Create a folder called HOMEPAGE in your C: drive's root directory.

2. Type Listing 2.7 and save it as an ASCII file called HOMEPAGE.HTML in your HOMEPAGE directory. (If you don't want to type the listing, just copy it from the CHAP02 directory of this book's CD-ROM.)

Listing 2.7   HOMEPAGE.HTML: An HTML Script for a Home Page.

```
<title>My Home Page</title>
<h1>The TicTacToe Home Page</h1>
This may be a dumb home page, but it gives
you a chance to play the TicTacToe applet
every time you start Netscape Navigator 2.0!<h>
<hr>
<applet
    codebase=TicTacToe
    code=TicTacToe.class
    width=120
    height=120
    alt="This is the TicTacToe applet."
    name=TicTacToe>
</applet>
<hr>
```

3. Copy the entire TICTACTOE folder (not just the folder's contents) from your JAVA\DEMO folder to your HOMEPAGE folder.

4. Start up Netscape Navigator 2.0, and click Navigator's Stop button to stop loading the currently set home page.

5. Select Options, General Preferences from Navigator's menu bar. The Preferences property sheet appears (Figure 2.9).

Figure 2.9

You can set your own starting home page in Navigator's Preferences property sheet.

6. Enter `C:\HOMEPAGE\HOMEPAGE.HTML` into the Start With text box.

7. Click the Home button to load your new TicTacToe home page (Figure 2.10).

Figure 2.10

Here's your new
TicTacToe home
page, up and
running.

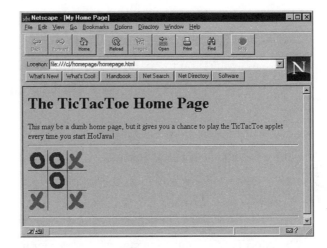

Figure 2.10

Here's your new TicTacToe home page, up and running.

> **Tip:** When running under Netscape Navigator 2.0, the TicTacToe applet seems to respond slowly to mouse clicks at first. If the applet doesn't respond right away, try moving your mouse pointer off the applet. This trick wakes things up most of the time.

Summary

As you learned in this chapter, Java applets are relatively easy to add to your HTML documents. However, folks without Web browsers aren't completely left out of the fun. They can create and view applets using the handy Appletviewer application that comes as part of the JDK. Because HTML was designed long before there were Java applets, Sun Microsystems had to create an extension to HTML in order to accommodate applets in Web pages. The extension takes the form of the `<applet>` tag, which enables you to not only provide values for an applet's attributes, but also to include a list of parameters and even offer alternate content for non-Java browsers.

Review Questions

1. How can someone without a Java-compatible browser run applets?

2. What are the three required attributes for the `<applet>` tag?

3. What does the optional `codebase` attribute do?

4. Name two other optional applet attributes.

5. Why would you use parameters with an applet?

6. How can your applet-enhanced HTML documents accommodate non-Java browsers?

Review Exercises

1. Use Appletviewer to view the BouncingHeads applet (or any other demo applet in which you're interested).

2. Change the size of the BarChart applet in the HTML code from Listing 2.5.

3. Modify the home page you created earlier in this chapter so that it displays both the NervousText and TicTacToe demo applets. The code for NervousText is found in the file NervousText.class. In addition to the applet's standard attributes, you'll also need to include one parameter called `text`, whose value is the text you want displayed.

CHAPTER 3

Applets and the Internet

Now that you have some idea how you can add Java applets to your Web pages, you need to discover how applets are handled on the Internet. After all, it is an applet's ability to hitch a ride on the Information Superhighway that makes it so unique. In fact, applets are really the first step towards making the Internet a true extension of your computer's local storage system. When you view a Web page containing applets, those applets may be coming to you from just about anywhere on the Web—from the office down the street or from a software distributor in Hong Kong. In this chapter, you discover just how this interaction works.

Local and Remote Applets

One of Java's major strengths is that you can use the language to create dynamic content for your Web pages. That is, thanks to Java applets, your Web pages are no longer limited to the tricks you can perform with HTML. Now your Web pages can do just about anything you want them to. All you need to do is write the appropriate applets.

But writing Java applets is only half the story. How your Web page's users obtain and run the applets is equally as important. It's up to you to not only write the applet (or use someone else's applet), but also to provide users access to the applet. Basically, your Web pages can contain two types of applets: local and remote. In this section, you learn the difference between these applet types, which are named after the location at which they are stored.

Local Applets

A local applet is one that is stored on your own computer system (Figure 3.1). When your Web page must find a local applet, it doesn't need to retrieve information from the Internet—in fact, your browser doesn't even need to be connected to the Internet at that time. As you can see in Listing 3.1, a local applet is specified by a path name and a file name.

Figure 3.1

Local applets are stored on and loaded from your computer system.

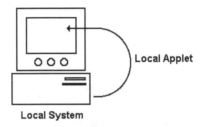

Local Applet

Local System

Listing 3.1   LST3_1.TXT: Specifying a Local Applet.

```
<applet
    codebase="tictactoe"
    code="TicTacToe.class"
    width=120
    height=120>
</applet>
```

In Listing 3.1, the codebase attribute specifies a path name on your system for the local applet, whereas the code attribute specifies the name of the byte-code file that contains the applet's code. The path specified in the codebase attribute is relative to the folder containing the HTML document that references the applet. (See the "Optional Attributes for Applets" section of Chapter 2 for more information.)

Remote Applets

A *remote applet* is one that is located on another computer system (Figure 3.2). This computer system may be located in the building next door or it may be on the other side of the world—it makes no difference to your Java-compatible browser. No matter where the remote applet is located, it's downloaded onto your computer via the Internet. Your browser must, of course, be connected to the Internet at the time it needs to display the remote applet.

Figure 3.2

Remote applets are stored on another system and are downloaded onto your computer via the Internet.

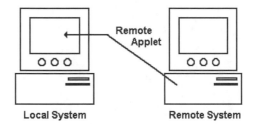

Local System   Remote System

To reference a remote applet in your Web page, you must know the applet's URL (where it's located on the Web) and any attributes and parameters that you need to supply in order to display the applet correctly. If you didn't write the applet, you'll need to find the document that describes the applet's attributes and parameters. This document is usually written by the applet's author. Listing 3.2 shows how to compose an HTML <applet> tag that accesses a remote applet.

Listing 3.2   LST3_2.TXT: Specifiying a Remote Applet.

```
<applet
    codebase="http://www.myconnect.com/applets/"
    code="TicTacToe.class"
    width=120
    height=120>
</applet>
```

The only difference between Listing 3.1 and Listing 3.2 is the value of the codebase attribute. In the first case, codebase specifies a local folder, and in the second case, it specifies the URL at which the applet is located.

Clients and Servers

If a required applet is not located on your system, it can be downloaded automatically to your system and then run. To the user, this exchange of applets over the Internet is mostly transparent. All the user knows is that she's looking at a page that contains a game of TicTacToe, an animated image of Duke, or some other Java-based content. In this way, the Internet becomes almost an extension of the user's basic system, sort of a gigantic hard drive that contains a practically infinite number of accessible applets and applications.

Currently, there's a *client/server relationship* between a browser that wants to display an applet and the system that can supply the applet. The *client* is a computer that requires services from another system; the *server* is the computer that provides those services. In the case of a Java applet, the client is the computer that's trying to display an HTML document that contains a reference to an applet. The server is the computer system that uploads the applet to the client, thereby allowing the client to use the applet. In Figure 3.2, you could call the local computer the client and the remote computer the server.

It won't be long, however, before the difference between a client and a server begins to get muddy. When Java browsers can send as well as receive applets, computers will constantly switch between being a client and a server. For example, suppose a user loads up his favorite Java-compatible browser and connects to a Web site. The home page on the Web site contains an animated title, so your system downloads the applet that displays this title. For the time being, your system is the client and the remote system is the server.

Now, however, you decide that you want to search the remote system's public databases for a particular file. Because you've just written a handy search application that can do the job for you, your system transmits the application to the remote computer, where it sets to work finding the file you specified. Suddenly, your computer is the server and the remote computer is the client.

This sort of switching between client and server tasks is a step toward making the Internet a huge extension of your computer. That is, more and more, the Internet will seem to be a part of your own local system, rather than a collection of computers located all over the world. You'll be able to access the Internet almost as easily as your own hard drive. In fact, you might not even need a hard drive at all! You can just run applications located somewhere else on the Internet and store your data in any number of special storage sites.

Security

You may have heard horror stories about people who have downloaded programs from the Internet only to find, after running the program, that it infected their system with a virus or otherwise wreaked havoc with their computer. Therefore, you may be reluctant to jump on the applet bandwagon. After all, with so many applets flying around the Internet, trouble could rear its ugly head like a demon from a Clive Barker movie.

The truth, however, is that Java applets are a secure way to transmit programs on the Internet. This is because the Java interpreter will not allow an applet to run until the interpreter has confirmed that the applet's byte-code has not been corrupted or changed in some way (Figure 3.3). Moreover, the interpreter determines whether the byte-code representation of the applet sticks to all of Java's rules. For example, a Java applet can never use a pointer to gain access to portions of computer memory for which it doesn't have access. The bottom line is that, not only are Java applets secure, they are virtually guaranteed not to crash the system.

Figure 3.3

Applets are verified before they are run, so they are virtually guaranteed to be safe and secure.

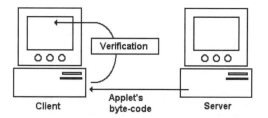

Example: Your Pages on the Web

Because you bought this book to learn how to write applets, you're probably also interested in setting up your own Web pages. (Of course, you may be interested only in creating applets that other people can use. That's okay, too.) To set up your own Java-compatible Web site, you need to create publicly accessible folders on your hard drive. You also need to gather all the applets you need so you can store them together in one place on your hard drive. That is, you'll want your Web pages to contain local applets. The instructions in this section will get you started on organizing a public folder.

First, create a folder on your hard drive's root directory. Name this folder something like PUBLIC. The PUBLIC folder will contain all of the files that are accessible to Web users who connect to your pages. Inside the PUBLIC folder, create a folder called something like APPLETS. The APPLETS folder will contain the applets that are referenced in your Web pages.

Now that you have your folders created, copy all the applets you need into the APPLETS folder. The applets' .CLASS files should be in the APPLETS directory, with their support files (such as graphics and sounds) in appropriately named folders within the APPLETS directory. For example, if you wanted to use the BouncingHeads applet in one of your pages, you'd copy the contents of the JAVA\DEMO\BOUNCINGHEADS folder to your APPLETS folder, ending up with the directory structure shown in Figure 3.4.

Figure 3.4

You need to set up your public directories properly.

The next step is to create the HTML files for your pages. When you've written these pages, they should be placed in the PUBLIC folder. Listing 3.3 shows the HTML file for a simple home page that displays the BouncingHeads applet and enables the user to view the applet's source code. The corresponding Web page is shown in Figure 3.5. Notice that the user can view the applet's source code by clicking on the link at the bottom of the page. When she does, she sees a window similar to Figure 3.6.

Listing 3.3   HOMEPAGE.HTML: A Home Page Displaying a Java Applet.

```
<title>Big Benny</title>
<h1>Welcome to Big Benny's Home Page</h1>
<b>We're hot wired for Java!</b>
<p>
<applet
    codebase="applets"
    code="BounceItem.class"
    width=400
    height=150>
</applet>
<p>
<a href="applets/BounceItem.java">The source code</a>
for this applet is available for your viewing pleasure.
```

Figure 3.5

A simple, Java-powered home page.

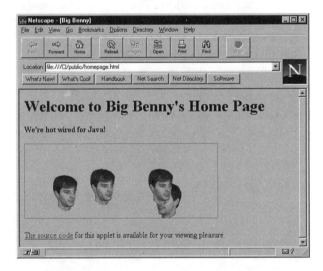

Note: Generally, you do not need to copy Java source code files to your APPLETS folder. Source code is not required in order to load and run applets.

Figure 3.6

The user can view the applet's source code by clicking the link.

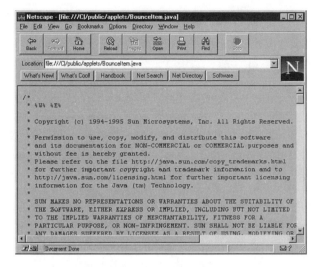

By placing all the publicly accessible files in one root directory, you can more easily set up your system's security to ensure that the rest of your system is kept safe from prying eyes. Moreover, you know exactly where you need to store any additional files that you may add to your site. Exactly how you create the folders for your Web pages will depend upon the applets and files you need to use, but the previous example should get you going fairly easily.

> **Note:** Of course, to create a Web site, you need to be connected to the Internet either directly or through an Internet provider that enables you to set up your own Web pages. If you are currently unable to have your own Web site, you can still set one up on your hard drive and then use your Java-compatible Web browser to load and view your Web pages. Then, when you get your Internet access, you'll be all ready to go. To find more information on setting up your own Web site, crank up your browser and log onto the handy Lycos directory at `http://www.lycos.com`; then fish around under the Computers, Web Publishing & HTML subdirectory.

Summary

Thanks to a Java-compatible browser's ability to download applets, users who log onto Java-powered Web pages can enjoy the Java experience without even realizing what's going on behind the scenes. This is unlike other types of applications on the Internet that the user must explicitly download before they can be run. When more and more applets start running rampant on the Information Superhighway, the Internet will become a virtual extension of your own computer system, one that's almost as easily accessed as your local hard drive. When this happens, the Internet will start living up to its hype.

Review Questions

1. What is a local applet?

2. What is a remote applet?

3. Explain the client/server relationship as it applies to Java applets.

4. How will the client/server focus of the Internet change as applications start to flow two ways, both from and to a remote computer?

5. Explain why Java applets are secure and guaranteed not to crash the system on which they're executing.

Review Exercises

1. Add additional applets to the simple Web site you set up in this chapter. You can copy the applets from the JAVA\DEMO folder.

2. Modify the HOMEPAGE.HTML file to display the additional applets you added in exercise 1.

3. Log onto the Internet and then find and download additional applets that you can use in your own pages. Start off at this URL:
   `http://www.javasoft.com/applets/appletsites.html`

Part II

Java Language Basics

CHAPTER 4

Object-Oriented Programming Concepts

Programming languages, like their spoken-language kin, evolve over time. They are constantly refined and focused to meet the ever-changing needs of their users. Like other modern programming languages such as C++, Java is an amalgamation of all the techniques developed over the years. Therefore, we'll start exploring object-oriented programming (OOP) by briefly looking at the history of programming languages. Knowing where object-oriented ideas came from will help you to better understand why they are an important part of modern programming languages. Once you understand why OOP was developed, you'll learn exactly what makes a programming language object-oriented.

From Switches to Objects

Back in the dark ages of computing, technicians programmed computers by flipping banks of switches, with each switch representing a single bit of information. In those days, even the simple programs required agonizing patience and precision. As the need for more sophisticated programs grew, so did the need for better ways to write these programs. The need to make computer programming quicker and simpler spurred the invention of assembly language and, shortly thereafter, high-level languages such as FORTRAN.

High-level languages enable programmers to use English-like commands in their programs and to be less concerned with the details of programming a computer and more concerned with the tasks that need to be completed. For example, in assembly language—a low-level language—it might take several instructions to display a line of text on the screen. In a high-level language, there's usually a single command such as PRINT that accomplishes this task.

With the advent of high-level languages, programming became accessible to more people; writing program code was no longer exclusively the domain of specially trained scientists. As a result, computing was used in increasingly complex roles. It was soon clear, however, that a more efficient way of programming was needed, one that would eliminate the obscure and complex "spaghetti code" that the early languages produced.

Programmers needed a new way of using high-level languages, one that enabled them to partition their programs into logical sections that represented the general tasks to be completed. Thus, the structured-programming paradigm was born. Structured programming encourages a *top-down* approach to programming, in which the programmer focuses on the general functions that a program must accomplish rather than the details of how those functions are implemented. When programmers think and program in top-down fashion, they can more easily handle large projects without producing tangled code.

For an analogy, consider an everyday task such as cleaning a house. If you wanted to write out the steps needed to complete this task, you'd write something like this:

Go to the living room.
Dust the coffee table.
Dust the end tables.
Vacuum the rug.
Go to the Kitchen.
Wash the dishes.
Wipe the counters.
Clean the stove.
Wipe off the refrigerator.
Sweep the floor.
Go to the bedroom.
Make the bed.
Dust the bureau.
Vacuum the rug.

The preceding list of steps is similar, in theory, to how you'd program a computer without using a top-down approach. Using the top-down programming approach, you'd revise the "program" as follows:

TOP LEVEL
Clean the Living Room.
Clean the Kitchen.
Clean the Bedroom.

SECOND LEVEL
Clean the Living Room
START
   Go to the living room.
   Dust the coffee table.
   Dust the end tables.
   Vacuum the rug.
END

Clean the Kitchen
START
   Go to the Kitchen.
   Wash the dishes.
   Wipe the counters.
   Clean the stove.
   Wipe off the refrigerator.
   Sweep the floor.
END

Clean the Bedroom
START
   Go to the bedroom.
   Make the bed.
   Dust the bureau.
   Vacuum the rug.
END

Now, if you're only interested in seeing what the "program" does, you can glance at the top level and see that these are instructions for cleaning the living room, kitchen, and bedroom. If that's all you need to know, you need to look no further. If, however, you want to know exactly how to clean the living room, you can go down one level in the top-down structure and find the detailed instructions for cleaning the living room. Yes, the top-down approach tends to make programs longer, but it also adds clarity to the program, because you can hide the details until you really need them.

Today, the need for efficient programming methods is more important than ever. The size of the average computer program has grown dramatically and now consists of hundreds of thousands of code lines. (It's rumored that Windows 95 comprises as much as 15 million lines of code. It boggles the mind!) With these huge programs, reusability is critical. Again, a better way of programming is needed—and that better way is object-oriented programming.

An Obvious, Yet Brilliant, Solution

The world consists of many objects, most of which manipulate other objects or data. For example, a car is an object that manipulates its speed and direction to transport people to a different location. This car object encapsulates all the functions and data that it needs to get its job done. It has a switch to turn it on, a wheel to control its direction, and brakes to slow it down. These functions directly manipulate the car's data, including direction, position, and speed.

When you travel in a car, however, you don't have to know the details of how these operations work. To stop a car, for example, you simply step on the brake pedal. You don't have to know how the pedal stops the car. You simply know that it works.

All these functions and data work together to define the object called a car. Moreover, all these functions work very similarly from one car to the next. You're not likely to confuse a car with a dishwasher, a tree, or a playground. A car is a complete unit—an object with unique properties.

You can also think of a computer program as consisting of objects. Instead of thinking of a piece of code that, for example, draws a rectangle on-screen, and another piece of code that fills the rectangle with text, and still another piece of code that enables you to move the rectangle around the screen, you can think of a single object: a window. This window object contains all the code that it needs in order to operate. Moreover, it also contains all the data that it needs. This is the philosophy behind OOP.

Object-Oriented Programming

Object-oriented programming enables you to think of program elements as objects. In the case of a window object, you don't need to know the details of how it works, nor do you need to know about the window's private data fields. You need to know only how to call the various functions (called *methods* in Java) that make the window operate. Consider the car object discussed in the previous section. To drive a car, you don't have to know the details of how a car works. You need to know only how to drive it. What's going on under the hood is none of your business. (And, if you casually try to make it your business, plan to face an amused mechanic who will have to straighten out your mess!)

But OOP is a lot more than just a way to hide the details of a program. To learn about OOP, you need to understand three main concepts that are the backbone of OOP. These concepts, which are covered in the following sections, are: *encapsulation, inheritance*, and *polymorphism*.

> **Note:** If you're new to programming, you might want to stop reading at this point and come back to this chapter after you've studied Chapters 5 through 14. It's not possible to discuss concepts such as encapsulation, inheritance, and polymorphism without dealing with such subjects as data types, variables, and variable scope. If these terms are unfamiliar, move on now to Chapter 5.

Encapsulation

One major difference between conventional structured programming and object-oriented programming is a handy thing called encapsulation. Encapsulation enables you to hide, inside the object, both the data fields and the methods that act on that data. (In fact, data fields and methods are the two main elements of an object in the Java programming language.) After you do this, you can control access to the data, forcing programs to retrieve or modify data only through the object's interface. In strict object-oriented design, an object's data is always private to the object. Other parts of a program should never have direct access to that data.

How does this data-hiding differ from a structured-programming approach? After all, you can always hide data inside functions, just by making that data local to the function. A problem arises, however, when you want to make the data of one function available to other functions. The way to do this in a structured program is to make the data global to the program, which gives any function access to it. It seems that you could use another level of scope—one that would make your data global to the functions that need it—but still prevent other functions from gaining access. Encapsulation does just that. In an object, the encapsulated data members are global to the object's methods, yet they are local to the object. They are not global variables.

Classes as Data Types

An object is just an instance of a data type. For example, when you declare a variable of type int, you're creating an instance of the int data type. A *class* is like a data type in that it is the blueprint upon which an object is based. When you need a new object in a program, you create a class, which is a kind of template for the object. Then, in your program, you create an instance of the class. This instance is called an object.

Classes are really nothing more than user-defined data types. As with any data type, you can have as many instances of the class as you want. For example, you can have more than one window in a Windows application, each with its own contents.

For example, think again about the integer data type (int). It's absurd to think that a program can have only one integer. You can declare many integers, just about all you want. The same is true of classes. After you define a new class, you can create many instances of the class. Each instance (called an object) normally has full access to the class's methods and gets its own copy of the data members.

Inheritance

Inheritance enables you to create a class that is similar to a previously defined class, but one that still has some of its own properties. Consider a car-simulation program. Suppose that you have a class for a regular car, but now you want to create a car that has a high-speed passing gear. In a traditional program, you might have to modify the existing code extensively and might introduce bugs into code that worked fine before your changes. To avoid these hassles, you use the object-oriented approach: Create a new class by inheritance. This new class inherits all the data and methods from the tested base class. (You can control the level of inheritance with the public, private, and protected keywords. You'll see how all this works with Java in Chapter 14, "Classes.") Now, you only need to worry about testing the new code you added to the derived class.

> **Note:** The designers of OOP languages didn't pick the word "inheritance" out of a hat. Think of how human children inherit many of their characteristics from their parents. But the children also have characteristics that are uniquely their own. In object-oriented programming, you can think of a base class as a parent and a derived class as a child.

Polymorphism

The last major feature of object-oriented programming is *polymorphism*. By using polymorphism, you can create new objects that perform the same functions as the base object but which perform one or more of these functions in a different way. For example, you may have a shape object that draws a circle on the screen. By using polymorphism, you can create a shape object that draws a rectangle instead. You do this by creating a new version of the method that draws the shape on the screen. Both the old circle-drawing and the new rectangle-drawing method have the same name (such as `DrawShape()`) but accomplish the drawing in a different way.

Example: Encapsulation, Inheritance, and Polymorphism

Although you won't actually start using Java classes until later in this book, this is a good time to look at OOP concepts in a general way. As an example, you'll extend the car metaphor you read earlier this chapter.

In that section I described a car as an object having several characteristics (direction, position, and speed) and several means (steering wheel, gas pedal, and brakes) to act on those characteristics. In terms of constructing a class for a car object, you can think of direction, position, and speed as the class's data fields and the steering wheel, gas pedal, and brakes as representing the class's methods.

The first step in creating an object is to define its class. For now, you'll use pseudocode to create a `Car` class. You'll learn about Java classes in Chapter 14, "Classes." The base `Car` class might look like Listing 4.1.

Listing 4.1   LST4_1.TXT: The Pseudocode for a Base Car Class.

```
class Car
{
    data direction;
    data position;
    data speed;

    method Steer();
    method PressGasPedal();
    method PressBrake();
}
```

In this base `Car` class, a car is defined by its direction (which way its pointed), position (where it's located), and speed. These three data fields can be manipulated by the three methods `Steer()`, `PressGasPedal()`, and `PressBrake()`. The `Steer()` method changes the car's direction, whereas the `PressGasPedal()` and `PressBrake()` change the car's speed. The car's position is affected by all three methods, as well as by the direction and speed settings.

The data fields and methods are all encapsulated inside the class. Moreover, the data fields are private to the class, meaning that they cannot be directly accessed from outside of the class. Only the class's three methods can access the data fields. In short, Listing 4.1 not only shows what a class might look like, it also shows how encapsulation works.

Now, suppose you want to create a new car that has a special passing gear. To do this, you can use OOP inheritance to derive a new class from the Car base class. Listing 4.2 is the pseudocode for this new class.

Listing 4.2   LST4_1.TXT: Deriving a New Class Using Inheritance.

```
Class PassingCar inherits from Car
{
    method Pass();
}
```

You may be surprised to see how small this new class is. It's small because it implicitly inherits all the data fields and methods from the Car base class. That is, not only does the PassingCar class have a method called Pass(), but it also has the direction, position, and speed data fields, as well as the Steer(), PressGasPedal(), and PressBrake() methods. The PassingCar class can use all these data fields and methods exactly as if they were explicitly defined in Listing 4.2. This is an example of inheritance.

The last OOP concept that you'll apply to the car classes is polymorphism. Suppose that you now decide that you want a new kind of car that has all the characteristics of a PassingCar, except that its passing gear is twice as fast as PassingCar's. You can solve this problem as shown in Listing 4.3.

Listing 4.3   LST4_3.TXT: Using Polymorphism to Create a Faster Car.

```
class FastCar inherits from PassingCar
{
    method Pass();
}
```

The FastCar class looks exactly like the original PassingCar class. However, rather than just inheriting the Pass() method, it defines its own version. This new version makes the car move twice as fast as PassingCar's Pass() method does (the code that actually implements each method is not shown). In this way, the FastCar class implements the same functionality as the PassingCar() class, but it implements that functionality a little differently.

> **Note:** Because the FastCar class inherits from PassingCar, which itself inherits from Car, a FastCar also inherits all the data fields and methods of the Car class. There are ways that you can control how inheritance works (using the public, protected, and private keywords), but you won't get into that until much later in this book.

Summary

Java is an object-oriented language, meaning that it can not only enable you to organize your program code into logical units called objects, but also that you can take advantage of encapsulation, inheritance, and polymorphism. Learning OOP, however, can be a little tricky. If you're a novice programmer, this chapter has probably left you confused. If so, read on to learn more about the Java language. Once you start writing Java programs, much of what you read here will make more sense. After finishing this part of the book, you might want to reread this chapter and so reinforce any concepts that may be shady now.

Review Questions

1. What is top-down programming?

2. What's the advantage of top-down programming?

3. How is OOP better than top-down programming?

4. What are the two main elements of a class?

5. How does a class relate to an object?

6. What are the three major concepts used in OOP?

7. Define each of these three concepts.

Review Exercises

1. Take an everyday task such as making a cake or driving a car and break the task down into a top-down "program." Try to create three levels of detail.

2. Consider a real-world object such as a stereo receiver or an oven. List the object's data fields and functions. Then, create a class for the object, using similar pseudocode to that used in Listing 4.1.

CHAPTER 5

Constants and Variables

If there's one thing that every computer program has in common, it's that they always process data input and produce some sort of output based on that data. And because data is so important to a computer program, it stands to reason that there must be plenty of different ways to store data so that programs can do their processing correctly and efficiently. In order to keep track of data, programs use constants and variables. In this chapter, you discover what constants and variables are, as well as learn to use them in the Java language.

Constants

If you think about the term "constant" for a few moments, you might conclude that constants must have something to do with data that never changes. And your conclusion would be correct. A constant is nothing more than a value, in a program, that stays the same throughout the program's execution. However, while the definition of a constant is fairly simple, constants themselves can come in many different guises. For example, the numeral 2, when it's used in a line of program code, is a constant. If you place the word "Java" in a program, the characters that comprise the word are also constants. In fact, these constant characters taken together are often referred to as a string constant.

> **Note:** To be entirely accurate, I should say that text and numerals that are placed in program code are actually called *literals*, because the value is literally, rather than symbolically, in the program. If this literal and symbolic stuff is confusing you, you'll probably have it figured out by the end of this chapter. For now, just know that I'm lumping literals in with constants to simplify the discussion.

Such values as the numeral 2 and the string constant "Java" are sometimes called hard-coded values because the values that represent the constants are placed literally in the program code. For example, suppose you were writing a program and wanted to calculate the amount of sales tax on a purchase. Suppose further that the total purchase in question is $12.00 and the sales tax in your state is 6 percent. The calculation that'll give you the sales tax would look like this:

```
tax = 12 * .06;
```

Suppose now that you write a large program that uses the sales tax percentage in many places. Then, after you've been happily using your program for a few months, the state suddenly decides to raise the sales tax to seven percent. In order to get your program working again, you have to go through every line of code, looking for the .06 values that represent the sales tax and changing them to .07. Such a modification can be a great deal of work in a large program. Worse, you may miss one or two places in the code that need to be changed, leaving your program with some serious bugs.

To avoid these situations, programmers often use something called *symbolic constants*, which are simply words that represent values in a program. In the case of your sales tax program, you could choose a word like SALESTAX (no spaces) to represent the current sales tax percentage for your state. Then, at the beginning of your program, you set SALESTAX to be equal to the current state sales tax. In the Java language, such a line of program code might look like this:

```
final float SALESTAX = 0.06;
```

In the preceding line, the word `final` tells Java that this data object is going to be a constant. The `float` is the data type, which, in this case, is a floating point. (You'll learn more about data types later in this chapter.) The word SALESTAX is the symbolic constant. The equals sign tells Java that the word on the left should be equal to the value on the right, which, in this case, is 0.06.

After defining the symbolic constant SALESTAX, you can rewrite any lines that use the current sales tax value to use the symbolic constant rather than the hard-coded value. For example, the calculation for the sales tax on that $12.00 purchase might now look something like this:

```
tax = 12 * SALESTAX;
```

> **Tip:** In order to differentiate symbolic constants from other values in a program, programmers often use all uppercase letters when naming these constants.

Now, when your state changes the sales tax to 7 percent, you need only change the value you assign to the symbolic constant and the rest of the program automatically fixes itself. The change would look like this:

```
final float SALESTAX = 0.07;
```

Variables

If constants are program values that cannot be changed throughout the execution of a program, what are variables? Variables are values that can change as much as needed during the execution of a program. Because of a variable's changing nature, there's no such thing as a hard-coded variable. That is, hard-coded values in a program are always constants (or, more accurately, literals).

Why do programs need variables? Think back to the sales tax program from the previous section. You may recall that you ended up with a program line that looked like this:

```
tax = 12 * SALESTAX;
```

In this line, the word `tax` is a variable. So, one reason you need variables in a program is to hold the results of a calculation. In this case, you can think of the word `tax` as a kind of digital bucket into which the program dumps the result of its sales tax calculation. When you need the value stored in `tax`, you can just reach in and take it out—figuratively speaking, of course. As an example, to determine the total cost of a $12.00 purchase, plus the sales tax, you might write a line like this:

```
total = 12 + tax;
```

In this line, the word `total` is yet another variable. After the computer performs the requested calculation, the variable `total` will contain the sum of 12 and whatever value is stored in `tax`. For example, if the value 0.72 is stored in `tax`, after the calculation, `total` would be equal to 12.72.

Do you see another place where a variable is necessary? How about the hard-coded value 12? Such a hard-coded value makes a program pretty useless because every person that comes into your store to buy something isn't going to spend exactly $12.00. Because the amount of each customer's purchase will change, the value used in your sales tax calculation must change, too. That means you need another variable. How about creating a variable named `purchase`? With such a variable, you can rewrite the calculations like this:

```
tax = purchase * SALESTAX;
total = purchase + tax;
```

Now you can see how valuable variables can be. Every value in the preceding lines is represented by a variable. (Although you're using SALESTAX as a symbolic constant, because of Java's current lack of true constants, it's really a variable, too.) All you have to do to get the total to charge your customer is plug the cost of his purchase into the variable purchase, something you'll see how to do in Chapter 6, "Simple Input and Output."

Math-savvy readers may have already figured that the preceding two lines can be easily simplified into one, like this:

```
total = purchase + (purchase * SALESTAX);
```

This revised line of code, however, is not as easy to understand as the original two lines were. In programming, you must constantly decide between longer, simpler code and shorter, more complex code. I tend to go for the longer, easy-to-understand approach, except when the longer code might bog down the program.

Naming Constants and Variables

The first computer languages were developed by mathematicians. For that reason, the calculations and the variables used in those calculations were modeled after the types of equations mathematicians were already accustomed to working with. For example, in the old days, the lines in your tax program might have looked like this:

```
a = b * c;
d = b + a;
```

As you can see, this type of variable-naming convention left a lot to be desired. It's virtually impossible to tell what type of calculations are being performed. In order to understand their own programs, programmers had to use tons of comments mixed in with their source code so they could remember what the heck they were doing from one programming session to the next. Such a section of source code in Java might look like Listing 5.1.

Listing 5.1   LST5_1.TXT: An Example of Mathematician's Variables.

```
// Calculate the amount of sales tax.
a = b * c;

// Add the sales tax to the purchase amount.
d = b + a;
```

Although adding comments to the program lines helps a little, the code is still pretty confusing, because you don't really know what the variables a, b, c, and d stand for. After a while (probably when mathematicians weren't the only programmers), someone came up with the idea of allowing more than one character in a variable name, which would enable the programmer to create mathematical expressions that read more like English. Thus, the confusing example above would be written as Listing 5.2.

Listing 5.2   LST5_2.TXT: Using English-like Variable Names.

```
// Calculate the amount of sales tax.
tax = purchase * SALESTAX;

// Add the sales tax to the purchase amount.
total = purchase + tax;
```

By using carefully chosen variable names, you can make your programs *self documenting*, which means that the program lines themselves tell whoever might be reading the program what the program does. If you strip away the comments from the preceding example, you can still see what calculations are being performed.

Of course, there are rules for choosing constant and variable names (also known as *identifiers* because they identify a program object). You can't just type a bunch of characters on your keyboard and expect Java to accept them. First, every Java identifier must begin with one of these characters:

A-Z

a-z

–

$

The preceding characters are any uppercase letter from A through Z, any lowercase letter from a through z, an underscore, and the dollar sign.

Following the first character, the rest of the identifier can use any of these characters:

A-Z

a-z

–

$

0-9

As you may have noticed, this second set of characters is very similar to the first. In fact, the only difference is the addition of the digits from 0 through 9.

> **Note:** Java identifiers can also use Unicode characters above the hexadecimal value of 00C0. If you don't know about Unicode characters, don't panic; you won't be using them in this book. Briefly put, Unicode characters expand the symbols that can be used in a character set to include characters that are not part of the English language.

Using the rules given, the following are valid identifiers in a Java program:

```
number
number2
amount_of_sale
$amount
```

The following identifiers are not valid in a Java program:

```
1number
amount of sale
&amount
item#
```

Example: Creating Your Own Identifiers

Suppose that you're now ready to write a program that calculates the total number of parking spaces left in a parking garage. You know that the total number of spaces in the garage is 100. You further know that the vehicles in the garage are classified as cars, trucks, and vans. The first step is to determine which values would be good candidates for constants. Because a constant should represent a value that's not likely to change from one program run to another, the number of vehicles that the garage can hold would make a good constant. Thinking hard (someone smell wood burning?), you come up with an identifier of TOTALSPACES for this value. In Java, the constant's definition looks like this:

```
final int TOTALSPACES = 100;
```

In this line, the keyword int represents the data type, which is integer. You should be able to understand the rest of the line.

Now, you need to come up with the mathematical formula that'll give you the answer you want. First, you know that the total number of vehicles in the garage is equal to the sum of the number of cars, trucks, and vans in the garage. Stating the problem in this way not only clarifies what form the calculation must take, but also suggests a set of good identifiers for your program. Those identifiers are cars, trucks, vans, and total_vehicles. So, in Java, your first calculation looks like this:

```
total_vehicles = cars + trucks + vans;
```

The next step is to subtract the total number of vehicles from the total number of spaces that the garage holds. For this calculation, you need only one new identifier to represent the remaining spaces, which is the result of the calculation. Again, stating the problem leads to the variable name, which might be `remaining_spaces`. The final calculation then looks like this:

```
remaining_spaces = TOTALSPACES - total_vehicles;
```

Data Types

In attempting to give you a quick introduction to constants and variables, the preceding sections skipped over a very important attribute of all constants and variables: data type. You may remember my mentioning two data types already, these being floating point (represented by the `float` keyword) and integer (represented by the `int` keyword). Java has eight different data types, all of which represent different kinds of values in a program. These data types are `byte`, `short`, `int`, `long`, `float`, `double`, `char`, and `boolean`. In this section, you'll learn what kinds of values these various data types represent.

Integer Values

The most common values used in computer programs are integers, which represent whole number values such as 12, 1988, and -34. Integer values can be both positive or negative, or even the value 0. The size of the value that's allowed depends on the integer data type you choose. Java features four integer data types, which are `byte`, `short`, `int`, and `long`. Although some computer languages allow both signed and unsigned integer values, all of Java's integers are signed, which means they can be positive or negative. (Unsigned values, which Java does not support, can hold only positive numbers.)

The first integer type, `byte`, takes up the least amount of space in a computer's memory. When you declare a constant or variable as `byte`, you are limited to values in the range -128 to 127. Why would you want to limit the size of a value in this way? Because the smaller the data type, the faster the computer can manipulate it. For example, your computer can move a `byte` value, which consumes only eight bits of memory, much faster than an `int` value, which, in Java, is four times as large.

In Java, you declare a `byte` value like this:

```
byte identifier;
```

In the preceding line, `byte` is the data type for the value, and *identifier* is the variable's name. You can also simultaneously declare and assign a value to a variable like this:

```
byte count = 100;
```

After Java executes the preceding line, your program will have a variable named count that currently holds the value of 100. Of course, you can change the contents of count at any time in your program. It only starts off holding the value 100.

The next biggest type of Java integer is short. A variable declared as short can hold a value from –32,768 to 32,767. You declare a short value like this:

```
short identifier;
```

or

```
short identifier = value;
```

In the preceding line, *value* can be any value from –32,768 to 32,767, as described previously. In Java, short values are twice as big in memory—16 bits (or two bytes)—as byte values.

Next in the integer data types is int, which can hold a value from –2,147,483,648 to 2,147,483,647. Now you're getting into some big numbers! The int data type can hold such large numbers because it takes up 32 bits (four bytes) of computer memory. You declare int values like this:

```
int identifier;
```

or

```
int identifier = value;
```

The final integer data type in the Java language is long, which takes up a whopping 64 bits (eight bytes) of computer memory and can hold truly immense numbers. Unless you're calculating the number of molecules in the universe, you don't even have to know how big a long number can be. I'd figure it out for you, but I've never seen a calculator that can handle numbers that big. You declare a long value like this:

```
long identifier;
```

or

```
long identifier = value;
```

> **Tip:** How do you know which integer data type to use in your program? Choose the smallest data type that can hold the largest numbers you'll be manipulating. Following this rule keeps your programs running as fast as possible. However, having said that, I should tell you that most programmers (including me) use the int data type a lot, even when they can get away with a byte.

Floating-Point Values

Whereas integer values can hold only whole numbers, the floating-point data types can hold values with both whole number and fractional parts. Examples of floating-point values include 32.9, 123.284, and –43.436. As you can see, just like integers, floating-point values can be either positive or negative.

Java includes two floating-point types, which are `float` and `double`. Each type allows greater precision in calculations. What does this mean? Floating-point numbers can become very complex when they're used in calculations, particularly in multiplication and division. For example, when you divide 3.9 by 2.7, you get 1.44444444. In actuality, though, the fractional portion of the number goes on forever. That is, if you were to continue the division calculation, you'd discover that you keep getting more and more fours in the fractional part of the answer. The answer to 3.9 divided by 2.7 is not really 1.44444444, but rather something more like 1.4444444444444444. But even that answer isn't completely accurate. A more accurate answer would be 1.44444444444444444444444444444444. The more 4s you add to the answer the more accurate the answer becomes—yet, because the 4s extend on into infinity, you can never arrive at a completely accurate answer.

Dealing with floating-point values frequently means deciding how many decimal places in the answer is accurate enough. That's where the difference between the `float` and `double` data types shows up. In Java, a value declared as `float` can hold a number in the range from around -3.402823×10^{38} to around 3.402823×10^{38}. These types of values are also known as *single-precision* floating-point numbers and take up 32 bits (four bytes) of memory. You declare a single-precision floating-point number like this:

```
float identifier;
```

or

```
float identifier = value;
```

In the second line, *value* must be a value in the range given in the previous paragraph, followed by an upper- or lowercase `F`. However, you can write floating-point numbers in a couple of ways, using regular digits and a decimal point or using scientific notation. This value is the type of floating-point number you're used to seeing:
356.552

Now, here's the same number written using Java's rules, in both the number's normal form and in the form of scientific notation:

356.552f

3.56552e2f

Both of the preceding values are equivalent, and you can use either form in a Java program. The e2 in the second example is the equivalent of writing x 102 and is a short form of scientific notation that's often used in programming languages.

> **Note:** If you're not familiar with scientific notation, the value 3.402823 x 10³⁸ is equal to 3.402823 times a number that starts with a 1 and is followed by 38 zeroes. Computer languages shorten this scientific notation to 3.402823e38.

The second type of floating-point data, double, represents a *double-precision* value, which is a much more accurate representation of floating-point numbers because it allows for more decimal places. A double value can be in the range from $-1.79769313486232 \times 10^{308}$ to $1.79769313486232 \times 10^{308}$ and is declared like this:

```
double identifier;
```

or

```
double identifier = value;
```

Floating-point values of the double type are written exactly as their float counterparts, except you use an upper- or lowercase D as the suffix, rather than an F. Here's a few examples:

3.14d

344.23456D

3.4423456e2d

> **Tip:** When using floating-point numbers in your programs, the same rule that you learned about integers applies: Use the smallest data type you can. This is especially true for floating-point numbers, which are notorious for slowing computer programs to a crawl. Unless you're doing highly precise programming, such as 3-D modeling, the single-precision float data type should do just fine.

Character Values

Often in your programs, you'll need a way to represent character values rather than just numbers. A character is a symbol that's used in text. The most obvious examples of characters are the letters of the alphabet, in both upper- and lowercase varieties. There are, however, many other characters, including not only things such as spaces, exclamation points, and commas, but also tabs, carriage returns, and line feeds. The symbols 0 through 9 are also characters when they're not being used in mathematical calculations.

In order to provide storage for character values, Java features the char data type, which is 16 bits. However, the size of the char data type has little to do with the values it can hold. Basically, you can think of a char as being able to hold a single character. (The 16 bit length accommodates Unicode characters, which you don't need to worry about in this book.) You declare a char value like this:

```
char c;
```

or

```
char c = 'A';
```

In the second example, you're not only declaring the variable c as a char, but also setting its value to an uppercase A. Notice that the character that's being assigned is enclosed in single quotes.

Some characters cannot be written with only a single symbol. For example, the tab character is represented in Java as \t, which is a backslash followed by a lowercase t. There are several of these special characters, as shown in Table 5.1.

Table 5.1   Special Character Literals.

Character	Symbol
Backslash	\\
Backspace	\b
Carriage return	\r
Double quote	\"
Form feed	\f
Line feed	\n
Single quote	\'
Tab	\t

Although the special characters in Table 5.1 are represented by two symbols, the first of which is always a backslash, you still use them as single characters. For example, to define a char variable as a backspace character, you might write something like the following in your Java program:

```
char backspace = '\b';
```

When Java's compiler sees the backslash, it knows that it's about to encounter a special character of some type. The symbol following the backslash tells the compiler which special character to use. Because the backslash is used to signify a special character, when you want to specify the backslash character yourself, you must use two backslashes, which keeps the compiler from getting confused. Other special characters that might confuse the compiler because they are used as part of the Java language are single and double quotes. When you want to use these characters in your program's data, you must also precede them with a backslash.

Boolean Values

Many times in a program, you need a way to determine if a specific condition has been met. For example, you might need to know whether a part of your program executed properly. In such cases, you can use Boolean values, which are represented in Java by the `boolean` data type. Boolean values are unique in that they can be only one of two possible values: true or false. You declare a `boolean` value like this:

```
boolean identifier;
```

or

```
boolean identifier = value;
```

In the second example, *value* must be `true` or `false`. In an actual program, you might write something like this:

```
boolean file_okay = true;
```

Boolean values are often used in `if` statements, which enable you to do different things depending on the value of a variable. You'll learn about `if` statements in Chapter 9, "The `if` and `switch` Statements."

Table 5.2 summarizes Java's various data types. Take some time now to look over the table and make sure you understand how the data types differ from each other. You might also want to think of ways you might use each data type in an actual program.

Table 5.2   Summary of Java's Data Types.

Type	Value
byte	−128 to 127
short	−32,768 to 32,767
int	−2,147,483,648 to 2,147,483,647
long	Huge
float	−3.402823e38 to 3.402823e38
double	−1.79769313486232e308 to 1.79769313486232e308
char	Symbols used in text
boolean	True or false

Variable Scope

When you write your Java programs, you can't just declare your variables willy-nilly all over the place. You first have to consider how and where you need to use the variables. This is because variables have an attribute known as *scope*, which determines where in your program variables can be accessed. In Java, a variable's scope is determined by the program block in which the variable first appears. The variable is "visible" to the program only from the beginning of its program block to the end of the program block. When a program's execution leaves a block, all the variables in the block disappear, a phenomenon that programmers call "going out of scope."

Now you're probably wondering, "What the devil is a program block?" Generally, a program block is a section of program code that starts with an opening curly brace ({) and ends with a closing curly brace (}). (Sometimes, the beginning and ending of a block are not explicitly defined, but you don't have to worry about that just yet.) Specifically, program blocks include things like classes, functions, and loops, all of which you'll learn about later in this book.

Of course, things aren't quite as simple as all that (you're dealing with computers, after all). The truth is that you can have program blocks within other program blocks. When you have one block inside another, the inner block is considered to be *nested*. Figure 5.1 illustrates the concept of nested program blocks.

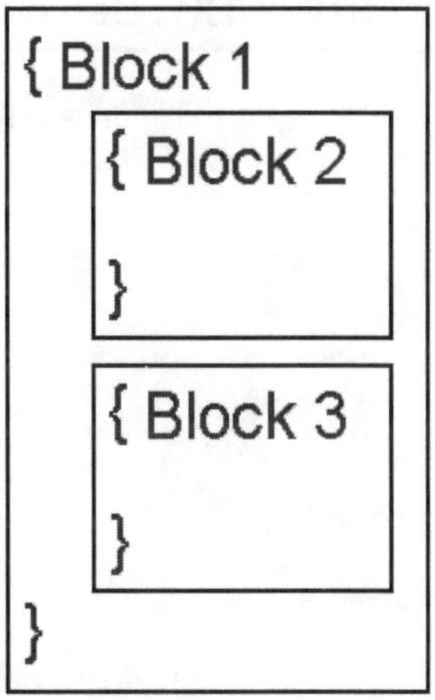

Figure 5.1

Program blocks can be nested inside other program blocks.

In the figure, Block 1 encloses both Block 2 and Block 3. That is, Block 2 and Block 3 are nested within Block 1, because these blocks occur after Block 1's opening brace but before Block 1's closing brace. If you wanted, you could also create a Block 4 and nest it within Block 2 or Block 3, and thus create even another level of nesting. As you'll see when you start writing full-length Java programming, all programs have a lot of nesting going on.

The ability to nest program blocks adds a wrinkle to the idea of variable scope. Because a variable remains in scope from the beginning of its block to the end of its block, such a variable is also in scope in any blocks that are nested in the variable's block. For example, looking back at Figure 5.1, a variable that's defined in Block 1 is accessible in not just Block 1, but also in Block 2 and Block 3. However, a variable defined inside Block 2 is accessible only in Block 2, because such a variable goes into scope at the start of Block 2 and goes out of scope at the end of Block 2. If you're a little confused, the following example ought to clear things up.

Example: Determining a Variable's Scope

Suppose you've written the small Java program shown in Listing 5.3. (Nevermind, at this point, that you don't know much about writing Java programs. Such minor details will be remedied by the time you complete this book.) The program shown in the listing follows the same program structure as that shown in Figure 5.1. That is, there is one large main block that contains two nested blocks. The main block begins with the opening brace on the second line and ends with the closing brace at the end of the program. The first inner block begins with the opening brace after the line labeling `Function1` and ends with the closing brace three lines below the opening brace. The second inner block is defined similarly, with its own opening and closing braces.

Listing 5.3   LST5_3.TXT: Determining Variable Scope.

```
public class Block1 extends Applet
{
    int value1 = 32;

    void Block2()
    {
        float value2 = 4.5f;
        value1 = 45;
    }

    void Block3()
    {
        value1 = 100;

        // The following line causes an error.
        value2 = 55.46f;
    }
}
```

Now look at the variables being used in this program. The first variable defined in the program is `value1`, which is found right after the main block's opening brace. This means that `value1` is accessible in all three blocks, as you can see by looking at the `Block2` and `Block3` blocks, both of which assign new values to `value1`.

The second variable in the program, value2, is defined inside the Block2 block, where it's both declared and assigned the value 4.5f. In the Block3 block, the program tries to assign a value to value2. If you tried to compile this program, you'd see that this line creates an error message, as shown in Figure 5.2. In the figure, the compiler is insisting that value2 in the Block3 block is undefined, which, of course, is true as far as the Block3 block is concerned. You'd get a similar message if you tried to access value2 anywhere but within the scope of the Block2 block.

Figure 5.2

When you try to access a variable that's out of scope, Java's compiler thinks that the variable is undefined.

You can use variable scope to simplify the access of variables in a program. For example, you will usually declare variables that you need in many places, so that they are in scope in the entire class. That way, you can access the variables without having to pass them as arguments to functions. (If you don't know about argument passing just yet, you will after you read Chapter 12, "Functions.") On the other hand, you'll have lots of variables that you use only inside one particular program block. You can keep your program uncluttered by being sure to declare these types of variables only in the blocks in which they're used. You'll learn more about setting up variables with the proper scope as you write Java programs later in this book.

Summary

All computers must manipulate data in order to produce output. Java, like all programming languages, features many data types that you can use for constants and variables in your programs. These data types enable you to store everything from simple integers like 23 and −10 to strings and complex floating-point numbers. There's a lot to know about variables, so your head may be spinning a bit at this point. Rest assured, however, that once you start writing programs and using variables, all the theoretical stuff will make sense.

Review Questions

1. What is a constant?

2. What is a variable?

3. How do constants and variables make writing programs easier?

4. Name the eight data types used in Java.

5. What is variable scope?

Review Exercises

1. Suppose you need to write a Java program that calculates an employee's paycheck for a given number of hours of work. Write declarations for the variables you'll need.

2. Using the variables you declared in exercise 1, write the program lines needed to perform the paycheck calculations.

3. Using Figure 5.1 as a guide, create a new figure that adds a program block to the class such that any variables declared in the new block cannot be accessed in any other program block.

4. Using the modified figure, add yet another program block, this time adding an additional level of block nesting.

CHAPTER 6

Simple Input and Output

In the previous chapter, you learned how you can store various types of values in your Java programs. It may have occurred to you that it doesn't do much good to store data in a computer's memory if you have no way of actually seeing that data. Also, you need a way to request and receive data from users of your programs. Both of these tasks—displaying and retrieving data—are accomplished through simple input and output, or I/O (as it's commonly called). In this chapter, you'll learn how Java enables you to perform simple I/O in your applets.

Windows and Graphics

Because you'll be writing your applets for a graphical user interface (GUI) such as Windows, you can't use the same kinds of data input/output that you may have been accustomed to using under another operating system, such as MS-DOS. This is because, under a system such as Windows, everything that appears on the screen is graphical (unlike MS-DOS, which displays plain old text).

Still, displaying graphical text doesn't require a whole lot of work, as long as you're not concerned with things like fonts and the size of the text string you want to display. You have to remember, though, that almost all graphical text is proportional, meaning that each letter in a line of graphical text takes up a different amount of space. Under an operating system like MS-DOS, most text output uses non-proportional characters. The difference is illustrated in Figure 6.1.

Figure 6.1

In a proportional font, each character takes up only as much space as it needs.

NON-PROPORTIONAL
PROPORTIONAL

Look at the letter "I" in the proportional font. You can see that it takes up much less space than other letters in the word. On the other hand, the letter "I" in the non-proportional font, as well as the hyphen, takes up exactly the same amount of space as every other letter.

The point is that, because of the different fonts that are used to print text in a graphical user interface, you can't assume much about the size of the text that'll be used. There are ways to figure out the actual size of a text string, but you don't have to be concerned with these details for now. Just be aware that text output in your applets is going to be graphical.

Displaying Text in an Applet

The easiest thing to display is a line of text. But because the text output will be graphical, you need to use one of Java's graphical-text functions. The most commonly used is drawString(), which is part of the Graphics class contained in the awt package. Listing 6.1 shows a simple applet that uses this method to display a single line of text. Figure 6.1 shows what the applet looks like when viewed with the Appletviewer application. Finally, Listing 6.2 is an HTML document that tests the Applet1 applet.

> **Note:** A *package* is nothing more than a collection of related classes. The awt (abstract windows toolkit) package contains all the classes that handle graphical windows. You'll learn a lot more about classes, packages, and the awt later in this book.

Listing 6.1   Applet1.java: An Applet That Displays a Single Line of Text.

```
import java.awt.*;
import java.applet.*;

public class Applet1 extends Applet
{
    public void paint(Graphics g)
```

```
        {
            g.drawString("Hello from Java!", 60, 75);
        }
    }
}
```

Tell Java that the program uses classes in the awt *package.*
Tell Java that the program uses classes in the applet *package.*
Derive the Applet1 *class from Java's* Applet *class.*
Override the Applet *class's* paint() *method.*
Draw a text string on the applet's surface.

Figure 6.2

When you run the
Applet1 applet,
you'll see a single
line of text in the
applet's display.

Listing 6.2   APPLET1.HTML: An HTML Document for Testing Applet1.

```
<title>Applet Test Page</title>
<h1>Applet Test Page</h1>
<applet
    code="Applet1.class"
    width=200
    height=150
    name="Applet1">
</applet>
```

Example: Creating and Running Applet1

In the next section, you'll see exactly how the Applet1 applet works. But before you get too much farther, you need to know how to create and run the many applets that you'll find in this book. All the applets that follow use the same sort of procedure. This procedure involves creating the applet's source code, compiling the code, and then writing the HTML document that demonstrates the applet. Follow the steps below to get the Applet1 applet up on your screen.

1. Create a folder called CLASSES on the root directory of your hard drive.

2. Type Listing 6.1 and save it in the CLASSES folder as an ASCII file. Name the file Applet1.java. (Use uppercase and lowercase letters exactly as shown for the program's file name.) Note that you can also copy the listing from this book's CD-ROM, if you don't want to type it.

> **Note:** Java insists that the name of a Java source-code file is the same name as the class contained in the file. If you try to use different names, even if the difference is only the case of a letter or two, the Java compiler will complain and refuse to compile the program.

3. Start an MS-DOS session by selecting Start/Programs/MS-DOS Prompt. If the MS-DOS screen takes over the entire screen, press Alt+Enter to display the MS-DOS session in a window.

4. If you haven't added the JAVA\BIN path to your AUTOEXEC.BAT file, type `PATH=JAVA\BIN` at the MS-DOS prompt. This ensures that the system will be able to find Java's executables.

5. Type `cd c:\classes` to move to your CLASSES folder.

6. Type `javac Applet1.java` to compile the Applet1 applet. You should receive no error messages, as shown in Figure 6.3. If you do receive error messages, carefully check your typing of Listing 6.1. Also, make sure you typed the command line `javac Applet1.java` properly. When the compiler finishes, you'll have the file `Applet1.class` in your CLASSES directory. This is the applet's byte-code file.

Figure 6.3

The Applet1.class file must compile with no errors.

7. Type Listing 6.2 and save it as an ASCII file to your CLASSES folder. Name the file APPLET1.HTML. (This time, the case of the letters doesn't matter.)

8. At the MS-DOS prompt, type `appletviewer applet1.html` (case doesn't matter). When you do, Appletviewer will load and display the applet.

How Applet1 Works

By now, you have the source code for Applet1 properly typed and compiled. You've even run the applet using Appletviewer. You know that the call to the drawString() method prints a string as graphical text in the applet's display area. But what are the values between drawString()'s parentheses? And how does the program know when to execute the call to drawString()?

First, look at the paint() method. Java calls paint() whenever the applet's display area (or *canvas*, as it's often called) needs to be redrawn. The paint() method always gets called when the applet first appears on the screen, which is exactly what's happening in Applet1. You run the applet, Java calls paint() when the applet appears, and paint() calls drawString(), which displays the text string "Hello from Java."

> **Note:** The Java compiler is case-sensitive, meaning that it can differentiate between upper- and lowercase letters. For this reason, you have to be extra careful to type method names properly. For example, if you type Paint() instead of paint(), Java will not recognize the method and will not call it when the applet needs to be redrawn.

What's that "g" followed by a period in front of the call to drawString()? Remember that I said drawString() is a method of the Graphics class. If you look at the first line of the paint() method, you'll see Graphics g in the parentheses. This means that Java is sending an object of the Graphics class to the paint() method and that object is called g. Whenever you need to call an object's method, you must preface the method's name with the object's name followed by a period. So, the line

```
g.drawString("Hello from Java!", 60, 75);
```

tells Java to call the g object's drawString() method. The values in the parentheses are called *arguments*, which are values that you need to send to the method. The arguments in the above call to drawString() tell Java to draw the text "Hello from Java!" at column 60 and row 75 of the display area. (The position is measured in pixels, not characters. A *pixel* is the smallest dot that can be displayed on the screen.) To display the text at a different location, just change the second and third arguments. For example, Figure 6.4 shows the text positioned at 25,25.

Figure 6.4

Here, Applet1 displays the text at position 25,25.

Getting Input from the User

Again, because you are now programming in a graphical environment, getting input from the user isn't as easy as just calling an input command. You must first create an area of the screen in which the user can type and edit his response to your request. There are several ways to do this, but one of the easiest is to add a control of the TextField class in your applet. A TextField control is much like the edit boxes you see when using Windows. You might, for example, see a number of edit controls in a dialog box. Listing 4.3 shows how to include a TextField control in your applet. Figure 6.5 shows the Applet2 applet in action.

Listing 6.3   Applet2.java: Getting Input from the User.

```java
import java.awt.*;
import java.applet.*;

public class Applet2 extends Applet
{
    TextField textField;

    public void init()
    {
        textField = new TextField(20);
        add(textField);
    }
}
```

Tell Java that the program uses classes in the awt *package.*
Tell Java that the program uses classes in the applet *package.*
Derive the Applet2 *class from Java's* Applet *class.*
  Declare textField *as an object of the* TextField *class.*
  Override the Applet *class's* init() *method.*
    Create the new TextField *object.*
    Add the TextField *object to the applet's display.*

Figure 6.5

The Applet2 applet displays an area in which you can type.

To run the Applet2 applet yourself, you'll need to type and save the source code, naming it `Applet2.java`. (You can copy the source code from the CD-ROM, if you like, and thus save on typing. Of course, you won't learn as much that way.) Then compile the source code (type **javac Applet2.java** at the MS-DOS prompt), which gives you the `Applet2.class` file. Next, create a new HTML document from the one shown in Listing 6.2, changing all instances of Applet1 to Applet2. You can then run Applet2 by typing **appletviewer applet2.html** at the DOS prompt.

How Applet2 Works

Applet2 looks quite a bit different from Applet1. First, it declares a data field named `textField` as an object of the `TextField` class, which represents a control very much like a standard Windows edit box. The program declares the control like this:

```
TextField textField;
```

Notice that the `textField` object is declared just as you would declare any other kind of data object such as an integer or a floating-point value. Next, notice that, although the name of the class and the name of the object are spelled identically, the object's name starts with a lowercase letter. This makes all the difference in the world to Java, which is a case-sensitive language.

Another difference between Applet1 and Applet2 is that Applet2 has an `init()` method instead of `paint()`. The `Init()` method is another of those methods that Java calls automatically—in this case, as soon as you run the Applet2 applet. Because Java calls `init()` almost immediately, it's a great place to initialize the applet. (Guess that's why they called it `init()`, huh?)

In Applet2, when `init()` gets called, `textField` has already been declared as an object of the `TextField` class, but `textField` hasn't yet been assigned a value. The first line of code in `init()` creates the `TextField` object and assigns it to `textField`, like this:

```
textField = new TextField(20);
```

After Java executes this line, `textField` refers to an actual `TextField` object. The value in the parentheses is the width of the `TextField` control; the larger this number, the wider the control. Keep in mind that a `textField` control can hold more text than its width allows. If you type past the end of the control's text box, the text scrolls horizontally.

The next step is to add the object to the applet's display area, like this:

```
add(textField);
```

The `add()` method's single argument is the control you want to add to the applet.

After creating the control and adding it to the applet, the control will automatically appear when Java draws the applet. You don't need a `paint()` method to draw a control, because the control can take care of itself.

Once the `TextField` control is on the screen, you can type in it. First, click the control to give it the focus, then type and edit to your heart's content.

Example: Retrieving text from a *TextField* control

In the Applet2 applet, you can type all you like in the TextField control, but how do you get the text out of the control and actually do something with it? Follow the steps below to create Applet3, a new version of Applet2 that can retrieve and display any text entered into the TextField control.

1. Type Listing 6.4 and save it in the CLASSES folder as an ASCII file. Name the file Applet3.java. Note that you can copy the listing from this book's CD-ROM if you don't want to type it.

Listing 6.4   Applet3.java: Source Code for the Applet3 Applet.

```java
import java.awt.*;
import java.applet.*;

public class Applet3 extends Applet
{
    TextField textField;

    public void init()
    {
        textField = new TextField(20);
        add(textField);
    }

    public void paint(Graphics g)
    {
        String s = textField.getText();
        g.drawString(s, 40, 50);
    }

    public boolean action(Event event, Object arg)
    {
        repaint();
        return true;
    }
}
```

Tell Java that the program uses classes in the awt *package.*
Tell Java that the program uses classes in the applet *package.*
Derive the Applet3 *class from Java's* Applet *class.*
  Declare textField *as an object of the* TextField *class.*
  Override the Applet *class's* init() *method.*
    Create the new TextField *object.*
    Add the TextField *object to the applet's display.*

> *Override the `Applet` class's `paint()` method.*
>   *Get the text string from the `TextField` control.*
>   *Display the text in the applet's display area.*
> *Override the `Applet` class's `action()` method.*
>   *Force the applet to redraw its display area.*
>   *Tell Java that the `action()` method finished successfully.*

2. Start an MS-DOS session by selecting Start/Programs/MS-DOS Prompt. If the MS-DOS screen takes over the entire screen, press Alt+Enter to display the MS-DOS session in a window.

3. Type **cd c:\classes** to move to your CLASSES folder.

4. Type **javac Applet3.java** to compile the Applet3 applet. You should receive no error messages. If you do receive error messages, carefully check your typing of Listing 6.4. Also, make sure you typed the command line **javac Applet3.java** properly.

5. Modify Listing 6.2 by replacing all occurrences of Applet1 with Applet3 and save it as an ASCII file to your CLASSES folder. Name the file APPLET3.HTML.

6. At the MS-DOS prompt, type **appletviewer applet3.html**. When you do, Appletviewer will load and display the applet.

When you run Applet3, go ahead and type some text into the `TextField` control. When you press Enter, the text appears in the applet's display area, right below the control (Figure 6.6).

Figure 6.6

Applet3 can display the text you type into the TextField control.

How Applet3 Works

If you look at the Applet3 program code, you can see that you've added a `paint()` method. This is where the text that the user types into the `TextField` control gets displayed. First, `paint()` extracts the text from the control, like this:

```
String s = textField.getText();
```

This line declares a variable called s to be an object of the String class, and then it sets s equal to the text string in the control. (The String class is another of Java's built-in classes that you'll learn more about later. For now, just know that this class represents text strings.) You can see in this line that you're calling the textField object's getText() method, because of the object and method name separated by the dot. The getText() method simply returns the text string that's stored in the textField control.

Displaying the string is as easy as calling on your old friend drawString(), as follows:

```
g.drawString(s, 40, 50);
```

One big difference between Applet2 and Applet3 is the action() method. Java calls this method whenever the user performs some action with controls in the applet. In this case, the action that action() responds to is the user's pressing Enter after typing text. In Applet3, the action() method does nothing more than call the applet's repaint() method, which tells Java that you want to redraw the applet's display area. (You'll learn more about using the action() method later in the book.) This causes Java to call the paint() method, which very neatly displays the control's string.

Displaying Numerical Values

In the previous chapter, you learned to declare and define a number of different variable types, including int, byte, short, float, and other numerical values. The problem with numerical values in a computer is that you can't display them without first converting them to text strings. Luckily, this task is pretty easy to perform. You need only call the String class's valueOf() method, as shown in Listing 6.5. Figure 6.7 shows Appletviewer running Applet4.

Listing 6.5   Applet4.java: The Source Code for Applet4.

```
import java.awt.*;
import java.applet.*;

public class Applet4 extends Applet
{
    public void paint(Graphics g)
    {
        int x = 10;
        String s = String.valueOf(x);
        g.drawString(s, 40, 50);
    }
}
```

Tell Java that the program uses classes in the awt *package.*
Tell Java that the program uses classes in the applet *package.*
Derive the Applet4 *class from Java's* Applet *class.*
  Override the Applet *class's* paint() *method.*
    Declare the integer x *and set its value to 10.*
    Convert x *to a string.*
    Display the string that represents x*'s value.*

As you can see in Listing 6.5, the String class has a method called valueOf() that can convert numerical values to strings. The method's single argument is the value you want to convert, which can be any of Java's numerical data types.

Figure 6.7

The Applet4 applet converts and displays an integer value.

Summary

All computer programs must deal with some form of I/O. At the very least, a program must be able to display information to the user, as well as retrieve data from the user. Java has several ways to handle this basic form of I/O, a couple of which you learned in this chapter. As you dig deeper into the art of writing Java applets, you'll see other ways to perform I/O.

Review Questions

1. What is graphical text?

2. What's the difference between proportional and non-proportional fonts?

3. What are arguments?

4. Describe the three arguments used with the drawString() method.

5. What does the paint() method do?

6. Describe one way to get user input in your applets.

7. Describe how the init() method works.

8. Describe how the action() method works.

9. How can you convert a numerical value to a text string?

Review Exercises

1. Modify Applet1 so that it displays the text string "Out to lunch!" at position 30, 50 in the applet's display area.

2. Modify Applet2 so that it displays a `TextField` control half as wide as the one displayed in the original program.

3. Write an applet that displays the days of the week in a column down the center of the applet's display area.

4. Using Applet3 as a model, write a new applet called NameApplet that asks the user for her name and age and then prints the answers in the applet's display area. The finished applet should look like Figure 6.8. (This one's tough, so, if you get stumped, check out the file NameApplet.java in the CHAP06 folder of this book's CD-ROM. First try to solve the problem yourself, though.)

Figure 6.8

This is what the NameApplet applet should look like when it is run with Appletviewer.

CHAPTER 7

Math Operators

In Chapter 5, "Constants and Variables," you got a quick look at a few math operators, including the times (*), plus (+), and minus (-) signs. You even got a chance to use these operators in a few simple mathematical formulas. There's still a lot more to learn about math operators, though, as you'll discover as you read this chapter. Here, you'll not only learn a few more operators, but also learn about *operator precedence*, which determines the order in which operations are performed.

The Addition Operator

In case you were sleeping during second grade, you might like to know that the addition operator (+) is used to compute the sum of two values. As with all mathematical operations, Java performs these summing tasks just as you did in your second-grade homework. For example, the following line shows the general form of an addition operation in Java:

```
result = expr1 + expr2;
```

Here, the values represented by expr1 and expr2 are added together (summed), with the result being assigned to the variable represented by result. The values expr1 and expr2 are actually expressions, which means that they can be anything from a literal number like 5 to a complex formula like 5*(3+7)^10. You'll get a closer look at expressions in the next chapter, "Expressions."

Example: Using the Addition Operator

Suppose you want to sum the values of two variables. For example, you're writing a program that asks the user for two values and then prints the sum of the values. Assuming that the user's values get stored in two variables called `value1` and `value2`, you might write a line of Java code that looks like this:

```
sum = value1 + value2;
```

In this example, if the user entered 12 as the value for `value1` and 15 as the value for `value2`, after Java executed the line, `sum` would be equal to 27.

Example: Multiple Additions

In the previous example, you saw the simplest way you can use the addition operator. However, you are not limited to adding only two values. You can, in fact, add as many expressions as you like. To extend the previous example, suppose you have four values you need to sum. You can use a line of code like this:

```
sum = value1 + value2 + value3 + value4;
```

As you'll see in Chapter 8, "Expressions," you can create all kinds of complicated mathematical formulas with Java.

The Subtraction Operator

You can use the subtraction operator, which looks like a minus sign (–), to subtract one value or expression from another. Although the subtraction operator yields a different result than the addition operator (thank heavens for that), it's used in exactly the same way, as you can see by this general example:

```
result = expr1 - expr2;
```

Here, the value represented by `expr2` is subtracted from `expr1`, with the result being assigned to the variable `result`. Just as you learned with the addition operator, the values `expr1` and `expr2` are expressions that can be anything that results in a numerical value.

Example: Using the Subtraction Operator

Suppose you want to subtract the value of one variable from another. For example, the program you're writing requires that you subtract a customer's monthly payment from the balance he owes. You might write a line of Java code that looks like this:

```
new_balance = current_balance - payment;
```

In this example, if the customer's current balance was $110 and he paid $25, after Java executed the line, new_balance would be equal to $85. (Of course, the subtraction is being done with the numbers 110 and 25, and the result is 85. The computer doesn't know anything about dollars, a fact that makes it tough for a computer to do its grocery shopping.)

> **Note:** Although the examples you've seen so far use integers, you can use mathematical operators with any type of numerical value, including floating-point.

Example: Multiple Subtractions Using Mixed Data Types

You know from your experience with the addition operator that you can use more than one mathematical operator in a calculation. The same is true with the subtraction operator. You can also use different types of values in the calculation. For example, suppose you needed to subtract both an integer and a floating-point value from another integer. You could perform this task with a calculation like this:

```
difference = 100 - 15 - 3.5f;
```

After Java executes the above line, the variable difference will be equal to 81.5. But do you see a potential problem? What type of value is 81.5? If you said "floating point," go to the head of the class. Because 81.5 is a floating-point value, difference must be a floating-point variable. If difference is an integer, Java's compiler will generate an error that tells you "Explicit cast needed to convert float to int." What Java is really saying here is, "If you want to have an integer result, you've got to tell me." In the next example, you see how to tell Java this important information.

Example: Casting a Result to a Different Data Type

When you *cast* a value, you're telling Java that it's okay to convert one type of value to another. You do this by placing in front of the calculation, in parentheses, the data type you want. For example, look at this line of Java code:

```
difference = 100 - 15 - 3.5f;
```

Because the calculation on the right side of the equals sign results in a floating-point number, difference must be a floating-point variable. After all, computers are very fussy. They refuse to do things like try to stuff a floating-point number into an integer. If difference is an integer, then the result of the calculation must also be an integer. In the above case, you can satisfy Java's compiler by using a type cast, which looks like this:

```
difference = (int)(100 - 15 - 3.5f);
```

Now, when Java executes the above line, it first calculates the result of 100-15-3.5f, which is 81.5. Then, it converts the result to an integer by dropping the decimal portion of the value. This gives a result of 81. Finally, Java assigns the value of 81 to difference, which is an integer variable. In short, when you use a type cast, you're telling the compiler, "Yes, I know what I'm doing. I want the result converted."

> **Note:** Sometimes the minus sign is used as a negation operator, rather than a subtraction operator. For example, if you want to write a negative number, like negative ten, you'd use the negation operator like this: –10. This is a case where the same symbol is used to mean different things. Java can tell the difference between the negation and a subtraction operators by the context in which the operator is used.

The Multiplication Operator

By now, you should be getting used to using mathematical operations in simple expressions. The multiplication operator (*) is no different from the addition and subtraction operators, except that it performs a different type of operation. When you want to multiply two numbers together, you use the multiplication operator like this:

```
result = expr1 * expr2;
```

After Java executes this line, result contains the product of expr1 times expr2. The most important thing to remember about multiplication is that you can run into some pretty big numbers fast. If the result of a multiplication is larger than the data type of the variable that'll hold the answer, you've got trouble, as you'll see in the following example.

Example: Multiplication and Data Types

Try to determine the result of the following calculation:

```
byte product = (byte)(20 * 20);
```

If you said the answer is 400, you'd be both right and wrong. While it is true that 20 times 20 is 400, product is only a byte variable, which means it can only hold values from –128 to 127. Unfortunately, Java just goes ahead and stuffs the answer into product whether it fits or not. (The byte type-cast, in fact, converts the answer to a byte before it's stuffed into product, but that's a minor complication.) In the preceding case, you'd end up with an answer of –112.

Be especially careful when you're performing more than one multiplication in a calculation. In such cases, numbers can really get out of hand if you're using the smaller data types like byte or short. Most Java programmers use the int data type for their integer variables, which ensures that their variables have plenty of room for large numbers.

Of course, as I've said before, you should choose the smallest data type that is large enough for the values you'll be using, since the computer must work harder, and thus slower, when it uses larger data types. Still, if you're not performing tons of calculations, using larger data types for safety sake probably won't make a noticeable change in the speed of your applet.

> **Tip:** When a mathematical calculation gives you an answer that seems way out of whack, check to make sure that you're using data types that are large enough to hold the values used in the calculation. This is especially true for the result of the calculation. Many hard-to-find program bugs result from using the wrong data types for large values.

The Division Operator

As you may have guessed, the next operator on the list is the division operator (/), which enables you to divide one value by another. The division operator is used exactly like the other operators you've studied so far, as you can see by this line:

```
result = expr1 / expr2;
```

Here, `result` ends up as the result of `expr1` divided by `expr2`. As with multiplication, there's a trap lurking here, but this time it doesn't have as much to do with the size of the numbers as it does in the division operation itself. The problem is that almost all division calculations end up with floating-point values as answers. The following example demonstrates this potential problem.

Example: Integer Versus Floating-Point Division

Look at this calculation:

```
int result = 3 / 2;
```

When you divide 3 by 2, you may start out with integers, but you end up with 1.5 for an answer, and 1.5 is, of course, a floating-point number. But when Java performs the division shown above, it performs integer division. That is, it drops any decimal portion in the answer, leaving `result` equal to 1. There are times when this is the type of division you want to perform. But if you want the precise answer to `3 / 2`, you're going to have to change something. Maybe changing `result` to a floating-point variable will make a difference:

```
float result = 3 / 2;
```

When Java performs this calculation, you still end up with 1 as the answer. Why? Because, as I mentioned before, Java performs integer division on integer values like 3 and 2. To solve the problem, you must also convert 3 and 2 to floating-point values, like this:

```
float result = 3f / 2f;
```

Now, you'll get the correct result of 1.5. Actually, only one of the numbers to the right of the equals sign needs to be floating-point in order to get a floating-point answer. This line will work, too:

```
float result = 3f / 2;
```

The Modulo Operator

In the previous section, you learned that integer division gives you a result that's equal to the number of times one number fits into another, regardless of the remainder. For example, you now know that, in Java, the answer to "3 divided by 2" is 1, meaning that 2 fits into 3 only once. Integer division throws away the remainder, but what if it's the remainder you're looking for? Then, you can use the modulo operator (%) like this:

```
result = expr1 % expr2;
```

This line results in the remainder of expr1 divided by expr2. For example, the calculation

```
int result = 11 % 3;
```

makes result equal to 2, because 3 goes into 11 three times with a remainder of 2. You probably won't use the modulo operator much, but it can be handy for special types of calculations.

The Increment Operator

Many times in a program, you want to increase a value by a specific amount. For example, if you were using the variable count to keep track of how many times a part of your program executed, you need to add 1 to count each time you reached that part of the program. Programmers used to do this kind of incrementing like this:

```
count = count + 1;
```

Here, the computer takes the value stored in count, increases it by 1, and then assigns the new value to count. If you've ever programmed in C or C++, you know that those languages have a shortcut way of incrementing a value. Because Java is much like C++, its creators also included this shortcut operator. Using the increment operator (++), you can replace the previous line with this one:

```
++count;
```

Another way to write the preceding line is like this:

```
count++;
```

There is, however, a subtle difference in the way the increment operator works when it's placed before (pre-increment) or after (post-increment) the value it's incrementing. The difference crops up when you use the operator in expressions. For example, look at these lines of Java program code:

```
int num1 = 1;
int num2 = ++num1;
```

Here, Java first sets the variable num1 to 1. In the second line, Java increments num1 to 2 and then assigns 2 to num2.

Now, look at these lines:

```
int num1 = 1;
int num2 = num1++;
```

This time, num2 ends up as 1. Why? In the second line, Java doesn't increment num1 until after it assigns the current value of num1 (1) to num2. Watch out for this little detail when you get started writing your own applets.

What if you want to increment a value by more than 1? The old-fashioned way would be to use a line like this:

```
num = num + 5;
```

Java has a special shortcut operator that handles the above situation, too. You use the shortcut operator like this:

```
num += 5;
```

The above line just says, "Add 5 to num."

The Decrement Operator

In computer programs, you don't always count forwards. Often, you need to count backwards as well. That's why Java has the decrement operator (--), which works just like the increment operator, except it subtracts 1 instead of adding it. You use the decrement operator like this:

```
- -num;
```

The above example uses the pre-decrement version of the operator. If you want to decrement the value after it's been used in an expression, use the post-decrement version, like this:

```
num- -;
```

The set of operators wouldn't be complete without a decrement operator that enables you to subtract any value from a variable. The following line

```
num -= 5;
```

tells Java to decrement num by 5.

Example: Using Mathematical Calculations in an Applet

It's one thing to learn about mathematical operators and how they're used to perform calculations. It's quite another to actually use these operators in an actual program. This is because, when performing calculations in programs, you frequently have to do a lot of conversions from numerical values to strings and vice versa. For example, suppose you ask the user for a number that you need in order to perform a calculation. When you retrieve the number from the user, it's still in string form. You can't use the text character "3" in a calculation. You need to convert the string form of "3" to the numerical form.

Once you have all your values converted to the right form, you can go ahead and do the calculations as you learned in this chapter. But what about when you want to show the answers to your applet's user? Again, you need to perform a conversion, this time from numerical form back to string form. Listing 7.1 shows an applet called Applet5 that demonstrates how these conversion tasks work. Figure 7.1 shows Applet5 running in the Appletviewer application.

Listing 7.1 Applet5.java: Source Code for the Applet5 Applet.

```java
import java.awt.*;
import java.applet.*;

public class Applet5 extends Applet
{
    TextField textField1;
    TextField textField2;

    public void init()
    {
        textField1 = new TextField(5);
        textField2 = new TextField(5);
        add(textField1);
        add(textField2);
        textField1.setText("0");
        textField2.setText("0");
```

```
    }

    public void paint(Graphics g)
{

        int value1;
        int value2;
        int sum;

        g.drawString("Type a number in each box.", 40, 50);
        g.drawString("The sum of the values is:", 40, 75);
        String s = textField1.getText();
        value1 = Integer.parseInt(s);
        s = textField2.getText();
        value2 = Integer.parseInt(s);
        sum = value1 + value2;
        s = String.valueOf(sum);
        g.drawString(s, 80, 100);
    }

    public boolean action(Event event, Object arg)
    {
        repaint();
        return true;
    }
}
```

Tell Java that the program uses classes in the awt *package.*
Tell Java that the program uses classes in the applet *package.*
Derive the Applet5 *class from Java's* Applet *class.*
  Declare TextField *objects called* textField1 *and* textField2.
  Override the Applet *class's* init() *method.*
    Create the two TextField *objects.*
    Add the two TextField *objects to the applet.*
    Initialize the text in both TextField *objects to "0".*
  Override the Applet *class's* paint() *method.*
    Declare three integers called value1, value2, *and* sum.
    Display two text strings in the applet's display area.
    Get the text from first TextField *object.*
    Convert the text to an integer.
    Get the text from the second TextField *object.*
    Convert the text to an integer.
    Add the two converted values together.
      Convert the sum to a string.
    Draw the text string on the applet's surface.
  Override the Applet *class's* action() *method.*
    Tell Java to redraw the applet's display area.
    Tell Java that the action() *method finished successfully.*

Figure 7.1

The Applet5 applet sums two values.

Use the procedures you learned in the previous chapter to compile and run the Applet5 applet. Remember that to do this, you must follow these steps:

1. Type and save the program (or copy it from the CD-ROM).

2. Compile the applet.

3. Write an HTML document to test the applet.

4. Use Appletviewer to display the HTML document containing the applet.

When you have the Applet5 applet up and running, enter a number into each text box, and then press Enter. When you do, the applet sums the two numbers and displays the result.

How Applet5 Works

Although Applet5's source code is a little longer than other applets you've seen, it's really not much more complicated. It simply uses a few more variables in order to store the values needed to perform its calculations.

First, near the top of the program, Applet5 declares two TextField objects, like this:

```
TextField textField1;
TextField textField2;
```

These TextField objects represent the text boxes in which the user types the values to be summed.

Next, the program overrides the Applet class's init() method. In this method, it first creates two new TextField objects:

```
textField1 = new TextField(5);
textField2 = new TextField(5);
```

The program then adds the TextField objects to the applet:

```
add(textField1);
add(textField2);
```

Finally, in order to be sure the program doesn't try to sum two non-existent values, `init()` initializes the text contained in the `TextField` objects to "0":

```
textField1.setText("0");
textField2.setText("0");
```

The `TextField` class's `setText()` method sets the text contained in the control to the text string given as the method's single argument.

> **Note:** Overriding a method is the process of replacing a method found in the base class with a version specific to the new class. In other words, the Applet class from which Applet5 is derived also has an `init()` method. If you didn't override `init()` in Applet5, Java would call the original version in Applet instead. (See the example called "Encapsulation, Inheritance, and Polymorphism" in Chapter 4 for more information.)

The `paint()` method is where all the action takes place. In `paint()`, the program first declares three integer variables:

```
int value1;
int value2;
int sum;
```

> **Note:** Because it takes a certain amount of time for a computer to allocate memory for variables, it's not always a good idea to declare variables inside the `paint()` method, which must run as quickly as possible. I chose to use this generally frowned upon practice in order to keep the programming examples simple and easy-to-understand. However, keep in mind that the `paint()` method must do as little processing as possible in order to keep it up to speed.

After declaring its variables, `paint()` displays two lines of text on the applet's display area:

```
g.drawString("Type a number in each box.", 40, 50);
g.drawString("The sum of the values is:", 40, 75);
```

Then, the program extracts the text from the first `TextField` object and converts that text from a string to a numerical value (in this case, an integer):

```
String s = textField1.getText();
value1 = Integer.parseInt(s);
```

You've seen the `TextField` class's `getText()` method before. The second line above, however, introduces you to a new class and method. The `Integer` class offers many methods that make working with integers easier. For example, the `parseInt()` method used in the second line above enables you to convert the contents of a string to an integer (assuming, of course, that the string contains numerical digits).

After converting the first string to an integer, `paint()` handles the second `TextField` object in exactly the same way:

```
s = textField2.getText();
value2 = Integer.parseInt(s);
```

Now the program has two integer values, stored in the variables `value1` and `value2`, that it can sum, which it does like this:

```
sum = value1 + value2;
```

After Java executes the above lines, the answer to the calculation is stored in `sum`. The program now needs to display the answer to the applet's user. However, before it can do that, it must convert the numerical value in `sum` to a text string that can be displayed on the screen. You know that the `String` class's `valueOf()` method handles this task. The last thing `paint()` does, then, is convert `sum` to a string and display the string on the screen:

```
s = String.valueOf(sum);
g.drawString(s, 80, 100);
```

The last method in Applet3 is `action()`, which you learned about in the previous chapter. To review, Java calls `action()` whenever the user performs some action with the applet's controls. In this case, `action()` responds when the user presses Enter in one of the `TextField` objects.

The Order of Operations

Now that you know how to use mathematical operators, you need to know about the complications you can run into when you use different operators in the same calculation. The *order of operations*, which is also called *operator precedence*, determines the order in which mathematical computations are performed. If you've ever taken algebra, you know that mathematicians long ago set up a standard set of symbols for mathematical operations as well as defined the order in which they're performed. These mathematical rules are also observed in programming languages like Java. Table 7.1 lists Java's mathematical operators in order of precedence.

Table 7.1 Operator Order of Operations.

Operator	Description
−	Negation
++	Increment
− −	Decrement
*	Multiplication

Operator	Description
/	Division
%	Modulus
+	Addition
–	Subtraction
=	Assignment

As I mentioned previously, operator precedence comes into play when you use several different operators in the same calculation. For example, look at this line of Java source code:

```
answer = 3 + 5 * 3;
```

Go ahead and do the calculation. What did you get for an answer? If you got 18, you already know how operator precedence works. If you're new to this sort of thing, you probably got 24 for an answer, which is incorrect. The reason 18 is the correct answer is because operator precedence dictates that the multiplication be performed before the addition. If you look at Table 7.1, you can see that multiplication comes before addition.

If you really wanted to get 24 for an answer, you could use parentheses to change the order of operations, like this:

```
answer = (3 + 5) * 3;
```

Now, the answer would be 24, because the parentheses tell Java to do the addition first.

Example: Order of Operations

If you've never dealt with order of operations before, you'll probably need a little practice to get the hang of it. Look at this calculation:

```
answer = 5 + 3 - 2 + 7;
```

You should get 13 for an answer. Because addition and subtraction have the same order of precedence in this calculation (yes, I know the table lists subtraction after addition, but if you do the subtraction first, you'll still get 13 for an answer), you can just work from left to right to solve this problem.

Example: More Order of Operations

The previous example was pretty easy. Ready to try something a little tougher? Look at this calculation:

```
answer = 4 * 5 + 4 / 2;
```

What do you get for an answer? You should have gotten 22. If you got 12, you forgot that multiplication and division are performed before addition.

Example: Still More Order of Operations

Suppose I change the previous example to this:

```
answer = 4 * (5 + 4) / 2;
```

You should get 18 for an answer, because the added parentheses tell you to perform the addition first.

Example: One Last Order of Operations

Okay, now you're going to get a chance to prove that you really know your stuff. Solve this calculation:

```
answer = 2 * 3 + 6 * 3 - (4 + 2) * 2;
```

The answer is 12. You solve the problem as shown below:

answer = 2 * 3 + 6 * 3 – (4 + 2) * 2;

answer = 2 * 3 + 6 * 3 – 6 * 2;

answer = 6 + 6 * 3 – 6 * 2;

answer = 6 + 18 – 6 * 2;

answer = 6 + 18 – 12;

answer = 12;

Summary

Almost all computer programs perform mathematical calculations. So that you can specify the types of calculations you want performed, computer languages such as Java feature mathematical operators for standard operations such as addition, subtraction, multiplication, and division. However, when using these operators, always remember operator precedence (or order of operations), which determines the order in which calculations are completed.

Review Questions

1. What symbols does Java use for the addition, subtraction, multiplication, and division operators?

2. What does `5*3` equal?

3. What is the answer to `3 - 2 + 5 + 6 - 1`?

4. If `num` equals 12, what does the expression `++num` do?

5. What result do you get from `12 % 5`?

6. If `num` equals 25, what does the expression `num += 5` do?

7. How do you set the text in a `TextField` object?

8. What is the answer to `12 + 3 * 6 / 2`?

9. How do you change the calculation `3 / 5` so that is uses floating-point division?

10. How do you use casting to change the result of `56 - 34.56f` from floating point to integer?

11. How do you convert digits in a string to an integer value?

12. What is the answer to `(12 - 8) * 10 / 2 * 2`?

Review Exercises

1. On a piece of paper, write an expression that sums five numbers.

2. Write an expression that uses both addition and multiplication with four numbers.

3. Use parentheses to change the order of operations in the expression you wrote in the previous exercise.

4. Modify Applet5 so that it accepts three values from the user. Divide the second value by the third and then add the first value. Rename the program `MathApplet.java`. Figure 7.2 shows what the final applet should look like. (You can find the solution to this programming problem in the CHAP07 folder of this book's CD-ROM.)

Figure 7.2

MathApplet should
look like this.

CHAPTER 8

Expressions

Without a doubt, expressions are the main building blocks of a program. This is because there are so many different kinds of expressions that a majority of the source-code lines in a program end up being—you guessed it—expressions. There are expressions that result in numerical values. There are expressions that result in strings. There are simple expressions, complex expressions, and all manner of expressions in between.

In the previous chapter, you got a quick look at some kinds of expressions as you put the mathematical operators to work. Now you'll learn not only more about those types of expressions, but also about logical expressions, which help a computer seem to be able to think and make choices. Along the way, you'll discover comparison and logical operators, which make logical expressions possible.

Types of Expressions

To put it simply, an *expression* is a line of code that can be reduced to a value or that assigns a value. For example, you know that the addition operator adds one expression to another, like this:

```
sum = expr1 + expr2;
```

In the preceding line, expr1 can be something as simple as the variable x or as complex as (4 + 5) * 2 * 5 / 7 + x / y. The same goes for expr2, of course. And, in fact, the first example containing expr1 and expr2 is an expression itself!

But no matter how complicated, all expressions can be classified into one of three main categories:

♦ *Numerical expressions* combine numbers, variables, or constants using mathematical operators. An example is 2 + 3 / x.

♦ *Assignment expressions* assign a value to a variable. An example is num = 3.

♦ *Logical expressions* are unique in that they result in a value of true or false. An example is x < 3 (which reads "x is less than 3").

Expressions Within Expressions

In the previous chapter, whether you were aware of it or not, you used lots of numerical and assignment expressions as you learned about mathematical operators. And if you look closely at some of those expressions, you'll make a neat discovery: Like a bunch of boxes that fit into each other, expressions often contain other simpler expressions. For example, look at the following assignment expression:

```
num = (5 - x) * (2 + y);
```

This is an assignment expression because it assigns a value to the variable num. However, the stuff on either side of the equals sign contains these other expressions:

```
num
(5 - x) * (2 + y)
```

Both of the above lines are numerical expressions because they can be reduced to a numerical value (assuming that you know the values of num, x, and y.

But, wait a second—you're not done yet. You can still find more sub-expressions. Look at the multiplication operation. Can you see that it's multiplying two expressions together? Those two expressions look like this:

```
(5 - x)
(2 + y)
```

And the above simplified expressions contain yet more sub-expressions. Those expressions are:

```
5
x
2
y
```

Expressions are what programmers like to call *recursive*, meaning that the definition of an expression keeps coming back on itself. An expression contains expressions that contain other expressions, which themselves contain other expressions. How deep you can dig depends on the complexity of the original expression. But, as you saw demonstrated, even the relatively simple expression num = (5 - x) * (2 + y) has four levels of depth.

Comparison Operators

Now that you've dug into the secrets of expressions, it's time to learn about a new type of operator. So far, you've gotten some practice with mathematical operators, which enable you to build various types of numerical and assignment expressions. Another type of operator you can use to build expressions is the comparison operator. Comparison operators are used to create logical expressions, which, if you recall, result in a value of `true` or `false`. Table 8.1 lists the logical expressions used in Java programming. C and C++ programmers will find these operators very familiar.

Table 8.1   Java's Logical Operators.

Operators	Description
==	Equal to
<	Less than
>	Greater than
<=	Less than or equal to
>=	Greater than or equal to
!=	Not equal to

Example: Using Comparison Operators

Just how do you use comparison operators? As their name suggests, you use them to compare two expressions, with the result of the comparison being either `true` or `false`. For example, look at this logical expression:

```
3 == 2 + 1
```

The result of the above expression is `true` because the `==` operator determines whether the expressions on either side are equal to each other. If you were to change the expression to

```
3 == 2 + 2
```

the result would be `false`. That is, 3 does not equal 4. However, the previous sentence suggests a way to rewrite the expression, like this:

```
3 != 2 + 2
```

This expression results in a value of `true`, because 3 does not equal 4.

The other logical expressions work similarly. Table 8.2 lists a number of logical expressions and the results they produce.

Table 8.2　Examples of Logical Expressions.

Expression	Result
3 + 4 == 7	true
3 + 4 != 7	false
3 + 4 != 2 + 6	true
3 + 4 < 10	true
3 + 4 <= 10	true
3 + 4 == 4 + 4	false
3 + 4 > 10	false
3 + 4 >= 7	true
3 + 4 >= 8	false

Logical Operators

The comparison operators enable you to compare two expressions. But another type of operator—logical operators—supercharges comparison operators so that you can combine two or more logical expressions into a more complex logical expression. Even if you've never programmed a computer before, you're already familiar with logical operators because you use them in everyday speech. For example, when you say, "Do you have a credit card or ten dollars in cash?" you're using the logical operator OR. Similarly, when you say, "I have a dog and a cat," you're using the AND operator. Table 8.3 lists Java's logical operators and what they mean.

Table 8.3　Java's Logical Operators.

Operator	Description
&&	AND
||	OR
^	Exclusive OR
!	NOT

The AND (&&) operator requires all expressions to be true for the entire expression to be true. For example, the expression

```
(3 + 2 == 5) && (6 + 2 == 8)
```

is true because the expressions on both sides of the && are true. However, the expression

```
(4 + 3 == 9) && (3 + 3 == 6)
```

is false because the expression on the left of the && is not true. Remember this when combining expressions with AND: If any expression is false, the entire expression is false.

The OR operator (¦¦) requires only one expression to be true for the entire expression to be true. For example, the expressions

```
(3 + 6 == 2) ¦¦ (4 + 4 == 8)
```

and

```
(4 + 1 == 5) ¦¦ (7 + 2 == 9)
```

are both true because at least one of the expressions being compared is true. Notice that in the second case both expressions being compared are true, which also makes an OR expression true.

The exclusive OR operator (^) is used to determine if one and only one of the expressions being compared is true. Unlike a regular OR, with an exclusive OR, if both expressions are true, the result is false (weird, huh?). For example, the expression

```
(5 + 7 == 12) ^ (4 + 3 == 8)
```

evaluates to true, whereas these expressions evaluate to false:

```
(5 + 7 == 12) ^ (4 + 3 == 7)
(5 + 7 == 10) ^ (4 + 3 == 6)
```

The NOT (!) operator switches the value of (or negates) a logical expression. For example, the expression

```
(4 + 3 == 5)
```

is false; however, the expression

```
!(4 + 3 == 5)
```

is true.

Example: Using Logical Operators

Take a look at the following expression:

```
(4 + 5 == 9) && !(3 + 1 = 3)
```

Is this expression true or false? If you said true, you understand the way the logical operators work. The expressions on either side of the && are both true, so the entire expression is true. If you said false, you must go to bed without any dinner.

Example: Using Multiple Logical Operators

Just as with mathematical operators, you can use multiple logical operators to compare several logical expressions. For example, look at this expression:

```
(4 == 4) && (5 == 5) && (6 == 6)
```

This expression gives a result of true because each expression to the left and right of each AND operator is true. However, this expression yields a value of false:

```
(4 == 4) && (5 == 6) && (6 == 6)
```

Remember that, when using AND, if any sub-expression is false, the entire expression is false. This is kind of like testifying in court. To be true, it's got to be the truth, the whole truth, and nothing but the truth.

Example: Combining Different Comparison and Logical Operators

Again, just like mathematical operators, there's no restriction on how you can combine the different comparison and logical operators, although if you build a very complex expression, you may have trouble evaluating it yourself. Check out this expression:

```
(3 < 5) && (2 == 2) && (9 > 6)
```

Here you've used four different comparison and logical operators in the same complex expression. But because you're comparing the sub-expressions with the AND operator, and because each of the sub-expressions is true, the result of the above expression is true.

Now, look at this expression:

```
((3 < 5) && (2 == 1)) || (7 == 7)
```

Yep, things are getting tricky. Is the above expression true or false? (Hey, give it a shot. You've got a fifty-fifty chance.) Ready for the answer? The above expression is true. First, look at the parentheses. The outermost parentheses, on the left, group the two expressions being compared by the AND operator into a single expression, so evaluate it first. The value 3 is less than 5, but 2 does not equal 1, so the entire expression on the left of the OR operator is false. On the right of the OR operator, however, 7 does indeed equal 7, so this sub-expression is true. Because one of the expressions in the OR comparison is true, the entire expression is true. Here's how the expression breaks down, step-by-step:

```
((3 < 5) && (2 == 1)) || (7 == 7)
((true) && (false)) || (7 == 7)
false || (7 == 7)
false || true
true
```

Writing Logical Expressions

You wouldn't write expressions such as

```
(4 + 5 == 9) && !(3 + 1 == 3)
```

in your programs. They would serve no purpose because you already know how the expressions evaluate. However, when you use variables, you have no way of knowing in advance how an expression may evaluate. For example, is the expression

```
(num < 9) && (num > 15)
```

true or false? You don't know without being told the value of the numerical variable num. By using logical operators, though, your program can do the evaluation, and, based on the result—true or false—take the appropriate action. In the next chapter, which is about if and switch statements, you'll see how your programs can use logical expressions to make decisions.

Order of Operations

Like all operators, comparison and logical operators have an order of operations, or operator precedence. When you evaluate a complex expression, you must be sure to evaluate any sub-expressions in the correct order. As you learned in the previous example, however, you can use parentheses to group expressions so that they're easier to understand or to change the order of operations. Table 8.4 lists the comparison and logical operators in order of precedence.

Table 8.4 Comparison and Logical Operators' Order of Operations.

Operators	Description
!	NOT
< > <= >=	Relational
== !=	Equality
^	Exclusive OR
&&	Logical AND
| |	Logical OR

Summary

Expressions, which are lines of Java code that can be reduced to a value or that assign a value, come in several types. In this chapter, you not only experimented with numerical and assignment expressions, but you also learned about logical expressions, which you create using the comparison and logical operators. Now that you know how to use comparison and logical operators to build logical expressions, you're ready to discover how computers make decisions. You'll make that discovery in the next chapter, where you'll also start using the operators you learned in order to write actual applets. Before you turn to that chapter, however, test your knowledge of expressions, comparison operators, and logical operators by answering the following review questions and by completing the review exercises.

Review Questions

1. What is an expression?

2. What are the three types of expressions?

3. What is the result of the logical expression (3 < 5)?

4. What is the result of the logical expression (3 < 5) && (5 == 4 + 1)?

5. Explain why expressions are recursive in nature.

6. What are the six comparison operators?

7. What are the four logical operators?

8. What is the result of the logical expression `(3 < 5) || (6 == 5) || (3 != 3)`?

9. What's the result of the logical expression `(5 != 10) && ((3 == 2 + 1) || (4 < 2 + 5))`?

10. What's the result of the logical expression `!(5 == 2 + 3) && !(5 + 2 != 7 - 5)`?

Review Exercises

1. Write an expression that compares three numbers for equality.

2. Write an expression that determines whether one number is less than or equal to another.

3. Write an expression that uses three different types of comparison operators and two different types of logical operators. The expression must be false.

4. Suppose you have three variables, called num1, num2, and num3, in a program. Write an expression that compares the variables for equality.

5. If the variable num1 is equal to 5 and the variable num2 is equal to 10, how would you evaluate the logical expression `((num1 != 5) || (num2 == 10)) && !(num1 == 5)`? Show each step of the evaluation.

CHAPTER 9

The *if* and *switch* Statements

In previous chapters, you've learned a lot about the way Java works. You now know how to type and compile programs, how to input and output simple data, how to perform mathematical operations, and how to perform comparisons using logical expressions. But these techniques are merely the building blocks of a program. To use these building blocks in a useful way, you have to understand how computers make decisions.

In this chapter, you learn how your programs can analyze data in order to decide what parts of your program to execute. Until now, your applets have executed their statements in strict sequential order, starting with the first line of a method and working, line by line, to the end of the method. Now it's time to learn how you can control your program flow—the order in which the statements are executed—so that you can do different things based on the data your program receives.

Controlling Program Flow

Program flow is the order in which a program executes its statements. Most program flow is sequential, meaning that the statements are executed one by one in the order in which they appear in the program or method. However, there are Java commands that make your program jump forward or backward, skipping over program code not currently required. These commands are said to control the program flow.

If the idea of computers making decisions based on data seems a little strange, think about how you make decisions. For example, suppose you're expecting an important letter. You go out to your mailbox and look inside. Based on what you find, you choose one of two actions:

♦ If there's mail in the mailbox, you take the mail into the house.

♦ If there's no mail in the mailbox, you complain about the postal system.

In either case, you've made a decision based on whether there is mail in the mailbox. This is called *conditional branching*.

Computers use this same method to make decisions (except they never complain and they don't give a darn how late your mail is). You will see the word `if` used frequently in computer programs. Just as you might say to yourself, "If the mail is in the mailbox, I'll bring it in," a computer also uses an `if` statement to decide what action to take.

Program Flow and Branching

Most programs reach a point where a decision must be made about a piece of data. The program must then analyze the data, decide what to do about it, and jump to the appropriate section of code. This decision-making process is as important to computer programming as pollen is to a bee. Virtually no useful programs can be written without it.

When a program breaks the sequential flow and jumps to a new section of code, it is called *branching*. When this branching is based on a decision, the program is performing *conditional branching*. When no decision-making is involved and the program always branches when it encounters a branching instruction, the program is performing *unconditional branching*. Unconditional branching is rarely used in modern programs, so this chapter deals with conditional branching.

The *if* statement

Most conditional branching occurs when the program executes an `if` statement, which compares data and decides what to do next based on the result of the comparison. For example, you've probably seen programs that print menus on-screen. To select a menu item, you often type the item's selection number. When the program receives your input, it checks the number you entered and decides what to do. You'd probably use an `if` statement in this type of program.

A simple `if` statement includes the keyword `if` followed by a logical expression, which, as you learned in the previous chapter, is an expression that evaluates to either `true` or `false`. These expressions are surrounded by parentheses. You follow the parentheses with the statement that you want executed if the logical expression is true. For example, look at this `if` statement:

```
if (choice == 5)
    g.drawString("You chose number 5.", 30, 30);
```

In this case, if the variable `choice` is equal to 5, Java will execute the call to `drawString()`. Otherwise, Java will just skip the call to `drawString()`.

Example: The Form of an *if* Statement

The syntax of languages such as Java are tolerant of the styles of various programmers, enabling programmers to construct programs that are organized in a way that's best suited to the programmer and the particular problem. For example, the Java language is not particular about how you specify the part of an `if` statement to be executed. For example, the statement

```
if (choice == 1)
    num = 10;
```

could also be written like this:

```
if (choice == 1) num = 10;
```

In other words, although the parentheses are required around the logical expression, the code to be executed can be on the same line or the line after the `if` statement.

In the case of an `if` statement that contains only one program line to be executed, you can choose to include or do away with the curly braces that usually mark a block of code. With this option in mind, you could rewrite the preceding `if` statement like Listing 9.1.

Listing 9.1   LST9_1.TXT: The *if* Statement with Braces.

```
if (choice == 1)
{
    num = 10;
}
```

Another way you'll often see braces used with an `if` statement is shown here:

```
if (choice == 1) {
    num = 10;
}
```

In this case, the opening brace is on the `if` statement's first line.

> **Note:** Logical expressions are also called *Boolean* expressions. That is, a Boolean expression is also an expression that evaluates to either `true` or `false`. Now you understand why Java has a `boolean` data type, which can hold the value `true` or `false`. Having the `boolean` data type enables you to assign the result of a logical expression to a variable.

Multiple *if* Statements

You can use a number of `if` statements to choose between several conditions. For example, look at the group of `if` statements in Listing 9.2.

Listing 9.2   LST9_2.TXT: A Group of *if* Statements.

```
if (choice == 1)
    num = 1;
if (choice == 2)
    num = 2;
if (choice == 3)
    num = 3;
```

How do these `if` statements work? Let's say that when Java executes the program code in Listing 9.2, the variable `choice` equals 1. When the program gets to the first `if` statement, it checks the value of `choice`. If `choice` equals 1 (which it does, in this case), the program sets the variable `num` to 1 and then drops down to the next `if` statement. This time, the program compares the value of `choice` with the number 2. Because `choice` doesn't equal 2, the program ignores the following part of the statement and drops down to the next `if` statement. The variable `choice` doesn't equal 3 either, so the code portion of the third `if` statement is also ignored.

Suppose `choice` equals 2 when Java executes the code in Listing 9.2. When the program gets to the first `if` statement, it discovers that `choice` is not equal to 1, so it ignores the `num = 1` statement and drops down to the next program line, which is the second `if` statement. Again, the program checks the value of `choice`. Because `choice` equals 2, the program can execute the second portion of the statement; that is, `num` gets set to 2. Program execution drops down to the third `if` statement, which does nothing because `choice` doesn't equal 3.

> **Note:** The `if` statement, no matter how complex it becomes, always evaluates to either `true` or `false`. If the statement evaluates to `true`, the second portion of the statement is executed. If the statement evaluates to `false`, the second portion of the statement is not executed.

Multiple-Line *if* Statements

Listings 9.1 and 9.2 demonstrate the simplest `if` statement. This simple statement usually fits your program's decision-making needs just fine. Sometimes, however, you want to perform more than one command as part of an `if` statement. To perform more than one command, enclose the commands within curly braces. Listing 9.3 is a revised version of Listing 9.2 that uses this technique.

Listing 9.3   LST9_3.LST: Multiple-Line *if* Statements.

```
if (choice == 1)
{
    num = 1;
    num2 = 10;
}

if (choice == 2)
{
    num = 2;
    num2 = 20;
}

if (choice == 3)
{
    num = 3;
    num2 = 30;
}
```

> **Tip:** Notice that some program lines in Listing 9.3 are indented. By indenting the lines that go with each `if` block, you can more easily see the structure of your program. Listing 9.3 also uses blank lines to separate blocks of code that go together. The compiler doesn't care about the indenting or the blank lines, but these features make your programs easier for you (or another programmer) to read.

What's happening in Listing 9.3? Suppose `choice` equals 2. When Java gets to the first `if` statement, it compares the value of `choice` with the number 1. Because these values don't match (or, as programmers say, the statement doesn't evaluate to `true`), Java skips over every line until it finds the next `if` statement.

This brings Java to the second `if` statement. When Java evaluates the expression, it finds that `choice` equals 2, and it executes the second portion of the `if` statement. This time the second portion of the statement is not just one command, but two. The program sets the values of both `num` and `num2`.

This brings the program to the last `if` statement, which Java skips over because `choice` doesn't equal 3. Notice that, when you want to set up an `if` statement that executes multiple lines of code, you must use the curly braces—{ and }—to denote the block of instructions that should be executed.

The *else* Clause

You might think it's a waste of time for Listing 9.3 to evaluate other `if` statements after it finds a match for the value of `choice`. You'd be right, too. When you write programs, you should always look for ways to make them run faster; one way to make a program run faster is to avoid all unnecessary processing. But how, you may ask, do you avoid unnecessary processing when you have to compare a variable with more than one value?

One way to keep processing to a minimum is to use Java's `else` clause. The `else` keyword enables you to use a single `if` statement to choose between two outcomes. When the `if` statement evaluates to `true`, the second part of the statement is executed. When the `if` statement evaluates to `false`, the `else` portion is executed. (When the `if` statement evaluates to neither `true` nor `false`, it's time to get a new computer!) Listing 9.4 demonstrates how `else` works.

Listing 9.4   LST9_4.LST: Using the *else* Clause.

```
if (choice == 1)
{
    num = 1;
    num2 = 10;
}
else
{
    num = 2;
    num2 = 20;
}
```

In Listing 9.4, if `choice` equals 1, Java sets `num` to 1 and `num2` to 10. If `choice` is any other value, Java executes the `else` portion, setting `num` to 2 and `num2` to 20. As you can see, the `else` clause provides a default outcome for an `if` statement. A default outcome doesn't help much, however, if an `if` statement has to deal with more than two possible outcomes (as in the original Listing 9.3). Suppose you want to rewrite Listing 9.3 so that it works the same but doesn't force Java to evaluate all three `if` statements unless it really has to. No problem. Listing 9.5 shows you how to use the `else if` clause:

Listing 9.5   LST9_5.LST: Using *if* and *else* Efficiently.

```
if (choice == 1)
{
    num = 1;
    num2 = 10;
}
else if (choice == 2)
{
    num = 2;
    num2 = 20;
}
else if (choice == 3)
{
    num = 3;
    num2 = 30;
}
```

When Java executes the program code in Listing 9.5, if `choice` is 1, Java will look at only the first `if` section and skip over both of the `else if` clauses. That is, Java will set `num` to 1 and `num2` to 10 and then continue on its way to whatever part of the program followed the final `else if` clause. Note that, if `choice` doesn't equal 1, 2, or 3, Java must evaluate all three clauses in the listing but will not do anything with `num` or `num2`.

Example: Using the *if* Statement in a Program

Now that you've studied what an `if` statement looks like and how it works, you probably want to see it at work in a real program. Listing 9.6 is a Java program that uses the menu example you studied earlier in this chapter, whereas Listing 9.7 is the HTML document that runs the applet. Figure 9.1 shows the applet running in the Appletviewer application.

Listing 9.6   Applet6.java: Using an *if* Statement in a Program.

```
import java.awt.*;
import java.applet.*;

public class Applet6 extends Applet
{
    TextField textField1;

    public void init()
    {
        textField1 = new TextField(5);
        add(textField1);
```

continues

Listing 9.6 Continued

```
g.drawString("3. Green", 40, 115);
        String s = textField1.getText();
        int choice = Integer.parseInt(s);

        if (choice == 1)
            g.setColor(Color.red);
        else if (choice == 2)
            g.setColor(Color.blue);
        else if (choice == 3)
            g.setColor(Color.green);
        else
            g.setColor(Color.black);

        if ((choice >= 1) && (choice <= 3))
            g.drawString("This is the color you chose.", 60, 140);
        else
            g.drawString("Invalid menu selection.", 60, 140);
    }

    public boolean action(Event event, Object arg)
    {
        repaint();
        return true;
    }
}
```

Tell Java that the program uses classes in the awt *package.*
Tell Java that the program uses classes in the applet *package.*
Derive the Applet6 *class from Java's* Applet *class.*
  Declare a TextField *object called* textField1.
  Override the Applet *class's* init() *method.*
    Create the TextField *object.*
    Add the TextField *object to the applet.*
    Initialize the text in the TextField *object to "1".*
  Override the Applet *class's* paint() *method.*
    Display user instructions in the applet's display area.
    Display the color menu on three lines.
    Get the text from the TextField *object.*
    Convert the text to an integer.
    Select a color based on the value the user entered.
    Display a message in the appropriate color.
  Override the Applet *class's* action() *method.*
    Tell Java to redraw the applet's display area.
    Tell Java that the action() *method finished successfully.*

Listing 9.7   APPLET6.HTML: The HTML Document That Runs Applet6.

```
<title>Applet Test Page</title>
<h1>Applet Test Page</h1>
<applet
    code="Applet6.class"
    width=250
    height=150
    name="Applet6">
</applet>
```

Figure 9.1

The Applet6 applet enables you to choose colors.

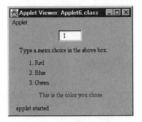

If you were awake at all during Chapter 7, you should already know how most of the Applet6 applet works. But, there's some new stuff in the paint() method that warrants a close look. First, after converting the user's typed selection from text to an integer, the program uses the integer in an if statement to match up each menu selection with the appropriate color. The setColor() method is part of the Graphics object; you call it to set the color of graphical elements, such as text, that the program draws in the applet's display area. The setColor() method's single argument is the color to set. As you can see, Java has a Color object that you can use to select colors. You'll learn more about the Color object in Chapter 36, "The Java Class Libraries." Notice that, if the user's selection does not match a menu selection, the color is set to black.

After the program sets the color, a second if statement determines which text to display, based on whether the user entered a valid selection. If the user's selection is valid, the program displays "This is the color you chose." in the selected color. Otherwise, the program displays "Invalid menu selection" in black.

The *switch* Statement

Another way you can add decision-making code to your programs is with the switch statement. The switch statement gets its name from the fact that it enables a computer program to switch between different outcomes based on a given value. The truth is, a switch statement does much the same job as an if statement, but it is more appropriate for situations where you have many choices, rather than only a few. Look at the if statement in Listing 9.8:

Listing 9.8   LST9_8.TXT: A Typical *if* Statement.

```
if (x == 1)
    y = 1;
if (x == 2)
    y = 2;
if (x == 3)
    y = 3;
else
    y = 0;
```

You could easily rewrite the preceding if statement as a switch statement, as shown in Listing 9.9:

Listing 9.9   LST9_9.TXT: Changing an *if* to a *switch*.

```
switch(x)
{
    case 1:
        y = 1;
        break;
    case 2:
        y = 2;
        break;
    case 3:
        y = 3;
        break;
    default:
        y = 0;
}
```

The first line of a switch statement is the keyword switch followed by the variable whose value will determine the outcome. This variable is called the *control variable*. Inside the main switch statement (which begins and ends with curly braces) are a number of case clauses, one for each possible value of the switch control variable (the x, in this case). In the above example, if x equals 1, Java jumps to the case 1 and sets y equal to 1. Then, the break statement tells Java that it should skip over the rest of the switch statement.

If x is 2, the same sort of program flow occurs, except Java jumps to the case 2, sets y equal to 2, and then breaks out of the switch. If the switch control variable is not equal to any of the values specified by the various case clauses, Java jumps to the default clause. The default clause, however, is optional. You can leave it out if you want, in which case Java will do nothing if there's no matching case for the control variable.

Example: Using the *break* Statement Correctly

One tricky thing about switch statements is the various ways that you can use the break statement to control program flow. Look at Listing 9.10:

Listing 9.10   LST9_10.TXT: Using *break* to Control Program Flow.

```
switch(x)
{
    case 1:
        y = 1;
    case 2:
        y = 2;
        break;
    case 3:
        y = 3;
        break;
    default:
        y = 0;
}
```

In this example, funny things happen, depending on whether the control variable x equals 1 or 2. In the former case, Java first jumps to case 1 and sets y equal to 1. Then, because there is no break before the case 2 clause, Java continues executing statements, dropping through the case 2 and setting y equal to 2. Ouch! The moral of the story is: Make sure you have break statements in the right places.

If the outcome of Listing 9.10 was really what you wanted to happen, you'd probably rewrite the switch statement is to look like Listing 9.11:

Listing 9.11   LST9_11.TXT: Rewriting Listing 9.10.

```
switch(x)
{
    case 1:
    case 2:
        y = 2;
        break;
    case 3:
        y = 3;
        break;
    default:
        y = 0;
}
```

Here, just as in Listing 9.10, y will end up equal to 2 if x equals 1 or 2. You'll run into this type of switch statement a lot in Java programs. If you're a C or C++ programmer, you've already seen a lot of this sort of thing, so you should feel right at home.

Example: Using the *switch* Statement in a Program

You've seen that a switch statement is similar in many ways to an if statement. In fact, if and switch statements can easily be converted from one to the other. Listing 9.12 is a new version of Applet6 (called Applet7) that incorporates the menu example by using a switch statement instead of an if statement.

Listing 9.12 APPLET7.JAVA: Using a *switch* Statement in a Program.

```java
import java.awt.*;
import java.applet.*;

public class Applet7 extends Applet
{
    TextField textField1;

    public void init()
    {
        textField1 = new TextField(5);
        add(textField1);
        textField1.setText("1");
    }

    public void paint(Graphics g)
    {
        g.drawString("Type a menu choice in the above box.", 20, 50);
        g.drawString("1. Red", 40, 75);
        g.drawString("2. Blue", 40, 95);
        g.drawString("3. Green", 40, 115);
        String s = textField1.getText();
        int choice = Integer.parseInt(s);

        switch(choice)
        {
            case 1:
                g.setColor(Color.red);
                break;
            case 2:
                g.setColor(Color.blue);
                break;
            case 3:
                g.setColor(Color.green);
                break;
            default:
                g.setColor(Color.black);
        }
```

```
if ((choice >= 1) && (choice <= 3))
        g.drawString("This is the color you chose.", 60, 140);
    else
        g.drawString("Invalid menu selection.", 60, 140);
    }

    public boolean action(Event event, Object arg)
    {
        repaint();
        return true;
    }
}
```

When you run this program, you'll see the same display as the one you saw with Applet6. In fact, from the user's point of view, the program works exactly the same as the previous version. The differences are completely internal.

Summary

Making decisions based on the state of data is an important part of a computer program, and now that you have this chapter behind you, you've made a giant leap forward in your Java programming career. You now have enough Java programming savvy to write simple, yet useful, applets. Of course, that's not to say that there isn't a lot left to learn. But by now you should have a good idea of what a Java applet looks like and how it works. The remainder of this book will fill out the details that make Java applets so powerful.

Review Questions

1. What is program flow?

2. Define conditional and unconditional branching.

3. What are two ways to control program flow?

4. In the following Java example, if num equals 5, will the second line execute?

```
if (choice == 3)
    num2 = choice;
```

5. Are there times when you don't need braces with an if statement? Explain.

6. What's the difference between a logical expression and a Boolean expression?

7. In Listing 9.13, what happens when choice equals 5?

Listing 9.13 LST9_13.LST: Listing for Question 7.

```
if (choice == 1)
{
    num = 1;
    num2 = 10;
}
else if (choice == 2)
{
    num = 2;
    num2 = 20;
}
```

8. Compare and contrast the if and switch statements.

9. What value is assigned to num in Listing 9.14 when choice equals 2?

Listing 9.14 LST9_14.TXT: Listing for Question 10.

```
switch(choice)
{
    case 1:
        num = 1;
        break;
    case 2:
        num = 2;
    case 3:
        num = 3;
        break;
    default:
        num = 0;
}
```

Review Exercises

1. Write an if statement that sets the variable num to 1 when choice equals 10.

2. Write an if statement that sets the variable num to the same value as the control variable choice when choice equals 5, but sets num to 0 in every other case.

3. Write an if statement that sets the variable num to twice the value of the control variable choice. Valid values for choice are 3, 4, 5, and 6.

4. Convert the if statement in exercise 3 to a switch statement.

5. Modify Applet7 so that it displays the text string "One," "Two," "Three," or "Four" when the user enters 1, 2, 3, or 4, respectively. Have the program display "Invalid value" for any other user entry. Figure 9.2 shows what the final applet, called SwitchApplet, should look like. (You can find the solution to this programming problem in the CHAP09 folder of this book's CD-ROM.)

Figure 9.2

The SwitchApplet applet converts numbers to words.

CHAPTER 10

The *while* and *do-while* Loops

A computer handles repetitive operations especially well—it never gets bored, and it can perform a task as well the 10,000th time as it did the first. Consider, for example, a disk file containing 10,000 names and addresses. If you tried to type labels for all those people, you'd be seeing spots before your eyes in no time. On the other hand, a printer (with the aid of a computer) can tirelessly spit out all 10,000 labels—and with nary a complaint to the union.

Every programming language must have some form of looping command to instruct a computer to perform repetitive tasks. Java features three types of looping: `for` loops, `while` loops, and `do-while` loops. In this chapter, you learn about the latter two types of loops. In the next chapter, you'll cover `for` loops.

> **Note:** In computer programs, looping is the process of repeatedly running a block of statements. Starting at the top of the block, the statements are executed until the program reaches the end of the block, at which point the program goes back to the top and starts over. The statements in the block may be repeated any number of times, from none to forever. If a loop continues on forever, it is called an infinite loop.

The *while* Loop

One type of loop you can use in your programs is the `while` loop, which continues running until its control expression becomes false. The control expression is a logical expression, much like the logical expressions you used with `if` statements. In other words, any expression that evaluates to `true` or `false` can be used as a control expression for a `while` loop. Here's an example of simple `while` loop:

```
num = 1;
while (num < 10)
    ++num;
```

Here the loop's control variable `num` is first set to 1. Then, at the start of the `while` loop, the program compares the value in `num` with 10. If `num` is less than 10, the expression evaluates to `true`, and the program executes the body of the loop, which in this case is a single statement that increments `num`. The program then goes back and checks the value of `num` again. As long as `num` is less than 10, the loop continues. But once `num` equals 10, the control expression evaluates to `false` and the loop ends.

> **Note:** Notice how, in the previous example of a `while` loop, the program first sets the value of the control variable (`num`) to 1. Initializing your control variable before entering the `while` loop is extremely important. If you don't initialize the variable, you don't know what it might contain, and therefore the outcome of the loop is unpredictable. In the above example, if `num` happened to be greater than 10, the loop wouldn't happen at all. Instead, the loop's control expression would immediately evaluate to `false`, and the program would branch to the statement after the curly braces. Mistakes like this make programmers growl at their loved ones.

Example: Using a *while* Loop

Although the previous example has only a single program line in the body of the `while` loop, you can make a `while` loop do as much as you want. As usual, to add more program lines, you create a program block using braces. This program block tells Java where the body of the loop begins and ends. For example, suppose you want to create a loop that not only increments the loop control variable, but also displays a message each time through the loop. You might accomplish this task as shown in Listing 10.1.

Listing 10.1   LST10_1.TXT: Using a *while* Loop.

```
num = 0;
while (num < 10)
{
    ++num;
    String s = String.valueOf(num);
    g.drawString("num is now equal to:", 20, 40);
    g.drawString(s, 20, 55);
}
```

Initialize the loop control variable.
Check whether num is less than 10.
  Increment the loop control variable.
  Create a string from the value of num.
  Display a message on the screen.
  Display the value of num.

> **Note:** The *body* of a loop comprises the program lines that are executed when the loop control expression is true. Usually, the body of a loop is enclosed in braces, creating a program block.

The pseudocode given after the listing illustrates how this while loop works. The thing to notice is how all the statements that Java should execute if the loop control expression is true are enclosed by braces. As I mentioned previously, the braces create a program block, telling Java where the body of the loop begins and ends.

> **Caution:** Always initialize (set the starting value of) any variable used in a while loop's control expression. Failure to do so may result in your program skipping over the loop entirely. (Initializing a variable means setting it to its starting value. If you need a variable to start at a specific value, you must initialize it yourself.) Also, be sure to increment or decrement the control variable as appropriate in the body of a loop. Failure to do this could result in an *infinite loop*, which is when the loop conditional never yields a true result, causing the loop to execute endlessly.

Example: Using a *while* Loop in a Program

As with most things in life, you learn best by doing. So, in this example, you put together an applet that uses a while loop to create its display. Listing 10.2 is the applet's source code, whereas Listing 10.3 is the HTML document that loads and runs the applet. Figure 10.1 shows the Applet8 applet running in Appletviewer. If you need a reminder on how to compile and run an applet, follow these steps:

1. Type the source code shown in Listing 10.2 and save it in your CLASSES folder, naming the file Applet8.java. (You can copy the source code from the CD-ROM, if you like, and thus save on typing.)

2. Compile the source code by typing **javac Applet8.java** at the MS-DOS prompt, which gives you the Applet8.class file.

3. Type the HTML document shown in Listing 10.3, and save it to your CLASSES folder under the name APPLET8.HTML.

4. Run the applet by typing, at the MS-DOS prompt, `appletviewer applet8.html`.

Listing 10.2   Applet8.java: An Applet That Uses a *while* Loop.

```java
import java.awt.*;
import java.applet.*;

public class Applet8 extends Applet
{
    TextField textField1;
    TextField textField2;

    public void init()
    {
        textField1 = new TextField(5);
        textField2 = new TextField(5);
        add(textField1);
        add(textField2);
        textField1.setText("1");
        textField2.setText("10");
    }

    public void paint(Graphics g)
    {
        g.drawString("Enter start and end values above.", 50, 45);
        String s = textField1.getText();
        int start = Integer.parseInt(s);
        s = textField2.getText();
        int end = Integer.parseInt(s);

        int row = 0;
        int count = start;
        while (count <= end)
        {
            s = "Count = ";
            s += String.valueOf(count++);
            g.drawString(s, 80, row * 15 + 70);
            ++row;
        }
    }

    public boolean action(Event event, Object arg)
    {
        repaint();
        return true;
    }
}
```

Tell Java that the program uses classes in the awt *package.*
Tell Java that the program uses classes in the applet *package.*
Derive the Applet8 *class from Java's* Applet *class.*
  Declare TextField *objects called* textField1 *and* textField2.
  Override the Applet *class's* init() *method.*
    Create the two TextField *objects.*
    Add the two TextField *objects to the applet.*
    Initialize the TextField *objects to "1" and "10."*
  Override the Applet *class's* paint() *method.*
    Print a prompt for the user.
    Get the number from the first TextField *object.*
    Convert the number from text to an integer.
    Get the number from the second TextField *object.*
    Convert the number from text to an integer.
    Initialize the row counter.
    Initialize the loop control variable, count.
    Loop from the starting value to the ending value.
      Initialize a string to "Count = ".
      Add the loop counter to the text string.
      Draw the text string in the applet's display area.
      Increment the row counter.
  Override the Applet *class's* action() *method.*
    Tell Java to redraw the applet's display area.
    Tell Java that the action() *method finished successfully.*

Listing 10.3   APPLET8.HTML: Applet8's HTML Document.

```
<title>Applet Test Page</title>
<h1>Applet Test Page</h1>
<applet
    code="Applet8.class"
    width=250
    height=350
    name="Applet8">
</applet>
```

When you run Applet8, type the starting value for the loop in the first box and the ending value for the loop in the second box. (Don't press enter until you've entered both values.) When you do, the program's while loop runs for the values you selected, printing the value of the loop control variable each time through the loop. For example, in Figure 10.1, the while loop has counted from 1 to 10 (the default values for the TextField controls). You can type any numbers you like, however. If you typed 15 in the first box and 30 in the last box, the while loop will count from 15 to 30, as shown in Figure 10.2.

Figure 10.1

Applet8 running in
Appletviewer.

Figure 10.2

Applet8 will count
however you tell
it to.

Note: If you enter a pair of numbers with a wide range, the applet's output will run off the bottom of the applet. This won't hurt anything, but you'll be unable to see the entire output. In addition, if you make the starting value greater than the ending value, no output will appear in the applet's display area. This is because the `while` loop's conditional expression never evaluates to true.

The *do-while* Loop

Java also features `do-while` loops. A `do-while` loop is much like a `while` loop, except a `do-while` loop evaluates its control expression at the end of the loop rather than at the beginning. So the body of the loop—the statements between the beginning and end of the loop—is always executed at least once. In a `while` loop, the body of the loop may or may not ever get executed. Listing 10.4 shows how a `do-while` loop works.

Listing 10.4 LST10_4.TXT: Using a *do-while* Loop.

```
num = 0;

do
    ++num;
while (num < 10);
```

The difference between a `do-while` loop and a `while` loop are readily apparent when you look at the listing. As you can see, the loop's conditional expression is at the end instead of the beginning. That is, in the example listing, `num` will always be incremented at least once. After Java increments `num`, it gets to the `while` line and checks whether `num` is less than 10. If it is, program execution jumps back to the beginning of the loop, where `num` gets incremented again. Eventually, `num` becomes equal to 10, causing the conditional expression to be false, and the loop ends.

Example: Using a *do-while* Loop

Near the beginning of this chapter, you saw an example of a `while` loop whose body contained multiple statements. By using braces to mark off a program block, you can do the same thing with a `do-while` loop. Listing 10.5 shows how to create a multiple line `do-while` loop:

Listing 10.5 LST10_5.TXT: A Multiple-Line *do-while* loop.

```
num = 0;

do
{
    ++num;
    String s = String.valueOf(num);
    g.drawString("num is now equal to:", 20, 40);
    g.drawString(s, 20, 55);
}
while (num < 10);
```

Initialize the loop control variable.
Begin the `do-while` loop.
   Increment the loop control variable.
   Create a string from the value of `num`.
   Display a message on the screen.
   Display the value of `num`.
   Determine whether to repeat the loop.

Example: Using a *do-while* Loop in a Program

Now it's time to put your knowledge of do-while loops to the test. If you haven't yet picked up on the pattern, you may be surprised to learn that the next applet is called Applet9. Applet9 looks and acts a lot like Applet8. In fact, as far as the user is concerned, they are almost exactly the same program. However, the clever among you may have already guessed that Applet9 uses a do-while loop in place of the while loop. This means that regardless of the values the user enters into the applet's TextField controls, the applet will always display at least one line of text. Listing 10.6 is the applet. Modify the HTML document from Listing 10.3, replacing all occurrences of Applet8 with Applet9, in order to run the new version of the applet.

Listing 10.6   Applet9.java: Source Code for Applet9.

```java
import java.awt.*;
import java.applet.*;

public class Applet9 extends Applet
{
    TextField textField1;
    TextField textField2;

    public void init()
    {
        textField1 = new TextField(5);
        textField2 = new TextField(5);
        add(textField1);
        add(textField2);
        textField1.setText("1");
        textField2.setText("10");
    }

    public void paint(Graphics g)
    {
        g.drawString("Enter start and end values above.", 50, 45);
        String s = textField1.getText();
        int start = Integer.parseInt(s);
        s = textField2.getText();
        int end = Integer.parseInt(s);

        int row = 0;
        int count = start;

        do
        {
            s = "Count = ";
            s += String.valueOf(count++);
            g.drawString(s, 80, row * 15 + 70);
            ++row;
        }
```

```
        while (count <= end);
    }

    public boolean action(Event event, Object arg)
    {
        repaint();
        return true;
    }
}
```

As long as the user always enters a lower value in the first box and a higher value in the second, the Applet9 applet will perform exactly as Applet8 did. However, the difference appears when the starting value is greater than the ending value. Applet8 produced no text output at all under these conditions, because the `while` loop evaluates the condition before it executes the body of the loop. As Figure 10.3 shows, Applet9 always displays at least one line of text output, because the loop is evaluated after its body is executed rather than before. In the figure, the user has entered a starting value that's higher than the ending value.

Figure 10.3

The *do-while* loop always executes at least once.

Summary

By using loops, you can easily program your applets to perform repetitive operations. Although loops may seem a little strange to you at this point, you'll find more and more uses for them as you write your own applets. Just remember that a `while` loop may or may not ever execute depending on how the conditional expressions works out. On the other hand, a `do-while` loop always executes at least once because its conditional is evaluated at the end of the loop rather than at the start. In the next chapter, you'll learn about one last type of loop, called a `for` loop. As you'll see, you use a `for` loop when you know exactly how many times a loop must execute.

Review Questions

1. When do you use loops in a program?

2. What is the body of a loop?

3. How does Java determine when to stop looping?

4. How many times is a while loop guaranteed to execute?

5. Why is it important to initialize a loop control variable?

6. What's an infinite loop?

7. Compare and contrast while and do-while loops?

8. How many times will the loop shown in Listing 10.7 execute? What will count equal when the loop finishes?

Listing 10.7   LST10_7.TXT: The Loop for Review Question 8.

```
int count = 10;

do
{
    ++count;
}
while (count <= 15);
```

Review Exercises

1. Write a while loop that executes 20 times.

2. Convert the while loop you wrote in exercise 1 to a do-while loop.

3. Write a while loop that will result in an infinite loop.

4. Write a do-while loop that can never execute more than once.

5. Write a while loop that counts backwards from 20 to 10.

6. Modify Applet8 so that it totals all the numbers from the user's selected starting value to the ending value. That is, if the user enters 10 and 15 as the starting and ending values, the applet should sum 10, 11, 12, 13, 14, and 15, and then display the result. Name the program WhileApplet.java. Figure 10.4 shows what the final applet should look like. (You can find the solution to this programming problem in the CHAP07 folder of this book's CD-ROM.)

Figure 10.4

This is what the
WhileApplet
applet should
look like.

CHAPTER 11

The *for* Loop

In the previous chapter, you got an introduction to looping. Along the way, you learned about while and do-while loops, which are an important part of the Java language. Java also supports another type of loop, called a for loop, that enables you to specify exactly how many times the loop should be executed. In this chapter, you learn to write for loops, as well as how to incorporate them into your Java programs.

Introducing the *for* Loop

Probably the most often-used loop in programming is the for loop, which instructs a program to perform a block of code a specified number of times. There are many applications for a for loop, including tasks such as reading through a list of data items or initializing an array. (You'll learn about arrays in Chapter 13, "Arrays.") You could, for example, use a for loop to instruct your computer to print 10,000 address labels, reading a new address from a file each time through the loop and sending that address to the printer. Because you don't currently have an address file, however, let's say you want to print a name on the screen 10 times. Listing 11.1 shows one way to do this.

Listing 11.1 LST11_1.TXT: Printing a Name 10 Times.

```
g.drawString("Alfred Thompson", 50, 50);
g.drawString("Alfred Thompson", 50, 65);
g.drawString("Alfred Thompson", 50, 80);
g.drawString("Alfred Thompson", 50, 95);
g.drawString("Alfred Thompson", 50, 110);
g.drawString("Alfred Thompson", 50, 125);
g.drawString("Alfred Thompson", 50, 140);
```

continues

Listing 11.1 Continued

```
g.drawString("Alfred Thompson", 50, 155);
g.drawString("Alfred Thompson", 50, 170);
g.drawString("Alfred Thompson", 50, 185);
```

If you were to add the lines shown in Listing 11.1 to your Java applet's `paint()` method, you'd see something like Figure 11.1. As you can see, you've accomplished the task at hand, which is printing a name 10 times. However, you haven't done it in the most efficient way.

Figure 11.1

This applet prints a name 10 times without using a loop.

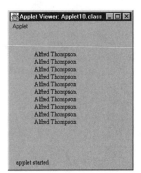

Look at Listing 11.1. See all those calls to `drawString()`? As a computer programmer, whenever you see program code containing many identical instructions, a little bell should go off in your head. When you hear this little bell, you should do one of two things:

1. Answer your telephone.

2. Say to yourself, "This looks like a good place for a loop."

Having many lines in your program containing identical instructions makes your program longer than necessary and wastes valuable memory. It also shows poor programming style. Unless you want your programming friends to snicker behind your back, learn to replace redundant program code with program loops.

> **Tip:** To produce programs that are tightly written, shorter, and faster, always try to replace repetitive program code with program loops.

Example: Using a *for* Loop

Listing 11.1 can be streamlined easily by using a `for` loop, as shown in Listing 11.2. The output of the second version is identical to the first, but now the listing is shorter and contains no redundant code.

Listing 11.2   LST11_2.TXT: Using a *for* Loop to Print a Name 10 Times.

```
int row = 0;

for (int x=0; x<10; ++x)
    g.drawString("Al Thompson", 25, 50 + (x * 15));
```

Look at the program line beginning with the keyword `for`. The loop starts with this line. The word `for` tells Java that you're starting a `for` loop. There are actually three elements inside the parentheses. The first part, `x=1`, is called the initialization section. The second part, `x<10`, is called the condition; the last part, `++x`, is called the increment.

All three sections of the `for` loop, which are separated by semicolons, reference the loop-control variable `x`. The loop-control variable, which can have any integer-variable name, is where Java stores the current loop count. Notice that the loop-control variable must have been previously declared as an `int` (integer) variable. You can place this declaration as part of the initialization part of the command.

The initialization section of the `for` statement is used to initialize the loop-control variable that controls the action. The condition section represents a Boolean condition that should be equal to true for the loop to continue execution. Finally, the increment, which is the third part of the statement, is an expression describing how to increment the control variable. The statement after the `for` statement is executed each time the loop's conditional expression is found to be true.

Suppose you want to modify Listing 11.2 to print the name 20 times. What would you change? If you answered, "I'd change the 10 in the `for` line to 20," you win the Programmer of the Week award. If you answered, "I'd change my socks," you better find a different book to read.

Example: Using a *for* Loop in a Program

The best way to learn about any programming construct is to use it in a program. Listing 11.3 is a short applet called Applet10 that uses a `for` loop to display a given name 10 times. Listing 11.4 is the HTML document that runs the applet, whereas Figure 11.2 shows the applet running under Appletviewer.

Listing 11.3   Applet10.java: Using a *for* Loop in an Applet.

```java
import java.awt.*;
import java.applet.*;

public class Applet10 extends Applet
{
    TextField textField1;

    public void init()
    {
        textField1 = new TextField(20);
        add(textField1);
        textField1.setText("Moe Howard");
    }

    public void paint(Graphics g)
    {
        g.drawString("Enter a name above.", 70, 45);
        String s = textField1.getText();

        for (int x=0; x<10; ++x)
            g.drawString(s, 80, x * 15 + 70);
    }

    public boolean action(Event event, Object arg)
    {
        repaint();
        return true;
    }
}
```

Tell Java that the program uses classes in the awt *package.*
Tell Java that the program uses classes in the applet *package.*
Derive the Applet10 *class from Java's* Applet *class.*
  Declare a TextField *object called* textField1.
  Override the Applet *class's* init() *method.*
    Create the TextField *object.*
    Add the TextField *object to the applet.*
    Initialize the text in the TextField *object to "Moe Howard."*
  Override the Applet *class's* paint() *method.*
    Display a prompt for the user.
    Get the name from the TextField *object.*
    Loop ten times.
      Draw the name in the applet's display area.
  Override the Applet *class's* action() *method.*
    Tell Java to redraw the applet's display area.
    Tell Java that the action() *method finished successfully.*

Listing 11.4   APPLET10.HTML: The HTML Document That Runs Applet10.

```
<title>Applet Test Page</title>
<h1>Applet Test Page</h1>
<applet
    code="Applet10.class"
    width=250
    height=250
    name="Applet10">
</applet>
```

Figure 11.2

This applet
displays, 10
times, whatever
name the user
types.

The Applet10 applet is well explained in the pseudocode following Listing 11.3. However, notice how the loop counter x works in this program. Although the `for` loop executes 10 times, the largest value stored in x will be 9. This is because the loop counter starts at 0, and counts 0, 1, 2, 3, 4, 5, 6, 7, 8, and 9. You might at first expect x to end up being equal to 10, Watch out for this sort of thing in your Java programs, especially if you use the value of the loop counter within the body of the loop or elsewhere in the program. Applet10 uses the loop counter to determine the row at which to print the next name. Keep in mind that, because x is declared as part of the `for` loop's program block, it can't be accessed outside of that block.

Changing the Increment Value

The previous example of a `for` loop increments the loop counter by 1. But suppose you want a `for` loop that counts from 5 to 50 by fives? This could be useful if you need to use the loop counter to display a value, which needs to be incremented by a different number. You can do this by changing the sections of the `for` loop, like this.

```
for (x=5; x<=50; x+=5)
```

This loop doesn't start counting at 1. Rather, the loop variable begins with a value of 5. Then, thanks to the x+=5 statement, the loop variable is incremented by 5 each time through the loop. Therefore, x goes from 5 to 10, from 10 to 15, and so on up to 50, resulting in ten loops.

You can also use a `for` loop to count backwards, like this:

```
for (x=50; x>=5; x-=5)
```

Notice that in the initialization part of the `for` statement, the higher value is used. Notice also that the increment clause uses a decrement operator, which causes the loop count to be decremented (decreased) rather than incremented.

Example: Looping with Different Increments

If you're a little confused, take a look at Listing 11.5, which shows the Java source code for a small applet called Applet11. This applet's `paint()` method contains two `for` loops, one that counts upward by fives and one that counts downward by fives. Each time through the loop, the program prints out the value of the loop control variable, so that you can see exactly what's going on inside the loops. To run this applet, use the HTML document from the previous applet, but replace all occurrences of Applet10 with Applet11. Figure 11.3 shows Appletviewer running the Applet11 applet.

Listing 11.5 Applet11.java: Using Different Increments with *for* Loops.

```java
import java.awt.*;
import java.applet.*;

public class Applet11 extends Applet
{
    public void paint(Graphics g)
    {
        int row = 0;

        for (int x=5; x<=40; x+=5)
        {
            String s = "Loop counter = ";
            s += String.valueOf(x);
            g.drawString(s, 80, row * 15 + 15);
            ++row;
        }

        for (int x=40; x>=5; x-=5)
        {
            String s = "Loop counter = ";
            s += String.valueOf(x);
```

```
        g.drawString(s, 80, row * 15 + 15);
                ++row;
            }
        }
}
```

Tell Java that the program uses classes in the awt *package.*
Tell Java that the program uses classes in the applet *package.*
Derive the Applet11 *class from Java's* Applet *class.*
   Override the Applet *class's* paint() *method.*
      Initialize the row counter.
      Begin the first for *loop.*
         Create the basic display string.
         Add the loop counter value to the display string.
         Show the string in the applet's display area.
         Increment the row counter.
      Start the second for *loop.*
         Create the basic display string.
         Add the loop counter value to the display string.
         Show the string in the applet's display area.
         Increment the row counter.

Figure 11.3

You can use *for* loops to count forward or backward by any amount that you like.

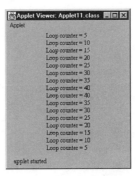

Using Variables in Loops

Just as you can substitute variables for most numerical values in a program, you can also substitute variables for the literals in a for loop. In fact, you'll probably use variables in your loop limits as often as you use literals, if not more. Here's an example of how to use variables to control your for loops:

```
for (x=start; x<=end; x+=inc)
```

In this partial `for` loop, the loop control variable x starts off at the value of the variable `start`. Each time through the loop, Java increments x by the value stored in the variable `inc`. Finally, when x is greater than the value stored in `end`, the loop ends. As you can see, using variables with `for` loops (or any other kind of loop, for that matter) enables you to write loops that work differently based on the state of the program.

Example: Controlling *for* Loops with Variables

For this chapter's last applet, you'll apply everything you've learned about `for` loops. The Applet12 applet, shown in Listing 11.6, enables you to experiment with different starting, ending, and increment values for the `for` loop contained in the applet's `paint()` method. Enter the starting value for the loop in the first box, then enter the ending and increment values in the second and third boxes. Don't press Enter until you've filled in all three boxes with the values you want. When you press Enter, the `action()` method takes over, telling Java to repaint the applet's display area using the new values. Figure 11.5 shows Applet12 running under the Appletviewer application.

Listing 11.6   Applet12.java: Advanced *for* Loops.

```java
import java.awt.*;
import java.applet.*;

public class Applet12 extends Applet
{
    TextField textField1;
    TextField textField2;
    TextField textField3;

    public void init()
    {
        textField1 = new TextField(5);
        textField2 = new TextField(5);
        textField3 = new TextField(5);

        add(textField1);
        add(textField2);
        add(textField3);

        textField1.setText("1");
        textField2.setText("10");
        textField3.setText("1");
    }
```

```
public void paint(Graphics g)
    {
        g.drawString("Enter loop starting, ending,", 50, 45);
        g.drawString("and increment values above.", 50, 60);

        String s = textField1.getText();
        int start = Integer.parseInt(s);
        s = textField2.getText();
        int end = Integer.parseInt(s);
        s = textField3.getText();
        int inc = Integer.parseInt(s);

        int row = 0;

        for (int x=start; x<=end; x+=inc)
        {
            String s2 = "Loop counter = ";
            s2 += String.valueOf(x);
            g.drawString(s2, 50, row * 15 + 85);
            ++row;
        }
    }

    public boolean action(Event event, Object arg)
    {
        repaint();
        return true;
    }
}
```

Tell Java that the program uses classes in the awt *package.*
Tell Java that the program uses classes in the applet *package.*
Derive the Applet12 *class from Java's* Applet *class.*
  Declare three TextField *objects as fields of the class.*
  Override the Applet *class's* init() *method.*
    Create the three TextField *objects.*
    Add the three TextField *objects to the applet.*
    Initialize the TextField *objects with their starting text.*
  Override the Applet *class's* paint() *method.*
    Display a prompt to the user.
    Get the entered text and convert it to integers.
    Initialize the row counter.
    Begin the for *loop.*
      Create the basic display string.
      Add the loop counter value to the display string.
      Show the string in the applet's display area.
      Increment the row counter.
  Override the Applet *class's* action() *method.*
    Tell Java to redraw the applet's display area.
    Tell Java that the method finished successfully.

Figure 11.4

Applet12 enables
you to experiment
with different
starting, ending,
and increment
values.

Summary

The for loop is a versatile programming construct that enables you to create loops that run from a given starting value to a given ending value. The loop's operation also depends on the value of the loop's increment value, which enables you to use the loop control variable to count forward or backward by any given amount. As you'll see, for loops are used a lot in Java programs. (In fact, they're a standard part of virtually all programming languages.) To be sure you understand for loops, look over the following questions and exercises.

Review Questions

1. How do you know when to use a for loop?

2. What are the three parts of a for loop?

3. When does a for loop stop looping?

4. How can a for loop count backward?

5. How can a for loop count by tens?

6. Is it possible to create an infinite loop with a for loop?

7. How many times will the loop shown below execute? What will x equal when the loop finishes?

```
for (int x=3; x<12; x+=2)
{
    ++count;
}
```

Review Exercises

1. Write a for loop that executes 15 times.

2. Write a for loop that counts by twos.

3. Write a for loop that can never execute.

4. Write a for loop that counts backwards from 20 to 10.

5. Modify Applet12 so that it contains two loops, one counting forward and the other counting backwards. Name the program ForApplet.java. Figure 11.5 shows what the final applet should look like. (You can find the solution to this programming problem in the CHAP11 folder of this book's CD-ROM.)

Figure 11.5

This is what ForApplet should look like.

Functions

Until now, your programs have been pretty short, each designed to demonstrate a single programming technique. When you start writing real programs, however, you'll quickly discover that they can grow to many pages of code. When programs get long, they also get harder to organize and read. To overcome this problem, professional programmers break their programs down into individual functions, each of which completes a specific and well-defined task.

The Top-Down Approach to Programming

As I said, long programs are hard to organize and read. A full-length program contains many pages of code, and trying to find a specific part of the program in all that code can be tough. You can use *modular program-design* techniques to solve this problem. Using modular programming techniques, you can break a long program into individual modules, each of which performs a specific task.

In Chapter 4, "Object-Oriented Programming Concepts," you got a quick look at modular program design, which is also known as structured programming. In that chapter, I used the example of cleaning a house as a way to understand the process of breaking tasks up into specific steps. (The only reasonable way to clean my house is to douse it with gasoline and throw in a lighted match, but we won't get into that now.) You'll use that metaphor again here, in preparation for learning about functions.

When cleaning a house, the main task might be called CLEAN HOUSE. Thinking about cleaning an entire house, however, can be overwhelming. So, to make the task easier, you can break it down into a number of smaller steps. These steps might be CLEAN LIVING ROOM, CLEAN BEDROOM, CLEAN KITCHEN, and CLEAN BATHROOM.

After breaking the housecleaning task down into room-by-room steps, you have a better idea of what to do. But cleaning a room is also a pretty big task—especially if it hasn't been done in a while or if you have cats coughing up fur balls all over the place. So why not break each room step down, too? For example, cleaning the living room could be broken down into PICK UP ROOM, DUST AND POLISH, CLEAN FURNITURE, and VACUUM RUG.

After breaking each room's cleaning down into steps, your housecleaning job is organized much like a pyramid, with the general task on the top. As you work your way down the pyramid, from the main task to the room-by-room list and finally to the tasks for each room, the tasks get more and more specific.

Of course, when cleaning a house, you don't usually write a list of steps. If you're an efficient housecleaner, the steps are organized in your mind. (If you clean house like I do, there are only two steps: TURN ON TV and COLLAPSE ON COUCH.) However, when writing a program, which is a more conceptual task, you may not have a clear idea of exactly what needs to be done. This can lead to your being overwhelmed by the project.

Breaking programming tasks down into steps, or modules, is called modular programming. And when you break your program's modules down into even smaller modules—as we did with the task of cleaning a house—you're using a top-down approach to program design. By using top-down programming techniques, you can write any program as a series of small, easy-to-handle tasks. In Java, the basic unit for organizing code in a top-down manner is the function.

Example: Using Functions as Subroutines

When programmers talk about subroutines, they usually mean program modules that return no value to your program. In a way, a subroutine is like a small program within your main program. If you write a housecleaning program, the subroutines in the main module might be called `CleanLivingRoom()`, `CleanBedroom()`, `CleanKitchen()`, and `CleanBathroom()`. The `CleanLivingRoom()` subroutine would contain all the steps needed to clean the living room, the `CleanBedroom()` subroutine would contain all the steps needed to clean a bedroom, and so on.

Of course, it takes an extremely talented programmer to get a computer to clean a house. (If you manage that trick, contact me immediately.) We need a more computer-oriented example. Suppose you want to write a program that displays game instructions on-screen. Listing 12.1 shows one way you might accomplish this task in a Java applet. Figure 12.1 shows what the applet looks like.

Listing 12.1   Applet13.java: Printing Instructions in an Applet.

```
import java.awt.*;
import java.applet.*;

public class Applet13 extends Applet
{
    public void paint(Graphics g)
    {
        g.drawString("Try to guess the number I am", 48, 65);
        g.drawString("thinking of. The number will be", 48, 80);
        g.drawString("between 0 and 100. You have an", 48, 95);
        g.drawString("unlimited number of tries.", 48, 110);
        g.drawString("Good Luck.", 95, 140);
    }
}
```

Applet13 is about the simplest applet you can write. All it does is display text. The text comprises instructions for playing a simple number game. If you had to sum up in a couple of words the task performed by Applet13's paint() method, you might come up with something like "Draw Instructions," which is an excellent name for a function to handle that task. Listing 12.2 is a new version of the applet that isolates the instruction-display task in its own function. When you run this applet, it looks identical to Applet13.

Figure 12.1

This is the Applet13 applet running under Appletviewer.

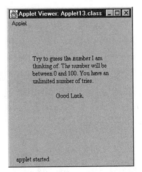

Listing 12.2   Applet14.java: Placing the Instructions in a Function.

```
import java.awt.*;
import java.applet.*;

public class Applet14 extends Applet
{
    public void paint(Graphics g)
```

continues

Listing 12.2 Continued

```
    {
        DrawInstructions(g);
    }

    void DrawInstructions(Graphics g)
    {
        g.drawString("Try to guess the number I am", 48, 65);
        g.drawString("thinking of. The number will be", 48, 80);
        g.drawString("between 0 and 100. You have an", 48, 95);
        g.drawString("unlimited number of tries.", 48, 110);
        g.drawString("Good Luck.", 95, 140);
    }
}
```

Now for the million-dollar question: How does this Applet14 work? The program is divided into two functions. The first is the `paint()` method, which Java calls whenever the applet's display area must be redrawn. In this applet, `paint()` is at the highest level of your top-down design. That is, no other part of the program calls `paint()`, but `paint()` calls functions that are lower in level.

> **Note:** You might be confused about the difference between methods, functions, and subroutines. The truth is that they are very similar. Specifically, a method is a function that is part of a class. So, in Applet14, both `paint()` and `DrawInstructions()` are methods of the `Applet14` class. (They are also functions.) A subroutine is a function that returns no value. That is, it has the word `void` in front of its name.

The second function in Listing 12.2 is the `DrawInstructions()` subroutine, which is really just a Java function that returns no value to the calling function (`paint()`, in this case). `DrawInstructions()` is one level down from the main program in the top-down design. In `paint()`, instead of having all the code that's needed to display the instructions, you only have a line that calls the function that handles this task. This makes it easier to see what's going on in `paint()`. If you need to see more detail, you can always drop down a level in your program and take a look at `DrawInstructions()`.

Defining and Calling Functions

There are two things you must do to use a function in a program. The first thing you must do is define the function, which means that you must write all the program instructions that make up the function, placing the instructions between curly braces. You must also determine what arguments the function must have in order to perform its task. In Applet14, the `DrawInstructions()` function definition looks like Listing 12.3.

Listing 12.3   LST12_3.TXT: The *DrawInstructions( )* Subroutine.

```
void DrawInstructions(Graphics g)
{
    g.drawString("Try to guess the number I am", 48, 65);
    g.drawString("thinking of. The number will be", 48, 80);
    g.drawString("between 0 and 100. You have an", 48, 95);
    g.drawString("unlimited number of tries.", 48, 110);
    g.drawString("Good Luck.", 95, 140);
}
```

The first line of Listing 12.3 tells Java the type of value returned from the function, the name of the function, and the arguments that must be sent to the function when it's called. In this case, the type of return value is `void`, which means the function returns no value. The name of the function is `DrawInstructions`, and its argument is a `Graphics` object called `g`. (Notice that, in the function's first line, you must list both the argument type and argument name.) If you look at the `paint()` method, you can see that Applet14 calls the `DrawInstructions()` function like this:

```
DrawInstructions(g);
```

This line tells Java that you want to execute the program code in the `DrawInstructions()` function and that you want to pass the `Graphics` object `g` to the function. `DrawInstructions()` needs access to `g` because it is the `Graphics` object that has the `drawString()` method. Without access to the `Graphics` object, `DrawInstructions()` cannot perform its task in the same way that the `drawString()` method cannot display a string unless you give it the string and the location at which to display the string.

The second thing you must do to use a function is to call the function. When you call a function, program execution jumps to the commands that make up the function. All commands in the function are executed, after which the program returns to the line after the function call.

> **Note:** The arguments you place between the parentheses of a function call must be of the same type and in the same order as the arguments given in the function's first line. That is, the call `DrawInstructions(g)` and the first line of the function, `DrawInstructions(Graphics g)`, match perfectly because the function call sends a `Graphics` object and the function expects a `Graphics` object. The names of the arguments, however, don't have to match. For example, the function call `DrawInstructions(g)` and the function name `DrawInstructions(Graphics graph)` are still a match. The only difference is that you'd have to refer to `graph` inside the `DrawInstructions()` function, rather than to `g`.

Example: Using Functions to Return Values

In Java, functions are the main way you can break up your programs into modules. But unlike when you used functions as subroutines, some types of functions return a value to the main program. You've used this type of Java function before in this book. The `String` class' `valueOf()` method is one. The value it returns is the numerical value of a string containing digits.

You can assign a function's return value to a variable. Suppose you have a function named `GetNum()` that calculates a number and returns it to your program. A call to the function might look something like this:

```
int num = GetNum();
```

The function might look something like Listing 12.4.

Listing 12.4   LST12_4.TXT: An Example of a Function.

```
int GetNum()
{
    ++value;
    return value;
}
```

Listing 12.4 shows some of the differences between using functions as subroutines (which return no value) and using functions to return values. While functions being used as subroutines always start with the keyword `void`, functions that return values start with the keyword `int`, `char`, `float` or whatever type of return value you need. Also, since subroutines return no value, they need no `return` statement. But as you can see, the `GetNum()` function returns a value by using the `return` keyword along with the value to be returned. If you fail to include the `return` command in the body of a function that returns a value, Java's compiler will give you an error message.

> **Note:** Normally, arguments passed into a function are *passed by value*, which means that a copy of the passed value is given to the function. When you change the value of the argument in the function, you are changing the copy, while the original value stays the same. However, some arguments are *passed by reference*, which means that the original object is passed to the function. In this case, changing the argument's value in the function changes the original value, too. You learn about passing by reference in Chapter 13, "Arrays."

Example: Putting Functions to Work

Think you understand functions now? The applet you'll build in this example will put your knowledge to the test. Listing 12.5 is the applet's source code, whereas Listing 12.6 is the HTML document that'll load and run the applet. Figure 12.2 shows what the applet looks like when it's running under Appletviewer.

Listing 12.5   APPLET15.JAVA: Using Functions in a Java Applet.

```java
import java.awt.*;
import java.applet.*;
import java.lang.Math;

public class Applet15 extends Applet
{
    /////////////////////////////////////////
    // Data fields.
    /////////////////////////////////////////
    TextField textField1;
    int guesses;
    int number;

    /////////////////////////////////////////
    // Overridden methods.
    /////////////////////////////////////////
    public void init()
    {
        textField1 = new TextField(10);
        add(textField1);
        textField1.setText("50");
        guesses = 0;
        number = CreateNumber();
    }

    public void paint(Graphics g)
    {
        DrawInstructions(g);
        int guess = GetGuess();
        ShowMessage(g, guess);
    }

    public boolean action(Event event, Object arg)
    {
        ++guesses;
        repaint();
        return true;
    }

    /////////////////////////////////////////
    // Private methods.
```

continues

Listing 12.5 Continued

```
/////////////////////////////////////////
void DrawInstructions(Graphics g)
{
    g.drawString("Try to guess the number I am", 48, 65);
    g.drawString("thinking of. The number will be", 48, 80);
    g.drawString("between 0 and 100. You have an", 48, 95);
    g.drawString("unlimited number of tries.", 48, 110);
    g.drawString("Good Luck.", 95, 140);
}

int GetGuess()
{
    String s = textField1.getText();
    int num = Integer.parseInt(s);
    return num;
}

int CreateNumber()
{
    float n = (float)Math.random();
    number = (int)(n * 100 + 1);
    return number;
}

void ShowMessage(Graphics g, int guess)
{
    String s = "Guesses so far: ";
    s += String.valueOf(guesses);
    g.drawString(s, 80, 170);

    if (guess < number)
        g.drawString("Your guess is too low.", 70, 185);
    else if (guess > number)
        g.drawString("Your guess is too high.", 70, 185);
    else
        g.drawString("You guessed the number!", 65, 185);
}
}
```

Tell Java that the program uses classes in the awt *package.*
Tell Java that the program uses classes in the applet *package.*
Tell Java that the program uses the lang package's Math *class.*
Derive the Applet15 *class from Java's* Applet *class.*
   Declare the class's data fields.
   Override the Applet *class's* init() *method.*

Create the TextField *object.*
Add the TextField *object to the applet.*
Initialize the text in the TextField *object to "50."*
Initialize the guess counter to zero.
Create the number that the player must guess.
Override the Applet *class's* paint() *method.*
  Print the game's instructions.
  Get the player's guess.
  Show the appropriate message based on the guess.
Override the Applet *class's* action() *method.*
  Increment the guess counter.
  Tell Java to redraw the applet's display area.
  Tell Java that the action() *method finished successfully.*
Define the private DrawInstructions() *method.*
  Display the game instructions in the applet.
Define the private GetGuess() *method.*
  Get the text from the TextField *object.*
  Convert the text to an integer.
  Return the integer to the calling function.
Define the private CreateNumber() *method.*
  Calculate a random number from 0 to 1.
  Convert the random number to an integer between 1 and 100.
  Return the random number to the calling function.
Define the private ShowMessage() *method.*
  Display the number of guesses so far.
  Display the results of the player's latest guess.

Listing 12.6 APPLET15.HTML: Applet15's HTML Document.

```
<title>Applet Test Page</title>
<h1>Applet Test Page</h1>
<applet
    code="Applet15.class"
    width=250
    height=250
    name="Applet15">
</applet>
```

Figure 12.2

This is the
Applet15 applet
running under
Appletviewer.

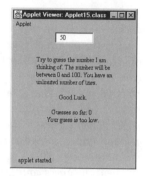

When you run Applet15, the program selects a random numeral from 1 to 100. Your task is to guess the numeral in the least number of tries. You type your guesses into the box at the top of the applet. When the program starts, this box contains the number 50, and the hint at the bottom of the screen tells you whether the number is high or low. Each time you enter a new number, the hint tells you whether the guess is high or low.

Yes, it's true that Applet15 is much larger than the example applets you've used so far in this book, but the program needs to be long in order to accommodate several different functions. By analyzing the program's flow, you can determine whether or not you understand how functions work.

Start with the paint() method. By examining the function calls it contains, you can get a good idea of what the program does. Specifically, the program displays the game's instructions, gets a guess from the user, and then displays a message to the user. If you were only interested in examining the paint() method, you wouldn't have to go any further; the details of how these other functions work are tucked out of your way.

If you wanted to see exactly how the program prints the game's instructions, however, you could find the DrawInstructions() method in the source code. The same is true for the other functions called in the paint() method.

You can see that some of the functions return values and others don't. Similarly, some functions require arguments and others don't. How the function is constructed depends on whether it must calculate and return a value to the program (such as in CreateNumber()) and whether the function requires values from the program in order to perform its task (such as ShowMessage(), which needs the Graphics object and the player's latest guess).

There are probably several lines of Java source code in Listing 12.5 that don't make sense to you right now. The pseudocode section following the listing describes, in general, what the program is doing. You'll learn about many of the details in other chapters. At this point, you only need to worry about being able to follow the function calls.

Summary

Functions enable you to break complicated programs down into easy-to-handle chunks. Moreover, by using a top-down structure, your programs can organize code with functions that start off being general in nature but get more detailed as you work your way deeper into the hierarchy. When a function doesn't return a value (has a return type of void), it is used as a subroutine, which simply performs some task before program execution jumps back to the line after the line that called the function. A function with a return type other than void enables your programs to calculate a value and return the value to the calling function. Either type of function can have one or more arguments, which enable the program to pass values into the function.

Review Questions

1. What is top-down programming?

2. How do functions make top-down programming possible?

3. Do all functions return values?

4. What are arguments and how are they used?

5. What is meant by "defining a function"?

6. How do you return a value from a function?

7. How do the arguments given in a function call relate to the arguments accepted by the function?

8. How do you determine how to break a program up into functions?

Review Exercises

1. Write a function that prints a two-line message to the user.

2. Write a function that returns the number 1 as an integer.

3. Write a function that accepts two integer arguments and returns the sum of the arguments.

4. Modify the function from exercise 3 so that it sums the two arguments, calls yet another function that multiplies the two arguments, sums the product and the original sum, and returns the result. Write the function that performs the multiplication.

5. Modify Applet15 by adding a function that starts the game over each time the user guesses the number. That is, after the user guesses the number, the program should select a new random number and continue the game. Name the program GuessApplet.java. (You can find the solution to this programming problem in the CHAP12 folder of this book's CD-ROM.)

CHAPTER 13

Arrays

As you've learned by now, using variables makes your programs flexible. Thanks to variables, you can conveniently store data in your programs and retrieve it by name. You can also get input from your program's user. The best thing about variables is that they can constantly change value. (They're called variables, after all, because they're *variable*.)

Until now, you've learned about various types of numerical variables, including integers, long integers, floating-point, and double floating-point variables. You also know about string variables, which can hold text. Now that you have a good understanding of these data types, it's time to explore one last data type—a handy data structure called an array.

An Introduction to Arrays

Often in your programs, you'll want to store many values that are related in some way. Suppose you manage a bowling league, and you want to keep track of each player's average. One way to do this is to give each player a variable in your program, as shown in Listing 13.1. Figure 13.1 shows the applet running under Appletviewer.

Listing 13.1   Applet16.java: Using Variables to Track Scores.

```
import java.awt.*;
import java.applet.*;

public class Applet16 extends Applet
```

continues

Listing 13.1 Continued

```
{
    TextField textField1, textField2, textField3;
    int avg1, avg2, avg3;

    public void init()
    {
        textField1 = new TextField(5);
        textField2 = new TextField(5);
        textField3 = new TextField(5);
        add(textField1);
        add(textField2);
        add(textField3);
        textField1.setText("0");
        textField2.setText("0");
        textField3.setText("0");
    }

    public void paint(Graphics g)
    {
        g.drawString("Your bowlers' averages are: ", 50, 80);
        String s = textField1.getText();
        g.drawString(s, 75, 110);
        avg1 = Integer.parseInt(s);
        s = textField2.getText();
        g.drawString(s, 75, 125);
        avg2 = Integer.parseInt(s);
        s = textField3.getText();
        g.drawString(s, 75, 140);
        avg3 = Integer.parseInt(s);
    }

    public boolean action(Event event, Object arg)
    {
        repaint();
        return true;
    }
}
```

Figure 13.1

This is Applet16 running under Appletviewer.

When you run Applet16, you can enter bowling scores into the three boxes at the top of the applet's display area. After you enter these averages, they're displayed on-screen as well as copied into the three variables avg1, avg2, and avg3.

Nothing too tricky going on here, right?

Now examine the listing. Remember in Chapter 10, "The while and do-while Loops," when you learned to keep an eye out for repetitive program code? How about all those calls to getText(), drawString(), and valueOf() in Listing 13.1? The only real difference between them is the specific bowler's score that's being manipulated. If you could find some way to make a loop out of this code, you could shorten the program significantly. How about a for loop that counts from 1 to 3?

But how can you use a loop when you're stuck with three different variables? The answer is an array. An array is a variable that can hold more than one value. When you first studied variables, you learned that a variable is like a box in memory that holds a single value. Now, if you take a bunch of these boxes and put them together, what do you have? You have an array. For example, to store the bowling averages for your three bowlers, you'd need an array that can hold three values. You could call this array avg. You can even create an array for a set of objects like the TextField objects Applet16 uses to get bowling scores from the user. You could call this array textField.

Now you have an array called avg that can hold three bowling averages and an array called textField that can hold three TextField objects. But how can you retrieve each individual average or object from the array? You do this by adding something called a *subscript* to the array's name. A subscript (also called an *index*) is a number that identifies the element of an array in which a value is stored. For example, to refer to the first average in your avg array, you'd write avg[0]. The subscript is the number in square brackets. In this case, you're referring to the first average in the array (array subscripts always start from zero.) To refer to the second average, you'd write avg[1]. The third average is avg[2].

If you're a little confused, look at Figure 13.2, which shows how the avg[] array might look in memory. In this case, the three bowling averages are 145, 192, and 160. The value of avg[0] is 145, the value of avg[1] is 192, and the value of avg[2] is 160.

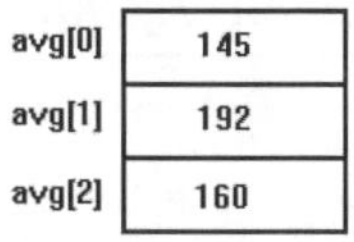

Figure 13.2

An array can hold many values of the same type.

avg[0]	145
avg[1]	192
avg[2]	160

Example: Creating an Array

Suppose that you need an array that can hold 30 floating-point numbers. First, you'd declare the array like this:

```
float numbers[];
```

Another way to declare the array is to move the square brackets to after the data type, like this:

```
float[] numbers;
```

After declaring the array, you need to create it in memory. Java lets you create arrays only using the new operator, like this:

```
numbers = new float[30];
```

The last step is to initialize the array, a task that you might perform using a for loop:

```
for (int x=0; x<30; ++x)
    numbers[x] = (float)x;
```

These lines of Java source code initialize the numbers[] array to the numbers 0.0 to 29.0. Notice how the loop only goes up to 29. This is because, although there are 30 elements in the numbers[] array, those elements are indexed starting with 0, rather than 1. That is, the subscript is always one less than the number of the element you're accessing. The first element has a subscript of 0, the second a subscript of 1, the third a subscript of 2, and so on.

Example: Using a Variable as a Subscript

As you learned in a previous chapter, most numerical literals in a Java program can be replaced by numerical variables. Suppose you were to use the variable x as the subscript for the array avg[]. Then (based on the averages in Figure 13.2) if the value of x is 1, the value of avg[x] is 192. If the value of x is 3, the value of avg[x] is 160.

Now take one last, gigantic, intuitive leap (c'mon, you can do it) and think about using your subscript variable x as both the control variable in a for loop and the subscript for the avg[] and textField arrays. If you use a for loop that counts from 0 to 2, you can handle all three averages with much less code than in the original program. Listing 13.2 shows how this is done.

Listing 13.2 Applet17.java: Using Arrays.

```
import java.awt.*;
import java.applet.*;

public class Applet17 extends Applet
{
    TextField textField[];
    int avg[];

    public void init()
    {
        textField = new TextField[3];
```

```
        avg = new int[3];

        for (int x=0; x<3; ++x)
        {
            textField[x] = new TextField(5);
            add(textField[x]);
            textField[x].setText("0");
        }
    }

    public void paint(Graphics g)
    {
        g.drawString("Your bowlers' averages are: ", 50, 80);

        for (int x=0; x<3; ++x)
        {
            String s = textField[x].getText();
            g.drawString(s, 75, 110 + x*15);
            avg[x] = Integer.parseInt(s);
        }
    }

    public boolean action(Event event, Object arg)
    {
        repaint();
        return true;
    }
}
```

Tell Java that the program uses classes in the awt *package.*
Tell Java that the program uses classes in the applet *package.*
Derive the Applet17 *class from Java's* Applet *class.*
 Declare TextField *and* int *arrays.*
 Override the Applet *class's* init() *method.*
  Create the textField *and* int *arrays with three elements each.*
  Loop from 0 to 2.
   Create a new TextField *object and store it in the array.*
   Add the new TextField *object to the applet.*
   Set the new TextField *object's text.*
 Override the Applet *class's* paint() *method.*
  Display a line of text.
  Loop from 0 to 2.
   Get the text from the currently indexed TextField *object.*
   Draw the retrieve text on the applet's display area.
   Convert the value and store it in the integer array.
 Override the Applet *object's* action() *method.*
  Force Java to redraw the applet's display area.
  Tell Java everything went okay.

At the beginning of Listing 13.2, you'll see a couple of strange new variable declarations that look like this:

```
TextField textField[];
int avg[];
```

These declarations are much like other declarations you've seen, except both of the variable names end with a set of square brackets. The square brackets tell Java that you're declaring arrays rather than conventional variables.

Once you have the arrays declared, you must create them. In Applet17, this is done like this:

```
textField = new TextField[3];
avg = new int[3];
```

Here you use the new operator to create the arrays. To tell Java the type of arrays to create, you follow new with the data type and the size of the array in square brackets. In other words, the first line above creates an array that can hold three TextField objects. The second line creates an array that can hold three integers.

Once you have your arrays created, you can use a loop to reduce the amount of code needed to initialize the arrays. For example, the long way to initialize the arrays (without using a loop) would look something like Listing 13.3:

Listing 13.3   LST13_3.TXT: Initializing an Array without Looping.

```
textField[0] = new TextField(5);
add(textField[0]);
textField[0].setText("0");
textField[1] = new TextField(5);
add(textField[1]);
textField[1].setText("0");
textField[2] = new TextField(5);
add(textField[2]);
textField[2].setText("0");
```

As you learned, however, you can use a variable—specifically, a loop control variable—as the array subscript. That's what Applet17 does, which enables it to initialize the textField array as shown in Listing 13.4.

Listing 13.4   LST13_4.TXT: Initializing an Array Using a Loop.

```
for (int x=0; x<3; ++x)
{
    textField[x] = new TextField(5);
    add(textField[x]);
    textField[x].setText("0");
}
```

The first time through the loop, x is equal to 0, so that element 0 (the first element) of the `textField` array is being manipulated. The next time through the loop, x is 1, so that element 1 of the array is being manipulated in the body of the loop. Finally, when x is 2, the program takes care of the third array element. As you can see, using a loop with an array can greatly simplify handling a group of related values. Imagine how many lines of source code you'd save if the array had 1,000 elements instead of only three. To accommodate the larger array, you'd only have to change `x<3` to `x<1000` in the first line of the `for` loop.

> **Caution:** Be careful not to try accessing a nonexistent array element. For example, in Listing 13.4, if you tried to access `textField[3]`, you'd be beyond the boundaries of the array. Java will generate an exception when this happens, which means your applet may or may not perform the way you want it to. (You'll learn more about exceptions in Chapter 30, "Exceptions.")

The `init()` method isn't the only place Applet17 takes advantage of a loop to handle the program's arrays. In the `paint()` method, you can see the loop shown in Listing 13.5.

Listing 13.5   LST13_5.TXT: The *for* Loop from the *paint( )* Method.

```
for (int x=0; x<3; ++x)
{
    String s = textField[x].getText();
    g.drawString(s, 75, 110 + x*15);
    avg[x] = Integer.parseInt(s);
}
```

This loop simplifies the printing of the bowlers' scores and the loading of the `avg[]` array with the scores. Again, imagine how much time and space you'd save if the arrays in question had thousands of elements rather than only three. It's at times like those that you really learn to appreciate arrays.

> **Note:** The memory locations that make up an array are called *elements* of the array. For example, in an array named `numbers[]`, `numbers[0]` is the first element of the array, `numbers[1]` is the second element, and so on. The reason `numbers[0]` is the first element of the array is because of the number 0 inside the subscript. It is the number inside the subscript that defines which array location is being referred to.

Multidimensional Arrays

So far, you've looked at simple arrays that hold their data in a list. However, most programming languages also support multidimensional arrays, which are more like tables than lists. For example, take a look at Figure 13.3. The first array in the figure is a one-dimensional array, which is like the arrays you've used so far in this chapter. The next type of array in the figure is two-dimensional, which works like the typical spreadsheet type of table you're used to seeing.

Figure 13.3

Arrays can have more than one dimension.

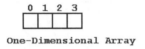

One-Dimensional Array

Two-Dimensional Array

Although Java doesn't support multidimensional arrays in the conventional sense, it does enable you to create arrays of arrays, which amount to the same thing. For example, to create a two-dimensional array of integers like the second array in Figure 13.3, you might use a line of code like this:

```
int table[][] = new int[4][4];
```

This line of Java code creates a table that can store 16 values—four across and four down. The first subscript selects the column and the second selects the row. To initialize such an array with values, you might use the lines shown in Listing 13.6, which would give you the array shown in Figure 13.4.

Listing 13.6 LST13_6.TXT: Initializing a Two-Dimensional Array.

```
table[0][0] = 0;
table[1][0] = 1;
table[2][0] = 2;
table[3][0] = 3;
table[0][1] = 4;
table[1][1] = 5;
table[2][1] = 6;
table[3][1] = 7;
table[0][2] = 8;
table[1][2] = 9;
```

```
table[2][2] = 10;
table[3][2] = 11;
table[0][3] = 12;
table[1][3] = 13;
table[2][3] = 14;
table[3][3] = 15;
```

Figure 13.4

Here's the two-dimensional array as initialized in Listing 13.6.

	0	1	2	3
0	0	1	2	3
1	4	5	6	7
2	8	9	10	11
3	12	13	14	15

You refer to a value stored in a two-dimensional array by using subscripts for both the column and row in which the value you want is stored. For example, to retrieve the value 11 from the `table[][]` array shown in Figure 13.4, you use a line like this:

```
int value = table[3][2];
```

A quick way to initialize a two-dimensional array is to use nested `for` loops, as shown in Listing 13.7.

Listing 13.7 LST13_11.TXT: Using Loops to Initialize a Two-Dimensional Array.

```
for (int x=0; x<3; ++x)
{
    for (int y=0; y<3; ++y)
    {
        table[x][y] = 5;
    }
}
```

If you've never seen nested loops before, you're about to discover how handy they can be. In the case of Listing 13.7, the outside loop (the `x` loop) starts first, setting `x` to 0. But the body of the loop is another loop. So the inside loop (the `y` loop) starts, setting `y` to 0, which brings the program to the line that initializes an element of the array. Because `x` and `y` both equal 0, the array element `table[0][0]` gets set to 5. Then the inside loop sets `y` to 1, which means `table[0][1]` gets set to 5. When the inner loop finishes, the program branches back to the outer loop, setting `x` to 1. The inner loop repeats again, only this time with `x` equal to 1 and `y` going from 0 to 2. Finally, when both loops finish, the entire array is initialized.

Of course, to create the array shown in Figure 13.4 with loops, you have to be a little more tricky, as shown in Listing 13.8. Work through each loop to see how the array gets initialized.

Listing 13.8   LST13_8.TXT: Initializing the Array Elements to Different Values.

```
for (int x=0; x<3; ++x)
{
    for (int y=0; y<3; ++y)
    {
        table[x][y] = x + y * 4;
    }
}
```

Example: Creating a Two-Dimensional Array

Suppose that you need a table-like array that can hold 80 integers in eight columns and 10 rows. First, you'd declare the array like this:

```
int numbers[][];
```

After declaring the array, you need to create it in memory, like this:

```
numbers = new int[8][10];
```

The last step is to initialize the array, probably using nested `for` loops:

```
for (int x=0; x<8; ++x)
    for (int y=0; y<10; ++y)
        numbers[x][y] = 0;
```

These lines initialize the `numbers[][]` array to all zeroes.

Example: Using Two-Dimensional Arrays in an Applet

To be sure you understand how arrays work, you'll put a two-dimensional array to work in a program called Applet18. The Applet18 applet creates and initializes a two-dimensional array with six columns and eight rows. (Try to imagine the elements of this array as the rows and columns of a spreadsheet.) The program then prints the contents of the array in the Applet's display area, so you can see that the array truly holds the values to which it was initialized. Listing 13.9 is the program, whereas Figure 13.5 shows the applet running under the Appletviewer application.

Listing 13.9   Applet18.java: Using a Two-Dimensional Array.

```java
import java.awt.*;
import java.applet.*;

public class Applet18 extends Applet
{
    int table[][];

    public void init()
    {
        table = new int[6][8];

        for (int x=0; x<6; ++x)
            for (int y=0; y<8; ++y)
                table[x][y] = x+y*6;
    }

    public void paint(Graphics g)
    {
        for (int x=0; x<6; ++x)
            for (int y=0; y<8; ++y)
            {
                String s = String.valueOf(table[x][y]);
                g.drawString(s, 50+x*25, 50+y*15);
            }
    }
}
```

Tell Java that the program uses classes in the awt *package.*
Tell Java that the program uses classes in the applet *package.*
Derive the Applet18 *class from Java's* Applet *class.*
  Declare a two-dimensional integer array.
  Override the Applet *class's* init() *method.*
    Create an array with six columns and eight rows.
    Loop from 0 to 5.
      Loop from 0 to 7.
        Initialize the currently indexed array element.
  Override the Applet *class's* paint() *method.*
    Loop from 0 to 5.
      Loop from 0 to 7.
        Convert the array element to a string.
        Display the array element's value.

Figure 13.5

This is Applet18 running under Appletviewer.

Notice in `init()` and `paint()` how the nested loops don't have curly braces like the example shown in Listing 13.8. This is because when you have only one statement in a program block, the curly braces are optional. In Applet18's `init()` method, the outside loop contains only one statement, which is the inner `for` loop. The inner `for` loop also contains only a single statement, which is the line that initializes the currently indexed element of the array. In the `paint()` method, the outer loop contains only one statement, which is the inner `for` loop. However, the inner loop contains two statements, so the curly braces are required in order to mark off that program block.

Summary

Arrays are a powerful data structure that enable you to store many related values using the same variable name. A one-dimensional array is a lot like a list of values that you can access by telling Java the appropriate subscript (or index). But because array subscripts always start at 0, the subscript is always one less than the number of the associated element. You can also create multidimensional arrays (or, to be more precise, arrays of arrays). A two-dimensional array is organized much like a table. To access the elements of a two-dimensional array, you need two subscripts. The first subscript identifies the column of the table and the second identifies the row.

Review Questions

1. What is an array?

2. Why are arrays easier to use than a bunch of related variables?

3. What is an array subscript? How is a subscript like an index?

4. What is a two-dimensional array?

5. If you had an array of 50 integers, what is the largest valid subscript?

6. What happens if you try to access a nonexistent array element?

7. Describe why a `for` loop is appropriate for accessing an array?

8. How would you use `for` loops to initialize a two-dimensional array?

Review Exercises

1. Declare an array that can hold 50 integers.

2. Write the code that creates the array you declared in exercise 1.

3. Write a `for` loop that initializes the array to the values 50 through 99.

4. Write the Java code to declare and create a two-dimensional array with 10 columns and 15 rows.

5. Write nested `for` loops that initialize the array from exercise 4 to the values 0 through 149.

6. Write the Java code needed to display, in table form, the values in the array from exercise 5.

7. Modify Applet17 so that it stores and displays not only the bowlers' scores, but also the bowlers' names. Create three `TextField` objects to enable the user to enter names and three for entering the scores. Name the program `ScoreApplet.java`. Figure 13.6 shows what the final applet should look like at startup. (You can find the solution to this programming problem in the CHAP13 folder of this book's CD-ROM.)

Figure 13.6

This is the ScoreApplet applet running under Appletviewer.

CHAPTER

Classes

Way back in Chapter 4, you got a general introduction to object-oriented programming concepts. In that chapter, you took a first look at classes and how they're used to organize source code into logically defined modules. Since then, you've been using various classes included as part of the Java language, but you haven't explored the implications of using a class or of creating your own classes. In this chapter, you plug up that hole in your understanding of Java and how it uses classes to create applets.

Classes and Objects

In Chapter 4, you learned that a class is the template for an object and that a class is a way to encapsulate both data (called fields in Java) and the functions (called methods) that operate on that data. You also learned about inheritance, which enables a class (called the *subclass*) to inherit the capabilities of a base class (called a *superclass* in Java). Finally, you discovered that polymorphism enables you to create virtual methods that can be implemented differently in derived classes. In this section, you'll apply what you know about object-oriented programming towards creating Java classes.

Defining a Simple Class

As I said, a class is sort of a template for an object. In this way, a class is equivalent to a data type such as int. The main difference is that Java already knows what an integer is. However, when you create a class, you must tell Java about the class's characteristics. You define a class by using the `class` keyword along with the class name, like this:

```
class MyClass
{
}
```

Believe it or not, the preceding lines are a complete Java class. If you save the lines in a file called `MyClass.java`, you could even compile the class into a .CLASS file, although the file won't actually do anything if you tried to run it. As you can see, the class definition begins with the keyword `class` followed by the name of the class. The body of the class is marked off by curly braces just like any other program block. In this case, the class's body is empty.

Because its body is empty, this example class doesn't do anything. You can, however, compile the class and even create an object from it. To create an object from a class, you type the class's name followed by the name of the object. For example, the line below creates an object from the `MyClass` class:

```
MyClass myObject = new MyClass();
```

Declaring Fields for a Class

As I said, the `MyClass` example class doesn't do much yet. In order to be useful, it needs both data fields and methods. You declare fields for your class in much the same way you declare any variable in a program, by typing the data type of the field followed by the name of the field, like this:

```
int myField;
```

The above line declares a data field of type integer. However, looking at the above line doesn't tell you much about how data fields are used with classes. In fact, you can't tell from the above line whether `myField` is actually part of an object or just a normal variable. To clear up this ambiguity, you can plug the above line into the `MyClass` class definition, as shown in Listing 14.1.

Listing 14.1   LST14_1.TXT: Adding a Data Field to a Class.

```
class MyClass
{
    int myField;
}
```

Now you can see that `myField` is a data field of the `MyClass` class. Moreover, this data field is by default accessible only by methods in the same package. (For now, you can think of a package as a file.) You can change the rules of this access by using the `public`, `protected`, and `private` keywords. A `public` data field can be accessed by any part of a program, inside or outside of the class in which it's defined. A `protected` data field can only be accessed from within the class or from within a derived class (a subclass). A `private` data field cannot even be accessed by a derived class.

Defining a Constructor

You have now added a data field to `MyClass`. However, the class has no methods and so can do nothing with its data field. The next step in defining the class, then, is to create methods. One special type of method, called a *constructor*, enables an object to initialize itself when it's created. A constructor is a `public` method (a method that can be accessed anywhere in a program) with the same name as the class. Listing 14.2 shows the `MyClass` class with its constructor in place.

Listing 14.2   LST14_2.TXT: Adding a Constructor to a Class.

```
class MyClass
{
    int myField;

    public MyClass(int value)
    {
        myField = value;
    }
}
```

As you can see, the class's constructor starts with the `public` keyword. This is important because you want to be able to create an object from the class anywhere in your program, and when you create an object, you're actually calling its constructor. After the `public` keyword comes the name of the constructor followed by the constructor's arguments in parentheses. When you create an object of the class, you must also provide the required arguments.

Example: Creating an Object by Calling a Constructor

If you want to create an object from `MyClass`, you must supply an integer value that the class uses to initialize the `myField` data field. This integer is the `MyClass` constructor's single argument. You'd create an object of the class like this:

```
MyClass myObject = new MyClass(1);
```

This line not only creates an object of the `MyClass` class, but also initializes the `myField` data field to 1. The first word in the line tells Java that `myObject` is going to be an object of the `MyClass` class. The next word is the object's name. After the equals sign comes the keyword `new` and the call to the class's constructor.

Defining Methods

Other methods that you add to a class are just like the methods you've been writing in previous chapters. You just need to be sure to provide the proper type of access to your methods. That is, methods that must be called from outside the class, should be defined as public, methods that must be callable only from the class and its derived classes should be defined as protected, and methods that must be callable only from within the class should be declared as private.

Suppose myField is defined as private, and you now want to be able to set the value of myField from outside the MyClass class. Because that data field is defined as private, meaning it can be accessed only from within the same class, you cannot access it directly by name. To solve this problem, you can create a public method that can set the value for you. You might also want to create a method that returns the value of the field, as well, as shown in Listing 14.3.

Listing 14.3   LST14_3.TXT: Adding a Method to the Class.

```
class MyClass
{
    private int myField;

    public MyClass(int value)
    {
        myField = value;
    }

    public void SetField(int value)
    {
        myField = value;
    }

    public int GetField()
    {
        return myField;
    }
}
```

Start defining the MyClass class.
  Declare the class's myField data field.
  Define the class's constructor.
    Initialize the data field.
  Start defining the SetField() method.

Set the data field to the value passed to SetField()*.*
Start Defining the GetField() *method.*
Return the value of the myField *data field.*

> **Note:** According to the rules of strict object-oriented design, all class data fields should be declared as private. Some programmers would go so far as to say that you should not even provide access to data fields through public methods. However, you'll see these rules broken a lot, even by programmers hired by big companies like Microsoft, Borland, and Sun. As you become more familiar with object-oriented programming, you'll better understand why the rules were made and when it's appropriate to break them.

Example: Using Classes in Applets

Up till now, you've been writing applets using the classes already supplied as part of Java. Now, you'll see how to use your own classes in applets. This will help you understand not only how your own classes work, but also help you to understand why you used Java's classes as you did. Follow the steps below to see how all this class stuff works.

1. Type Listing 14.3 and save it to your CLASSES folder under the name MyClass.java. (If you don't want to type, you can find the listing on this book's CD-ROM, in the CHAP14 folder.)

2. Start a DOS session by selecting Programs/MS-DOS Prompt from the Start menu. The DOS window appears, as shown in Figure 14.1.

Figure 14.1

This is the DOS prompt window.

3. Type CD C:\CLASSES to switch to your CLASSES folder.

4. Type `javac MyClass.java` to compile the `MyClass` class. You'll then find the `MyClass.class` file in your CLASSES folder.

5. Type Listing 14.4 and save it as `Applet19.java` in your CLASSES folder.

Listing 14.4   Applet19.java: An Applet That Uses the *MyClass* Class.

```java
import java.awt.*;
import java.applet.*;
import MyClass;

public class Applet19 extends Applet
{
    MyClass myObject;
    TextField textField1;

    public void init()
    {
        myObject = new MyClass(1);
        textField1 = new TextField(10);
        add(textField1);
        textField1.setText("1");
    }

    public void paint(Graphics g)
    {
        String s = textField1.getText();
        int value = Integer.parseInt(s);
        myObject.SetField(value);
        value = myObject.GetField();
        s = String.valueOf(value);
        g.drawString("The data field of the object", 30, 80);
        g.drawString("is now set to this value:", 40, 95);
        g.drawString(s, 90, 125);
    }

    public boolean action(Event event, Object arg)
    {
        repaint();
        return true;
    }
}
```

Tell Java that the program uses the awt *package.*
Tell Java that the program uses the applet *package.*
Tell Java that the program uses the MyClass *class.*
Derive the Applet19 *class from the* Applet *class.*
Declare an object of the MyClass *class.*
Declare a TextField *object.*

Override the Applet *class's* init() *method.*
   Create an object of the MyClass *class.*
   Create a TextField *object.*
   Add the TextField *object to the applet.*
   Set the TextField *object's text.*
Override the Applet *class's* paint() *method.*
   Get the text from the TextField *object.*
   Convert the text to an integer.
   Set myObject*'s* myField *data field.*
   Get the value of myField *from* myObject.
   Convert the value to a string.
   Draw the applet's display area.
Override the Applet *class's* action() *method.*
   Repaint the applet's display area.
   Tell Java the method executed okay.

6. Type javac Applet19.java to compile the Applet19 applet. You'll then have the Applet19.class file in your CLASSES folder.

7. Type Listing 14.5 and save the file as APPLET19.HTML.

Listing 14.5   APPLET19.HTML: The HTML Document for Applet19.

```
<title>Applet Test Page</title>
<h1>Applet Test Page</h1>
<applet
    code="Applet19.class"
    width=200
    height=200
    name="Applet19">
</applet>
```

You're now ready to run the Applet19 applet, which uses the MyClass class. To run the program, type **APPLETVIEWER APPLET19.HTML**. When you do, you see the window shown in Figure 14.2.

Figure 14.2

This is Applet19 running under Appletviewer.

The applet's display area shows the current setting of MyClass's data field, myField. You can change this setting by typing a new value into the text box and pressing Enter.

Understanding the Applet

By now, you should have a good idea of how classes work, at least generally. Still, you'll now examine parts of Applet19's source code. First, near the top of the source code is this line:

```
import MyClass;
```

Because the MyClass class is located in a different file than Applet19, you need to tell Java where to find it. The above line tells Java that it can find everything it needs to know about MyClass in the MyClass.class file, which you created when you compiled MyClass.java.

The next line of interest is this one, which is located at the top of Applet19's definition:

```
MyClass myObject;
```

This line tells Java that you'll be creating an object of the MyClass class and that the object will be called myObject.

At this point, you don't have the object created yet. You have to create the object, which Applet19 does in its init() method, using the new operator, like this:

```
myObject = new MyClass(1);
```

After the above line executes, Java has created the object, which means you can now call the object's public methods to manipulate the object as appropriate. Objects of the MyClass class have only two public methods (not counting the constructor). Applet19 calls these methods in its paint() method, like this:

```
myObject.SetField(value);
value = myObject.GetField();
```

In the first line, Applet19 calls the object's SetField() method, whose single argument is the value to which to set the myField data field. Due to its private access, this is the only way to set the value of myField outside of the class. If you tried to access myField with the line

```
myObject.myField = value;
```

you wouldn't even be able to compile the file. The compiler will generate an error telling you that you cannot access myField in this way (Figure 14.3).

Figure 14.3

The compiler complains when you ignore rules of access.

Using Inheritance

You may not know it, but throughout the second part of this book, you've been using inheritance to create your applets. Specifically, you've been deriving your applet classes (i.e, Applet10, Applet11, and so on) from Java's Applet superclass. By using inheritance in this way, you can take an existing class and create a new similar class that does things a little differently. The new class will have all the characteristics of its superclass, but will also have any new characteristics that you choose to add.

Creating a Subclass

You derive a new class from a superclass by using the extends keyword, an apt name for a keyword because by deriving a new class you usually extend the abilities of the original class. For example, when you create a new applet, you start the applet's class with a line that looks something like this:

```
public class MyApplet extends Applet
```

First, Java insists that all applet classes be declared as public. Next in the line, you can see the class keyword followed by the name of the class. Finally comes the extends keyword followed by the name of the superclass. In English, the above line means that the public class MyApplet is derived from (is a subclass of) the existing Applet class. As you've probably already figured out, Applet is a class that the Java makers created for you. This class contains all the basic functionality you need to create an applet. You need only extend (there's that word again) the specifics of the class in order to create your own applet class. Again, you've been doing that in every applet you've written so far.

Adding Fields and Methods to the Subclass

One thing you can do when you create a subclass is to add your own data fields and methods. For example, when you derive your own applet class from Java's `Applet` class, although your class inherits tons of data fields and methods from the superclass, you'll undoubtedly need fields and methods not supplied in the superclass. Maybe your new applet is designed to play Tic-Tac-Toe. (Hmmmm. Where have I seen that before?) Obviously, when the fine programmers at Sun created the `Applet` class, they didn't think to add the methods needed to play Tic-Tac-Toe. You'll have to add those methods yourself.

Example: Adding Fields and Methods

Take the `MyClass` class that you created earlier in this chapter (shown in Listing 14.3). Suppose you want to create a new class that has a new data field called `myNewField`, as well as a constructor and methods for setting and retrieving the value of this new data field. You might come up with something like Listing 14.6.

Listing 14.6   MYSUBCLASS.JAVA: Creating a Subclass.

```
import MyClass;

class MySubClass extends MyClass
{
    private int myNewField;

    public MySubClass(int value)
    {
        super(value);
        myNewField = value;
    }

    public void SetNewField(int value)
    {
        myNewField = value;
    }

    public int GetNewField()
    {
        return myNewField;
    }
}
```

The file containing the `MySubClass` class first imports the `MyClass` file, because Java will need the information contained in that file. In the constructor, the class first calls

```
super(value);
```

which ensures that the superclass (MyClass) is properly initialized by calling its constructor. The keyword super refers to the class's superclass. After calling the superclass's constructor, the MySubClass constructor initializes the new data field, myNewField. The new class also supplies new methods for setting and getting the value of myNewField. In short, MySubClass now has two data fields—myField, which it inherited from MyClass, and the new myNewField—and four methods—SetField() and GetField, which it inherited from MyClass, and the new SetNewField() and GetNewField() methods.

Example: Using a Subclass in a Program

Now that you have the MySubClass subclass, it might be nice to see how it works in a real programming situation. Applet20, which is shown in Listing 14.7, does the honors of putting MySubClass to work. In most places, compared to Applet19, the applet merely replaces occurrences of MyClass with MySubClass. The paint() method has to work a bit harder, though, calling all four of MySubClass's methods to prove they work.

Listing 14.7   APPLET20.JAVA: Using a Subclass in a Program.

```
import java.awt.*;
import java.applet.*;
import MySubClass;

public class Applet20 extends Applet
{
    MySubClass mySubObject;
    TextField textField1;
    TextField textField2;

    public void init()
    {
        mySubObject = new MySubClass(1);
        textField1 = new TextField(10);
        add(textField1);
        textField1.setText("1");
        textField2 = new TextField(10);
        add(textField2);
        textField2.setText("2");
    }

    public void paint(Graphics g)
    {
        String s = textField1.getText();
        int value = Integer.parseInt(s);
```

continues

Listing 14.7 Continued

```
        mySubObject.SetField(value);
        value = mySubObject.GetField();
        s = String.valueOf(value);
        g.drawString("The myField data field", 30, 80);
        g.drawString("is now set to this value:", 40, 95);
        g.drawString(s, 90, 125);

        s = textField2.getText();
        value = Integer.parseInt(s);
        mySubObject.SetNewField(value);
        value = mySubObject.GetNewField();
        s = String.valueOf(value);
        g.drawString("The myNewField data field", 30, 155);
        g.drawString("is now set to this value:", 40, 170);
        g.drawString(s, 90, 200);
    }

    public boolean action(Event event, Object arg)
    {
        repaint();
        return true;
    }
}
```

When you run Applet20 under Appletviewer, you see the window shown in Figure 14.4. Use the first text box to enter values for the original myField data field. Use the second text box to enter values for myNewField. Whenever you press Enter, the applet reads the values from the boxes and calls MySubClass's methods to set the new values and to retrieve the set values from the object.

Figure 14.4

This is
Appletviewer
running the
Applet20 applet.

Overriding Methods of the Superclass

If you've been reading the pseudocode sections that follow many of the listings in this book, you've seen the term "overriding" many times. When you *override* a method, you are creating a new version of a method that's part of the superclass. For example, in many of the applets you've created, you've overridden methods like `init()`, `paint()`, and `action()`. All of these methods are defined in some general way in the `Applet` superclass. When you derive a new class from applet, you can override these methods to perform the tasks you want them to perform, rather than the general tasks assigned to them by the `Applet` class.

> **Note:** In general object-oriented programming discussions, the term "derive" means exactly the same thing as "subclass" (when the latter is used as a verb). Ditto for the terms "base class" and "superclass," which are the same thing. In other words, when you derive a new class from a base class, you are subclassing a new class from a superclass.

For example, you know that, when Java starts up an applet, it calls the applet's `init()` method. Here's how the `Applet` class defines `init()`:

```
public void init()
{
}
```

No, your eyes aren't fooling you. In the `Applet` class, the `init()` method does nothing at all. It's only there so you can override it in your own class. Here's how it all works: When you derive your applet class from `Applet`, your applet class inherits all of `Applet`'s data fields and methods. If you don't override a method, Java calls the original version as necessary. In other words, if you don't override `init()` in your applet class, when Java starts your applet, it calls the `Applet` class's version of `init()`, which does nothing. However, if you override `init()` in your class, Java is smart enough to call the new version rather than the original do-nothing version. Cool, eh?

The *this* Keyword

There may be times when you need to explicitly refer to an object from within the object's methods. For example, you might need to pass a reference to the object as an argument in a method call. When you need to refer to the object explicitly, use the `this` keyword. In many cases, the `this` keyword is implicit in the method call or variable reference. For example, inside an object that has the data field `dataField`, the line

```
dataField = 1;
```

is the same as

```
this.dataField = 1;
```

In the first case, the `this` keyword is implicit, whereas in the second case, you've included it explicitly. If you needed to pass a reference to the object as an argument, you might write something like this:

```
SomeMethod(this);
```

Of course, the `SomeMethod()` method would have been written to accept an object of `this`'s type as its single argument.

Summary

If you've never done any object-oriented programming, it might take you a while to get used to using classes. Classes are the single biggest hurdle to jump when making the transition from normal procedural programming to object-oriented programming (OOP). Just think of classes as a way to provide another level of abstraction to your programs. In your non-OOP programs, you had program elements called programs, files, and procedures, listed in the order of their level of abstraction. Now, you can add classes to the end of the list, right between files and procedures.

Review Questions

1. What is a class?

2. How do classes help you to organize your programs?

3. What are the three parts of a simple, empty class?

4. What two elements do you add to complete the class?

5. How do you create an object from a class?

6. How do you use a class that's defined in a different file than the file that accesses the class?

7. What is inheritance and how does it help you create new classes quickly?

8. What is a subclass and a superclass?

9. How do you create a subclass?

10. How do you override a method inherited from a superclass?

Review Exercises

1. Write a basic, empty class called TestClass.

2. Add to TestClass a string data field called data1. This data field should be private to the class.

3. Add to TestClass a constructor that accepts a starting value for data1 as its single argument, and public methods for setting and retrieving the value of data1. Call these methods SetData() and GetData().

4. Compile the finished class.

5. Write a subclass called TestSubClass that is derived from TestClass and that adds an integer data field called data2 (declared as private) and a public method called CreateDataString() that creates a string object from data1 and data2. That is, if data1 is equal to Java is cool! and data2 is equal to 15, the CreateDataString() method should return Java is cool! 15 as a single string object. Also, create public methods called SetData2() and GetData2() for setting and retrieving the value of data2, as well as a constructor that accepts arguments for the starting values of data1 and data2.

6. Modify Applet20 so that it creates an object of the TestSubClass class. You should provide text boxes for enabling the user to set data1 and data2, as well as write paint() so that it displays the string returned by CreateDataString(). Figure 14.5 shows what the ClassApplet applet should look like. (You can find the solutions for these exercises in the CHAP14 folder of this book's CD-ROM.)

Figure 14.5

This is ClassApplet running under Appletviewer.

Part III

Putting Java to Work

CHAPTER 15

Writing a Simple Applet

Throughout Part II of this book, you've been writing applets that demonstrate the various features of the Java language. Along the way, you learned a few things about how applet works, including how Java calls the `init()` method when the applet starts, how the `paint()` method draws the applet's display, and how Java calls the `action()` method in response to some action by the user (for example, pressing Enter when typing in a `TextField` object). In this chapter, you'll extend your knowledge of applets by looking more closely at the construction of an applet, as well as discovering some other methods that are important to Java applets.

The Simplest Java Applet

The Java programming language and libraries enable you to create applets that are as simple or as complex as you like. In fact, you can write the simplest Java applet in only a few lines of code, as shown in Listing 15.1.

Listing 15.1   MyApplet.java: The Simplest Java Applet.

```
import java.applet.*;

public class MyApplet extends Applet
{
}
```

The first line of Listing 15.1 tells the Java compiler that this applet will be using some or all of the classes defined in the `applet` package (the asterisk acts as a wildcard, just as in DOS file names). All of the basic capabilities of an applet are provided for in these classes, which is why you can create a usable applet with so few lines of code.

The second line of code declares a new class called `MyApplet`. This new class is declared as `public` so that the class can be accessed when the applet is run in a Web browser or in the Appletviewer application. If you fail to declare the applet class as `public`, the code will compile fine, but the applet will refuse to run. In other words, all applet classes must be `public`.

As you can see, you take advantage of object-oriented programming (OOP) inheritance to declare your applet class by subclassing Java's `Applet` class. This inheritance works exactly the same as when you created your own classes in Chapter 14, "Classes." The only difference is that `Applet` is a class that's included with the Java Developer's Kit (JDK), rather than a class you created yourself.

You can actually compile the applet shown in Listing 15.1. When you do, you'll have the `MyApplet.class` file, which is the byte-code file that can be executed by the Java system. To run the applet, just create an HTML document like the one shown in Listing 15.2. You've already used similar HTML documents with the many applets you created in part II of this book. However, if you need a refresher course on using the `<applet>` tag, turn back to Chapter 2, "Running Java Applets." If you were to run the MyApplet applet, however, you wouldn't see anything much in Appletviewer or in your Web browser.

Listing 15.2   MYAPPLET.HTML: MyApplet's HTML Document.

```
<title>Applet Test Page</title>
<h1>Applet Test Page</h1>
<applet
    code="MyApplet.class"
    width=250
    height=250
    name="MyApplet">
</applet>
```

The Five Stages of an Applet's Life Cycle

Every Java applet you create inherits a set of default behaviors from the `Applet` class. In most cases, these default behaviors do nothing, unless you override some of `Applet`'s methods in order to extend the applet's basic functionality. However, although a simple applet like `MyApplet` in Listing 15.1 doesn't seem to do much, a lot is going on in the background. Some of this activity is important to your understanding of applets, and some of it can stay out of sight and out of mind.

Part of what goes on in a simple applet is the execution of the applet's life cycle. There are five parts to this cycle, each of which has a matching method that you can override to gain access to that cycle of the applet's life. The five stages of an applet's life cycle are listed here:

♦ *Initialization stage.* This is the part of an applet's life cycle in which the applet object is created and loaded. At this point, it's appropriate to create objects needed by the applet, as well as initialize values that must be valid when the applet runs. The initialization stage occurs only once in the applet's life cycle. You can tap into the initialization stage by overriding the Applet class's init() method.

♦ *Start stage.* This stage occurs when the system starts running the applet. The start stage can occur right after the initialization stage or when an applet is restarted. This usually happens when the user switches back to the applet's page after viewing a different page in his or her Web browser. Unlike the initialization stage, the start stage can occur several times over the life of the applet. To provide your own start code, override the Applet class's start() method.

♦ *Paint stage.* The paint stage occurs whenever the applet's display must be drawn on the screen. This happens right after the applet's start stage, as well as whenever the applet's display must be restored or changed. This can happen when the applet is exposed from underneath another window or when the program changes the applet's display in some way and explicitly repaints the applet. Almost every applet you write will have a paint() method, which is the method you override to provide your applet with its display.

♦ *Stop stage.* As you may have guessed, the stop stage is the counterpart to the start stage. Java executes this stage of the applet's life cycle when the applet is no longer visible on the screen, such as when the user switches to a different Web page. The default behavior for this cycle, however, is to keep the applet running in the background. If you want to handle the stop cycle differently, you should override the Applet class's stop() method.

♦ *Destroy stage.* This is the counterpart to the initialization stage and occurs when the system is about to remove the applet from memory. Like the initialization cycle, the destroy cycle occurs only once. If your applet has resources that need to be cleaned up before the applet exits, this is the place to do it. You tap into this cycle by overriding the Applet class's destroy() method.

> **Note:** To be entirely accurate, the paint stage isn't considered an actual applet life cycle, but because an applet without a display is likely useless (not always, though), I thought I'd include the paint cycle. Truth is, the `paint()` method isn't even defined in the `Applet` class. Rather, `Applet` inherits `paint()` from the `Component` class, a superclass in `Applet`'s long chain of inheritance, which goes from `Applet` to `Panel` to `Container` and finally to `Component`.

Example: Overriding the Life Cycle Methods

All this talk about life cycles and overriding methods may have left you a little confused as to how all this actually applies to the applets you want to create. In previous chapters, you managed to create applets without dealing with most of this stuff because the `Applet` class, from which you derived your own applet classes, handled the life-cycle methods in the default manner proscribed by the Java system. If you look at Listing 15.3, you'll see a small applet that overrides all the methods needed to provide custom behaviors for all the applet's life-cycle stages.

Listing 15.3   MyApplet2.java: Overriding the Applet Life-Cycle Methods.

```java
import java.applet.*;
import java.awt.*;

public class MyApplet2 extends Applet
{
    public void init()
    {
        // Place initialization cycle code here.
    }

    public void start()
    {
        // Place start cycle code here.
    }

    public void paint(Graphics g)
    {
        // Place paint cycle code here.
    }

    public void stop()
    {
        // Place stop cycle code here.
    }
```

```
public void destroy()
    {
        // Place destroy cycle code here.
    }
}
```

Notice that in order to override the `paint()` method, you must import the `java.awt.*` libraries, which contain information about the `Graphics` class. As you learned when writing previous applets in this book, the `Graphics` class enables you to display information and graphics in an applet's *display area* (or *canvas*, as the display area is sometimes called).

If you look for the previous methods in Java's source code, you'll discover that the default implementations of `init()`, `start()`, `paint()`, `stop()`, and `destroy()` all do nothing at all. If you want your applet to do something in response to these cycles, you have to provide the code yourself by overriding the appropriate method.

Summary

In this chapter, you got a quick look at the basic applet and the methods you can call at various stages during the applet's life cycle. Over the rest of the chapters in this book, you'll use this knowledge to develop applets that can do anything from display text in various fonts to execute animation sequences with sound.

Review Questions

1. What is the superclass for all applets?

2. Why do applet classes need to be declared as `public`?

3. What are the five life-cycle stages of an applet?

4. How is the paint cycle different from the rest of the life-cycle stages?

5. What's the difference between the initialize and start life-cycle stages?

6. What do the life-cycle methods in the `Applet` superclass do?

Review Exercises

1. Write a simple do-nothing applet called `TestApplet`.

2. Override the `paint()` method in `TestApplet` so that the applet displays the text string "Hello there!." The final applet should look like Figure 15.1.

You can find the solution for these exercises in the CHAP15 folder of this book's CD-ROM.

Figure 15.1

This is TestApplet running under Appletviewer.

CHAPTER 16

Drawing Graphics

Almost all applets need to create some sort of display, whether that display is as simple as a line of text or as sophisticated as an animation sequence. Because Windows is a graphical system, everything you see on the screen during a Windows session is displayed graphically. This is true even of text. Because of its graphical nature, a system like Java's must include the capability to handle device-independent graphics. In this chapter, you see not only how you can display various graphical shapes, but also how to query the system about the characteristics of the display.

The Applet's Canvas

Every applet has an area of the screen, called the *canvas*, in which it can create its display. The size of an applet's canvas depends on the size of the applet, which is in turn controlled by the parameters included in an HTML document's `<applet>` tag. Generally, the larger the applet appears in the HTML document, the larger the applet's visible canvas. Anything that you try to draw outside of the visible canvas doesn't appear on the screen.

You draw graphical images on the canvas by using coordinates that identify pixel locations. Chances are good that you've had some sort of computer-graphics experience before Java, so you know that the coordinates that define pixel locations on a computer screen can be organized in various ways. Windows, for example, supports a number of different mapping modes that determines how coordinates are calculated in a window.

Thankfully, Java does away with the complications of displaying graphics in a window by adopting a single coordinate system. This coordinate system has its origin (point 0,0) in the upper-left corner, with the X axis increasing to the right, and the Y axis increasing downward, as shown in Figure 16.1.

Figure 16.1

An applet's canvas uses the typical computer-display coordinate system.

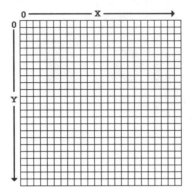

Example: Using the Coordinate System

When you want to draw something on an applet's canvas, you use the coordinate system shown in Figure 16.1. This coordinate system situates the system's origin in the applet's upper-left corner, just as it's shown in Figure 16.1. For example, Figure 16.2 shows an applet displaying a single line in its canvas. This line was drawn starting at coordinates 5,10, as shown in Figure 16.3.

Figure 16.2

This applet displays a single line.

Figure 16.3

The line in Figure 16.2 is drawn at the coordinates 5,10.

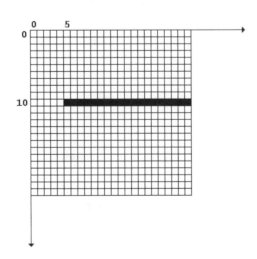

Drawing Shapes

Java's Graphics class includes methods for drawing many different types of shapes, everything from straight lines to polygons. You were introduced to the Graphics class in Part II of this book when you displayed text in an applet's paint() method. As you may recall, a reference to a Graphics object is passed to the paint() method as its single argument. Because the Graphics class is part of the awt package, you have to include one of the following lines at the top of your applet's code to use the class:

```
import java.awt.Graphics
import java.awt.*
```

The first line in the preceding imports only the Graphics class, whereas the second line imports all the classes included in the awt package. Table 16.1 lists the most commonly used drawing methods in the Graphics class.

Table 16.1   Drawing Methods of the *Graphics* Class.

Method	*Description*
clearRect()	Erases a rectangular area of the canvas.
copyArea()	Copies a rectangular area of the canvas to another area.
drawArc()	Draws a hollow arc.
drawLine()	Draws a straight line.
drawOval()	Draws a hollow oval.
drawPolygon()	Draws a hollow polygon.
drawRect()	Draws a hollow rectangle.
drawRoundRect()	Draws a hollow rectangle with rounded corners.
drawString()	Displays a text string.
fillArc()	Draws a filled arc.
fillOval()	Draws a filled oval.
fillPolygon()	Draws a filled polygon.
fillRect()	Draws a filled rectangle.
fillRoundRect()	Draws a filled rectangle with rounded corners.
getColor()	Retrieves the current drawing color.
getFont()	Retrieves the currently used font.

continues

Table 16.1 Continued

Method	Description
getFontMetrics()	Retrieves information about the current font.
setColor()	Sets the drawing color.
setFont()	Sets the font.

To draw a shape in an applet's display area, you only need to call the appropriate method and supply the arguments required by the method. These arguments are based on the coordinates at which you want to draw the shape. For example, the following code example draws a straight line from coordinate 5,10 to 20,30:

```
g.drawLine(5, 10, 20, 30);
```

The g in the preceding code line is the Graphics object passed to the paint() method. As you can see, the drawLine() method takes four arguments, which are X,Y coordinate pairs that specify the starting and ending points of the line.

> **Tip:** There may be times when you need to retrieve information about the system's currently set graphical attributes. Java's Graphics class supplies methods like getColor(), getFont(), and getFontMetrics() to enable you to obtain this information.

Example: Drawing a Rectangle

Most of the shape-drawing methods are as easy to use as the drawLine() method is. Suppose that you want to write an applet that draws a filled rounded rectangle inside a hollow rectangle. You'd then add calls to the Graphics class's fillRoundRect() and drawRect() to the applet's paint() method. Listing 16.1 is just such an applet, whereas Listing 16.2 is the HTML document that displays the applet. Figure 16.4 shows the applet running under Appletviewer.

Listing 16.1 RECTAPPLET.JAVA: Drawing Rectangles.

```
import java.awt.*;
import java.applet.*;

public class RectApplet extends Applet
{
    public void paint(Graphics g)
```

```
    {
        g.drawRect(35, 15, 125, 200);
        g.fillRoundRect(50, 30, 95, 170, 15, 15);
    }
}
```

Listing 16.2   RECTAPPLET.HTML: HTML Document for RectApplet.

```
<title>Applet Test Page</title>
<h1>Applet Test Page</h1>
<applet
    code="RectApplet.class"
    width=200
    height=250
    name="RectApplet">
</applet>
```

Figure 16.4

This is RectApplet
running under
Appletviewer.

In RectApplet's paint() method, you can see the method calls that produce the graphical display. The first line creates the outside rectangle. That method call looks like this:

```
g.drawRect(35, 15, 125, 200);
```

The drawRect() method's four arguments are the X,Y coordinates of the rectangle's upper-left corner and the width and height of the rectangle. The rounded filled rectangle is almost as easy to draw:

```
g.fillRoundRect(50, 30, 95, 170, 15, 15);
```

The first four arguments of the fillRoundRect() method are the same as those for the drawRect() method. The fifth and sixth arguments are the size of the rectangle that represents the rounded corners. Think of this rectangle as being placed on each corner of the main rectangle and a curved line drawn between its corners, as shown in Figure 16.5.

Figure 16.5

The coordinates for the rounded corners are given as the width and height of the rectangle that encloses the rounded corner.

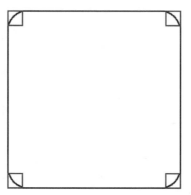

Example: Drawing Other Shapes

Some shapes you can draw with the Graphics class are more complex than others. For example, the drawArc() method requires six arguments in order to draw a simple curved line. To see how drawing other shapes works, you'll now create the ShapeApplet applet, which enables you to switch from one shape to another in the applet's display. Listing 16.3 is ShapeApplet's source code. Figures 16.6 and 16.7 show what the applet looks like running under the Appletviewer application.

Listing 16.3   ShapeApplet.java: An Applet That Draws Various Shapes.

```
import java.awt.*;
import java.applet.*;

public class ShapeApplet extends Applet
{
    int shape;
    Button button;

    public void init()
    {
        shape = 0;
        button = new Button("Next Shape");
        add(button);
    }

    public void paint(Graphics g)
    {
        int x[] = {35, 150, 60, 140, 60, 150, 35};
        int y[] = {50, 80, 110, 140, 170, 200, 230};
        int numPts = 7;

        switch(shape)
```

```
        {
            case 0:
                g.drawLine(35, 50, 160, 230);
                break;
            case 1:
                g.drawRect(35, 50, 125, 180);
                break;
            case 2:
                g.drawRoundRect(35, 50, 125, 180, 15, 15);
                break;
            case 3:
                g.drawOval(35, 50, 125, 180);
                break;
            case 4:
                g.drawArc(35, 50, 125, 180, 90, 180);
                break;
            case 5:
                g.drawPolygon(x, y, numPts);
                break;
            case 6:
                g.fillPolygon(x, y, numPts);
                break;
        }
    }

    public boolean action(Event event, Object arg)
    {
        ++shape;
        if (shape == 7)
            shape = 0;
        repaint();
        return true;
    }
}
```

Tell Java that the applet uses the classes in the awt *package.*
Tell Java that the applet uses the classes in the applet *package.*
Derive the ShapeApplet *class from Java's* Applet *class.*
  Declare the class's shape data field.
  Declare the class's button data field.
  Override the init() *method.*
    Initialize the shape counter.
    Create the applet's Button *object.*
    Add the Button *object to the applet.*
  Override the paint() *method.*
    Initialize the X and Y coordinates for the polygons.
    Initialize the polygon point count.
    Display a shape based on the value of the shape counter.
  Override the action() *method.*

Increment the shape counter.
Reset the shape counter if it has reached its maximum value.
Force the applet to repaint its canvas with the next shape.
Tell Java that the method executed okay.

Figure 16.6

This is what
ShapeApplet looks
like when it first
runs.

Figure 16.7

This is
ShapeApplet
displaying an oval.

To run ShapeApplet, use the HTML document shown in Listing 16.2, except change all occurrences of RectApplet to ShapeApplet. When you run the applet with Appletviewer, you see the window shown in Figure 16.6. To change the shape displayed in the applet's canvas, click the Next Shape button.

Understanding the ShapeApplet Applet

You don't need to concern yourself at this point with the button control that ShapeApplet uses to switch shapes, except to know that just like the `TextField` controls you've been using, clicking the button causes Java to call the applet's `action()` method. The `action()` method increments the shape counter, `shape`, and tells the applet to redraw itself. In the `paint()` method, the value of `shape` is used in a `switch` statement to determine which shape gets drawn. You learned about `switch` statements back in Chapter 9, "The `if` and `switch` Statements."

Drawing Ovals

The real meat of this program are the calls to the Graphics object's various shape-drawing methods. You already know about the first three: drawLine(), drawRect(), and drawRoundRect(). The call to drawOval(), however, is new and looks like this:

```
g.drawOval(35, 50, 125, 180);
```

As you can see, this method, which draws ovals and circles, takes four arguments. These arguments are the X,Y coordinates, width, and height of a rectangle that can enclose the oval. Figure 16.8 shows how the resultant oval relates to its enclosing rectangle.

Figure 16.8

An oval's coordinates are actually the coordinates of an enclosing rectangle.

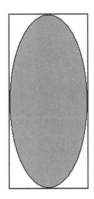

Drawing Arcs

Next in paint() is the drawArc() method, which is the most complicated (at least, from an understanding point of view) of the shape-drawing methods. The call to drawArc() looks like this:

```
g.drawArc(35, 50, 125, 180, 90, 180);
```

The first four arguments are the same as the arguments for drawOval(): the X,Y coordinates, width, and height of the enclosing rectangle. The last two arguments are the angle at which to start drawing the arc and the number of degrees around the arc to draw.

To understand all this angle nonsense, take a look at figure 16.9, which shows how Java relates the arc's starting angle to the degrees of an oval. In the preceding example call to drawArc(), the fifth argument is 90, which means Java starts drawing the arc, within the arc's enclosing rectangle, at the 90-degree point. The sixth argument of 180 tells Java to draw around the arc 180 degrees (or halfway around the full 360 degrees). It doesn't mean that the ending point should be at the 180-degree point. Figure 16.10 shows the resultant arc.

Figure 16.9

The degrees of an oval start on the right side and travel counter-clockwise around the arc.

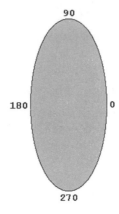

Figure 16.10

The arc shown here starts at the 90-degree point and sweeps 180 degrees around the arc.

Example: Drawing Arcs in an Applet

Because understanding the angles involved in drawing arcs can be a little confusing, in this example you'll create an applet called ArcApplet that enables you to enter different values for drawArc()'s fifth and sixth arguments and immediately see the results. Listing 16.4 is the source code for the applet. Use Listing 16.2 to create ArcApplet's HTML document, by changing each occurrence of RectApplet to ArcApplet.

Listing 16.4   ARCAPPLET.JAVA: An Arc-Drawing Applet.

```
import java.awt.*;
import java.applet.*;

public class ArcApplet extends Applet
{
    TextField textField1, textField2;
```

```
    public void init()
    {
        textField1 = new TextField(10);
        textField2 = new TextField(10);

        add(textField1);
        add(textField2);

        textField1.setText("0");
        textField2.setText("360");
    }

    public void paint(Graphics g)
    {
        String s = textField1.getText();
        int start = Integer.parseInt(s);

        s = textField2.getText();
        int sweep = Integer.parseInt(s);

        g.drawArc(35, 50, 125, 180, start, sweep);
    }

    public boolean action(Event event, Object arg)
    {
        repaint();
        return true;
    }
}
```

Tell Java that the applet uses the classes in the awt *package.*
Tell Java that the applet uses the classes in the applet *package.*
Derive the ArcApplet *class from Java's* Applet *class.*
   Declare the class's TextField *objects.*
   Override the init() *method.*
     Create the two TextField *objects.*
     Add the TextField *objects to the applet.*
     Set the text for the TextField *objects.*
   Override the paint() *method.*
     Get the starting angle and convert it to an integer.
     Get the sweep angle and convert it to an integer.
     Display the selected arc.
   Override the action() *method.*
     Force the applet to repaint its canvas with the next shape.
     Tell Java that the method executed okay.

When you run ArcApplet using Appletviewer, you see the window shown in Figure 16.11. (Looks kind of like a guy with shifty eyes and a big nose, doesn't it?)

Because the starting angle (in the first text box) is 0 and the drawing degrees (the second box) is 360, the arc is actually a full oval. By changing the values in the two boxes and pressing Enter, you can cause the applet to display different arcs. For example, Figure 16.12 shows an arc that has a starting angle of 120 degrees and drawing degrees of 245.

Figure 16.11

This is ArcApplet at startup.

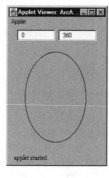

Figure 16.12

You can use ArcApplet to experiment with different arc angle settings.

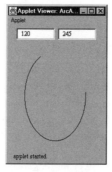

> **Note:** Most of the shape-drawing methods come in two versions, one that draws a hollow shape and one that draws a filled shape. The method that draws the filled shape has the same name as the one that draws the hollow shape, except you change the word `draw` in the name to `fill`. For example, because `drawArc()` draws a hollow arc, the method `fillArc()` draws a filled arc.

Drawing Polygons

Polygons are simply many-sided shapes. For example, a triangle is a polygon (it is, in fact, the simplest polygon). Squares, rectangles, and hexagons are all polygons, as well. Because a polygon comprises many different lines, before you can draw a polygon in Java, you need to create arrays that contain the X,Y coordinates for each line in the polygon. In Listing 16.3, ShapeApplet defines those arrays like this:

```
int x[] = {35, 150, 60, 140, 60, 150, 35};
int y[] = {50, 80, 110, 140, 170, 200, 230};
int numPts = 7;
```

The first array, called x[] in the preceding, is the X coordinates for each X,Y pair, and the second array, called y[], is the Y coordinates for each X,Y pair. By looking at the values defined in the arrays, you can see that the first line gets drawn from 35,50 to 150,80. Because all the lines in a polygon are connected, Java can continue drawing lines by using the previous ending point (in this case, 150,80) and the next coordinate pair, which is 60,110. Java will continue to work through the arrays until it uses all the given coordinates. The actual method call that draws the polygon looks like this:

```
g.drawPolygon(x, y, numPts);
```

The drawPolygon() method's three arguments are the array holding the X coordinates, the array holding the Y coordinates, and the number of points defined in the arrays. You can use a literal value for the third argument, but it's often handy to define a variable as shown in the example (numPts). Then, if you change the arrays, you can change the variable at the same time and not have to worry about correcting any method calls that use the arrays along with point count.

Figure 16.13 shows the polygon drawn by the values given in the x[] and y[] arrays in the preceding. Looks more like a squiggly line than a polygon. That's because when you draw a hollow polygon, Java doesn't connect the starting and ending point. If you draw a filled polygon, though, you'll see that the connecting side is really there, as shown in Figure 16.14.

Figure 16.13

A hollow polygon is always missing one side.

Figure 16.14

A filled polygon actually looks like a polygon instead of a squiggly line.

Note: If you need more control over your polygons, Java includes a `Polygon` class from which you can create polygon objects from the coordinate arrays. The `Polygon` class includes handy methods that enable you to add points to a polygon, determine whether a point is inside the polygon, and retrieve the polygon's bounding rectangle. You create a `Polygon` object with a line like `Polygon polygon = new Polygon(x, y, numPts)`. The arguments for the class's constructor are the same as those for the `drawPolygon()` method. The `Polygon` class's public methods are `addPoint(x, y)`, `getBoundingBox()` (which returns a `Rectangle` object), and `inside()` (which returns a `boolean` value).

Summary

Java's `Graphics` class enables you to draw many types of shapes, including lines, rectangles, ovals, and arcs. You can use these shape-drawing methods to enhance the appearance of your applets, drawing frames around objects, and even putting together simple illustrations. In addition, you can set the drawing color used by the `Graphics` class, as well as query the system for its current graphics settings. In the next chapter, you add to your graphics knowledge by learning how to create, manipulate, and display graphical text.

Review Questions

1. What do you call the area of an applet in which you can draw?

2. How is Java's graphical coordinate system organized?

3. What is the difference in the shapes drawn by the `drawRect()` and `fillRect()` methods?

4. What are the four arguments for the `drawRect()` method?

5. How do the arguments for the `drawRoundRect()` method differ from the arguments for `drawRect()`?

6. Why does the `drawPolygon()` method require that you set up arrays of coordinates?

7. What are the six arguments required by the `drawArc()` method?

8. Why would you want to use the `polygon` class?

Review Exercises

1. Write the code needed to draw a 100×200 rectangle at the coordinates 50,75.

2. Write an applet that displays a square inside a circle.

3. Write an applet that enables the user to choose the width, height, and location of a rectangle. The applet should display the rectangle at the given coordinates.

4. Modify the ArcApplet applet so that the user can select not only the arc's drawing points, but also the size of the arc's bounding rectangle.

5. Write an applet called FaceApplet that displays a face made from ovals and arcs. The final applet should look like Figure 16.15. (You can find the solution to this problem in the CHAP16 folder of this book's CD-ROM.)

Figure 16.15

This is what FaceApplet should look like when running under Appletviewer.

CHAPTER 17

Graphical Text

Now that you know how to draw all kinds of shapes in your applets, it's time to see how to use text and text fonts, as well. By combining graphical text with other drawing methods, you can create attractive applets for your Web pages. In this chapter, you'll review how to display text, as well as how to create fonts and retrieve information about those fonts.

Dealing with Graphical Text

Earlier in this book, I said that because Windows is a device-independent graphical environment, you can't assume much about how the user's system is set up. At the time, I was talking about fonts and how different fonts take up different amounts of space in the display. After giving you this good advice, I then proceeded to ignore it. All the programs so far in this book display text strings without considering the font being used. Hopefully, you didn't run into any troubles. If you did, you'll be delighted to know that in this section, you'll learn how to solve such problems.

Getting Font Attributes

Every font that you can use with your Java applets is associated with a group of attributes that determines the size and appearance of the font. The most important of these attributes is the font's name, which determines the font's basic style. As shown in Figure 17.1, there is a big difference between the Arial and Times Roman fonts as far as how they look. When you're setting up a font for use, the name of the font is usually the first thing with which you're concerned.

Figure 17.1

The appearance of text is determined mostly by the font you choose.

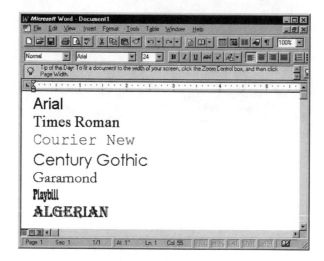

You can easily get information about the currently active font. Start by calling the Graphics object's getFont() method, like this:

```
Font font = g.getFont();
```

The getFont() method returns a Font object for the current font. Once you have the Font object, you can use the Font class's various methods to obtain information about the font. Table 17.1 shows the most commonly used public methods of the Font class and what they do.

Table 17.1   The *Font* Class's Most Commonly Used Public Methods.

Methods	Description
getFamily()	Returns the family name of the font.
getName()	Returns the name of the font.
getSize()	Returns the size of the font.
getStyle()	Returns the style of the font, where 0 is plain, 1 is bold, 2 is italic, and 3 is bold italic.
isBold()	Returns a boolean value indicating whether the font is bold.
isItalic()	Returns a boolean value indicating whether the font is italic.
isPlain()	Returns a boolean value indicating whether the font is plain.
toString()	Returns a string of information about the font.

Example: Displaying Font Information

As always, the best way to see how something works is to try it out yourself. With that end in mind, Listing 17.1 is an applet that displays information about the currently active font using many of the methods described in Table 17.1. Listing 17.2 is the HTML document used to run the applet, and Figure 17.2 shows the applet running under Appletviewer.

Listing 17.1 FontApplet.java: Getting Information About a Font.

```java
import java.awt.*;
import java.applet.*;

public class FontApplet extends Applet
{
    public void paint(Graphics g)
    {
        Font font = getFont();
        String name = font.getName();
        String family = font.getFamily();

        int n = font.getStyle();
        String style;
        if (n == 0)
            style = "Plain";
        else if (n == 1)
            style = "Bold";
        else if (n == 2)
            style = "Italic";
        else
            style = "Bold Italic";

        n = font.getSize();
        String size = String.valueOf(n);
        String info = font.toString();

        String s = "Name: " + name;
        g.drawString(s, 50, 50);
        s = "Family: " + family;
        g.drawString(s, 50, 65);
        s = "Style: " + style;
        g.drawString(s, 50, 80);
        s = "Size: " + size;
        g.drawString(s, 50, 95);
        g.drawString(info, 20, 125);
    }
}
```

Tell Java that the applet uses the classes in the awt *package.*
Tell Java that the applet uses the classes in the applet *package.*
Derive the FontApplet *class from Java's* Applet *class.*
   Override the paint() *method.*
      Get a Font object representing the active font.
      Get the name of the font.
      Get the family name of the font.
      Get the style of the font.
      Create a style string based on the value of the style integer.
      Get the size of the font.
      Convert the size to a string.
      Get an info string for the font.
      Display the font's attributes.

Listing 17.2 FONTAPPLET.HTML: The HTML Document for Running
FontApplet.

```
<title>Applet Test Page</title>
<h1>Applet Test Page</h1>
<applet
    code="FontApplet.class"
    width=380
    height=170
    name="FontApplet">
</applet>
```

Figure 17.2

This is FontApplet
running under
Appletviewer.

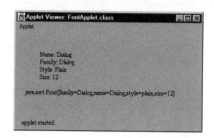

As you can see from Listing 17.1, using the Font class's methods is fairly straightforward. Just call the method, which returns a value that describes some aspect of the font represented by the Font object.

Getting Font Metrics

In many cases, the information you can retrieve from a Font object is enough to keep you out of trouble. For example, by using the size returned by the getSize() method, you can properly space the lines of text. Sometimes, though, you want to know more about the font you're using. For example, you might want to know the width of a particular character or even the width in pixels of an entire text string. In these cases, you need to work with text metrics.

True to form, the Java Developer's Kit includes the FontMetrics class, which makes it easy to obtain information about fonts. You create a FontMetrics object like this:

```
FontMetrics fontMetrics = getFontMetrics(font);
```

You may recall that getFontMetrics(), which returns a reference to a FontMetrics object for the active font, is a method of the Graphics class. Its single argument is the Font object for which you want the font metrics.

Once you have the FontMetrics object, you can call its methods in order to obtain detailed information about the associated font. Table 17.2 lists the most commonly used methods.

Table 17.2   Commonly Used *FontMetrics* Methods.

Method	Description
charWidth()	Returns the width of a character.
getAscent()	Returns the font's ascent.
getDescent()	Returns the font's descent.
getFont()	Returns the associated Font object.
getHeight()	Returns the font's height.
getLeading()	Returns the font's leading (line spacing).
stringWidth()	Returns the width of a string.
toString()	Returns a string of information about the font.

> **Note:** If you haven't used fonts before, some of the terms—*leading*, *ascent*, and *descent*—used in Table 17.2 may be unfamiliar to you. *Leading* (pronounced "ledding") is the amount of white space between lines of text. *Ascent* is the height of a character, from the baseline to the top of the character. *Descent* is the size of the area that accommodates the descending portions of letters, such as the tail on a lowercase *g*. *Height* is the sum of ascent, descent, and leading. See Figure 17.3 for examples of each.

Figure 17.3

Ascent, descent, and leading determine the overall height of a font.

Example: Displaying Font Metrics

Most of the methods listed in Table 17.2 are self-explanatory. However, you probably want a chance to see them in action. Listing 17.3 is the source code for the MetricsApplet, and Listing 17.4 is the applet's HTML document. When you run the MetricsApplet applet, you see the window shown in Figure 17.4. At the top of the window is a text box into which you can enter different strings of text. When you press Enter, the applet displays the length of the string in pixels. Immediately below the text box is information about the current font.

Listing 17.3   MetricsApplet.java: An Applet That Displays Text Metrics.

```java
import java.awt.*;
import java.applet.*;

public class MetricsApplet extends Applet
{
    TextField textField;

    public void init()
    {
        textField = new TextField(20);
        add(textField);
        textField.setText("Default string");
    }

    public void paint(Graphics g)
    {
        Font font = getFont();
```

```
        FontMetrics fontMetrics = g.getFontMetrics(font);
        int n = fontMetrics.getLeading();
        String leading = String.valueOf(n);
        n = fontMetrics.getAscent();
        String ascent = String.valueOf(n);
        n = fontMetrics.getDescent();
        String descent = String.valueOf(n);
        n = fontMetrics.getHeight();
        String height = String.valueOf(n);

        String s = textField.getText();
        n = fontMetrics.stringWidth(s);
        String width = String.valueOf(n);

        g.drawString("FONT INFO:", 55, 60);
        g.drawString("Leading: " + leading, 70, 80);
        g.drawString("Ascent: " + ascent, 70, 95);
        g.drawString("Descent: " + descent, 70, 110);
        g.drawString("Height: " + height, 70, 125);

        g.drawString("STRING INFO:", 55, 155);
        g.drawString("Width: " + width, 70, 175);
    }

    public boolean action(Event event, Object arg)
    {
        repaint();
        return true;
    }
}
```

Listing 17.4   METRICSAPPLET.HTML: MetricsApplet's HTML Document.

```
<title>Applet Test Page</title>
<h1>Applet Test Page</h1>
<applet
    code="MetricsApplet.class"
    width=200
    height=200
    name="MetricsApplet">
</applet>
```

Note: Because all of the applets you've written so far in this book haven't used text metrics when displaying text, you may wonder why you even need to bother with this stuff. Chances are that when you're running your applets under Windows 95 using the default font, everything will work fine. But remember that your applets may run on machines using other operating systems, and their default fonts may not be exactly the same size. Also, when you create your own fonts, you may not know the resultant font's size exactly. In order to position text accurately, you need to use font metrics, as you'll see later in this chapter.

Figure 17.4

This is
Appletviewer
running the
MetricsApplet
applet.

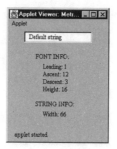

Creating Fonts

You may think an applet that always uses the default font is boring to look at. In many cases, you'd be right. An easy way to spruce up an applet is to use different fonts. Luckily, Java enables you to create and set fonts for your applet. You do this by creating your own font object, like this:

```
Font font = new Font("TimesRoman", Font.PLAIN, 20);
```

The constructor for the Font class takes three arguments: the font name, style, and size. The style can be any combination of the font attributes that are defined in the Font class. Those attributes are Font.PLAIN, Font.BOLD, and Font.ITALIC.

Example: Creating a Font with Multiple Styles

Although you can create fonts with the plain, bold, or italic styles, you may at times need to combine font styles. Suppose, for example, that you wanted to use both bold and italic styles. The line

```
Font font = new Font("Courier", Font.BOLD + Font.ITALIC, 18);
```

gives you an 18-point bold italic Courier font. (A *point* is a measurement of a font's height and is equal to 1/72 of an inch.)

Using the Font

After you've created the font, you have to tell Java to use the font. You do this by calling the Graphics class's setFont() method, like this:

```
g.setFont(font);
```

At this point, the next text you display in your applet will use the new font. However, although you request a certain type and size of font, you can't be sure of what you'll get. The system tries its best to match the requested font, but you still need to know at least the size of the font with which you ended up. You can get all the information you need by creating a FontMetrics object, like this:

```
FontMetrics fontMetrics = g.getFontMetrics(font);
```

To get the height of a line of text, call the FontMetrics object's getHeight() method, like this:

```
int height = fontMetrics.getHeight();
```

> **Caution:** When creating a font, be aware that the user's system may not have a particular font loaded. In that case, Java chooses a default font as a replacement. This possible font substitution is a good reason to use methods like Font.getName() in order to see whether you got the font you wanted. You especially need to know the size of the font, so you can be sure to position your text lines properly.

Example: Displaying Different Sized Fonts

You wouldn't create a font unless you had some text to display. The problem is that before you can display your text, you need to know at least the height of the font. Failure to consider the font's height may give you text lines that overlap or that are spaced too far apart. You can use the height returned from the FontMetrics class's getHeight() method as a row increment value for each line of text you need to print. Listing 17.5, which is the source code for the FontApplet2 applet, shows how this is done. Listing 17.6 is the applet's HTML document, and Figure 17.5 shows what the applet looks like.

Listing 17.5   FontApplet2.java: Displaying Different Sized Fonts.

```java
import java.awt.*;
import java.applet.*;

public class FontApplet2 extends Applet
{
    TextField textField;

    public void init()
    {
        textField = new TextField(10);
        add(textField);
        textField.setText("32");
    }
```

continues

Listing 17.5   Continued

```java
    public void paint(Graphics g)
    {
        String s = textField.getText();
        int height = Integer.parseInt(s);

        Font font = new Font("TimesRoman", Font.PLAIN, height);
        g.setFont(font);
        FontMetrics fontMetrics = g.getFontMetrics(font);
        height = fontMetrics.getHeight();

        int row = 80;
        g.drawString("This is the first line.", 70, row);
        row += height;
        g.drawString("This is the second line.", 70, row);
        row += height;
        g.drawString("This is the third line.", 70, row);
        row += height;
        g.drawString("This is the fourth line.", 70, row);
    }

    public boolean action(Event event, Object arg)
    {
        repaint();
        return true;
    }
}
```

Listing 17.6   FONTAPPLET2.HTML: FontApplet2's HTML Document.

```html
<title>Applet Test Page</title>
<h1>Applet Test Page</h1>
<applet
    code="FontApplet2.class"
    width=400
    height=200
    name="FontApplet2">
</applet>
```

Figure 17.5

This is
Appletviewer
running the
FontApplet2
applet.

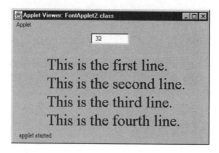

When you run FontApplet2, you see the window shown in Figure 17.5. The size of the active font is shown in the text box at the top of the applet, and a sample of the font appears below the text box. To change the size of the font, type a new value into the text box and press Enter. Figure 17.6, for example, shows the applet displaying 12-point font, whereas Figure 17.7 is the applet displaying 120-point characters. As you can see, no matter what font size you choose, the lines are properly spaced (although large fonts overrun the boundaries of the applet's canvas).

Figure 17.6

FontApplet2 can display any size characters you like. This is 12-point text.

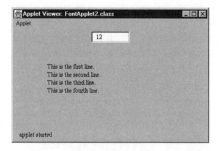

Figure 17.7

This is FontApplet2 displaying 120-point text.

The spacing of the lines is accomplished by first creating a variable to hold the vertical position for the next line of text:

```
int row = 80;
```

Here, the program not only declares the row variable, but also initializes it with the vertical position of the first row of text.

The applet then prints the first text line, using row for drawString()'s third argument:

```
g.drawString("This is the first line.", 70, row);
```

In preparation for printing the next line of text, the program adds the font's height to the row variable:

```
row += height;
```

Each line of text is printed, with row being incremented by the font's height in between, like this:

```
g.drawString("This is the second line.", 70, row);
row += height;
g.drawString("This is the third line.", 70, row);
```

Summary

In regular Windows programming, creating and using fonts is a meticulous and frustrating experience. Java, however, simplifies this task by offering the Font and FontMetrics classes. With just a few method calls, you can create the fonts you need for your applet. Displaying text with any font is as easy setting the font as the current font and getting the font's size. The font's height is especially important because a font's height determines the line spacing you must use. After you've created and set the font, any text you display will use the new font.

Review Questions

1. What method of the Graphics class do you call to get the active font?

2. What method of the Font class do you call to get a font's name?

3. What method of the Font class do you call to get a font's height?

4. Why is it important to determine the height of the current font?

5. How do you get a reference to a FontMetrics object?

6. When would you use a FontMetrics object to obtain information about a font instead of using the Font object?

7. How can you determine the width of an entire text string?

8. When referring to fonts, what is a *point*?

9. Define the terms *ascent*, *descent*, *baseline*, and *leading*.

10. How does a font's height relate to ascent, descent, and leading?

11. How do you create and use a new font?

12. What happens if the font you request is not available on the user's system?

Review Exercises

1. Write an applet that displays three lines of text using the 16-point Helvetica font. Use the height returned from the Font class's getHeight() method to space your lines of text.

2. Modify the applet you created in exercise 1 to display bold text.

3. Modify exercise 2's applet so that it uses a `FontMetric` object to determine the font's height.

4. Write an applet called FontApplet3 that provides a button that the user can click in order to switch between the Courier, TimesRoman, and Helvetica fonts. The final applet should look like Figure 17.8, displaying the text using the selected font with a height of 32 points and using the bold style. Figure 17.9 shows what the applet looks like when the user has clicked the button and switched to the TimesRoman font. (You can find the solution to this problem in the CHAP17 folder of this book's CD-ROM.)

Figure 17.8

This is FontApplet3 displaying the Courier font.

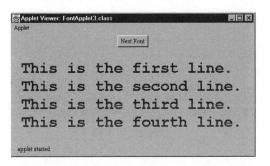

Figure 17.9

Here's FontApplet3 displaying the TimesRoman font.

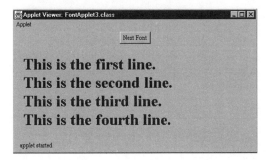

CHAPTER 18

Label and Button Controls

Many computer applications require that the user enter information that the program needs to perform its tasks. In a windowed, graphical environment, getting information from the user presents a challenge. This is because the currently executing application doesn't control the entire screen and so can't just take control of the keyboard or other input device in order to obtain information from the user. That's why the developers of graphical user interfaces created the various controls—such as *text boxes*, *buttons*, and *menus*—that enable applications to interact with the user without bringing the rest of the system to a halt.

Because Java applets must run under many different windowed operating systems, the Java Developer's Kit provides classes for creating the basic controls needed by most graphical user interfaces. These controls include *labels*, *text fields*, *buttons*, *radio buttons*, *check boxes*, and *choice menus*. In this chapter, you learn to program and manage the label and button controls. Other controls are covered in succeeding chapters.

Labels

Labels are the simplest of Java's controls, being little more than text strings you can place anywhere on your applet's display area. You create a label by calling the Label class's constructor, like this:

```
Label label = new Label(str, align);
```

The Label class's constructor takes two arguments, which are the text to display and an alignment value. The alignment value can be Label.LEFT, Label.CENTER, or Label.RIGHT. After creating the label, you add it to the applet by using the add() method, like this:

```
add(label);
```

Example: Creating a Label

Suppose that you want a centered label that displays the text Java does labels! To do this, you use a line of Java code something like this:

```
Label label = new Label("Java does labels!", Label.CENTER);
```

Of course, you can also store the text to display in a String object, like this:

```
String str = "Java does Labels!";
Label label = new Label(str, Label.CENTER);
```

One cool thing about labels is that they automatically retain their alignment when the size of an applet's display area changes. For example, Figure 18.1 shows an applet displaying the centered label created in the previous example. In Figure 18.2, the user has increased the size of the Appletviewer window. The label adjusts to the new space, automatically staying centered.

Figure 18.1

Labels are great for creating text strings that align automatically.

Figure 18.2

Here, the label has repositioned itself so that, in spite of the enlarged window, the label stays centered.

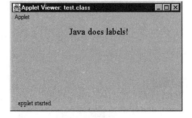

Methods of the *Label* Class

After you create a Label object, you can use the class's methods to manipulate the label. Specifically, you can get or set the label's text and alignment, as shown by the methods listed in Table 18.1.

Table 18.1   Methods of the *Label* class.

Method	*Description*
int getAlignment()	Retrieves a label's alignment setting.
String getText()	Retrieves a label's test string.
setAlignment(int align)	Sets a label's alignment.
void setText(String label)	Sets a label's text string.

The getAlignment() and getText() methods have no arguments. The argument for the setAlignment() is the alignment value (Label.LEFT, Label.CENTER, or Label.RIGHT), and the argument for setText() is the new text for the label.

> **Note:** A label's text is displayed using the currently set font. You can create labels that use different fonts by creating and setting the font before creating the label.

Buttons

In a few previous applets, you used *buttons* to enable the user to manipulate some feature of the applet. Buttons are a great way to trigger events in your applet because they're easy to create and manage, and, most importantly, they're easy for the user to use. To create a button, you first call the Button class's constructor, like this:

```
Button button = new Button(str);
```

Here, str is the text string that you want to appear on the button.

Like other Java classes, Button features methods you can use to manipulate a button object. You use these methods to retrieve or set the button's text, like this:

```
String button.getLabel();
button.setLabel(str);
```

Example: Adding a Button to an Applet

Adding buttons to your applets is painfully easy. Just create the button, and then call the add() method to add the button to the applet. When the applet runs, the user will be able to interact with the button, generating events that the applet can respond to as appropriate. For example, suppose that you want to add a button for setting a font. First, you create a button with an appropriate label, like this:

```
Button button = new Button("TimesRoman");
```

Then, you call the `add()` method to add the button object to the applet, like this:

```
add(button);
```

Now, when the applet appears in your Web page, the user can click the button to trigger an event that tells your applet which font to display.

Handling Multiple-Button Events

In previous applets that contained buttons, you responded to the button in the applet's `action()` method. When the user clicked the button, Java called `action()`, and you did whatever you needed to do in that method. However, what if you have more than one button? Then, you need some way to figure out which button was clicked so the applet can respond properly.

As it turns out, the `action()` method delivers two parameters to your program when it's called, as you can see by examining the function's signature:

```
public boolean action(Event evt, Object arg)
```

The first parameter, `evt`, is an `Event` object, and `arg`, the second parameter, is, in the case of a button, the button's label. (The value type of the second parameter changes depending on the interface object.) The `target` field of an `Event` object indicates the type of object that generated the event. To determine the object, you use the `instanceof` keyword, like this:

```
if (evt.target instanceof Button)
```

If this `if` statement is `true`, it was a button object that generated the event. To determine exactly which button caused the event, you examine the `arg` parameter, like this:

```
if (arg == str)
```

In this line, `str` is the button's label. If the comparison is true, you know exactly which button was clicked.

Example: Handling Multiple Buttons in an Applet

To get a better understanding of how button events work, take a look at the applet shown in Listing 18.1. ButtonApplet displays three buttons in its display area, as shown in Figure 18.3. Whenever you click a button with a normal label, its label reverses itself, as shown in Figure 18.4. When you click a button with an already reversed label, all the labels return to their normal state.

Listing 18.1   ButtonApplet.java: An Applet with Multiple Buttons.

```java
import java.awt.*;
import java.applet.*;

public class ButtonApplet extends Applet
{
    Button button1;
    Button button2;
    Button button3;

    public void init()
    {
        button1 = new Button("Button1");
        button2 = new Button("Button2");
        button3 = new Button("Button3");

        add(button1);
        add(button2);
        add(button3);
    }

    public boolean action(Event evt, Object arg)
    {
        if (evt.target instanceof Button)
            HandleButtons(arg);
        return true;
    }

    protected void HandleButtons(Object label)
    {
        if (label == "Button1")
            button1.setLabel("1nottuB");
        else if (label == "Button2")
            button2.setLabel("2nottuB");
        else if (label == "Button3")
            button3.setLabel("3nottuB");
        else
        {
            button1.setLabel("Button1");
            button2.setLabel("Button2");
            button3.setLabel("Button3");
        }
    }
}
```

Tell Java that the applet uses the classes in the awt *package.*
Tell Java that the applet uses the classes in the applet *package.*
Derive the ButtonApplet *class from Java's* Applet *class.*
   Declare three button objects.
   Override the init() *method.*

Create the three buttons.
Add the buttons to the applet's display.
Override the `action()` method.
 If a button was pressed, call the `HandleButtons()` method.
 Tell Java that the event was handled okay.
Define the `HandleButtons()` method.
 Convert the size to a string.
 if the button's label is normal, reverse it.
 Else set all the button's labels back to normal.

Figure 18.3

The ButtonApplet applet displays three buttons.

Figure 18.4

When you click a button with a normal label, the label reverses itself.

Summary

Because a program running in a windowed environment cannot take exclusive control of a computer's resources, applets require special controls to send and retrieve information to and from the user. Two such controls are labels, which enable you to display short text strings, and buttons, which enable the user to select commands with a single mouse click. When clicked, a button object triggers an event that you can capture and respond to in the applet's `action()` method. By writing Java source code to handle the button click, you can implement many types of button-controlled commands in your applets. In following chapters, you'll learn about other Java controls, including checkboxes, choice menus, and scroll bars.

Review Questions

1. What are the two arguments required by the Label class's constructor?

2. What happens to a label's alignment when the size of an applet changes?

3. How do you add controls to an applet?

4. What is the single argument needed by the Button class's constructor?

5. What are the values you can use to set a label's alignment?

6. What two attributes of a label object can be set using the class's methods?

7. How can you change the label displayed in a button control?

8. When a user clicks a button control, what arguments are received by the action() method?

9. In an applet with several button controls, how can you determine which button was clicked?

10. What happens when the user clicks a label?

Review Exercises

1. Write an applet that displays the label Java rules!

2. Write an applet that creates a button control with the label Command.

3. Write an applet that contains three button controls. When the user clicks a button, display the button's label in the area below the buttons.

4. Write an applet that contains two labels and two buttons organized into two rows. Each row should start with a label followed by a button. (Hint: The size of the applet given in its HTML document will determine how the controls are organized.)

5. Write an applet called LabelButtonApplet that contains three buttons and three labels. When the user clicks a button, the associated label should reverse its text. Clicking on a button that's associated with a changed label should reverse the text again, back to its original form. The final applet should look like Figure 18.5. Figure 18.6 shows the applet with two labels changed. (You can find the solution to this problem in the CHAP18 folder of this book's CD-ROM.)

Figure 18.5

This is the
ButtonLabelApplet
applet at startup.

Figure 18.6

Here's
ButtonLabelApplet
after two labels
have been
reversed.

CHAPTER 19

Checkbox and TextField Controls

As you learned in the previous chapter, label and button controls give you a couple of ways of presenting and retrieving information from the user. However, Java provides many other types of controls, each of which is adept at a certain type of interactivity with the user. *Checkboxes*, for example, are a lot like buttons, except that they enable the user to select from a list of options, whereas *textfield controls* enable the user to type information that your applet needs from the user. In this chapter, you learn about these important controls.

Checkboxes

Many applications (and applets) require that the user select from a list of options. Sometimes, the user can choose as many options as he or she likes (such as when combining various text attributes like bold and italic), and other times the user can select only one option in a list (such as when selecting a color). One way to provide these kinds of choices to your applet's users is to create and display checkbox controls.

To create a checkbox, you call the `Checkbox` class's constructor, like this:

```
Checkbox checkBox = new Checkbox(str, group, check);
```

Here, `str` is a text string for the checkbox's label, `group` is a reference to a `CheckboxGroup` object (used only for exclusive checkboxes), and a `boolean` value indicating whether the checkbox is selected (`true`) or not selected (`false`). After you create the checkbox, add it to the applet by calling the `add()` method, like this:

```
add(checkbox);
```

> **Note:** When the user can select many options from a list of checkboxes, the checkboxes are being used *nonexclusively*. When only one checkbox in a group can be selected simultaneously, the checkboxes are being used *exclusively*. Java's `Checkbox` class enables you to include both types of checkboxes in your applets.

Example: Creating Nonexclusive Checkboxes

Suppose that you're writing an applet that requires the user to select from a list of books. Because you want the user to be able to select any, all, or none of the books, you want to set up checkboxes in nonexclusive mode. First, you create the checkboxes, as shown in Listing 19.1

Listing 19.1   LST19_1.TXT: Creating Nonexclusive Checkboxes.

```
checkbox1 =
    new Checkbox("The Adventures of Javaman", null, false);
checkbox2 =
    new Checkbox("Java by Example", null, false);
checkbox3 =
    new Checkbox("Java and the Single Guy", null, false);
```

As you know, the Checkbox constructor takes three agruments, which are the box's label, a reference to the checkbox's group, and a boolean value indicating whether the box should be displayed as checked. After creating the checkboxes, you add them to the applet:

```
add(checkbox1);
add(checkbox2);
add(checkbox3);
```

Now, when you run your applet, the user sees a list of checkboxes, like those shown in Figure 19.1. In the figure, none of the checkboxes has been selected. To select a checkbox, the user needs only to click the checkbox with the mouse. Because these are nonexclusive checkboxes, the user can select as many options as desired, as shown in Figure 19.2.

Figure 19.1

Checkboxes enable the user to select from a list of options.

Figure 19.2

Nonexclusive
checkboxes enable
the user to select
as many options
as desired.

Checkbox Groups

In order to create a list of exclusive checkboxes, you must first associate the checkboxes in the list with a `CheckboxGroup` object. The first step is to create the `CheckboxGroup`, like this:

```
CheckboxGroup group = new CheckboxGroup();
```

The `CheckboxGroup` constructor takes no arguments. After you create the `CheckboxGroup` object, you create the checkboxes themselves, giving a reference to the `CheckboxGroup` object as the constructor's second argument, as shown in Listing 19.2.

Listing 19.2   LST19_2.TXT: Creating Exclusive Checkboxes.

```
checkbox1 =
    new Checkbox("The Adventures of Javaman", group, true);
checkbox2 =
    new Checkbox("Java by Example", group, false);
checkbox3 =
    new Checkbox("Java and the Single Guy", group, false);
```

In Listing 19.2, notice that the `CheckboxGroup` object, `group`, is given as the second argument of the `Checkbox` class's constructor for each of the checkboxes in the list. This tells Java that the three checkboxes should all be placed into the same group and that they should be treated as exclusive checkboxes, meaning only one can be selected at a time. Notice also that the third argument for the first checkbox is `true`. This value tells Java that you want the first checkbox to be selected when Java displays the list.

As always, after creating the checkboxes, you must add them to the applet, by calling the `add()` method for each checkbox in the group:

```
add(checkbox1);
add(checkbox2);
add(checkbox3);
```

Now, when the applet appears, the user sees a list something like that shown in Figure 19.3. In the figure, the first option is selected. If the user decides to click a different option, the first option becomes unselected and the new one selected. Notice that exclusive checkboxes are round rather than square.

Figure 19.3

Only one exclusive
checkbox can
be selected
simultaneously.

Checkbox **Methods**

Just like other controls supported by Java, the Checkbox class features a number of
methods that you can call in order to manipulate the control or obtain information
about it. Table 19.1 lists the public methods for the Checkbox class.

Table 19.1   Public Methods of the *Checkbox* Class.

Method	Description
CheckboxGroup getCheckboxGroup()	Returns the checkbox's group object.
String getLabel()	Returns the checkbox's label.
boolean getState()	Returns the checkbox's state.
void setCheckboxGroup(CheckboxGroup g)	Sets the checkbox's group object.
void setLabel(String label)	Sets the checkbox's label.
void setState(boolean state)	Sets the checkbox's state.

The get methods listed in Table 19.1 requires no arguments and return objects of
the appropriate type. The setCheckboxGroup() requires a reference to a CheckboxGroup
object as its single argument, whereas setLabel() and setState() require a text string
and a boolean value, respectively, as their single argument.

> **Note:** Checkboxes that are set to exclusive mode are also known as *radio
> buttons* because, like the station-selection buttons on a radio, only one can be
> selected at a time.

Example: Handling Checkboxes in an Applet

Depending on what your applet needs to do, checkboxes can be handled in a couple
of ways. The easiest way to handle checkboxes is to use their methods to determine
the information you need in an applet. Listing 19.3, for example, is an applet that

tracks the state of a set of checkboxes, displaying their current states every time there are changes. Listing 19.4 is the applet's HTML document, and Figure 19.4 shows the applet running under Appletviewer.

Listing 19.3   CheckboxApplet.java: Handling Checkboxes in an Applet.

```
import java.awt.*;
import java.applet.*;

public class CheckboxApplet extends Applet
{
    Checkbox checkbox1;
    Checkbox checkbox2;
    Checkbox checkbox3;

    public void init()
    {
        checkbox1 = new Checkbox("Option 1", null, true);
        checkbox2 = new Checkbox("Option 2", null, false);
        checkbox3 = new Checkbox("Option 3", null, false);

        add(checkbox1);
        add(checkbox2);
        add(checkbox3);
    }

    public void paint(Graphics g)
    {
        Font font = g.getFont();
        FontMetrics fontMetrics = g.getFontMetrics(font);
        int height = fontMetrics.getHeight();

        boolean checked = checkbox1.getState();
        if (checked)
            g.drawString("Option1 selected", 20, 120);
        else
            g.drawString("Option1 not selected", 20, 120);

        checked = checkbox2.getState();
        if (checked)
            g.drawString("Option2 selected", 20, 120 + height);
        else
            g.drawString("Option2 not selected", 20, 120 + height);

        checked = checkbox3.getState();
        if (checked)
            g.drawString("Option3 selected", 20, 120 + 2 * height);
        else
            g.drawString("Option3 not selected", 20, 120 + 2 * height);
    }

    public boolean action(Event evt, Object arg)
    {
        repaint();
        return true;
    }
}
```

Tell Java that the applet uses the classes in the awt *package.*
Tell Java that the applet uses the classes in the applet *package.*
Derive the CheckboxApplet *class from Java's* Applet *class.*
  Declare three checkbox objects.
  Override the init() *method.*
    Create the three checkboxes.
    Add the checkboxes to the applet's display.
  Override the paint() *method.*
    Get the height of the active font.
    Get the first checkbox's state and display the state.
    Get the second checkbox's state and display the state.
    Get the third checkbox's state and display the state.
  Override the action() *method.*
    Force Java to redraw the applet's display.
    Tell Java that the event was handled okay.

Listing 19.4   CHECKBOXAPPLET.HTML: The HTML Document That Runs CheckboxApplet.

```
<title>Applet Test Page</title>
<h1>Applet Test Page</h1>
<applet
    code="CheckboxApplet.class"
    width=135
    height=220
    name="CheckboxApplet">
</applet>
```

Figure 19.4

CheckboxApplet
running under
Appletviewer.

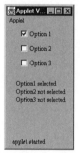

Responding to a Checkbox Event

Most of Java's user-interface controls generate events when they're clicked. The checkbox controls are no different. However, unlike button controls, which send both a reference to the control and the control's label as parameters to the action()

method, checkboxes send only a reference to the control, with the second action() parameter always being true. This anomaly makes it a little more difficult to handle checkbox controls when you need to respond directly to the event generated by the control.

To respond to a checkbox event, you must use the Event object's target field to call the checkbox's methods in order to determine which checkbox caused the event. If you don't remember, the Event object is passed as the action() method's first argument.

First, you obtain a reference to the checkbox, like this:

```
Checkbox checkbox = (Checkbox)evt.target;
```

Then, with a reference to the checkbox in hand, you can call whatever Checkbox class members you need in order to determine which checkbox caused the event and to deal with the event as appropriately. Probably the best way to determine which checkbox you're dealing with is to get the object's label, like this:

```
String label = checkbox.getLabel();
```

You can then compare the returned string to the labels for each checkbox object.

Example: Handling Checkbox Events in an Applet

To demonstrate how to use the previously presented technique in an actual programming situation, you'll now examine the CheckboxApplet2. The source code for the applet is shown in Listing 19.5. To create an HTML document for the applet, start with Listing 19.4 and then change all occurrences of CheckboxApplet with CheckboxApplet2.

Listing 19.5   CheckboxApplet2.java: Responding to Checkbox Events.

```java
import java.awt.*;
import java.applet.*;

public class CheckboxApplet2 extends Applet
{
    Checkbox checkbox1;
    Checkbox checkbox2;
    Checkbox checkbox3;

    public void init()
    {
        checkbox1 = new Checkbox("Option 1", null, true);
        checkbox2 = new Checkbox("Option 2", null, false);
        checkbox3 = new Checkbox("Option 3", null, false);
```

continues

Listing 19.5   Continued

```
        add(checkbox1);
        add(checkbox2);
        add(checkbox3);
    }

    public boolean action(Event evt, Object arg)
    {
        if (evt.target instanceof Checkbox)
            ChangeLabel(evt);
        repaint();

        return true;
    }

    protected void ChangeLabel(Event evt)
    {
        Checkbox checkbox = (Checkbox)evt.target;
        String label = checkbox.getLabel();

        if (label == "Option 1")
            checkbox.setLabel("Changed 1");
        else if (label == "Option 2")
            checkbox.setLabel("Changed 2");
        else if (label == "Option 3")
            checkbox.setLabel("Changed 3");
        else
        {
            checkbox1.setLabel("Option 1");
            checkbox2.setLabel("Option 2");
            checkbox3.setLabel("Option 3");
        }
    }
}
```

Tell Java that the applet uses the classes in the awt *package.*
Tell Java that the applet uses the classes in the applet *package.*
Derive the CheckboxApplet2 *class from Java's* Applet *class.*
  Declare three checkbox objects.
  Override the init() *method.*
    Create the three checkboxes.
    Add the checkboxes to the applet's display.
  Override the action() *method.*
    If a checkbox caused the event, call the ChangeLabel() *method.*
    Force Java to redraw the applet's display.
    Tell Java that the event was handled okay.
  Declare the ChangeLabel() *method.*

Cast the Event object to a Checkbox object.
Get the checkbox's label.
Change the label of the selected checkbox
Or else change all the labels back to their normal form.

When you run the CheckboxApplet2 applet, you see a display something like Figure 19.5. You can click on any of the checkboxes as normal, and their check state will change accordingly. However, when you click on a checkbox, its label will also change, as shown in Figure 19.6, proving that the applet is responding to the event generated by the checkbox. If you click on a checkbox that still has its original label, that label changes. If you click on a label that has already been changed, all the checkbox labels revert to their starting text.

Figure 19.5

This is
CheckboxApplet2
running under
Appletviewer.

Figure 19.6

Clicking the
checkboxes
changes their
labels.

TextFields

You've already had a lot of experience with textfield controls. You've used these handy controls to implement text input for many of your previous applets. As you already know, a *textfield object*, which is an object of the TextField class, is much like a Windows edit control, providing a small box into which the user can type text. To create a textfield control, you call the TextField class's constructor, like this:

```
TextField textField = new TextField(str, size);
```

The constructor's two arguments are the default text that should be displayed in the textfield control and the size in characters of the control. After you create the control, add it to the applet by calling the add() method, like this:

```
add(textField);
```

TextField Methods

The TextField class features a number of public methods that you can use to manipulate textfield objects. By using these methods, you can set a textfield object's characteristics and obtain information about the object. Table 19.2 lists the most commonly used methods and their descriptions.

Table 19.2   Methods of the *TextField* Class.

Method	Description
boolean echoCharIsSet()	Returns true if the object's echo character is set. When set, echo characters appear in place of any character the user types.
int getColumns()	Returns the size of the textfield object.
char getEchoChar()	Returns the object's echo character, if set.
String getText()	Gets the text from the textfield object.
void setEchoCharacter(char c)	Sets the object's echo character.
void setText(String str)	Sets the text in the textfield object.

Example: Using Echo Characters

You should already be pretty familiar with using textfield objects in applets because you've used them already many times in previous applets in this book. However, I've not yet mentioned *echo characters*, which enable you to create textfield objects that display a special character when the user types. The most common use for echo characters is to set up text entry for things like passwords.

Listing 19.6 is the source code for a short applet called EchoApplet that initializes a textfield object to use an asterisk as an echo character. Listing 19.7 is the applet's

HTML document. When you run the applet and type something in the textfield control, you see the display in Figure 19.7. You can change the echo character by clicking on the Change Echo button. Then, when you click on the textfield control to enter text, the text in the control changes to the new echo character, as shown in Figure 19.8. The program switches between three different echo characters: an asterisk (*), a pound sign (#), and a dollar sign ($).

Listing 19.6   EchoApplet.java: Using Echo Characters.

```
import java.awt.*;
import java.applet.*;

public class EchoApplet extends Applet
{
    TextField textField;
    Button button;

    public void init()
    {
        textField = new TextField("", 25);
        button = new Button("Change Echo");

        textField.setEchoCharacter('*');

        add(textField);
        add(button);
    }

    public boolean action(Event evt, Object arg)
    {
        if (evt.target instanceof Button)
            ChangeEcho();

        return true;
    }

    protected void ChangeEcho()
    {
        char c = textField.getEchoChar();

        if (c == '*')
            textField.setEchoCharacter('#');
        else if (c == '#')
            textField.setEchoCharacter('$');
        else
            textField.setEchoCharacter('*');
    }
}
```

Tell Java that the applet uses the classes in the `awt` package.
Tell Java that the applet uses the classes in the `applet` package.
Derive the `EchoApplet` class from Java's `Applet` class.
   Declare textfield and button objects.
   Override the `init()` method.
      Create the textfield and button objects.
      Set the textfield object's echo character to an asterisk.
      Add the textfield and button objects to the applet's display.
   Override the `action()` method.
      If the button caused the event, call the `ChangeEcho()` method.
      Tell Java that the event was handled okay.
   Declare the `ChangeEcho()` method.
      Get the current echo character.
      Reset the echo character to the next in the series.

Listing 19.7   ECHOAPPLET.HTML: EchoApplet's HTML Document.

```
<title>Applet Test Page</title>
<h1>Applet Test Page</h1>
<applet
    code="EchoApplet.class"
    width=200
    height=150
    name="EchoApplet">
</applet>
```

Figure 19.7

When you start typing, you see asterisks instead of regular text characters.

Figure 19.8

When you click the Change Echo button, the applet switches to a different echo character.

Note: Because you've already had a lot of experience with textfield controls, you know that a textfield control generates an event when the user presses Enter after typing in the control. You can capture this event in the applet's `action()` method.

Summary

In this chapter, you discovered two new controls that will help you build useful applets. Whenever you need the user to select from a list of items, you can use checkbox controls, which can be created in both nonexclusive and exclusive modes. TextField controls, on the other hand, enable the user to enter text data into an applet. You can even disguise the user's entry by substituting the typed text with echo characters.

Review Questions

1. What are the three arguments required by the `Checkbox` class's constructor?

2. What's another name for checkboxes that are set for exclusive mode?

3. What are the two arguments needed by the `TextField` class's constructor?

4. What method do you call in order to change the state of a checkbox?

5. What is the difference between the nonexclusive and exclusive modes for a checkbox control?

6. What additional object do you need to group the items in a checkbox control?

7. When would you use echo characters with a textfield control?

8. How do you set a textfield control's echo character?

9. How can you determine which checkbox in an applet generated an event?

Review Exercises

1. Write an applet that displays a checkbox with the label `Click here`.

2. Write an applet that displays a textfield control that displays the default text string `Type here`.

3. Write an applet that contains one checkbox and textfield control. Change the checkbox's label to whatever the user types in the textfield control.

4. Write an applet that contains three checkboxes in nonexclusive mode.

5. Revise the applet from exercise 4 so that the checkboxes operate in exclusive mode.

CHAPTER 20

Choice Menu, Text Area, and Scrolling List Controls

If your applet must handle only a couple of user commands, it's an easy matter to include button controls or checkbox groups in order to enable the user to select those commands. However, often, an applet's command set is sophisticated enough to warrant complete menus. Java features *choice menus* for just this eventuality. Java also features a *scrolling list control*, not unlike Windows' list box control, that enables the user to select items from a list. Finally, the *text area control* enables you to display paragraphs of text within your applet. You'll learn about all these controls in this chapter.

Choice Menus

Choice menus are very similar to the drop-down lists. When the user selects the menu, a list of commands appears from which the user can choose. After the user makes a choice, the menu disappears.

To create a choice menu, you must first create an instance of the Choice class, like this:

```
Choice menu = new Choice();
```

As you can see, the Choice class's constructor accepts no arguments.

After you have created the Choice object, you can add items to the menu by calling the object's addItem() method:

```
menu.addItem(str);
```

Here, str is the text that will appear as the command in the menu. You can call addItem() as often as you need to build a complete menu. When you have the complete menu created, you add it to the applet by calling the add() method.

Example: Creating a Choice Menu

Creating a menu is a fairly straightforward process. For example, to create a choice menu that enables the user to select between three font styles, you might use the code shown in Listing 20.1.

Listing 20.1 LST20_1.TXT: Creating a Choice Menu.

```
Choice menu = new Choice();
menu.addItem("Plain");
menu.addItem("Bold");
menu.addItem("Italic");
add(menu);
```

When the user runs the applet containing this menu, a menu like that shown in Figure 20.1 appears. To display the menu, the user clicks on the arrow to the right of the text box displaying the current choice, and the menu appears, as shown in Figure 20.2. To select a choice, the user merely clicks an entry in the menu.

Figure 20.1

Java displays a choice menu as a text box with an arrow.

Figure 20.2

Clicking the arrow displays the menu.

Choice Menu Methods

As you've no doubt guessed, the Choice class features a number of public methods that enable you to manipulate choice menus in various ways. Using these methods, you can do everything from determining the number of command entries in a menu to adding items to the menu. Table 20.1 lists the most commonly used methods and their descriptions.

Table 20.1   Methods of the *Choice* Class.

Method	Description
int countItems()	Returns the number of command items in the menu.
String getItem(int index)	Returns the command text for a given item.
void addItem(String item)	Adds an item to the menu.
String getSelectedItem()	Returns a string representing the selected item.
int getSelectedIndex()	Returns the index of the selected item.
void select(int index)	Selects the item at the given position.
void select(String str)	Selects the item with the given text string.

Example: Responding to Menu Events in an Applet

A menu isn't much good unless you can determine which item the user selected so that the applet can carry out the user's command. As with most controls, when the user makes a selection from a choice menu, Java generates an event that you can capture in the action() method. In the case of a choice menu, action()'s first parameter is the menu instance, and the second parameter is the text of the selected menu item. By comparing the text to the items you added to the menu, you can determine which menu item the user chose.

The ChoiceApplet applet, whose source code is shown in Listing 20.2, demonstrates creating and responding to choice menus in an applet. Listing 20.3 is the applet's HTML document. When you run the applet under Appletviewer, you see the window shown in Figure 20.3. The text in the window is displayed using the currently selected color in the choice menu. To change the text color, just select a new menu item.

Listing 20.2   ChoiceApplet.java: Using Menus in an Applet.

```java
import java.awt.*;
import java.applet.*;

public class ChoiceApplet extends Applet
{
    Choice menu;
    Color color;

    public void init()
    {
        Choice menu = new Choice();

        menu.addItem("Black");
        menu.addItem("Red");
        menu.addItem("Green");
        menu.addItem("Blue");

        add(menu);

        color = Color.black;
    }

    public void paint(Graphics g)
    {
        Font font = new Font("TimesRoman", Font.BOLD, 24);
        int height = font.getSize();
        g.setFont(font);

        g.setColor(color);

        g.drawString("This text is drawn in", 32, 75);
        g.drawString("the color selected from", 32, 75+height);
        g.drawString("the above choice menu.", 32, 75+2*height);
    }

    public boolean action(Event evt, Object arg)
    {
        if (evt.target instanceof Choice)
            HandleMenu(arg);

        return true;
    }

    protected void HandleMenu(Object item)
    {
        if (item == "Black")
            color = Color.black;
        else if (item == "Red")
            color = Color.red;
        else if (item == "Green")
```

```
                color = Color.green;
        else
                color = Color.blue;

        repaint();
    }
}
```

Tell Java that the applet uses the classes in the awt *package.*
Tell Java that the applet uses the classes in the applet *package.*
Derive the ChoiceApplet *class from Java's* Applet *class.*
    Declare menu and color objects.
    Override the init() *method.*
        Create the menu object.
        Add commands to the menu object.
        Add the menu to the applet.
        Initialize the starting color for the text.
    Override the paint() *method.*
        Create and set the display font.
        Set the selected color.
        Display text in the selected color.
    Override the action() *method.*
        If the menu caused the event, call the HandleMenu() *method.*
        Tell Java that the event was handled okay.
    Declare the HandleMenu() *method.*
        Set the color field based on the menu selection.
        Tell Java to repaint the applet's display area.

Listing 20.3   CHOICEAPPLET.HTML: ChoiceApplet's HTML Document.

```html
<title>Applet Test Page</title>
<h1>Applet Test Page</h1>
<applet
    code="ChoiceApplet.class"
    width=300
    height=150
    name="ChoiceApplet">
</applet>
```

Figure 20.3

ChoiceApplet displays text in the color selected from its choice menu.

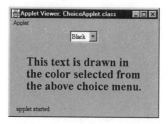

Scrolling Lists

Whereas choice menus usually display a set of commands or options, *scrolling lists* are best used to display a list of items from which the user can choose. For example, you might use a scrolling list to enable the user to choose a state when filling out an address form. The scrolling list in this case would contain all 50 states. The user would only need to double-click on his or her state in order to complete that section of the form. Scrolling lists not only make it easy for users to enter information, but also ensure that the user makes a choice from a valid set of responses.

To create a scrolling list, you first call the List class's constructor, like this:

```
List list = new List(num, false);
```

The constructor's two arguments are the number of visible lines in the list and a boolean value indicating whether the list will support multiple selections. The list created in the preceding will not allow the user to select more than one item simultaneously.

When you have the list object created, you can add items to the list. You do this by calling the List object's addItem() method:

```
list.addItem(str);
```

Here, str is the text string for the item to add to the list.

> **Note:** You can add as many items as you like to a list. You are not limited to the number of items given as the List constructor's first argument. That value specifies only the size of the list box; that is, the value determines how many items are visible on the screen at one time.

Example: Creating a Single-Selection List

Suppose that you need to create a list that contains musical artists from which the user must select only one. First, you create the list object, after which you add the names of the artists you want to include. Finally, you add the list to the applet.

Listing 20.4 shows the Java code that performs these tasks. Figure 20.4 shows the resultant list box.

Listing 20.4   LST20_4.TXT: Creating a Single-Selection List Box.

```
List list = new List(10, false);
list.addItem("Pearl Jam");
list.addItem("Dream Theater");
list.addItem("Joe Satriani");
list.addItem("Oasis");
list.addItem("Alanis Morissette");
list.addItem("Soul Asylum");
list.addItem("The Rembrandts");
list.addItem("Smashing Pumpkins");
list.addItem("Joan Osborne");
list.addItem("Bjork");
add(list);
```

Figure 20.4

In this list, only one item can be selected at a time.

Because the List constructor's first argument is 10 and there are only 10 items in the list, all of the items are visible on the screen. Moreover, because the List constructor's second parameter is false, in the list created by Listing 20.4, the user can select only a single artist at a time.

Example: Creating a Multiple-Selection List

When you display a list of musical artists such as that created by Listing 20.4, you may want the user to select more than one. In this case, you can create a multiple-selection list, just by changing the List constructor's second argument to true, like this:

```
List list = new List(10, true);
```

As Figure 20.5 shows, the new list enables the user to select as many artists as he or she likes.

Figure 20.5

Now the user can select more than one artist at a time.

Example: Creating a Scrolling List

You may have noticed that in this chapter's title, the list controls are called "scrolling lists." So far, though, none of your lists have scrolled. In fact, they haven't even had scroll bars. Whenever the size of the list box (given as the constructor's first argument) is greater than or equal to the number of items in the list, the list doesn't need to scroll, so no scroll bar appears. However, as soon as the number of items exceeds the size of the list box, Java enables scrolling.

As an example, suppose that you were to change the first line of Listing 20.4 to this:

```
List list = new List(5, false);
```

Now, you have a list that can display five items at a time. However, there are 10 items in your list, which means that, in order for the user to be able to see all then items, the list must scroll. Figure 20.6 shows the resultant scrolling list.

Figure 20.6

The user must scroll this list to see all the items.

Methods of the *List* Class

Because there's so much you can do with a scrolling list control, the List class has a large set of public methods that you can call to manipulate a list. The most useful of these methods are listed in Table 20.2. Although there are a lot of methods to learn in the table, the most important are addItem(), getSelectedIndex(), getSelectedIndexes(), getSelectedItem(), and getSelectedItems(). Using these five methods, you can create a basic scrolling list and enable the user to make selections from it. In the next section, in fact, you'll see how to determine which item the user selected.

Table 20.2 Most Useful Methods of the *List* Class.

Method	Description
void addItem(String item)	Adds an item to the end of the list.
void addItem(String item, int index)	Adds an item to a specific position in the list.
boolean allowsMultipleSelections()	Returns a boolean value indicating whether the list supports multiple selection.
void clear()	Clears all items from the list.
int countItems()	Returns the number of items in the list.
void delItem(int position)	Deletes the item at the given position from the list.
void delItems(int start, int end)	Deletes a group of items from the list.
void deselect(int index)	Deselects the item at the given index.
String getItem(int index)	Returns the item at the given index.
int getRows()	Returns the size of the list box.
int getSelectedIndex()	Gets the index of the selected item.
int[] getSelectedIndexes()	Gets the indexes of a multiple selection.
String getSelectedItem()	Returns the selected item in a list.
String[] getSelectedItems()	Returns all the items in a multiple selection.
int getVisibleIndex()	Returns the index of the last item that was made visible.
boolean isSelected(int index)	Returns a boolean value indicating whether the item at the given index is selected.

continues

Table 20.2 Continued

Method	Description
void makeVisible(int index)	Ensures that the item at the given index is visible.
void replaceItem(String newValue, int index)	Replaces the item at the given index with a new item.
void select(int index)	Selects the item at the given index.
void setMultipleSelections(boolean v)	Toggles the multiple-selection mode.

Example: Using a Scrolling List in an Applet

By now, you've gotten used to working with the list of musical artists that I've used in the previous few examples. In this example, you put that list to the test by not only creating and displaying the list in an applet, but also by displaying the user's selection. Listing 20.5 is the source code for the ListApplet applet.

Listing 20.5 ListApplet.java: An Applet with a Scrolling List.

```java
import java.awt.*;
import java.applet.*;

public class ListApplet extends Applet
{
    List list;

    public void init()
    {
        list = new List(5, false);

        list.addItem("Pearl Jam");
        list.addItem("Dream Theater");
        list.addItem("Joe Satriani");
        list.addItem("Oasis");
        list.addItem("Alanis Morissette");
        list.addItem("Soul Asylum");
        list.addItem("The Rembrandts");
        list.addItem("Smashing Pumpkins");
        list.addItem("Joan Osborne");
        list.addItem("Bjork");

        add(list);
        resize(300, 150);
    }
```

```
    public void paint(Graphics g)
    {
        g.drawString("CHOSEN ITEM:", 100, 110);
        String s = list.getSelectedItem();

        if (s == null)
            s = "None";

        g.drawString(s, 100, 130);
    }

    public boolean action(Event evt, Object arg)
    {
        repaint();
        return true;
    }
}
```

Tell Java that the applet uses the classes in the awt *package.*
Tell Java that the applet uses the classes in the applet *package.*
Derive the ListApplet *class from Java's* Applet *class.*
   Declare the list object.
   Override the init() *method.*
      Create the list object.
      Add items to the list object.
      Add the list to the applet.
      Set the applet's size.
   Override the paint() *method.*
      Draw a label in the applet's display.
      Get the selected item from the list box.
      If there is no item selected, set the string to "None."
      Display the selected item.
   Override the action() *method.*
      Force the applet to repaint its display.
      Tell Java that the event was handled okay.

When you run ListApplet with Appletviewer, you see the window shown in Figure 20.7. When you double-click an item in the list, Java calls the applet's action() method in which the applet calls the repaint() method. This forces Java to call the paint() method, where the applet retrieves the selected item and displays it.

Notice the call to resize() in the init() method. The resize() method enables you to set the applet to any size you wish. This size overrides any size setting that's included in the HTML document that ran the applet.

Figure 20.7

The scrolling list in this applet lets you choose a single musical artist.

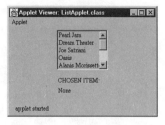

The *TextArea* Control

Throughout this book, you've been using the `TextField` control to retrieve information from the user. In most cases, the `TextField` control works great, but it does have some limitations, the most serious being the fact that it can display only one line of text at a time. There may be situations where you'd like to display one or more paragraphs of text in your applet, in a control that enables the user to edit existing text, as well as enter his or her own text. This is where the `TextArea` control is useful. The `TextArea` control is a text box that acts like a simple word processor. When you display a text box, the user can type and edit multiple lines of text.

To create a `TextArea` control, you call the class's constructor, like this:

```
TextArea textArea = new TextArea(str, rows, cols);
```

This constructor's three arguments are the string to display in the control, the number of rows in the control, and the number of columns. As with the other controls, after you create the `TextField` object, you add it to the applet by using the `add()` method.

Example: Creating a *TextArea* Control

As an example, suppose that you need to create a `TextArea` control that'll start off displaying eight lines of text. Listing 20.6 is an applet, called TextAreaApplet, that creates a `TextArea` control that displays eight lines of text. Figure 20.8 shows what the applet looks like running under Appletviewer. When you run the applet, click on the `TextArea` control's box and try editing the text in the window. As you'll discover, you not only can edit the existing text, but also add new text.

Listing 20.6   TEXTAREAAPPLET.JAVA: The TextAreaApplet Applet.

```
import java.awt.*;
import java.applet.*;

public class TextAreaApplet extends Applet
{
```

```
    TextArea textArea;

    public void init()
    {
        String s = "This is an example of a\n";
        s += "textarea control, which is not\n";
        s += "unlike a textfield control.\n";
        s += "The big difference is that a\n";
        s += "textarea control can hold many\n";
        s += "lines of text, whereas a\n";
        s += "textfield control deals with\n";
        s += "only one line of text at a time.\n";

        textArea = new TextArea(s, 9, 30);
        add(textArea);

        resize(300, 180);
    }
}
```

Tell Java that the applet uses the classes in the awt *package.*
Tell Java that the applet uses the classes in the applet *package.*
Derive the TextAreaApplet *class from Java's* Applet *class.*
　Declare the TextArea *object.*
　Override the init() *method.*
　　Create the string to display in the control.
　　Create the TextArea *object.*
　　Add the control to the applet.
　　Set the applet's size.

Figure 20.8

TextAreaApplet applet running under Appletviewer.

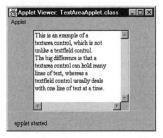

Tip: If you look at how the TextArea control's display string is created in TextAreaApplet, you'll see that you can store multiple lines of text into a single String object. You do this by placing the newline character (\n) at the end of each line that you add to the string.

When you run TextAreaApplet, notice how all the text fits within the text box. Because the text is fully displayed, the control's scroll bars are inactive. However, if you were to edit the text such that you added more lines than the control can display, or made a line longer that the control can display, the control's scroll bars become active. Figure 20.9 shows TextAreaApplet after the user has added text that forces the scroll bars to become active. You can use the scroll bars to view the portions of the text that are offscreen.

Figure 20.9

When the text contained in the control cannot be fully displayed, a `TextArea` control activates its scroll bars.

Methods of the *TextArea* Class

To enable you to easily manipulate the text, the `TextArea` class features a number of public methods. You can use these methods to modify the text in the control or to obtain information about the control. Table 20.3 shows the most useful methods and what they do.

Table 20.3   Useful Methods of the *TextArea* Class.

Method	Description
`void appendText(String str)`	Appends text to the control.
`int getColumns()`	Returns the number of columns in the control.
`int getRows()`	Returns the number of rows in the ` control.
`void insertText(String str, int pos)`	Inserts text at the given position.
`void replaceText(String str, int start, int end)`	Replaces text specified by the starting and ending points.

Summary

Choice menus are a powerful control that enable you to include a pop-up menu of commands for the user of your applet. By using such a menu, the user can more easily control the applet, as well as set options, without the controls' taking up a lot of screen space. Scrolling lists are a valuable tool for ensuring that the user always enters a response from a valid set of responses. You can even set up a list to accept multiple selections. Finally, the TextArea control provides a simple text editor that you can easily add to your applets.

Review Questions

1. How many arguments are accepted by the Choice class's constructor?

2. How do you add items to a choice menu?

3. What are the two arguments needed by the List class's constructor?

4. How do you add items to a scrolling list?

5. When would you use a TextArea control in place of a TextField control?

6. How can you determine which menu command the user selected?

7. How do you create a multiple-selection scrolling list?

8. How do you retrieve the selected item from a single-selection scrolling list?

9. How do you create a single string containing multiple lines of text?

10. How do you retrieve multiple selections from a scrolling list?

11. Can you delete items from a scrolling list?

Review Exercises

1. Write an applet that has a menu containing the commands On and Off.

2. Write an applet that displays a single-selection scrolling list containing the titles of five movies.

3. Write an applet that displays a TextArea control. The control should display five lines of text at startup.

3. Write an applet that changes the size of the applet based on five selections in a choice menu.

4. Revise the applet from exercise 3 such that the user uses a single-selection list to select the applet's size.

5. Write an applet called TextTransferApplet that includes a list box and a
TextArea control. The list box should contain 10 words. When the user
clicks a word, the word should appear in the TextArea control on a new
line. Figure 20.10 shows what the completed applet should look like, and
Figure 20.11 shows the applet after the user has transferred several words
to the TextArea control. You can find the solution for this problem in the
CHAP20 folder of this book's CD-ROM.

Figure 20.10

TextTransferApplet
should look like
this.

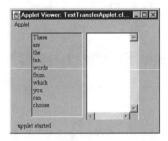

Figure 20.11

Here's the applet
after the user has
transferred a few
words to the text
area.

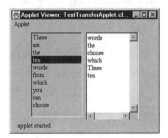

CHAPTER 21

Scrollbar and Canvas Controls

Next in the long list of Java controls are the scrollbar and canvas controls, which are represented by the Scrollbar and Canvas classes. Using a scrollbar, you can enable the user to choose values from a slider or even set up your own scrolling displays. The canvas control, on the other hand, enables you to draw and display graphics in an applet. In this chapter, you'll get a handle on both of these handy controls.

Scrollbars

Practically every application that runs under Windows supports scrollbars. In most cases, you use a scrollbar to move to different portions of a document. However, a good alternative use for these controls is selecting a value from a range. Although scrollbars are not as common in applets, Java does include a class for adding scrollbars to your programs. To create a scrollbar, you first call the Scrollbar class's constructor, like this:

```
Scrollbar scrollbar = new Scrollbar(orientation,
    start, page, min, max);
```

The constructor's five arguments are the scrollbar's orientation (can be Scrollbar.HORIZONTAL or Scrollbar.VERTICAL), the starting setting for the scrollbar, the scrollbar's page size (the amount the display scrolls when the user clicks above or below the scroll box), and the minimum and maximum values represented by the scrollbar.

After creating the scrollbar object, you add it to the applet by calling the `add()` method, like this:

```
add(scrollbar);
```

Example: Creating a Scrollbar

Suppose you need to create a scrollbar that'll enable the user to select a value from 1 to 100. You can create such a scrollbar like this:

```
Scrollbar scrollbar =
    new Scrollbar(Scrollbar.HORIZONTAL, 50, 0, 1, 100);
add(scrollbar);
```

The constructor's first argument tells Java that the scrollbar should be drawn horizontally on the display. The second argument tells Java that you want the scrollbar to start off set to the value of 50. The third argument is the page size, which represents the area in the slider covered by the scroll box. Finally, the fourth and fifth arguments give the scrollbar a minimum value of 1 and a maximum value of 100.

These settings enable the user to select a value from 1 to 100. So, why is the scrollbar's page size set to zero? Doing this forces the scroll box in the scrollbar to center on the selected value. It also enables the user to select the maximum value of 100. To understand why this is necessary, imagine that the scrollbar's scroll box represents the page of data that's currently displayed (such as in a word processor document). The scroll box then starts on the selected value and ends on the selected value plus the page size. Figure 21.1 illustrates this concept. The scrollbar in the figure was created like this:

```
Scrollbar scrollbar =
    new Scrollbar(Scrollbar.HORIZONTAL, 50, 10, 1, 100);
```

Because the scrollbar's starting value is 50, and the scrollbar's page size is 10, the scroll box covers the area of the slider from 50 to 60. If the user were to drag the scroll box to its maximum value, the scroll box would cover the area in the slider from 90 to 100, as shown in Figure 21.2. In this case, the page size of 10 makes it impossible for the user to actually select the value of 100. This is because, if the user could select the value 100, the scrollbox would have to cover the slider area from 100 to 110. But, the scrollbar's maximum value is 100.

Figure 21.1

The scroll box covers an area from the selected value to the selected value plus the page size.

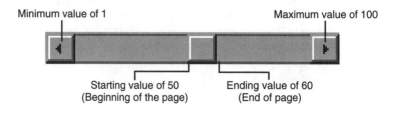

Minimum value of 1   Maximum value of 100

Starting value of 50
(Beginning of the page)

Ending value of 60
(End of page)

Figure 21.2

This maximum setting starts at 90 and goes to 90 plus the page size, which equals the maximum value of 100.

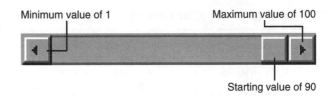

Minimum value of 1

Maximum value of 100

Starting value of 90

When using a scrollbar to select specific values rather than areas of a document, you can either set the page size to zero or set the maximum to the maximum you want plus the page size. Both of these scrollbars will operate the same way:

```
Scrollbar scrollbar =
    new Scrollbar(Scrollbar.HORIZONTAL, 50, 10, 1, 110);

Scrollbar scrollbar =
    new Scrollbar(Scrollbar.HORIZONTAL, 50, 0, 1, 100);
```

Figure 21.3 shows the scrollbar produced by either of the above examples. Notice that the scroll box is now centered on 50. When the scrollbox is at its maximum position now, it indicates a value of 100.

Figure 21.3

This scrollbar enables the user to select any value within its minimum and maximum range.

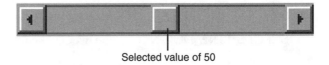

Selected value of 50

Responding to a Scrollbar

Because of the many different types of events a scrollbar generates, you need to capture its events in the class's handleEvent() method, rather than in action(), as you did with other controls. What's handleEvent()? Like action(), handleEvent() is a method that's defined in one of your applet's superclasses (in this case, Component). The handleEvent() method handles all the specific event messages that are generated by the typical windowing system. Table 21.1 lists some of the events to which the handleEvent() method can respond.

Table 21.1   Most Common Events That Can Be Handled by *handleEvent().*

Event Message	Description
ACTION_EVENT	An event that can be handled by action().
GOT_FOCUS	The component received the focus.

continues

Table 21.1   Continued

Event Message	Description
KEY_PRESS	A key on the keyboard was pressed.
KEY_RELEASE	A key on the keyboard was released.
LIST_DESELECT	An item in a list was deselected.
LIST_SELECT	An item in a list was selected.
LOST_FOCUS	The component lost the focus.
MOUSE_DOWN	The user pressed a mouse button.
MOUSE_DRAG	The user dragged the mouse pointer.
MOUSE_ENTER	The mouse pointer entered an area.
MOUSE_EXIT	The mouse pointer left an area.
MOUSE_MOVE	The user moved the mouse.
MOUSE_UP	The released a mouse button.
SCROLL_ABSOLUTE	The user moved a scrollbar's scroll box.
SCROLL_LINE_DOWN	The user clicked a scrollbar's down arrow.
SCROLL_LINE_UP	The user clicked a scrollbar's up arrow.
SCROLL_PAGE_DOWN	The user clicked in a scrollbar below the scroll box.
SCROLL_PAGE_UP	The user clicked in a scrollbar above the scroll box.
WINDOW_DEICONIFY	The window has been restored from an icon state.
WINDOW_DESTROY	The window has been destroyed.
WINDOW_EXPOSE	The window has been activated.
WINDOW_ICONIFY	The window has been reduced to an icon.
WINDOW_MOVED	The window has been moved.

As you can see from the list in Table 21.1, there are five event messages associated with a scrollbar. These messages are SCROLL_ABSOLUTE, SCROLL_LINE_DOWN, SCROLL_LINE_UP, SCROLL_PAGE_DOWN, and SCROLL_PAGE_UP. You can respond to these event messages when you want to customize how the scrollbar functions. (You learn how to handle event messages in Chapter 25, "Mouse and Keyboard Events.") However, you don't need to get into such details when you just need to know where the user set the scrollbar. Instead, you can override `handleEvent()` and check for the scrollbar object in that method. If the user generates an event with the scrollbar, you can then call the scrollbar's methods to determine what change was made. Table 21.2 lists the most useful methods of the `Scrollbar` class:

Table 21.2   Most Useful Methods of the Scrollbar Class.

Method	*Description*
`int getLineIncrement()`	Returns the line increment.
`int getMaximum()`	Returns the maximum value.
`int getMinimum()`	Returns the minimum value.
`int getOrientation()`	Returns the orientation.
`int getPageIncrement()`	Returns the page increment.
`int getValue()`	Returns the currently set value.
`int getVisible()`	Returns the page size.
`setLineIncrement(int inc)`	Sets the line increment.
`setPageIncrement(int inc)`	Sets the page increment.
`setValue(int value)`	Sets the selected value.
`setValues(int value, int pgsize, int min, int max)`	Sets all the slider's values.

Example: Using a Scrollbar in an Applet

Now that you know how to use a scrollbar, you can put together an applet that demonstrates the concepts involved. Listing 21.1 is just such an applet. Called ScrollbarApplet, this applet enables you to manipulate a scrollbar with your mouse and see the results on the screen. Figure 21.4 shows the applet when it first starts up.

Listing 21.1   ScrollbarApplet.java: An Applet That Uses a Scrollbar.

```
import java.awt.*;
import java.applet.*;

public class ScrollbarApplet extends Applet
{
```

continues

Listing 21.1 Continued

```
Scrollbar scrollbar;
String s;

public void init()
{
    BorderLayout layout = new BorderLayout();
    setLayout(layout);

    scrollbar = new Scrollbar(Scrollbar.HORIZONTAL,
        50, 0, 1, 100);
    add("North", scrollbar);

    s = "50";
    Font font = new Font("TimesRoman", Font.BOLD, 72);
    setFont(font);
    resize(200, 200);
}

public void paint(Graphics g)
{
    g.drawString(s, 60, 120);
}

public boolean handleEvent(Event evt)
{
    if (evt.target instanceof Scrollbar)
    {
        scrollbar = (Scrollbar)evt.target;
        int value = scrollbar.getValue();
        s = String.valueOf(value);
        repaint();
        return true;
    }
    else
    {
        boolean result = super.handleEvent(evt);
        return result;
    }
}
}
```

Tell Java that the applet uses the classes in the awt package.
Tell Java that the applet uses the classes in the applet package.
Derive the ScrollbarApplet class from Java's Applet class.
   Declare the scrollbar and display string.
   Override the init() method.
      Create and set the layout.
      Create and add the scrollbar.
      Initialize the display string, the font, and the applet size.

Override the `paint()` method.
Draw the display string.
Override the `handleEvent()` method.
If the toolbar caused the event...
Cast the target object to a scrollbar.
Get the scrollbar's current setting.
Convert the setting to a string.
Force Java to redraw the applet's display area.
Tell Java that the event was handled.
Else if this is not a scrollbar event...
Send the event on to the superclass's `handleEvent()`.
Return the result.

Figure 21.4

This is
ScrollbarApplet
running under
Appletviewer.

There are two things that you should be sure to notice in ScrollbarApplet. First, notice that the scrollbar isn't just added to the applet. It is, instead, added to the applet after the applet's layout manager has been set. This is because the size of the control bar is dependent upon the active layout manager and how the control is added to the manager. (For more information on layout managers, see Chapter 22, "Panels and the Layout Manager." By creating a BorderLayout manager and adding the horizontal scrollbar to the "North" position, you get a scrollbar the stretches across the top of the applet. Failure to place the scrollbar properly in an appropriate layout manager will result in a useless scrollbar like the one shown in Figure 21.5.

Figure 21.5

The scrollbar in
this applet was not
placed properly in
an appropriate
layout manager.

Canvases

Canvases are nothing more than areas on which you can draw. You can combine canvases with other types of components, such as buttons, in order to build layouts that that are attractive, as well as functional. The first step in creating a canvas is to call the Canvas class's constructor, like this:

```
Canvas canvas = new Canvas();
```

The Canvas constructor requires no arguments.

Once you have the canvas created, you add it to your layout just as you would any other component, by calling the add() method:

```
add(canvas);
```

Example: Using a Canvas in an Applet

To end this chapter, take a look at Listing 21.2, which is an applet that creates a canvas class and uses the class to display a colored area on the screen. When you run the applet with Appletviewer, you see the window shown in Figure 21.6. The applet displays two components: a button at the top of the applet and a canvas below the button. When you click the button, the canvas changes color.

Note: Often, you'll want to derive your own custom canvas class from Java's Canvas class. Then, you can more easily control what's drawn in the canvas, by overriding the canvas's paint() method. This is the approach that's used in the CanvasApplet applet.

Listing 21.2   CanvasApplet.java: An Applet That Displays a Canvas.

```
import java.awt.*;
import java.applet.*;

public class CanvasApplet extends Applet
{
    CustomCanvas canvas;

    public void init()
    {
        setLayout(new BorderLayout());

        Button button = new Button("Color");
        add("North", button);

        canvas = new CustomCanvas();
        add("Center", canvas);
```

```
        resize(200, 250);
    }

    public boolean action(Event evt, Object arg)
    {
        if (arg == "Color")
            canvas.swapColor();

        return true;
    }
}

class CustomCanvas extends Canvas
{
    Color color;

    public CustomCanvas()
    {
        color = Color.black;
    }

    public void paint(Graphics g)
    {
        Rectangle r = bounds();
        g.setColor(color);
        g.fillRect(0, 0, r.width, r.height);
        g.setColor(Color.white);
        g.drawString("CANVAS", 72, 90);
    }

    public void swapColor()
    {
        if (color == Color.black)
            color = Color.red;
        else if (color == Color.red)
            color = Color.green;
        else
            color = Color.black;

        repaint();
    }
}
```

Tell Java that the applet uses the classes in the awt *package.*
Tell Java that the applet uses the classes in the applet *package.*
Derive the CanvasApplet *class from Java's* Applet *class.*
   Declare the custom canvas object.
   Override the init() *method.*
     Create and set the layout.
     Create and add the button.
     Create and add the canvas.
     Size the applet.

Override the `action()` method.
 if the "Color" button was pressed...
  Tell the canvas to change color.
 Tell Java that the event was handled.
Define the `CustomCanvas` class.
 Declare the class's single data field.
 Declare the class's constructor.
  Set the initial canvas color.
 Override the `paint()` method.
  Get the canvas's size.
  Set the currently selected color.
  Fill the canvas with the selected color.
  Set the color for the text.
  Display the text string.
 Define the `swapColor()` method.
  Set color to the next color.
  Repaint the canvas with the new color.

Figure 21.6

This is
CanvasApplet
running under
Appletviewer.

Summary

Most often, you see scrollbars being used to manipulate such controls as scrolling
lists and text areas. However, scrollbars also enable you to create a reasonable
facsimile of a Windows 95 slider control, which enables the user to select a value
from a given range. Remember that you need to use the appropriate layout manager
in order for the scrollbar to be drawn properly. Unlike scrollbars, canvases aren't
usually used to obtain input from the user (although they do generate some types
of event messages). Instead, canvases enable you to create graphical areas in your
applets.

Review Questions

1. What are the Scrollbar constructor's five arguments?

2. What is a canvas?

3. What arguments are expected by the Canvas class's constructor?

4. With a scrollbar, when would you use a page size of zero?

5. What's the easiest way to respond to a scrollbar change?

6. What are the five event messages that are generated by a scrollbar?

7. How can you create a custom canvas component?

8. How do you draw in a custom canvas?

Review Exercises

1. Write an applet that displays a vertical scrollbar.

2. Write an applet that displays a scrollbar along with three buttons. Clicking the buttons should set the scrollbar's values to its minimum, middle, and maximum values. (Hint: You can set the scrollbar's value with its setValue() method.)

3. Modify CanvasApplet so that the display includes, besides the canvas, three buttons labeled "Black," "Green," and "Red." Clicking a button should change the canvas to the appropriate color. You'll probably want to use a GridLayout object for this applet's layout manager. (For more information on using a GridLayout object, see Chapter 22, "Panels and the Layout Manager." Figure 21.7 shows the resultant applet. (You can find the solution to this exercise in the CHAP21 folder of this book's CD-ROM. It's called CanvasApplet2.)

Figure 21.7

This is CanvasApplet2 running under Appletviewer.

CHAPTER 22

Panels and Layout Managers

Up until the previous chapter, when you've added controls to your applets, you've let Java place those controls wherever it felt like it. The only way you could control positioning was by changing the size of the applet. Obviously, if you're going to produce attractive applets that are organized logically, you need some way to tell Java exactly where you want things placed. Java's layout managers were created for exactly this purpose. Working in conjunction with layout managers are components called panels, which enable you to organize other applet components. In this chapter, you learn about these two important layout components.

Panels

A panel is a special type of container object that acts as a parent to other components that you want to organize in your applet. For example, you can add several panels to an applet, each with their own layout. By using panels in this way, you can create many different creative displays. Creating a panel is as easy as calling the `Panel` class's constructor, like this:

```
Panel panel = new Panel();
```

As you can see, the `Panel` class's constructor requires no arguments.

Once you create a panel, you add it to the applet in the normal way, by calling the `add()` method:

```
add(panel);
```

Example: Creating and Using Panels

Using panels can be a little confusing at first, so an example is in order. Suppose you need to create an applet that displays four buttons, but you don't want Java to place the buttons one after the other in the display, which Java will do with its default layout. Instead, you want the buttons displayed in two rows of two. One way to accomplish this feat is to add two panels to the applet and then add two buttons to each panel. Listing 22.1 shows how this is done, whereas Figure 22.1 shows what the display looks like.

Listing 22.1   PanelApplet.java: Using Panels.

```java
import java.awt.*;
import java.applet.*;

public class PanelApplet extends Applet
{
    Panel panel1, panel2;
    Button button1, button2, button3, button4;

    public void init()
    {
        panel1 = new Panel();
        panel2 = new Panel();

        add(panel1);
        add(panel2);

        button1 = new Button("Button1");
        button2 = new Button("Button2");
        button3 = new Button("Button3");
        button4 = new Button("Button4");

        panel1.add(button1);
        panel1.add(button2);
        panel2.add(button3);
        panel2.add(button4);
    }
}
```

Tell Java that the applet uses the classes in the awt *package.*
Tell Java that the applet uses the classes in the applet *package.*
Derive the PanelApplet *class from Java's* Applet *class.*
  Declare the panel and button objects.
  Override the init() *method.*
    Create the panels.
    Add the panels to the applet.
    Create the four buttons.
    Add the buttons to the panels.

Figure 22.1

Using panels,
you can more
easily organize
components in an
applet.

Notice how, when adding the panels to the applet, the program calls the `PanelApplet` class's `add()` method (which adds the panels to the applet's display). However, when adding the buttons, the program calls the panel objects' `add()` method (which adds the buttons to the panels). This is how you build a hierarchy of components into your applets. In this case, you've got a stack of components three high, with the applet's display on the bottom, the two panels on top of that, and the four buttons on top of the panels. As you create more sophisticated applets, this type of component stacking will be more common.

Panels are kind of a "plain vanilla" container for organizing components in an applet. As you'll discover in the next section, you can combine panels with layout managers to create truly complex displays.

Layout Managers

Layout Managers are special objects that determine how elements of your applet are organized in the applet's display. When you create an applet, Java automatically creates and assigns a default layout manager. In many of the applets you've created so far in this book, it's the default layout manager that's determined where your controls appear. You can, however, create different types of layout managers in order to better control how your applets look. The layout managers you can use are listed below:

- ◆ FlowLayout
- ◆ GridLayout
- ◆ BorderLayout
- ◆ CardLayout
- ◆ GridBagLayout

Each of these layout managers is represented by a class of the same name. To create a layout manager for your applet, you first create an instance of the appropriate layout class and then call the setLayout() method to tell Java which layout object you want to use. In the following sections, you get a chance to see the various layout managers in action.

The *FlowLayout* Manager

In the previous section, I mentioned that, when you create an applet, Java assigns to it a default layout manager. It just so happens that this default manager is an object of the FlowLayout class. The FlowLayout manager places controls, in the order in which they're added, one after the other in horizontal rows. When the layout manager reaches the right border of the applet, it begins placing controls on the next row. In its default state, the FlowLayout manager centers controls on each row. However, you can set the alignment when you create the layout manager for your applet, like this:

```
FlowLayout layout = new FlowLayout(align, hor, ver);
SetLayout(layout);
```

The FlowLayout constructor takes three arguments, which are the alignment (FlowLayout.LEFT, FlowLayout.CENTER, or FlowLayout.RIGHT), the horizontal spacing between components, and the vertical spacing.

Example: Creating a *FlowLayout* Manager

Suppose that you want to arrange three buttons in an applet using a FlowLayout manager set to left alignment. Listing 22.2 shows how you'd create the manager and the buttons for the applet. Figure 22.2 shows the resultant control layout. Figures 22.3, and 22.4 show the center and right alignments for the same controls.

Listing 22.2   LST22_2.TXT: Creating a *FlowLayout* Manager.

```
FlowLayout layout =
    new FlowLayout(FlowLayout.LEFT, 10, 10);
setLayout(layout);
button1 = new Button("Button1");
button2 = new Button("Button2");
button3 = new Button("Button3");
add(button1);
add(button2);
add(button3);
```

Figure 22.2

These buttons are left aligned by the `FlowLayout` manager.

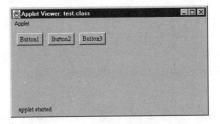

Figure 22.3

These buttons are center aligned by the `FlowLayout` manager.

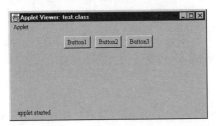

Figure 22.4

These buttons are right aligned by the `FlowLayout` manager.

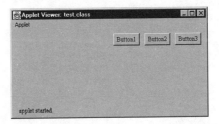

Note: The `FlowLayout()` constructor shown in this chapter takes four arguments. However, you can actually construct a `FlowLayout` object with no arguments, `FlowLayout()`, or with a single argument for the alignment, `FlowLayout(FlowLayout.LEFT)`. Many of Java's classes have multiple constructors.

The *GridLayout* Manager

Once you start creating more sophisticated applets, you'll quickly discover that the `FlowLayout` manager may not give you the control you need to create the kind of display you want for your applet. When you need more control over the placement of components, you can try out the `GridLayout` manager.

Java's `GridLayout` manager organizes your applet's display into a rectangular grid, similar to the grid used in a spreadsheet. Java then places the components you create for the applet into each cell of the grid, working from left to right and top to bottom. You create a `GridLayout` manager like this:

```
GridLayout layout = new GridLayout(rows, cols, hor, ver);
SetLayout(layout);
```

The constructor's four arguments are the number of rows in the grid, the number of columns, and the horizontal and vertical space between the grid cells.

Creating a *GridLayout* Manager

To test the GridLayout manager, suppose you want to place four buttons into a 2×2 grid, with no space between the buttons. Listing 22.3 shows how you'd create the manager and the buttons for the applet. Figure 22.5 shows the resultant control layout. Figure 22.6 shows the same layout manager, except created with horizontal and vertical spacing of 10, and Figure 22.7 shows the layout with a single row of four cells.

Listing 22.3 LST22_3.TXT: Creating a *GridLayout* Manager.

```
GridLayout layout =
    new GridLayout(2, 2, 0, 0);
setLayout(layout);
button1 = new Button("Button1");
button2 = new Button("Button2");
button3 = new Button("Button3");
button4 = new Button("Button4");
add(button1);
add(button2);
add(button3);
add(button4);
```

Figure 22.5

This GridLayout manager is set to two rows and two columns.

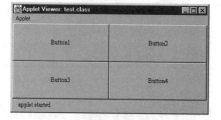

Figure 22.6

This is the same GridLayout manager with horizontal and vertical spacing.

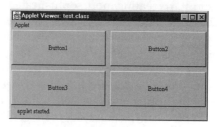

Figure 22.7

This GridLayout
manager has one
row and four
columns.

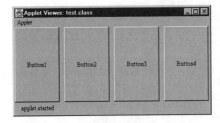

The *BorderLayout* Manager

You'll probably use the GridLayout manager most of the time, but there may be cases where you need to put together something a little more unusual. One layout you can try is provided by the BorderLayout manager, which enables you to position components using the directions north, south, east, west, and center. You create a BorderLayout manager object like this:

```
BorderLayout layout = new BorderLayout(hor, ver);
setLayout(layout);
```

This constructor's two arguments are the horizontal and vertical spacing between the cells in the layout.

After you create the BorderLayout object, you must add the components using a different version of the add() method:

```
add(position, object);
```

Here, position is where to place the component and must be the string North, South, East, West, or Center. The second argument, object, is the component you want to add to the applet.

Creating a *BorderLayout* Manager

Suppose you have five buttons that you want to place in the five areas supported by a BorderLayout manager. First, you create and set the manager. Then, you create the five buttons and add them to the applet, using the special version of add() that includes the object's position as the first argument. Listing 22.4 shows how this is done. Figure 22.8 shows the resultant display, whereas Figure 22.9 shows the same applet with the BorderLayout manager with horizontal and vertical spacing.

Listing 22.4   LST22_4.TXT: Creating a *BorderLayout* Manager.

```
BorderLayout layout = new BorderLayout(0, 0);
setLayout(layout);
button1 = new Button("Button1");
```

continues

Listing 22.4 Continued

```
button2 = new Button("Button2");
button3 = new Button("Button3");
button4 = new Button("Button4");
button5 = new Button("Button5");
add("North", button1);
add("South", button2);
add("East", button3);
add("West", button4);
add("Center", button5);
```

Figure 22.8

This applet displays five buttons using a `BorderLayout` manager.

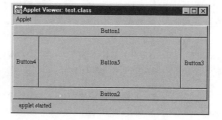

Figure 22.9

This is the same applet with horizontal and vertical spacing.

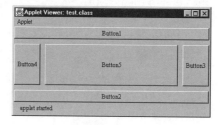

The *CardLayout* Manager

One of the most complex layout managers is CardLayout. Using this manager, you can create a stack of layouts not unlike a stack of cards and then flip from one layout to another. This type of display organization is not unlike Windows 95's tabbed dialogs, usually called property sheets. To create a layout with the CardLayout manager, you first create a parent panel to hold the "cards." Then, you create the CardLayout object and set it as the panel's layout manager. Finally, you add each "card" to the layout by creating the components and adding them to the panel.

To create a CardLayout manager, call its constructor and then add it to the applet, like this:

```
CardLayout cardLayout = new CardLayout(hor, ver);
panel.setLayout(cardLayout);
```

The constructor's two arguments are the horizontal and vertical spacing.

The *CardLayout* Manager Methods

Because the CardLayout manager enables you to switch between a stack of layouts, you need some way to tell the manager what to do. For this reason, the CardLayout manager has a number of public methods that you can call to specify which card is visible on the screen. Table 22.1 lists the most useful of these methods along with their descriptions.

Table 22.1 *CardLayout* Manager Methods.

Method	Description
first(Container parent)	Displays the first card.
last(Container parent)	Displays the last card.
next(Container parent)	Displays the next card.
previous(Container parent)	Displays the previous card.
show(Container parent, String name)	Displays the specified card.

Example: Creating a *CardLayout* Manager

Putting the CardLayout manager to work is a lot easier if you always keep in mind the hierarchy of components. At the bottom of the stack is the applet's display area. On top of this stack is the component (usually a panel) that will hold the "cards." On top of the parent component is the CardLayout manager, which you can think of as a deck of cards. The cards in this deck are the components that you add to the panel.

Listing 22.5 is an applet that demonstrates how all this works. The cards in this applet are the three buttons. When you run the applet, you see a single button in the display (Figure 22.10). Click the button to switch to the next button in the stack. When you get to button three and click it, you end up back at button one. You can cycle through the buttons as often as you like.

Listing 22.5 CardApplet.java: Using a *CardLayout* Manager.

```
import java.awt.*;
import java.applet.*;

public class CardApplet extends Applet
{
    CardLayout cardLayout;
    Panel panel;
```

continues

Listing 22.5 Continued

```java
    Button button1, button2, button3;

    public void init()
    {
        panel = new Panel();
        add(panel);

        cardLayout = new CardLayout(0, 0);
        panel.setLayout(cardLayout);

        button1 = new Button("Button1");
        button2 = new Button("Button2");
        button3 = new Button("Button3");

        panel.add("Button1", button1);
        panel.add("Button2", button2);
        panel.add("Button3", button3);
    }

    public boolean action(Event evt, Object arg)
    {
        cardLayout.next(panel);
        return true;
    }
}
```

Tell Java that the applet uses the classes in the awt *package.*
Tell Java that the applet uses the classes in the applet *package.*
Derive the CardApplet *class from Java's* Applet *class.*
  Declare the layout, panel, and button objects.
  Override the init() *method.*
    Create and add the parent panel.
    Create and set the layout.
    Create the buttons (which act as the cards).
    Add the buttons to the panel.
  Override the action() *method.*
    Switch to the next card (button).
    Tell Java that the event was handled okay.

Figure 22.10

Clicking the button switches the manager to a new card.

> **Note:** The stack of cards that are arranged by a `CardLayout` manager can be any
> type of component. For example, you can create several different panels, each
> with their own controls, and switch between the panels. This enables you to switch
> between whole sets of controls, just like Windows 95's property sheets.

The *GridBagLayout* Manager

The most complex of the layout managers is `GridBagLayout`, which pretty much lets
you organize objects any way you like. However, the price for this power is
meticulous planning and a lot of experimentation. At the time of this writing, the
documentation for the `GridBagLayout` manager was sketchy and incomplete. I did
the best I could to figure out exactly how this layout manager worked, but there's
no question that to get the best out of `GridBagLayout`, you're going to have to spend
some time experimenting with different layouts.

To create a layout using `GridBagLayout`, you must follow these steps:

1. Create a `GridBagLayout` object.

2. Set the layout manager.

3. Create a `GridBagConstraints` object.

4. Initialize and set the constraints for the object about to be added to the
layout.

5. Add the object to the layout.

6. Repeat steps 4 and 5 for each object you're adding to the layout.

Yep, there's much to be done to use a `GridBagLayout` manager. In the sections that
follow, you'll learn how to perform each of the required steps.

Creating and Setting the *GridBagLayout* Manager

To create a `GridBagLayout` manager, call the class's constructor, like this:

```
GridBagLayout layout = new GridBagLayout();
```

The constructor requires no arguments. When you've created the `GridBagLayout()`
object, set the manager by calling `setLayout()`:

```
setLayout(layout);
```

This method's single argument is a reference to the layout object.

Creating and Setting a *GridBagConstraints* Object

Because the position of each component in a layout controlled by a GridBagLayout object is determined by the currently set GridBagConstraints object, you must create the GridBagConstraints object before you can start building your layout. To do this, call the class's constructor:

```
GridBagConstraints constraints = new GridBagConstraints();
```

Like the GridBagLayout class, the GridBagConstraints constructor requires no arguments. However, although the class's fields start off initialized to default values, you'll almost always change some of those values before adding components to the layout. You perform this task with lines something like this:

```
constraints.fill = GridBagConstraints.BOTH;
```

This line sets the GridBagConstraints object's fill field to a constant defined in the class. Table 22.2 shows the fields of the GridBagConstraints class and what they mean.

Table 22.2   Fields of the *GridBagConstraints* Class.

Field	Description
anchor	Where within a component's area the component should be placed. Predefined values are GridBagConstraints.NORTH, GridBagConstraints.NORTHEAST, GridBagConstraints.EAST, GridBagConstraints.SOUTHEAST, GridBagConstraints.SOUTH, GridBagConstraints.SOUTHWEST, GridBagConstraints.WEST, GridBagConstraints.NORTHWEST, and GridBagConstraints.CENTER.
fill	Determines how to size a component when the display area is larger than the component. Predefined values you can use are GridBagConstraint.NONE, GridBagConstraint.HORIZONTAL, GridBagConstraint.VERTICAL, and GridBagConstraint.BOTH.
gridheight	The number of cells in each column of a component's display area.
gridwidth	The number of cells in each row of a component's display area.
gridx	The X coordinate of the cell at the upper left of a component's display area.
gridy	The Y coordinate of the cell at the upper left of the component's display area.

Field	Description
insets	The minimum amount of space between a component and the edges of its display area.
ipadx	The amount of horizontal space around a component.
ipady	The amount of vertical space around a component.
weightx	Determines whether components stretch horizontally to fill the applet's display area.
weighty	Determines whether components stretch vertically to fill the applet's display area.

Once you have the `GridBagConstraints` object created and initialized, you must set the constraints by calling the layout object's `setConstraints()` method:

```
layout.setConstraints(component, constraints);
```

This method's two arguments are a reference to the component whose constraints you're setting and a reference to the constraints object. You need to call `setConstraints()` for each component you add to the layout. After setting the constraints for the component, you add the component to the layout in the normal way, by calling the `add()` method.

Example: Using a *GridBagLayout* Manager in an Applet

As I said before, the only way to really understand how the `GridBagLayout` manager works is to experiment with it on your own. This book just doesn't have the room to cover every detail of using this complex manager. Still, I won't send you off without at least the basics. So, Listing 22.6 is an applet, called GridBagApplet, that demonstrates how to create and use a `GridBagLayout` manager. Figure 22.11 shows what the applet looks like when it's run under Appletviewer.

Listing 22.6   GridBagApplet.java: A *GridBagLayout* Applet.

```
import java.awt.*;
import java.applet.*;

public class GridBagApplet extends Applet
{
    public void init()
```

continues

```
{
        GridBagLayout layout = new GridBagLayout();
        setLayout(layout);

        GridBagConstraints constraints = new GridBagConstraints();

        Button button1 = new Button("Button1");
        Button button2 = new Button("Button2");
        Button button3 = new Button("Button3");
        Button button4 = new Button("Button4");
        Button button5 = new Button("Button5");
        Button button6 = new Button("Button6");
        Button button7 = new Button("Button7");
        Button button8 = new Button("Button8");
        Button button9 = new Button("Button9");

        constraints.fill = GridBagConstraints.BOTH;

        layout.setConstraints(button1, constraints);
        add(button1);

        constraints.gridwidth = GridBagConstraints.RELATIVE;
        layout.setConstraints(button2, constraints);
        add(button2);

        constraints.gridwidth = GridBagConstraints.REMAINDER;
        layout.setConstraints(button3, constraints);
        add(button3);

        constraints.gridwidth = GridBagConstraints.REMAINDER;
        layout.setConstraints(button4, constraints);
        add(button4);

        constraints.gridwidth = GridBagConstraints.RELATIVE;
        layout.setConstraints(button5, constraints);
        add(button5);

        constraints.gridwidth = GridBagConstraints.REMAINDER;
        layout.setConstraints(button6, constraints);
        add(button6);

        constraints.gridwidth = 1;
        constraints.gridheight = 2;
        layout.setConstraints(button7, constraints);
        add(button7);

        constraints.gridwidth = GridBagConstraints.REMAINDER;
        constraints.gridheight = 1;
        layout.setConstraints(button8, constraints);
        add(button8);
```

```
        layout.setConstraints(button9, constraints);
        add(button9);

        resize(300, 200);
    }
}
```

Tell Java that the applet uses the classes in the awt *package.*
Tell Java that the applet uses the classes in the applet *package.*
Derive the GridBagApplet *class from Java's* Applet *class.*
 Override the init() *method.*
  Create and set the layout.
  Create the constraints object.
  Create nine buttons.
  Initialize the fill for both vertical and horizontal.
  Set the constraints for the buttons and add the buttons.
  Set the applet's size.

Figure 22.11

GridBagLayout
manager enables
you to create
unusual layouts.

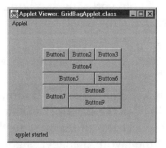

Understanding the *GridBagApplet* Applet

Although GridBagApplet contains only the init() method, there's a lot going on in the program. In this section, you'll see, line by line, exactly how the applet works. The first two lines in the init() method look like this:

```
GridBagLayout layout = new GridBagLayout();
setLayout(layout);
```

This is where the applet creates its GridBagLayout object and sets it as the applet's layout. In the next line, the applet creates its GridBagConstraints object, like this:

```
GridBagConstraints constraints = new GridBagConstraints();
```

The applet will use this single GridBagConstraints object in order to set the constraints for each component added to the layout. Before components can be added, however, they must be created, which the applet does as shown in Listing 22.7.

Listing 22.7 LST22_7.TXT: Creating the Applet's Buttons.

```
Button button1 = new Button("Button1");
Button button2 = new Button("Button2");
Button button3 = new Button("Button3");
Button button4 = new Button("Button4");
Button button5 = new Button("Button5");
Button button6 = new Button("Button6");
Button button7 = new Button("Button7");
Button button8 = new Button("Button8");
Button button9 = new Button("Button9");
```

After creating the buttons, the program can start adding them to the layout. But before the first button gets added, the constraints object must contain the appropriate values. In this case, only the `fill` field must be initialized, since the first button component will use all the other default values:

```
constraints.fill = GridBagConstraints.BOTH;
```

Setting the `fill` field to both ensures that the components (in this case, buttons) will expand both vertically and horizontally to completely fill their display areas. After initializing the constraints for the first button, the applet sets the constraints and adds the button:

```
layout.setConstraints(button1, constraints);
add(button1);
```

Now that you have the first button added, it's time to consider how the second button will fit in the layout. The value the applet initialized the `fill` field to will remain in effect for all buttons, so the applet doesn't need to change it again. However, the layout manager is going to want to know how `button2` should be placed. The following lines set the constraints and add the button:

```
constraints.gridwidth = GridBagConstraints.RELATIVE;
layout.setConstraints(button2, constraints);
add(button2);
```

By setting `gridwidth` to `GridBagConstraints.RELATIVE`, the applet tells the layout manager that this button is the next to the last component in this row, which will determine its width. The `button3` object is the last component for the first row, so it sets `gridwidth` to `GridBagConstraints.REMAINDER`:

```
constraints.gridwidth = GridBagConstraints.REMAINDER;
layout.setConstraints(button3, constraints);
add(button3);
```

The `REMAINDER` constant tells the layout manager that this control should fill the first row all the way to the end.

The `button4` component is the only object on its row, so it too uses a `gridwidth` of `REMAINDER`:

```
constraints.gridwidth = GridBagConstraints.REMAINDER;
layout.setConstraints(button4, constraints);
add(button4);
```

Yes, it's true that the first line above really isn't necessary, since `gridwidth` was already set to `REMAINDER`. However, I like leaving this kind of line around because it tells me that I haven't forgotten something here, that I do indeed want a width of `REMAINDER` for this button too.

Because `button5` is both the first and next-to-last button in its row, it uses a width of `RELATIVE`:

```
constraints.gridwidth = GridBagConstraints.RELATIVE;
layout.setConstraints(button5, constraints);
add(button5);
```

Because there's only two buttons in this row, the `button6` component gets a width of `REMAINDER`:

```
constraints.gridwidth = GridBagConstraints.REMAINDER;
layout.setConstraints(button6, constraints);
add(button6);
```

Now, things get a little tricky (like they weren't tricky enough, right?). If you look at Figure 22.11, you'll see that `button7` is one cell wide but two cells high. Buttons seven and eight, on the other hand are two cells wide but only one cell high. Even though `button7` is technically the next-to-last button in its row, you don't want to give it the `RELATIVE` width because then Java will make the button twice as wide. So, the applet sets the width of `button7` to 1 and the height to 2, as shown in Listing 22.8.

Listing 22.8   LST22_8.TXT: Setting *button7's* size.

```
constraints.gridwidth = 1;
constraints.gridheight = 2;
layout.setConstraints(button7, constraints);
add(button7);
```

Now, because `button8` is the last button in its row, it gets the `REMAINDER` width. However, the button also must be set back to a normal one-cell height, as shown in Listing 22.9.

Listing 22.9   LST22_9.LST: Creating *button8*.

```
constraints.gridwidth = GridBagConstraints.REMAINDER;
constraints.gridheight = 1;
layout.setConstraints(button8, constraints);
add(button8);
```

Finally, `button9` can use exactly the same restraints, which means simply setting the constraints and adding the button, like this:

```
layout.setConstraints(button9, constraints);
add(button9);
```

All of the lines described in this section work together to create the applet's layout. Every layout will work differently, requiring that you carefully plan ahead how you want the applet's components laid out. There's almost an infinite number of ways to use the constraints along with the `GridBagLayout` manager.

You may wonder how changes to this example layout will affect the appearance of the applet. Suppose, for example, you left the `fill` field set to its default value of `GridBagConstraints.NONE`. You would then end up with a layout like that shown in Figure 22.12. Figure 22.13 shows the applet with a `fill` setting of `GridBagConstraints.VERTICAL`.

Figure 22.12

The fill setting can make a huge difference in how a layout looks.

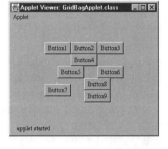

Figure 22.13

The vertical fill stretches sone controls vertically.

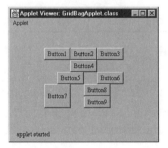

Another change you might make is to set `weightx` and `weighty`, which tells Java how to use the extra space that usually surrounds the controls in the layout. For example, in `GridBagApplet`, if you set `weightx` to 1, you get a display like Figure 22.14, because you've told Java that you want the layout to fill the entire horizontal space in the applet. Setting `weighty` stretches the layout in the vertical direction, as shown in Figure 22.15, which has both `weightx` and `weighty` set.

Figure 22.14

Setting the weightx field stretches the layout horizontally.

Figure 22.15

Setting both weightx and weighty stretches the layout in both directions.

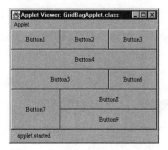

Summary

Java gives you many options when it comes to creating a layout for the components that make up your applet. However, having so many possibilities at your fingertips can be daunting at first, because there may be several ways to get the effect that you want. The better you learn to use Java's layout managers, the more easily you'll know which is the appropriate manager for a specific situation. Mastering the GridBagLayout manager especially requires time and patience.

Review Questions

1. Why would you add multiple Panel objects to an applet?

2. What are the names of Java's five layout managers?

3. Which layout manager is the default manager for an applet?

4. How does the FlowLayout manager organize components?

5. What are the arguments for the GridLayout manager's constructor?

6. What component positions can use with a BorderLayout manager?

7. How do you add a component to an applet that uses the `BorderLayout` manager?

8. How does the `CardLayout` manager enable you to mimic Windows 95's property sheets?

9. How do you switch from one card to another when using a `CardLayout` manager?

10. How does a `GridBagConstraints` object work in conjunction with a `GridBagLayout` manager?

11. What does the `GridBagConstraints.fill` field control?

12. How do you add a component to a layout controlled by a `GridBagLayout` manager?

Review Exercises

1. Write an applet that uses a `FlowLayout` manager to display a button on the left side of the applet.

2. Write an applet that displays nine buttons in a 3×3 grid.

3. Write an applet that uses a `BorderLayout` object to display a single button at the bottom of the applet.

4. Write an applet that uses two panels to group two sets of three buttons.

5. Write an applet called CardApplet2 that contains three pages of controls. The first page should contain three buttons, the second page should contain a scrolling list, and the third page should contain a `TextField` control. Clicking on any control should cause the applet to switch to the next page (except for the `TextField` control, which only sends an event when you press Enter). Figure 22.16 shows what CardApplet2 looks like when its scrolling list card is visible. (You can find the solution to this exercise in the CHAP22 folder of this book's CD-ROM.)

6. Write an applet called GridBagApplet2 that displays three rows of buttons. The first row should contain two buttons, with the first button twice as wide as the second. The second row should contain two buttons, with the second button twice as wide as the first. The third row should contain three normal-width buttons. Figure 22.17 shows the completed applet running under Appletviewer. (You can find the solution for this exercise in the CHAP22 folder of this book's CD-ROM.)

Figure 22.16

This is the second page of the CardApplet2 applet.

Figure 22.17

This is GridBagApplet2 running under Appletviewer.

CHAPTER 23

Windows and Menu Bars

So far in this book, when you created and displayed an applet, you had a single window on the screen. This window was either Appletviewer or the browser you were using to display the applet. However, applets can create additional windows. Although you probably won't use this feature a lot, it's nice to know it's around in case you need it. Moreover, when you create a window in Java, you can add a full-featured menu bar that can contain commands, checked options, and separator objects. In this chapter, you learn to display windows and their menu bars, as well as how to respond to menu commands.

Displaying a Window

Java's libraries include a class called Frame that represents a frame window that you can create and display from within an application. To create a frame window, you call the Frame class's constructor, like this:

```
Frame frame = new Frame("Frame Window");
```

This constructor's single argument is the window's title, which will appear in the window's title bar.

When you have the window created, you can display it by calling the window's show() method. To remove the window from the screen, you call the hide() method. You can even size the window by calling resize() or position the window by calling move().

Example: Displaying a Window in an Applet

To demonstrate the basics of using the Frame class, Listing 23.1 is the source code for an applet that can display a frame window. When you click the applet's button, the applet displays a frame window. When you click the button a second time, the applet removes the window from the screen. Figure 23.1 shows the applet and its frame window. Notice that, when the button is clicked, the button's label switches between "Show Window" and "Hide Window."

Listing 23.1   FrameApplet.java: Displaying a Frame Window.

```java
import java.awt.*;
import java.applet.*;

public class FrameApplet extends Applet
{
    Frame frame;
    Button button;

    public void init()
    {
        frame = new Frame("Frame Window");
        button = new Button("Show Window");
        add(button);
    }

    public boolean action(Event evt, Object arg)
    {
        boolean visible = frame.isShowing();
        if (visible)
        {
            frame.hide();
            button.setLabel("Show Window");
        }
        else
        {
            frame.show();
            frame.resize(200, 100);
            button.setLabel("Hide Window");
        }

        return true;
    }
}
```

Tell Java that the applet uses the classes in the awt package.
Tell Java that the applet uses the classes in the applet package.
Derive the FrameApplet class from Java's Applet class.
  Declare the frame-window and button objects.
  Override the init( ) method.

Create the frame window.
Create the button component.
Add the button to the applet.
Override the action( ) *method.*
Determine whether the window is visible.
If the window is visible...
Hide the window.
Change the button's label to "Show Window."
Else if the window is hidden...
Show the window.
Set the window's size.
Change the button's label to "Hide Window."
Tell Java that the message was handled okay.

Figure 23.1

Your Java applets
can display
additional
windows.

Example: Creating a Window Class

When you decide that your applet needs to display a frame window, you're usually better off creating a special class for the window. That way, you have complete control over how the window is constructed and displayed. To create a custom window class, you simply derive your window class from Java's Frame class. Listing 23.2 is a rewritten version of FrameApplet, called FrameApplet2, that gives the frame window its own class. This new frame window also takes advantage of having its own class by overriding the paint( ) method in order to display text in the window. Figure 23.2 shows FrameApplet2 running under Appletviewer.

Listing 23.2   FrameApplet2.java: Creating a Frame-Window Class.

```
import java.awt.*;
import java.applet.*;

public class FrameApplet2 extends Applet
{
    CustomFrame frame;
```

continues

Listing 23.2   Continued

```
  Button button;

    public void init()
    {
        frame = new CustomFrame("Custom Frame Window");
        button = new Button("Show Window");
        add(button);
    }

    public boolean action(Event evt, Object arg)
    {
        boolean visible = frame.isShowing();
        if (visible)
        {
            frame.hide();
            button.setLabel("Show Window");
        }
        else
        {
            frame.show();
            button.setLabel("Hide Window");
        }

        return true;
    }
}

class CustomFrame extends Frame
{
    CustomFrame(String title)
    {
        super(title);
    }

    public void paint(Graphics g)
    {
        resize(200, 100);
        g.drawString("This is a custom window.", 30, 30);
    }
}
```

Tell Java that the applet uses the classes in the awt *package.*
Tell Java that the applet uses the classes in the applet *package.*
Derive the FrameApplet2 *class from Java's* Applet *class.*
  Declare the custom frame-window and button objects.
  Override the init( ) *method.*
    Create the custom frame window.
    Create the button component.
    Add the button to the applet.

Override the action( ) method.
   Determine whether the window is visible.
   If the window is visible...
      Hide the window.
      Change the button's label to "Show Window."
   Else if the window is hidden...
      Show the window.
      Change the button's label to "Hide Window."
   Tell Java that the message was handled okay.
Derive the CustomFrame class from Java's Frame class.
   Define the class's constructor.
      Pass the title string on to the Frame class.
   Override the window's paint( ) method.
      Resize the window.
      Display a message in the window.

Figure 23.2

This is FrameApplet2 running under Appletviewer.

Note: When you compile FrameApplet2, notice that, although both the FrameApplet2 and CustomFrame classes are defined in the same file, the Java compiler creates two class files called FrameApplet2.class and CustomFrame.class.

Example: Adding Components to a Window

Frame windows are just like any other window you see when you create an applet. That is, you can add components organized into a variety of layouts and respond to the user's selections of these components. In fact, adding layouts and components to a frame window is not unlike doing the same thing with your applet's main window, which you did in the previous chapter. First you create and set the layout manager, and then you add the components as appropriate for the layout manager you've chosen.

Listing 23.3 is an applet called FrameApplet3 that not only creates a custom frame window, but also creates a simple layout for the window. This layout contains only a single button; however, you can create as sophisticated a layout as you like. Feel free to experiment further with this applet. Figure 23.3 shows FrameApplet3 running under Appletviewer, after the user has displayed the frame window. As you can see in the figure, the window has a single button labeled "Close Window." When you click this button, the frame window's `action()` method responds by calling the `dispose()` method, which not only removes the window from the screen, but also destroys the window in memory.

Listing 23.3   FrameApplet3.java: Adding Components to a Window.

```java
import java.awt.*;
import java.applet.*;

public class FrameApplet3 extends Applet
{
    CustomFrame frame;
    Button button;

    public void init()
    {
        frame = new CustomFrame("Custom Frame Window");

        button = new Button("Show Window");
        add(button);
    }

    public boolean action(Event evt, Object arg)
    {
        boolean visible = frame.isShowing();
        if (visible)
        {
            frame.hide();
            button.setLabel("Show Window");
        }
        else
        {
            frame.show();
            button.setLabel("Hide Window");
        }

        return true;
    }
}

class CustomFrame extends Frame
{
    Button button;
```

```
CustomFrame(String title)
    {
        super(title);

        FlowLayout layout = new FlowLayout();
        setLayout(layout);

        button = new Button("Close Window");
        add(button);
    }

    public void paint(Graphics g)
    {
        resize(200, 100);
        g.drawString("This is a custom window.", 30, 50);
    }

    public boolean action(Event evt, Object arg)
    {
        if (arg == "Close Window")
            dispose();

        return true;
    }
}
```

Figure 23.3

This is
FrameApplet3
running under
Appletviewer.

Table 23.1 shows some useful methods you can use to manipulate a frame window. Some of these methods are defined in the Frame class, whereas others are inherited from the class's superclasses, such as Window and Container.

Table 23.1   Useful Frame-Window Methods.

Methods	*Description*
void add( )	Adds components to the window.
void dispose( )	Deletes the window from memory.

continues

305

Table 23.1   Continued

Methods	Description
int getCursorType( )	Returns the window's cursor type.
Image getIconImage( )	Returns the window's icon object.
LayoutManager getLayout( )	Returns the window's layout manager.
MenuBar getMenuBar( )	Returns the window's menu bar object.
String getTitle( )	Returns the window's title.
void hide( )	Removes the window from the screen.
Boolean isResizable( )	Returns true if the window is resizable.
void remove( )	Removes components from the window.
void removeAll( )	Removes all components from the window.
void setCursor(int cursorType)	Sets the window's cursor type.
void setIconImage(Image image)	Sets the window's icon object.
void setLayout( )	Sets the window's layout manager.
void setMenuBar(MenuBar mb)	Sets the window's menu bar.
void setResizable(boolean resizable)	Sets the window's resizable attribute.
void setTitle(String title)	Sets the window's title.
void show( )	Displays the window on the screen.

Using Menu Bars

Most Windows applications have menu bars, which enable the user to more easily locate and select the various commands and options supported by the program. The frame windows you create from within your applets can also have menu bars. To create a menu bar in a window, you must follow a series of steps:

1. Create an object of the MenuBar class.

2. Call the window's setMenuBar( ) method to give the menu bar to the window.

3. Create objects of the `Menu` class for each menu you want in the menu bar.

4. Call the `MenuBar` object's `add()` method to add each menu object to the menu bar.

5. Create objects of the `MenuItem` or `CheckboxMenuItem` classes for each item you want to appear in the menus.

6. Call the menus' `add()` methods in order to add each item to its appropriate menu.

Each of the above steps is covered in the sections that follow.

Creating and Setting a MenuBar Object

The first step in adding a menu bar to a frame window is to create the `MenuBar` object that'll hold all the menus and commands. The menu bar in a window is the horizontal area near the top that contains the names of each of the menus in the menu bar. To create the `MenuBar` object, call the `MenuBar` class's constructor, like this:

```
MenuBar menuBar = new MenuBar( );
```

As you can see, the `MenuBar()` constructor requires no arguments.

After you've created the `MenuBar` object, you have to tell Java to associate the menu bar with the frame window. You do this by calling the window's `setMenuBar()` method:

```
setMenuBar(menuBar);
```

At this point, you have an empty menu bar associated with the window. In the next steps, you add menus to the menu bar.

Adding Menus to a Menu Bar

A menu bar is the horizontal area near the top of a window that contains the names of the menus contained in the menu bar. After creating and setting the `MenuBar` object, you have the menu bar, but it contains no menus. To add these menus, you first create objects of the `Menu` class for each menu you want in the menu bar, like this:

```
Menu fileMenu = new Menu("File");
Menu editMenu = new Menu("Edit");
Menu optionMenu = new Menu("Options");
```

The `Menu` class's constructor takes a single argument, which is the string that'll appear as the menu's name on the menu bar. The example lines above create three menus for the menu bar.

After creating the Menu objects, you have to add them to the menu bar, which you do by calling the MenuBar object's add( ) method, like this:

```
menuBar.add(fileMenu);
menuBar.add(editMenu);
menuBar.add(optionMenu);
```

After Java executes the above three lines, you have a menu bar with three menus, as shown in Figure 23.4. Note, however, that at this point the menus contain no commands. If you were to click on the menu names, no pop-up menus would appear.

Figure 23.4

This window's menu bar contains three empty menus.

Adding Menu Items to Menus

You may have empty menus at this point, but you're about to remedy that problem. To add items to your menus, you first create objects of the MenuItem or CheckboxMenuItem classes for each menu item you need. To add items to the Options menus you made previously, you might use Java code something like this:

```
MenuItem option1 = new MenuItem("Option 1");
MenuItem option2 = new MenuItem("Option 2");
MenuItem option3 = new MenuItem("Option 3");
```

The MenuItem constructor takes as its single argument the string that'll be displayed in the menu for this item.

If you're thinking that, after you create the menu items, you must call the appropriate Menu object's add( ) method, you're be exactly right. Those lines might look like this:

```
optionMenu.add(option1);
optionMenu.add(option2);
optionMenu.add(option3);
```

Now, when you display the frame window sporting the menu bar you've just created, you'll see that the Options menu contains a number of selections from which the user can choose, as shown in Figure 23.5.

Figure 23.5

Now the Options menu contains menu items.

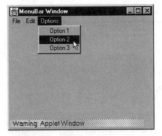

Tip: Sometimes, you may have several groups of related commands that you'd like to place under a single menu. You can separate these command groups by using menu separators, which appear as horizontal lines in a pop-up menu. To create a menu separator, just create a regular `MenuItem` object with a string of "-". That is, the string should contain a single hyphen.

Example: Using a Menu Bar in a Frame Window

Now that you have this menu bar business mastered, it's time to put what you've learned to work. Listing 23.4 is an applet called MenuBarApplet. This applet displays a single button, which, when selected, displays a frame window with a menu bar. This menu bar contains a single menu with three items. The first two items are regular `MenuItem` objects. The third item is `CheckboxMenuItem`, which is a menu item that can display a check mark. Figure 23.6 shows MenuBarApplet with its frame window displayed and the Test menu visible. (Notice the menu separator above the checked item.)

Listing 23.4   MenuBarApplet.java: An Applet That Uses a Menu Bar.

```
import java.awt.*;
import java.applet.*;

public class MenuBarApplet extends Applet
{
    MenuBarFrame frame;
    Button button;

    public void init()
    {
        frame = new MenuBarFrame("MenuBar Window");
```

continues

Listing 23.4 Continued

```java
        button = new Button("Show Window");
        add(button);
    }

    public boolean action(Event evt, Object arg)
    {
        boolean visible = frame.isShowing();
        if (visible)
        {
            frame.hide();
            button.setLabel("Show Window");
        }
        else
        {
            frame.show();
            button.setLabel("Hide Window");
        }

        return true;
    }
}

class MenuBarFrame extends Frame
{
    MenuBar menuBar;
    String str;

    MenuBarFrame(String title)
    {
        super(title);
        menuBar = new MenuBar();
        setMenuBar(menuBar);

        Menu menu = new Menu("Test");
        menuBar.add(menu);

        MenuItem item = new MenuItem("Command 1");
        menu.add(item);
        item = new MenuItem("Command 2");
        menu.add(item);

        item = new MenuItem("-");
        menu.add(item);

        CheckboxMenuItem checkItem =
            new CheckboxMenuItem("Check");
        menu.add(checkItem);

        str = "";
        Font font = new Font("TimesRoman", Font.BOLD, 20);
```

```
setFont(font);
    }

    public void paint(Graphics g)
    {
        resize(300, 250);
        g.drawString(str, 20, 100);
    }

    public boolean action(Event evt, Object arg)
    {
        if (evt.target instanceof MenuItem)
        {
            if (arg == "Command 1")
                str = "You selected Command 1";
            else if (arg == "Command 2")
                str = "You selected Command 2";
            else if (arg == "Check")
                str = "You selected the Check item";

            repaint();
            return true;
        }
        else
            return false;
    }
}
```

Tell Java that the applet uses the classes in the awt *package.*
Tell Java that the applet uses the classes in the applet *package.*
Derive the MenuBarApplet *class from Java's* Applet *class.*
  Declare the custom frame-window and button objects.
  Override the init( ) *method.*
    Create the custom frame window.
    Create and add the button component.
  Override the action( ) *method.*
    Determine whether the window is visible.
    If the window is visible...
      Hide the window.
      Change the button's label to "Show Window."
    Else if the window is hidden...
      Show the window.
      Change the button's label to "Hide Window."
    Tell Java that the message was handled okay.
Derive the MenuBarFrame *class from Java's* Frame *class.*
  Declare the class's menu bar and string objects.
  Define the class's constructor.
    Pass the title string on to the Frame *class.*

Create and set the menu bar.
Create and add the Test menu.
Create and add two regular menu items.
Create and add a menu separator.
Create and add a checkmark menu item.
Initialize the class's display string and font.
Override the window's paint( ) method.
   Resize the window.
   Show the display string in the window.
Override the action( ) method.
  if a menu item was selected...
    Respond to the selected menu.
    Repaint the window, so the new string is displayed.
    Return true if the message was handled.
  Or else return false so Java knows the event is unhandled.

Figure 23.6

This is
MenuBarApplet's
frame window and
menu bar.

> **Note:** To determine the state (checked or unchecked) of a CheckboxMenuItem
> object, you can call its getState( ) method. This method returns true if the item is
> checked and false if the item is unchecked. In addition, you can set the item's
> state by calling its setState( ) method.

As you can see from MenuBarApplet's source code, you respond to menu-item
selections in the same way you respond to other events in applets. This time,
however, you have overridden two action( ) methods. The first is in the MenuBarApplet
class and handles the applet's single button. The second overridden action( )
method, which is the one that handles the menu items, is in the MenuBarFrame class.

Summary

Although it's an ability you may not frequently take advantage of, Java applets can display windows. The `Frame` class makes this possible, by providing the functionality for frame windows, which can be sized, moved, used to display components, and much more. A frame window can, in fact, even have a full-featured menu bar, just like the menu bars you see in many Windows applications. Creating a menu bar, however, requires knowing how to create and manipulate `MenuBar`, `Menu`, `MenuItem`, and `CheckboxMenuItem` objects. Luckily, you learned about those classes in this chapter, so you're all ready to amaze the world with your Java frame windows.

Review Questions

1. How do you create a frame window?

2. How do you display a frame window after you create it?

3. How can you determine whether a frame window is currently visible?

4. What's the difference between `MenuItem` and `CheckboxMenuItem` objects?

5. Which Java class must you extend to create a custom frame-window class?

6. How do you ensure that a custom frame-window class has properly initialized its superclass?

7. How do you draw text or graphics in a frame window?

8. What are the six steps that must be completed in order to add a menu bar to a frame window?

9. How do you add components, such as controls, to a frame window?

10. How do you respond to selected menu items?

11. How do you create a menu separator object?

Review Exercises

1. Write an applet that displays a frame window as soon as the applet runs.

2. Write an applet that displays a frame window containing a 2x2 grid of buttons.

3. Modify the applet you wrote in exercise 2 so that the frame window contains a menu bar with two menus. Each menu should have a single menu item.

4. Modify the MenuBarApplet so that the menu bar has an additional menu called View. This menu should contain a single checkmarked option called Window that determines whether a second frame window is visible on the screen. When the user selects the Window command, the command should be checkmarked and the second window should appear. When the user clicks this command a second time, the second window should disappear and the command should be unchecked. Figure 23.7 shows the resultant applet in action. (You can find the solution to this exercise in the CHAP23 folder of this book's CD-ROM.)

Figure 23.7

This is MenuFrameApplet running under Appletviewer.

CHAPTER 24

Dialog Boxes

In most cases, you'll add controls to your applet's display in order to present information to the user or to obtain information from the user. However, there may be times when you prefer to create a dialog box. For example, when the applet encounters some sort of error, a pop-up dialog box not only supplies the user with important information, but also immediately draws his attention to that information. Although Java supports dialog boxes, they unfortunately can only be associated with a frame window. This requirement limits their usefulness, but you still may want to use a dialog box at one time or another. In this chapter, you'll see how.

Using a Dialog Box

To create, display, and handle a dialog box, you must perform the following steps:

1. Create the dialog box object.

2. Create and set a layout manager for the dialog box.

3. Create controls and add them to the dialog box.

4. Call the dialog's show() method to display the dialog box.

5. When the user clicks the OK or Cancel button, call the dialog's hide() method to remove the dialog box from the screen.

6. Extract and process the data, if any, entered into the dialog box's controls.

The following section discuss the above steps in greater detail.

Creating the Dialog Box

Java's dialog boxes are objects of the Dialog class. So, to create a dialog box object, you first call the Dialog class's constructor, like this:

```
Dialog dialog = new Dialog(frame, title, modal);
```

The constructor's three arguments refer to a frame window, the dialog box's title, and boolean value indicating whether the dialog box is modal (true) or modeless (false). A modal dialog box, which is the most common of the two types, retains the focus until the user dismisses it. This forces the user to respond to the dialog box before continuing with the program. A modeless dialog box can lose the focus to another window, which means that the user can switch to another window even while the dialog box is still on the screen.

> **Note:** Although Java claims to support both modal and modeless dialog boxes, the constructor's argument doesn't seem to make any difference. In my experience, every Java dialog box is modeless. Maybe this inconsistency will be corrected by the time you read this book.

Creating the Dialog Box's Layout

Once you have the dialog box object created, you must give it a layout manager. If you fail to do this, any components you try to place in the dialog box will not appear. You perform this step exactly as you would for any other type of window or applet, by creating and setting the layout object:

```
FlowLayout layout = new FlowLayout();
dialog.setLayout(layout);
```

The next step is to create and add whatever controls you want to appear in the dialog box. You'll always have at least an OK button, with which the user can dismiss the dialog box:

```
Button button = new Button("OK");
dialog.add(button);
```

Displaying the Dialog Box

Just like a frame window, a dialog box doesn't appear on the screen until you call its show() method, like this:

```
dialog.show();
```

Once the dialog box is on the screen, the user can manipulate its controls in order to enter information into the dialog box's fields or to dismiss the dialog box from the screen.

Removing the Dialog Box

When the user clicks a dialog box's OK or Cancel buttons, that's your applet's signal to remove the dialog box from the screen, which you do by calling its `hide()` method:

```
dialog.hide();
```

The `hide()` method removes the dialog box from the screen, but the dialog box and its controls remain in memory so that you can access them in order to extract whatever information the user may have entered into the dialog box.

After you've removed the dialog box from the screen, you can use a control's methods to extract whatever information the user may have entered into the dialog's controls. For example, to get the entry from a text field control, you'd call the control's `getText()` method.

Methods of the Dialog Class

Like any class, `Dialog` provides a set of public methods that you can use to control the dialog box. `Dialog` also inherits many methods from its superclasses, `Window` and `Container`. Table 24.1 lists the most useful methods of the `Dialog` class, including those methods inherited from the `Window` and `Container` classes.

Table 24.1 Useful Methods of the *Dialog* Class (Including Inherited).

Method	*Description*
`Component add(Component comp)`	Adds a component to the dialog box.
`void dispose()`	Removes the dialog box from memory.
`LayoutManager getLayout()`	Returns the dialog's layout manager.
`String getTitle()`	Returns the dialog box's title.
`void hide()`	Removes the dialog box from the screen.
`boolean isModal()`	Returns `true` if the dialog box is modal.
`boolean isResizable()`	Returns `true` if the dialog box is resizable.
`Component locate(int x, int y)`	Returns the component at the given location.

continues

Table 24.1   Continued

Method	Description
`void remove(Component comp)`	Removes a component from the dialog box.
`void removeAll()`	Removes all components.
`void setLayout(LayoutManager mgr)`	Sets the dialog's layout manager.
`void setResizable(boolean resizable)`	Sets the resizable attribute.
`void setTitle(String title)`	Sets the dialog box's title.
`void show()`	Displays the dialog box.

Example: A Dialog Box for Text Input

Your last task in this chapter is to put your newly acquired knowledge of dialog boxes to work. Listing 24.1 is an applet that enables you to display a frame window. From the frame window's menu bar, you can select a command that displays a dialog box. This dialog box contains an OK button for dismissing the dialog box and a text field for entering information. When you dismiss the dialog box, the text you entered into the text field control appears in the frame window. Figure 24.1 shows the applet, the frame window, and the dialog box.

Listing 24.1   DialogApplet.java: An Applet That Displays a Dialog Box.

```
import java.awt.*;
import java.applet.*;

public class DialogApplet extends Applet
{
    DialogFrame frame;
    Button button;

    public void init()
    {
        frame = new DialogFrame("Dialog Window");

        button = new Button("Show Window");
        add(button);
    }
```

```
    public boolean action(Event evt, Object arg)
    {
        boolean visible = frame.isShowing();
        if (visible)
        {
            frame.hide();
            button.setLabel("Show Window");
        }
        else
        {
            frame.show();
            button.setLabel("Hide Window");
        }

        return true;
    }
}

class DialogFrame extends Frame
{
    MenuBar menuBar;
    Dialog dialog;
    TextField textField;
    String str;

    DialogFrame(String title)
    {
        super(title);

        menuBar = new MenuBar();
        setMenuBar(menuBar);
        Menu menu = new Menu("Test");
        menuBar.add(menu);
        MenuItem item = new MenuItem("Dialog box");
        menu.add(item);

        str = "";
    }

    public void paint(Graphics g)
    {
        resize(300, 250);

        g.drawString("THE TEXT YOU ENTERED IS:", 70, 50);
        g.drawString(str, 70, 70);
    }

    public boolean action(Event evt, Object arg)
    {
        if (evt.target instanceof MenuItem)
```

continues

Listing 24.1   Continued

```
{
            if (arg == "Dialog box")
                ShowDialogBox();
        }
        else if (evt.target instanceof Button)
        {
            if (arg == "OK")
            {
                dialog.hide();
                str = textField.getText();
                repaint();
            }
        }

        return true;
    }

    protected void ShowDialogBox()
    {
        dialog = new Dialog(this, "Test Dialog", true);
        FlowLayout layout = new FlowLayout();
        dialog.setLayout(layout);

        textField = new TextField("", 20);
        Button button = new Button("OK");
        dialog.add(button);
        dialog.add(textField);

        dialog.show();
        dialog.resize(200, 100);
    }
}
```

Tell Java that the applet uses the classes in the awt *package.*
Tell Java that the applet uses the classes in the applet *package.*
Derive the DialogApplet *class from Java's* Applet *class.*
　Declare the frame-window and button objects.
　Override the init() *method.*
　　Create the frame window.
　　Create and add the button component.
　Override the action() *method.*
　　Determine whether the frame window is visible.
　　If the window is visible...

> *Hide the window.*
> *Change the button's label to "Show Window."*
> *Else if the window is hidden...*
> > *Show the window.*
> > *Set the window's size.*
> > *Change the button's label to "Hide Window."*
> *Tell Java that the message was handled okay.*

Define the frame window class.
> *Declare objects needed by the class.*
> *Define the class's constructor.*
> > *Initialize the superclass (Frame).*
> > *Create the window's menu bar.*
> > *Initialize the display string.*
> *Override the* paint() *method.*
> > *Resize the frame window.*
> > *Draw the display text in the window.*
> *Override the* action() *method.*
> > *If the "Dialog Box" command was selected, create the dialog.*
> > *Else if the OK button was selected*
> > > *Hide the dialog box.*
> > > *Get the contents of the dialog's test field.*
> > > *Tell Java to repaint the frame window.*
> > *Tell Java that the event was handled.*
> *Define the* ShowDialogBox() *method.*
> > *Create the new dialog box and set its layout.*
> > *Create and add components to the dialog box.*
> > *Display and resize the dialog box.*

Note: In addition to normal dialog boxes, Java supports file dialog boxes for loading and saving files. The file dialogs are represented by the FileDialog class. However, because Java applets have extremely limited access to files, file dialog boxes are not covered here.

Figure 24.1

This is
DialogApplet
running under
Appletviewer.

Summary

You probably won't have much call for dialog boxes in your Java applets, but it's always good to know they're there when you need them. Using dialog boxes in conjunction with a frame window, you can inform the user of critical problems, as well as obtain information from the user without cluttering your main window with controls. Because dialog boxes are much like other display windows in Java, you can set up layout managers, add components, and control the dialog box using the many methods defined in the `Dialog` class or inherited from the class's super-classes.

Review Questions

1. What are the three arguments accepted by the `Dialog` class's constructor?

2. How do you display and hide a dialog box?

3. Why are frame windows important to dialog boxes?

4. What is the one control every dialog box should have?

5. What's the difference between modal and modeless dialog boxes?

6. How do you add components to the dialog box?

Review Exercises

1. Write the code needed to create and display a dialog box with the title "Test Dialog" and with two button controls.

2. Write an applet that can display a dialog box with a 2×2 grid containing four buttons.

3. Modify DialogApplet so that the dialog box has both an OK and a Cancel button. If the user clicks the Cancel button, the dialog should be removed from the screen, but the string that was entered into the text field control should be ignored. Figure 24.2 shows the resultant applet, called DialogApplet2. (You can find the solution to this exercise in the CHAP24 folder of this book's CD-ROM.)

Figure 24.2

This is the DialogApplet2 applet running under Appletviewer.

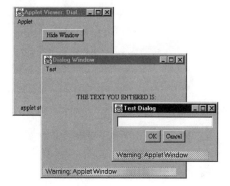

CHAPTER 25

Mouse and Keyboard Events

Up until now, your applets have responded to events generated by Java components like buttons, text fields, and list boxes. You've yet to examine how to respond to events generated by the most basic of a computer's controls, the mouse and the keyboard. Because virtually every computer has these important hardware controls, you can confidently take advantage of them in your applets to collect various types of input. In this chapter, you learn the secrets of mouse and keyboard handling in Java applets.

The Event Object

In order to understand how to respond to various types of events, you need to know more about Java's Event class, an object of which is passed to any event-handling method. When you want to respond to a Java button control, for example, you override the action() method, whose first argument is an Event object. You then examine the target field of the Event object to determine whether it was the button control that generated the event. The Event class, however, defines many constants and data fields that provide information about the event represented by the object.

First, the Event class defines constants for all of the events to which an event-handling method can respond. In this chapter, you'll learn about some of these constants, which include MOUSE_DOWN, MOUSE_UP, and KEY_PRESS. The class also defines constants for special keys, such as F1, PGUP, PGDN, HOME, and so on. Finally, the Event class defines the data fields shown in Table 25.1. How you use these data fields depends on the type of event represented by the Event object.

Table 25.1 Data Fields of the *Event* Class.

Field	Description
Object arg	Event-specific information. With a button event, for example, this field is the button's label.
int clickCount	The click count for mouse events. A value of 1 means a single click, and 2 means a double-click.
int id	The event's type, such as MOUSE_DOWN, MOUSE_MOVE, KEY_PRESS, etc.
int key	The key for a key-related event. For a KEY_PRESS event, for example, this would be the key that was pressed.
int modifiers	The key modifiers, including the shift and control keys. The Event class defines constants such as SHIFT_MASK and CTRL_MASK.
Object target	The type of object—such as Button, TextField, and so on—that generated the event.
long when	The event's time stamp.
int x	The X coordinate associated with the event, usually used with mouse events to indicate the mouse's position at the time of the event.
int y	The Y coordinate associated with the event, usually used with mouse events to indicate the mouse's position at the time of the event.

The Mouse

Most people use their computer's mouse darn near as much as its keyboard. I can vouch for this from first-hand experience, because my only bout with RSI (repetitive strain injury) came not from typing furiously all day, but from maneuvering my mouse to mark paragraphs, highlight words, click buttons, make list selections, bring up menus, and any number of other mousely tasks. I'm not looking for your sympathy, though. My point is that the mouse is one of the most important input devices attached to your computer. To write complete applets, you're going to have to master responding to mouse events in your Java programs.

Luckily, responding to mouse input is a simple matter. Because responding to the events generated by the mouse are such an important and common task in modern programming, Java's classes already include special methods for responding to these events. Exactly what events are you expected to handle? A mouse generates six types of event messages that you can capture in your applets. These events are listed below, along with their descriptions and the method that handles them:

- MOUSE_DOWN—This event, which is handled by the mouseDown() method, is caused when the user presses the mouse button.

- MOUSE_UP—This event, which is handled by the mouseUp() method, is caused when the user releases the left mouse button.

- MOUSE_MOVE—This event, which is handled by the mouseMove() method, occurs when the user moves the mouse pointer on the screen.

- MOUSE_DRAG—This event, which is handled by the mouseDrag() method, is generated when the user moves the mouse pointer while holding down the left mouse button.

- MOUSE_ENTER—This event, which is handled by the mouseEnter() method, is sent when the mouse pointer enters the area owned by an applet or component.

- MOUSE_EXIT—This event, which is handled by the mouseExit() method, occurs when the mouse pointer leaves the area owned by an applet or a component.

In the sections that follow, you'll learn more about the most commonly used of these mouse events.

Handling Mouse Clicks

Without a doubt, the most commonly used mouse event in Java programs (and any other program written for a graphical user interface) is the MOUSE_DOWN event, which is generated whenever the user clicks within an applet. It's the MOUSE_DOWN event, for example, that lets Java know when an on-screen button component has been clicked. You don't have to worry about clicks on on-screen buttons (usually), because they're handled by Java. However, you can respond to MOUSE_DOWN events in your applets in order to accomplish other input tasks.

Java provides a couple of methods by which you can respond to mouse events. The easiest way to capture a MOUSE_DOWN event is to override the applet's mouseDown() method. Java automatically calls mouseDown() whenever the MOUSE_DOWN event is generated, which makes responding to this event easier than melting butter with a blowtorch. The mouseDown() method's signature looks like this:

```
public boolean mouseDown(Event evt, int x, int y)
```

The arguments passed to the function are an Event object and the X,Y coordinates of the mouse event. Although Java has already extracted the X,Y mouse coordinates for you, you can also get them from the Event object by examining the values stored in the x and y data fields, as described in Table 25.1. (Because Java has already extracted the coordinates for you, though, it makes more sense to use the x and y parameters sent to the function.) What you do with these coordinates depends, of course, on your applet. In the next section, you'll see how to use the coordinates to display graphics on the screen.

> **Note:** Although most of Java's event-handling methods automatically receive as arguments the basic information you need about a specific event (such as the coordinates of a mouse click), you can extract whatever additional information you need from the Event object, which is always the first parameter in a message-handling method.

Example: Using Mouse Clicks in an Applet

As I was describing the mouseDown() method in the previous section, I felt an example coming on. And, sure enough, here it is. The applet in Listing 25.1 responds to mouse clicks by printing the word "Click!" wherever the user clicks in the applet. It does this by storing the coordinates of the mouse click in the applet's coordX and coordY data fields. The paint() method then uses these coordinates to display the word. Figure 25.1 shows MouseApplet running under Appletviewer.

Listing 25.1 MouseApplet.java: Using Mouse Clicks in an Applet.

```java
import java.awt.*;
import java.applet.*;

public class MouseApplet extends Applet
{
    int coordX, coordY;

    public void init()
    {
        coordX = -1;
        coordY = -1;

        Font font =
            new Font("TimesRoman", Font.BOLD, 24);
        setFont(font);

        resize(400, 300);
    }

    public void paint(Graphics g)
    {
        if (coordX != -1)
            g.drawString("Click!", coordX, coordY);
```

```
    }

    public boolean mouseDown(Event evt, int x, int y)
    {
        coordX = x;
        coordY = y;
        repaint();
        return true;
    }
}
```

Tell Java that the applet uses the classes in the awt *package.*
Tell Java that the applet uses the classes in the applet *package.*
Derive the MouseApplet *class from Java's* Applet *class.*
   Declare the class's data fields.
   Override the init() *method.*
     Initialize the click coordinates.
     Create and set the font for the applet.
     Size the applet.
   Override the paint() *method.*
     If the user has selected a coordinate...
       Draw the word Click! at the selected coordinate.
   Override the mouseDown() *method.*
     Save the mouse click's coordinates.
     Force Java to repaint the applet.
     Tell Java that the event was handled.

Figure 25.1

The MouseApplet
applet responds to
mouse clicks.

> **Note:** When you run MouseApplet, you'll discover that the applet window gets erased each time the `paint()` method is called. That's why only one "Click!" ever appears in the window.

Handling Mouse Movement

Although mouse clicks are the most common type of mouse event to which your applet may want to respond, tracking the mouse pointer's movement can also be useful. Drawing programs, for example, enable you to draw shapes by tracking the movement of the mouse and displaying the results on the screen.

Unlike mouse clicks, though, which are rare, only occurring when the user presses a mouse button, MOUSE_MOVE events come flooding into your applet by the hundreds as the user moves the mouse around the screen. Each one of these events can be handled in the `mouseMove()` method, whose signature looks like this:

```
public boolean mouseMove(Event evt, int x, int y)
```

Yep. Except for its name, the `mouseMove()` method looks exactly like the `mouseDown()` method, receiving as arguments an `Event` object and the X,Y coordinates at which the event occurred.

Example: Responding to Mouse Movement in an Applet

Responding to mouse movement isn't something you have to do often in your applets. Still, it's a handy tool to have on your belt. You might, for example, need to track mouse movement when writing a game applet that uses the mouse as input. A more common use is in graphics programs that enable you to draw on the screen. Listing 25.2 is just such an applet.

When you run MouseApplet2 with Appletviewer, you see a blank window. Click the mouse in the window to choose a starting point and then move the mouse around the window. Wherever the mouse pointer goes, it leaves a black line behind (Figure 25.2). Although this is a very simple drawing program, it gives you some idea of how you might use a mouse to accomplish other similar tasks.

Listing 25.2   MouseApplet2.java: An Applet That Tracks Mouse Movement.

```
import java.awt.*;
import java.applet.*;

public class MouseApplet2 extends Applet
{
    Point startPoint;
```

```
        Point points[];
        int numPoints;
        boolean drawing;

        public void init()
        {
            startPoint = new Point(0, 0);
            points = new Point[1000];
            numPoints = 0;
            drawing = false;
            resize(400, 300);
        }

        public void paint(Graphics g)
        {
            int oldX = startPoint.x;
            int oldY = startPoint.y;

            for (int x=0; x<numPoints; ++x)
            {
                g.drawLine(oldX, oldY, points[x].x, points[x].y);
                oldX = points[x].x;
                oldY = points[x].y;
            }
        }

        public boolean mouseDown(Event evt, int x, int y)
        {
            drawing = true;
            startPoint.x = x;
            startPoint.y = y;
            return true;
        }

        public boolean mouseMove(Event evt, int x, int y)
        {
            if ((drawing) && (numPoints < 1000))
            {
                points[numPoints] = new Point(x, y);
                ++numPoints;
                repaint();
            }

            return true;
        }
}
```

Tell Java that the applet uses the classes in the awt *package.*
Tell Java that the applet uses the classes in the applet *package.*
Derive the MouseApplet2 *class from Java's* Applet *class.*
  Declare the class's data fields.
  Override the init() *method.*

Initialize the starting point.
Create an array for storing the coordinates of line segments.
Create and set the font for the applet.
Set point count to zero.
Set drawing flag off.
Size the applet.
Override the `paint()` *method.*
  Initialize the drawing's starting point.
  Cycle through each element in the `points[]` *array.*
    Draw a line segment.
    Save ending point as the starting point for the next line.
Override the `mouseDown()` *method.*
  Set the flag in order to allow drawing to begin.
  Save the mouse click's coordinates.
  Tell Java that the event was handled.
Override the `mouseMove()` *method.*
  if it's okay to add another line segment...
    Create a new point and save the mouse's coordinates.
    Increment the point counter.
    Force Java to repaint the applet.
  Tell Java that the event was handled.

Figure 25.2

This applet draws by tracking the movement of the mouse.

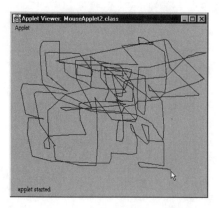

The Keyboard

The keyboard has been around even longer than the mouse and has been the primary interface between humans and their computers for decades. Given the keyboard's importance, obviously there may be times when you'll want to handle the keyboard events at a lower level than you can with something like a TextField control. Java responds to two basic key events, which are represented by the KEY_PRESS and KEY_RELEASE constants. As you'll soon see, Java defines methods that make it just as easy to respond to the keyboard as it is to respond to the mouse.

Responding to Key Presses

Whenever the user presses a key when an applet is active, Java sends the applet a KEY_PRESS event. In your applet, you can respond to this event by overriding the keyDown() method, whose signature looks like this:

```
public boolean keyDown(Event evt, int key)
```

As you can see, this method receives two arguments, which are an Event object and an integer representing the key that was pressed. This integer is actually the ASCII representation of the character represented by the key. In order to use this value in your programs, however, you must first cast it to a char value, like this:

```
char c = (char)key;
```

Predefined Key Constants

Some of the keys on your keyboard issue commands rather than generate characters. These keys include all the F keys, as well as keys like Shift, Ctrl, Page Up, Page Down, and so on. In order to make these types of keys easier to handle in your applets, Java's Event class defines a set of constants that represent these key's values. Table 25.2 lists these constants.

Table 25.2   Key Constants of the *Event* Class.

Constant	Key
DOWN	The down arrow key.
END	The End key.
F1	The F1 key.
F2	The F2 key.
F3	The F3 key.
F4	The F4 key.

continues

Table 25.2 Continued

Constant	Key
F5	The F5 key.
F6	The F6 key.
F7	The F7 key.
F8	The F8 key.
F9	The F9 key.
F10	The F10 key.
F11	The F11 key.
F12	The F12 key.
HOME	The Home key.
LEFT	The left arrow key.
PGDN	The Page Down key.
PGUP	The Page Up key.
RIGHT	The right arrow key.
UP	The up arrow key.

Key Modifiers

The Event class also defines a number of constants for modifier keys that the user might press along with the basic key. These constants include ALT_MASK, SHIFT_MASK, and CTRL_MASK, which represent the Alt, Shift, and Ctrl (or Control) keys on your keyboard. The SHIFT_MASK and CTRL_MASK constants are used in the Event class's methods shiftDown() and controlDown(), each which of returns a boolean value indicating whether the modifier key is pressed. (There currently is no altDown() method.) You can also examine the Event object's modifiers field to determine whether a particular modifier key was pressed. For example, if you wanted to check for the Alt key, you might use a line of Java code like this:

```
boolean altPressed = (evt.modifiers & Event.ALT_MASK) != 0;
```

By ANDing the mask with the value in the modifiers field, you end up with a non-zero value if the Alt key was pressed and a 0 if it wasn't. You convert this result to a boolean value by comparing the result with 0.

Example: Using Key Presses in an Applet

Although capturing key presses is a fairly simple process, there's nothing like an example applet to put the theoretical stuff to the test. Listing 25.3 is an applet called KeyApplet that displays whatever key the user presses. Figure 25.3 shows the applet running under Appletviewer.

> **Note:** If you run KeyApplet under a browser like Netscape Navigator, click on the applet with your mouse before you start typing. This ensures that the applet has the focus and will receive the key presses.

Listing 25.3   KeyApplet.java: An Applet That Captures Key Presses.

```java
import java.awt.*;
import java.applet.*;

public class KeyApplet extends Applet
{
    int keyPressed;

    public void init()
    {
        keyPressed = -1;

        Font font =
            new Font("TimesRoman", Font.BOLD, 144);
        setFont(font);

        resize(200, 200);
    }

    public void paint(Graphics g)
    {
        String str = "";

        if (keyPressed != -1)
        {
            str += (char)keyPressed;
            g.drawString(str, 40, 150);
        }
    }

    public boolean keyDown(Event evt, int key)
    {
        keyPressed = key;
        repaint();
        return true;
    }
}
```

Tell Java that the applet uses the classes in the awt *package.*
Tell Java that the applet uses the classes in the applet *package.*
Derive the KeyApplet *class from Java's* Applet *class.*
  Declare the class's data field.
  Override the init() *method.*
    Initialize keyPressed *to indicate no valid key received yet.*
    Create and set the font for the applet.
    Size the applet.
  Override the paint() *method.*
    Create the empty display string.
    Draw the character on the screen.
  Override the keyDown() *method.*
    Save the key that was pressed.
    Force Java to redraw the applet.
    Tell Java that the event was handled.

Figure 25.3

This applet displays the last character typed.

Handling Events Directly

All of the events received by your applet are processed by the handleEvent() method, which the Applet class inherits from the Component class. When this method is not overridden in your applet, the default implementation is responsible for calling the many methods that respond to events. Listing 25.4 shows how the handleEvent() method is implemented in the Component class. By examining this listing, you can easily see why you only have to override methods like mouseDown() to respond to events. In the next section, you see how to customize handleEvent() in your own programs.

Listing 25.4   LST25_4.TXT: The Default Implementation of *handleEvent( )*.

```java
public boolean handleEvent(Event evt) {
switch (evt.id) {
  case Event.MOUSE_ENTER:
    return mouseEnter(evt, evt.x, evt.y);

  case Event.MOUSE_EXIT:
    return mouseExit(evt, evt.x, evt.y);

  case Event.MOUSE_MOVE:
    return mouseMove(evt, evt.x, evt.y);

  case Event.MOUSE_DOWN:
    return mouseDown(evt, evt.x, evt.y);

  case Event.MOUSE_DRAG:
    return mouseDrag(evt, evt.x, evt.y);

  case Event.MOUSE_UP:
    return mouseUp(evt, evt.x, evt.y);

  case Event.KEY_PRESS:
  case Event.KEY_ACTION:
    return keyDown(evt, evt.key);

  case Event.KEY_RELEASE:
  case Event.KEY_ACTION_RELEASE:
    return keyUp(evt, evt.key);

  case Event.ACTION_EVENT:
    return action(evt, evt.arg);
  case Event.GOT_FOCUS:
    return gotFocus(evt, evt.arg);
  case Event.LOST_FOCUS:
    return lostFocus(evt, evt.arg);
}
return false;
}
```

Example: Overriding *handleEvent()* in an Applet

Although the default implementation of handleEvent() calls special methods that you can override in your applet for each event, you might want to group all your event handling in one method to conserve on overhead, change the way an applet responds to a particular event, or even create your own events. To accomplish any of these tasks (or any others you might come up with), you can forget the individual event-handling methods and override handleEvent() instead.

In your version of handleEvent(), you must examine the Event object's id field in order to determine which event is being processed. You can just ignore events in which you're not interested. However, be sure to return `false` whenever you ignore a message, so that Java knows that it should pass the event on up the object hierarchy. Listing 25.5 is a rewritten version of the MouseApplet2 applet, called MouseApplet3. This version overrides the `handleEvent()` method in order to respond to events.

Listing 25.5 MouseApplet3.java: Using the *handleEvent( )* Method.

```
import java.awt.*;
import java.applet.*;

public class MouseApplet3 extends Applet
{
    Point startPoint;
    Point points[];
    int numPoints;
    boolean drawing;

    public void init()
    {
        startPoint = new Point(0, 0);
        points = new Point[1000];
        numPoints = 0;
        drawing = false;
        resize(400, 300);
    }

    public void paint(Graphics g)
    {
        int oldX = startPoint.x;
        int oldY = startPoint.y;

        for (int x=0; x<numPoints; ++x)
        {
            g.drawLine(oldX, oldY, points[x].x, points[x].y);
            oldX = points[x].x;
            oldY = points[x].y;
        }
    }

    public boolean handleEvent(Event evt)
    {
        switch(evt.id)
        {
            case Event.MOUSE_DOWN:
                drawing = true;
                startPoint.x = evt.x;
                startPoint.y = evt.y;
                return true;
            case Event.MOUSE_MOVE:
                if ((drawing) && (numPoints < 1000))
```

```
            {
                points[numPoints] = new Point(evt.x, evt.y);
                ++numPoints;
                repaint();
            }
            return true;
        default:
            return false;
        }
    }
}
```

Summary

Because the keyboard and the mouse are two of the most important devices for accepting input from the user, it's important that you know how to handle these devices in your applets. Maybe most of your applets will work fine by leaving such details up to Java or maybe you'll want to have more control over the devices than the default behavior allows. You can capture most messages received by a Java applet by overloading the appropriate event handlers, such as mouseDown() and keyDown(). However, if you want to step back even further in your event-handling code, you can override the handleEvent() method, which receives all events sent to an applet.

Review Questions

1. What is the mouse event that's most commonly captured and responded to in Java applets?

2. What is the mouse message an applet receives the most of?

3. What are the six different mouse event messages that your applet may receive?

4. What are the two keyboard events your applet is likely to receive?

5. How can you determine what type of object generated an event?

6. How can you determine the type of event message that's being received?

7. When your applet receives a mouse-related message, how can you determine the coordinates of the mouse at the time of the event?

8. How can you tell whether the user single- or double-clicked his mouse?

9. What two methods are associated with the KEY_PRESS and KEY_RELEASE event messages?

10. What arguments are received by the keyDown() method?

11. What arguments are received by the mouseDown() method?

12. Why might you need to use the SHIFT_MASK and CTRL_MASK constants?

13. If you want to handle all events in a single method, what method should you override in your applet?

Review Exercises

1. Write an applet that displays a rectangle wherever the user clicks.

2. Write an applet that displays a rectangle, the color which changes whenever the user presses a key on his keyboard.

3. Write an applet that displays the current coordinates of the mouse as the mouse moves around the applet's window.

4. Write an applet that enables the user to type a string of characters on the screen. Use a String object to hold the characters, adding each new character to the string as the user types and displaying the string in the applet's paint() method.

5. Modify MouseApplet2 so that the first MOUSE_DOWN event selects a starting point, after which the applet remembers all the MOUSE_MOVE coordinates. However, the applet shouldn't draw the lines associated with these moves until the user presses his F2 key. Pressing F3 should erase the lines from the applet and signal the applet to start the process over again. (You can find the solution to this exercise, called MouseApplet4, in the CHAP25 folder of this book's CD-ROM.)

CHAPTER 26

Configurable Applets

All of the applets you've written so far have one thing in common. Outside of the starting size of the applet, none of your applets are configurable. That is, the user can't configure the applet to fit his needs. In many cases, it doesn't make sense to give the user configurable options. But, just as often, someone who wants to use your applet in his own home page will want to make minor changes without having to change and recompile the source code. In fact, the user probably won't even have access to the source code. In this chapter, you get a look at configurable applets, which enable the applet's user to modify how an applet looks and acts, all without having to change a line of Java code.

Types of Users

Before you read further, it might be a good idea to define exactly what a user is. When it comes to applets, you could say that there are two kinds of users. The first kind is a net surfer who logs onto your home page and sees all the cool applets you've spent the last six months creating. Because this user is not installing your applets on his own Web pages—he's just a casual observer—he doesn't need access to the applet's parameters. In fact, if you want your Web pages to look right for different users, it just doesn't make sense to enable the surfer to configure an applet.

The other kind of user is the guy who found your applet on a server somewhere and wants to incorporate the applet into his own Web pages. Assuming that you've released your applet into the world for others to use, you want this type of user to find your applet to be as flexible as possible. However, you probably don't want to give this user your source code and expect him to make changes that require recompiling. Hey, he could end up trashing the applet completely, right?

So, to make it easy for this user to modify the applet's appearance and functionality, you must build in support for parameters. To use these parameters, the user only needs to add a few lines to the HTML document that loads and runs the applet. For example, you may have written an applet that displays an awesome title on your home page. Now, you want to release the applet so that other netfolks can use it in their Web pages. However, these folks are going to want to display their own titles. So, you make the title string a parameter.

In the sections that follow, you'll not only learn how to support applet parameters, but you'll also learn how to make those parameters idiot-proof.

Parameters and Applets

When you want to use an applet that supports parameters, you must add the parameters and their values to the HTML document that loads and runs the applet. You do this using the <PARAM> tag, which has two parts. The NAME part of the tag specifies the parameter's name, and the VALUE part specifies the parameter's value. For example, suppose you want to provide a title parameter for that title applet you read about in the previous section. The parameter tag might look like this:

```
<PARAM NAME=title VALUE="Big Al's Home Page">
```

Here, the name of the parameter is title. The applet will use this name to identify the parameter. The value of the title parameter in the above line is the text string Big Al's Home Page. The applet will retrieve this text string in order to display the title the user wants. A complete HTML document for the title applet might look something like Listing 26.1.

Listing 26.1   LST26_1.TXT: Using a Parameter in an HTML Document.

```
<title>Applet Test Page</title>
<h1>Applet Test Page</h1>
<applet
    code="TitleApplet.class"
    width=250
    height=150
    name="TitleApplet">
    <PARAM NAME=title VALUE="Big Al's Home Page">
</applet>
```

As you can see, the <PARAM> tag is enclosed between the <applet> and </applet> tags. that is, the parameters are part of the applet's HTML code.

How does your applet retrieve the parameter at run time? An excellent question, and one for which I fortunately have the answer. To retrieve a parameter, you call the applet's getParameter() method, like this:

```
String param = getParameter(name);
```

The `getParameter()` method takes a single argument, which is a string containing the name of the parameter for which you want the value. The method always returns a string to your applet. This string is, of course, the part of the PARAM tag that follows the VALUE=.

Example: Setting and Retrieving a Parameter's Value

Suppose that you've written an applet that displays a fancy greeting to the viewer. (How fancy the greeting is displayed depends upon the code you've written for the applet. Because how the applet actually displays this greeting is not important at this point, just pretend it does something really cool.) The parameter is defined in the HTML document like this:

```
<PARAM NAME=greeting VALUE="All Web Surfers Welcome!">
```

When the applet runs, it has to find out what greeting to display. So, in the applet's `init()` method is the following line:

```
String str = getParameter("greeting");
```

Now that the applet has the text stored in the `str` variable, it can manipulate and display it any way it needs to.

Example: Using a Parameter in an Applet

Now that you know how to create HTML documents that set parameters, as well as how to obtain those parameters from within your applet, you'd probably like a real parameterized applet with which you can experiment. Listing 26.2 is an applet called ConfigApplet, which takes a single parameter. This parameter is the text string to display. Listing 26.3 is the HTML document that loads and runs the applet. Notice the <PARAM> tag. When you run the applet with Appletviewer, you see the window shown in Figure 26.1.

Listing 26.2   ConfigApplet.java: An Applet with a Single Parameter.

```java
import java.awt.*;
import java.applet.*;

public class ConfigApplet extends Applet
{
    String str;

    public void init()
    {
        str = getParameter("text");

        Font font = new Font("TimesRoman", Font.BOLD, 24);
```

continues

343

Listing 26.2 Continued

```
        setFont(font);
    }

    public void paint(Graphics g)
    {
        g.drawString(str, 50, 50);
    }
}
```

Tell Java that the applet uses the classes in the awt *package.*
Tell Java that the applet uses the classes in the applet *package.*
Derive the ConfigApplet *class from Java's* Applet *class.*
　　Declare the class's data field.
　　Override the init() *method.*
　　　Retrieve the value of the text parameter.
　　　Create and set the font for the applet.
　　Override the paint() *method.*
　　　Display the given string.

Listing 26.3 CONFIGAPPLET.HTML: HTML Document for ConfigApplet.

```
<title>Applet Test Page</title>
<h1>Applet Test Page</h1>
<applet
    code="ConfigApplet.class"
    width=250
    height=150
    name="ConfigApplet">
    <PARAM NAME=text VALUE="Display Text">
</applet>
```

Figure 26.1

This applet's display string is given as a parameter.

Once you get ConfigApplet compiled, try running the applet several times, each time changing the parameter in the HTML document to a new text string. This will give you a good example of how parameters work from the HTML document writer's point of view. Changing the value of the parameter in the HTML document is all you need to do to display a different text string. You don't have to change the applet's source code at all.

Multiple Parameters

When you're writing an application that others may use in their Web pages, it's important that you make the applet as flexible as possible. One way to do this is to use parameters for any applet value that the user might like to customize. Adding multiple parameters is just a matter of adding additional <PARAM> tags to the HTML document and then retrieving the values of the parameters in the applet. In the next example, you take a look at ConfigApplet2, which gives the user much more control over how the applet displays the text string.

Example: Using Multiple Parameters in an Applet

Suppose that you want to rewrite ConfigApplet so that the user can customize not just the text string the applet will display, but also the position of the text and the size of the font used to print the text. To do this, you need to create four parameters, one each for the text to display, the X position of the text, the Y position of the text, and the point size of the font. Listing 26.4 is an HTML document that loads and runs the ConfigApplet2 applet, which is a new version of ConfigApplet. Notice that the HTML document now specifies four parameters for the applet. You can specify as many parameters as you need for an applet.

Listing 26.4   CONFIGAPPLET2.HTML: HTML Document for ConfigApplet2.

```
<title>Applet Test Page</title>
<h1>Applet Test Page</h1>
<applet
    code="ConfigApplet2.class"
    width=350
    height=200
    name="ConfigApplet2">
    <PARAM NAME=text VALUE="Display Text">
    <PARAM NAME=typesize VALUE=72>
    <PARAM NAME=xpos VALUE=20>
    <PARAM NAME=ypos VALUE=100>
</applet>
```

In the above HTML document, the user is specifying that he wants to display the text string Display Text in 72-point type and at position 20,100. The applet, of course, must call `getParameter()` to read these values into the applet. Moreover, the applet must call `getParameter()` once for each parameter. After retrieving the parameters, the applet must initialize itself such that it displays the text as requested. Listing 26.5 is the Java source code for ConfigApplet2, which accomplishes all these tasks. Figure 26.2 shows the applet running under Appletviewer, using the parameters given in the HTML document in Listing 25.4.

Note: Because the `getParameter()` method always returns a string, you may have to convert some parameters before you can use them in your applet. For example, the ConfigApplet2 applet must convert its `typesize`, `xpos`, and `ypos` parameters from strings to integers.

Listing 26.5   ConfigApplet2.java: The ConfigApplet2 Applet.

```java
import java.awt.*;
import java.applet.*;

public class ConfigApplet2 extends Applet
{
    String str;
    Point position;

    public void init()
    {
        String s;

        str = getParameter("text");

        s = getParameter("typesize");
        int typeSize = Integer.parseInt(s);

        s = getParameter("xpos");
        int xpos = Integer.parseInt(s);

        s = getParameter("ypos");
        int ypos = Integer.parseInt(s);

        position = new Point(xpos, ypos);

        Font font = new Font("TimesRoman", Font.BOLD, typeSize);
        setFont(font);
    }

    public void paint(Graphics g)
    {
        g.drawString(str, position.x, position.y);
    }
}
```

Tell Java that the applet uses the classes in the awt *package.*
Tell Java that the applet uses the classes in the applet *package.*
Derive the ConfigApplet2 *class from Java's* Applet *class.*
  Declare the class's data fields.
  Override the init() *method.*
    Declare a local variable.
    Retrieve the value of the text parameter.
    Retrieve and convert the typesize parameter.
    Retrieve and convert the xpos parameter.
    Retrieve and convert the ypos parameter.
    Store the position in a Point object.
    Create and set the font for the applet, using typesize.
  Override the paint() *method.*
    Display the given string.

Figure 26.2

This applet accepts four parameters that determine how the text is displayed.

Suppose you were to change the parameters in the HTML file to those shown in Listing 26.6. You'd then completely change the way the text string is displayed in the applet, as shown in Figure 26.3. As you can see, parameters can have a profound effect on the way an applet looks and acts.

Listing 26.6   LST26_6.TXT: New Parameters for ConfigApplet2.

```
<PARAM NAME=text VALUE="New Text String">
<PARAM NAME=typesize VALUE=18>
<PARAM NAME=xpos VALUE=60>
<PARAM NAME=ypos VALUE=150>
```

Figure 26.3

Here's
ConfigApplet2
running with
different
parameters.

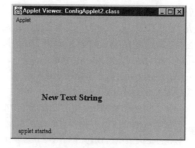

Default Parameter Values

You might have noticed by now that there's a big problem with the ConfigApplet and ConfigApplet2 applets. Neither applet checks to ensure that the parameters it tries to retrieve exist. For example, what happens when the user forgets to include the text parameter?

Relying on other people to provide your applet with the data it needs is a dangerous practice. Your applet should always check the validity of values returned from the getParameter() method. At the very least, you should be sure that the returned value is not null, which is the value getParameter() returns when a particular parameter doesn't exist (that is, the user forget to define it in the HTML document or deliberately left it out assuming that the applet will automatically use a default value for the missing one).

To ensure that your applet is in a runnable state after retrieving parameters, you must always check the parameter's values and supply default values for those parameters that are missing or invalid. For example, to make sure that your applet has a text string to display, you might use lines like this:

```
str = getParameter("text");
if (str == null)
    str = "Default Text";
```

Note: If you decide to release your applets so other people can use them in their Web pages, be sure that you include a separate documentation file that describes the applet's parameters and shows how to use them.

Example: Using Default Parameters in an Applet

You can now extend the ConfigApplet2 so that it provides default values for each parameter. When you've done this, the applet can run without generating errors no matter what parameters the user chooses to include or ignore. Listing 26.7 is the new version, called ConfigApplet3.

Notice that although the program now checks for missing parameters, it doesn't limit the values to any ranges or otherwise check their validity. Because the text parameter will always be a string, there's really nothing you need to check for (except null). However, you may want to limit the font size or make sure that the display location is inside the applet's window. Listing 26.8 is the HTML document used to load and run the applet as it's displayed in Figure 26.4.

Listing 26.7   ConfigApplet3.java: This Applet Provides Default Values for All Parameters.

```java
import java.awt.*;
import java.applet.*;

public class ConfigApplet3 extends Applet
{
    String str;
    Point position;

    public void init()
    {
        HandleTextParam();
        HandleTypeSizeParam();
        HandlePositionParam();
    }

    public void paint(Graphics g)
    {
        g.drawString(str, position.x, position.y);
    }

    protected void HandleTextParam()
    {
        str = getParameter("text");
        if (str == null)
            str = "Default Text";
    }

    protected void HandleTypeSizeParam()
    {
        String s = getParameter("typesize");
        if (s == null)
            s = "24";
        int typeSize = Integer.parseInt(s);

        Font font = new Font("TimesRoman", Font.BOLD, typeSize);
        setFont(font);
    }

    protected void HandlePositionParam()
    {
```

continues

Listing 26.7 Continued

```java
        String s = getParameter("xpos");
        if (s == null)
            s = "20";
        int xpos = Integer.parseInt(s);

        s = getParameter("ypos");
        if (s == null)
            s = "50";
        int ypos = Integer.parseInt(s);

        position = new Point(xpos, ypos);
    }
}
```

Tell Java that the applet uses the classes in the awt *package.*
Tell Java that the applet uses the classes in the applet *package.*
Derive the ConfigApplet3 *class from Java's* Applet *class.*
   Declare the class's data fields.
   Override the init() *method.*
      Call the methods that retrieve and validate the parameters.
   Override the paint() *method.*
      Display the given string.
   Define the HandleTextParam() *method.*
      Retrieve the text parameter.
      If the parameter is null, set str to the default text.
   Define the HandleTypeSizeParam() *method.*
      Retrieve the typesize parameter.
      If the parameter is null, set the parameter string to "24."
      Convert the parameter string to an integer.
      Create and set the font.
   Define the HandlePositionParam() *method.*
      Retrieve the xpos parameter.
      if xpos is null, set the parameter string to "20."
      Convert the parameter string to an integer.
      Retrieve the ypos parameter.
      if ypos is null, set the parameter string to "50."
      Convert the parameter string to an integer.
      Create the Point object with the position values.

Listing 26.8   CONFIGAPPLET3.HTML: The HTML Document for ConfigApplet3.

```
<title>Applet Test Page</title>
<h1>Applet Test Page</h1>
<applet
    code="ConfigApplet3.class"
    width=640
    height=200
    name="ConfigApplet3">
    <PARAM NAME=text VALUE="Hi there!">
    <PARAM NAME=typesize VALUE=144>
    <PARAM NAME=xpos VALUE=40>
    <PARAM NAME=ypos VALUE=140>
</applet>
```

Figure 26.4

This is
ConfigApplet3
running under
Appletviewer.

Summary

By supporting parameters, your applets are more flexible, which makes it easier for other people to incorporate them into their Web-page designs. Even if you don't plan to release your applets, using parameters can make your applets more powerful and your own Web pages easier to fine tune. Using the <PARAM> tag is more sensible than having to reprogram and recompile an applet every time you want it to do something slightly different. Keep in mind, though, that all parameters must have default values built into the applet's source code. Otherwise, you could end up with an error-ridden applet, something that won't do much for your reputation as a Java guru.

Review Questions

1. What kind of applet user is likely to appreciate parameterized applets?

2. What are the two parts of the <PARAM> tag?

3. How can your applet retrieve the value of a parameter?

4. Where do you specify the values for an applet's parameters?

5. Do you need to recompile an applet in order to take advantage of new parameters?

6. How many parameters can you have in a single applet?

7. Why do you need to convert the values of some parameters?

8. Why is it important to supply default values for all parameters?

Review Exercises

1. Write an applet that displays a rectangle on the screen. The rectangle's size should be specified using parameters.

2. Write an applet that uses a parameter to display a red, green, or blue background.

3. Modify ConfigApplet2 so that it not only checks for null parameters, but also checks for the parameters' validity. The type size should always be in the range of 10 to 72 points and the text should always be positioned so that it's never printed completely out of view. (You can find the solution to this exercise, called ConfigApplet4, in the CHAP26 folder of this book's CD-ROM.)

CHAPTER 27

Images and Sounds

If you've seen a lot of the applets that are floating around, you've undoubtedly noticed that many of them feature vivid graphics and even sound effects. When programming in a language such a C++, displaying graphics and playing sounds can be infamously difficult, thanks to the fact that these languages provide no direct support for handling these types of files. Even the Windows API, as immense as it is, provides little help when it comes to handling these graphical and aural chores. Java, on the other hand, was designed to make creating applets as easy as possible. For that reason, Java's classes handle almost all the difficulties associated with displaying images (commonly called bitmaps) and playing sounds. In this chapter, you use Java's power to add images and sounds to your applets.

Image Types

In the world of computers, there are many types of images, each of which is associated with a specific file format. These image types are usually identified by their file extensions, which include PCX, BMP, GIF, JPEG (or JPG), TIFF (or TIF), TGA, and more. Each of these file types was created by third-party software companies for use with their products, but many became popular enough to grow into standards. The PCX graphics file type, for example, began as the format for PC Paintbrush files, whereas BMP files are usually associated with the Windows graphical interface.

If you were writing your Internet applications using a more conventional language like C++, you could choose to support whatever image type was most convenient for your use. This is because you'd have to write all the file-loading code from scratch, anyway. Java, on the other hand, comes complete with classes that are capable of loading image files for you. This convenience comes with a small price, however, since Java can load only GIF and JPEG image file formats. In this book, you'll use GIF files, which are more common, although JPEG files are rapidly gaining a reputation, especially for high-resolution, true-color images.

Loading and Displaying an Image

The first step in displaying an image in your applet is to load the image from disk. To do this, you must create an object of Java's Image class. This is fairly easy to do; however, in order to do so, you need to create an URL object that holds the location of the graphics file. You could just type the image's URL directly into your Java source code. If you do this, however, you have to change and recompile the applet whenever you move the graphics file to a different directory on your disk. A better way to create the image's URL object is to call either the getDocumentBase() or getCodeBase() method. The former returns the URL of the directory from which the current HTML file was loaded, whereas the latter returns the URL of the directory from which the applet was run.

Example: Using the *getDocumentBase()* Method

As I said previously, the getDocumentBase() method returns the URL of the directory from which the HTML document was loaded. If you're storing your images in the same directory (or a subdirectory of that directory) as your HTML files, you'd want to use this method to obtain an URL for an image.

Suppose you have your HTML documents in a directory called PUBLIC and the image you want, called IMAGE.GIF, is stored in a subdirectory of PUBLIC called IMAGES. A call to getDocumentBase() will get you the appropriate base URL. That call looks like this:

```
URL url = getDocumentBase();
```

As you'll soon see, once you have the URL, you can load the file by using the URL along with the relative location of the image, which in this case would be IMAGES/IMAGE.GIF. The full URL to the file would then be FILE:/C:/PUBLIC/IMAGES/IMAGE.GIF. If you decided to move your public files to a directory called MYHOMEPAGE, the call to getDocumentBase() will give you the URL for that new directory, without your having to change the applet's source code. This new URL, once you included the relative location of the image file, would be FILE:/C:/MYHOMEPAGE/IMAGES/IMAGE.GIF.

Example: Using the *getCodeBase()* Method

The `getCodeBase()` method works similarly to `getDocumentBase()`, except that it returns the URL of the directory from which the applet was loaded. If you're storing your images in the same directory (or a subdirectory of that directory) as your CLASS files, you'd want to call `getCodeBase()` to obtain an URL for an image.

Suppose you have your CLASS files in a directory called CLASSES and the image you want (still called IMAGE.GIF) is stored in a subdirectory of CLASSES called IMAGES. A call to `getCodeBase()` will get you the base URL you need to load the image. That call looks like this:

```
URL url = getCodeBase();
```

Again, once you have the URL, you can load the file by using the URL along with the relative location of the image, which would still be IMAGES/IMAGE.GIF. The full URL to the file would then be FILE:/C:/CLASSES/IMAGES/IMAGE.GIF.

Loading an Image

Once you have the image's base URL, you're ready to load the image and create the `Image` object. You can complete both of these tasks at the same time, by calling your applet's `getImage()` method, like this:

```
Image image = getImage(baseURL, relLocation);
```

The `getImage()` method's two arguments are the URL returned by your call to `getCodeBase()` or `getDocumentBase()` and the relative location of the image. For example, assuming that you've stored your CLASS files in the directory C:\CLASSES and your images in the directory C:\CLASSES\IMAGES, you'd have a code that looks something like this:

```
URL codeBase = getCodeBase();
Image myImage = getImage(codeBase, "images/myimage.gif");
```

After Java has executed the above lines, your image is loaded into the computer's memory and ready to display.

Displaying an Image

Displaying the image is a simple matter of calling the `Graphics` object's `drawImage()` method, like this:

```
g.drawImage(myImage, x, y, width, height, this);
```

This method's arguments are the image object to display, the X and Y coordinates at which to display the image, the width and height of the image, and the applet's `this` reference.

> **Tip:** When you want to display an image with its normal width and height, you can call a simpler version of the `drawImage()` method, which leaves out the width and height arguments, like this: `drawImage(image, x, y, this)`. This version of the method actually draws the image faster because it doesn't have to worry about reducing or expanding the image to the given width and height. It just blasts it on to the screen exactly as the image normally appears.

You may be wondering where you can get the width and the height of the image. As it turns out (no doubt thanks to careful consideration by Java's programmers over hundreds of cups of coffee), the `Image` class has two methods, `getWidth()` and `getHeight()`, that return the width and height of the image. The complete code for displaying the image, then, might look like this:

```
int width = image.getWidth(this);
int height = image.getHeight(this);
g.drawImage(image, x, y, width, height, this);
```

As you can see, the `getWidth()` and `getHeight()` methods require a single argument, which is the applet's `this` reference.

Example: Displaying an Image in an Applet

You're now ready to write an applet that can display images. Listing 27.1 is the Java source code for an applet called ImageApplet that displays a small image using the techniques described previously in this chapter. When you run the applet with Appletviewer, you see the window shown in Figure 27.1. Make sure the SNAKE.GIF image is in the same directory as the ImageApplet.class file, since that's where the program expects to find it.

Listing 27.1   ImageApplet.java: An Applet That Displays an Image.

```
import java.awt.*;
import java.applet.*;
import java.net.*;

public class ImageApplet extends Applet
{
    Image snake;

    public void init()
    {
        URL codeBase = getCodeBase();
        snake = getImage(codeBase, "snake.gif");
        resize(250, 250);
    }
```

```
public void paint(Graphics g)
    {
        int width = snake.getWidth(this);
        int height = snake.getHeight(this);

        g.drawRect(52, 52, width+10, height+10);
        g.drawImage(snake, 57, 57, width, height, this);
    }
}
```

Tell Java that the applet uses the classes in the awt *package.*
Tell Java that the applet uses the classes in the applet *package.*
Tell Java that the applet uses the classes in the net *package.*
Derive the ImageApplet *class from Java's* Applet *class.*
  Declare the class's image data field.
  Override the init() *method.*
    Retrieve the base URL.
    Load the image.
    Size the applet.
  Override the paint() *method.*
    Get the image's width and height.
    Draw a framing rectangle for the image.
    Draw the image within the rectangle.

Figure 27.1

This is
ImageApplet
running under
Appletviewer.

Notice how the applet imports the classes in the net package, which is where the URL class lives. If you fail to include this line at the top of the program, Java will be unable to find the URL class and the applet will not compile.

Tip: By using different values for the drawImage() method's width and height arguments, you can display an image at any size you like. For example, to display an image at twice its normal size, just use 2*width and 2*height for the width and height arguments. To display the image at half its normal size, use `width/2` and `height/2`. Figure 27.2 shows the snake image displayed at twice its normal size. It doesn't even fit in the window any more!

Figure 27.2

Here's the snake image at twice its size.

Playing a Sound

Just as there are many types of image files, so too are there many types of sound files. But, when it comes to applets, the only type of sound file you need to know about are audio files, which have the file extension AU. These types of sound files were popularized on UNIX machines and are the only type of sound file Java can load and play.

When you want to play a sound from beginning to end, you only have to call `getDocumentBase()` or `getCodeBase()` for the URL and then call `play()` to play the sound. A call to `play()` looks like this:

```
play(baseURL, relLocation);
```

The `play()` method's two arguments are the URL returned from a call to `getDocumentBase()` or `getCodeBase()` and the relative location of the sound file.

Example: Using the *play()* Method

Suppose you have your CLASS files in the directory C:/MYHOMEPAGE and your AU files in the directory C:/MYHOMEPAGE/AUDIO. The following lines then will load and play an audio file called SOUND.AU:

```
URL codeBase = getCodeBase();
play(codeBase, "audio/sound.au");
```

Example: Playing a Sound in an Applet

Now get ready to write an applet that plays a sound file. Listing 27.2 is the applet in question, called SoundApplet. When you run the applet with Appletviewer, you'll see the window shown in Figure 27.3. Just click the button to hear the sound. Of course, you need to have a sound card properly installed on your system. You also must be sure that the SPACEMUSIC.AU sound file is in the same directory as the applet. (This sound file is included with the Java Developer's Kit and has been copied to this chapter's CD-ROM directory for your convenience.)

Listing 27.2   SoundApplet.java: An Applet That Plays a Sound File.

```
import java.awt.*;
import java.applet.*;
import java.net.*;

public class SoundApplet extends Applet
{
    Button button;

    public void init()
    {
        BorderLayout layout = new BorderLayout();
        setLayout(layout);

        Font font = new Font("TimesRoman", Font.BOLD, 32);
        setFont(font);

        button = new Button("Play Sound");
        add("Center", button);

        resize(250, 250);
    }

    public boolean action(Event evt, Object arg)
    {
        if (evt.target instanceof Button)
        {
            URL codeBase = getCodeBase();
            play(codeBase, "spacemusic.au");
        }

        return true;
    }
}
```

Tell Java that the applet uses the classes in the awt *package.*
Tell Java that the applet uses the classes in the applet *package.*
Tell Java that the applet uses the classes in the net *package.*
Derive the SoundApplet *class from Java's* Applet *class.*
   Declare the class's button object.
   Override the init() *method.*
     Create and set the applet's layout.
     Create and set the applet's font.
     Create and add the button.
     Size the applet.
   Override the action() *method.*
     If the user clicks the button...
       Get the base URL.
       Play the sound.
     Tell Java that the event was handled.

Figure 27.3

Click the button to hear the applet's sound file.

Controlling Sounds

Although the applet's play() method is the easiest way to load and play sounds, it doesn't give you much control. You have only one option: play the sound from beginning to end. If you want a little more control over your sounds, you can create an AudioClip object and use the object's methods to control the sound. Unfortunately, even the AudioClip class doesn't give you much power, although you can play, stop, and loop the sound.

To create the AudioClip object, you call the getAudioClip() method, like this:

```
AudioClip audioClip = getAudioClip(baseURL, relLocation);
```

This method's two arguments are the sound file's base URL and relative location.

Once you have the AudioClip object created and loaded, you can call its methods to control the sound. There are only three from which to choose: play(), stop(), and loop(). The play() method plays the sound once from beginning to end, stop() stops the sound whether or not it has finished playing, and `loop()` causes the sound to keep repeating until it's stopped.

Example: Using an AudioClip in an Applet

Although using audio clips is a little more complicated than simply loading and playing a sound using the applet's `play()` method, it's still a straightforward process. Listing 27.3 is an applet that creates an `AudioClip` object and enables the user to send commands to the object using the applet's command buttons. When you run the applet with Appletviewer, you see the window shown in Figure 27.4. To play the sound once from beginning to end, click the Play button. To stop the sound at any time, click the Stop button. Finally, to play the sound over and over, click the Loop button.

Listing 27.3   SoundApplet2.java: An Applet That Creates and Displays an *AudioClip* Object.

```
import java.awt.*;
import java.applet.*;
import java.net.*;

public class SoundApplet2 extends Applet
{
    AudioClip soundClip;

    public void init()
    {
        GridLayout layout = new GridLayout(1, 3, 10, 10);
        setLayout(layout);

        Font font = new Font("TimesRoman", Font.BOLD, 24);
        setFont(font);

        Button button = new Button("Play");
        add(button);
        button = new Button("Stop");
        add(button);
        button = new Button("Loop");
        add(button);

        URL codeBase = getCodeBase();
        soundClip = getAudioClip(codeBase, "spacemusic.au");

        resize(250, 250);
    }
```

continues

Listing 27.3 Continued

```
public boolean action(Event evt, Object arg)
    {
        if (arg == "Play")
            soundClip.play();
        else if (arg == "Stop")
            soundClip.stop();
        else if (arg == "Loop")
            soundClip.loop();

        return true;
    }
}
```

Tell Java that the applet uses the classes in the awt package.
Tell Java that the applet uses the classes in the applet package.
Tell Java that the applet uses the classes in the net package.
Derive the SoundApplet2 class from Java's Applet class.
   Declare the class's audio clip object.
   Override the init() method.
      Create and set the applet's layout.
      Create and set the applet's font.
      Create and add the three buttons.
      Get the base URL and create the audio clip.
      Size the applet.
   Override the 5 method.
      Respond to the appropriate button.
      Tell Java that the event was handled.

Figure 27.4

This is
Appletviewer
running
SoundApplet2.

Summary

Nothing spices up an applet more than vivid graphics and enjoyable sound effects.
That's why Java's creators went to such lengths to ensure that you can easily add

these important elements to your applets. Loading and displaying an image is as simple as obtaining the image's base URL, creating an Image object, and calling drawImage() to display the image on the screen. Sound effects are just as easy—if not easier—to handle. The simplest way is to call the applet's play() method, which will play the sound from beginning to end. However, if you want a little extra control over the sound, you can create an AudioClip object, whose method's enable you to play, stop, and loop the sound.

Review Questions

1. What two types of image files can be loaded by a Java applet?

2. What two parameters are required by methods such as getImage() and getAudioClip()?

3. What's the only type of audio file recognized by Java?

4. How do you display an image after it's loaded?

5. Do image and sound files always have to be stored in the same directory as the HTML or CLASS file?

6. How do you display an image larger or smaller than normal?

7. How can you determine the width and height of an image?

8. What's the difference between a document and code base URL?

9. Why does creating an AudioClip object give you more control over your sound effects?

Review Exercises

1. Write an applet that displays the SNAKE.GIF image at three times its normal size.

2. Write an applet that loops the SPACEMUSIC.AU file as soon as the applet starts up. The applet should have a Stop button that enables the user to stop the sound.

3. Write an applet that has three buttons for displaying an image at 50%, 100%, and 200% of its normal size. Use the SNAKE.GIF image that you used earlier in this chapter. When the user clicks a button, you should display the image at the selected size, reducing or enlarging the applet's size to accommodate the image. But make the applet's minimum horizontal size 150 so that the three buttons always fit across the top. Figures 27.6,

27.7, and 27.8 show the ImageApplet3 applet displaying the image in its three sizes. (You can find the solution for this exercise in the CHAP27 folder of this book's CD-ROM.)

Figure 27.5

Here's the image at 50%.

Figure 27.6

Here's the image at 100%.

Figure 27.7

And here's the image at 200%.

CHAPTER 28

Communications

Not to state the obvious, but because applets are used on the Internet, they have the ability to perform a few types of telecommunications tasks. One of these tasks, connecting to other Web sites, is a snap to implement. Other tasks, such as accessing data in files, are difficult to implement because you constantly stumble over the security restrictions built into applets. Dealing with the intricacies of Internet security is beyond the scope of this book. If you're interested in this topic, you should pick up an advanced Java book. In this chapter, though, you'll get a chance to use Java to communicate over the Internet by connecting to URLs that the user supplies.

URL Objects

In the previous chapter, you got a quick introduction to URL objects when you obtained the location of graphics and sound files by calling the getDocumentBase() and getCodeBase() methods. You used the URL objects returned by these methods in order to display images and play sounds that were stored on your computer. In that case, the locations of the files were on your own system. What you didn't know then is that you can create an URL object directly by calling its constructor. Using this technique, you can create URL objects that represent other sites on the World Wide Web.

Although the URL class's constructor has several forms, the easiest to use requires a string argument holding the URL from which you want to create the object. Using this constructor, you create the URL object like this:

```
URL url = new URL(str);
```

This constructor's single argument is the complete URL of the location to which you want to connect. This URL string must be properly constructed or the URL constructor will throw an exception (generate an error). You'll soon see what to do about such errors.

Example: Creating an URL Object

Suppose you want to create an URL object for the URL http://www.sun.com, which is where you can find lots of information about Java. You'd create the URL object like this:

```
URL url = new URL("http://www.sun.com");
```

If the URL construction goes okay, you can then use the URL object however you need to in your applet.

URL Exceptions

As I mentioned previously, if the argument for the URL constructor is in error (meaning that it doesn't use valid URL syntax), the URL class throws an exception. Because the URL class is designed to throw an exception when necessary, Java gives you no choice except to handle that exception properly. This prevents the applet from accidentally attempting to use a defective URL object. You'll learn all the details about handling exceptions in Chapter 30, "Exceptions." For now, though, you need to know how to handle the URL exception because your applets will not compile properly until you add the exception-handling code.

Basically, when you need to watch out for an exception, you enclose the code that may generate the error in a try program block. If the code in the block generates an exception, you handle that exception in a catch program block. (It's no coincidence that when code "throws" an exception, Java expects the program to "catch" that exception.) When you create an URL object from a string, you must watch out for the MalformedURLException exception, which is one of the many exceptions defined by Java. To do this, use the try and catch program blocks, as shown in Listing 28.1.

Listing 28.1   LST28_1.TXT: Handling URL Exceptions.

```
try
{
    URL url = new URL(str);
}
catch (MalformedURLException e)
{
    DisplayErrorMessage();
}
```

The Applet Context

Once you have the URL object created, you need a way to pass it on to the browser in which the applet is running. It is the browser, after all, that will make the Web connection for you. But, how do you refer to the browser from within your applet? You call the getAppletContext() method, which returns an AppletContext object. This AppletContext object represents the browser in which the applet is running. You call getAppletContext() like this:

```
AppletContext context = getAppletContext();
```

Once you have the context, you can link to the URL represented by the URL object you already created. You do this by calling the AppletContext object's showDocument() method, like this:

```
context.showDocument(url);
```

If all goes well, the above line will connect you to the requested URL.

Example: Using an AppletContext to Link to an URL

Suppose that you want to enable the user to enter an URL string in your applet and then use URL and AppletContext objects to link to that URL. Listing 28.2 shows how you might accomplish this feat of Internet prestidigitation:

Listing 28.2   LST28_2.TXT: Linking to an URL.

```
String str = GetURLStringFromUser();

try
{
    URL url = new URL(str);
    AppletContext context = getAppletContext();
    context.showDocument(url);
}
catch (MalformedURLException e)
{
    DisplayErrorMessage();
}
```

In Listing 28.2, the program first calls a method that retrieves a text string from the user. This text string is the URL to which the user wants to connect. Then, the try program block starts. The first line inside the try block attempts to create an URL object from the string the user entered. Of course, because user's often make mistakes when typing in long strings of characters, the string the user entered may not be a syntactically valid URL. In that case, program execution automatically jumps to the catch program block, where your applet displays an appropriate error message. If the URL object gets created okay, though, the program finishes the code in the try block, getting the AppletContext object and making the link to the URL. In this case, Java completely ignores the catch block.

Example: Using an AppletContext in an Applet

Ready for a full-fledged example? Listing 28.3 is a complete applet that enables the user to link to an URL. Listing 28.4 is the HTML document that loads the applet. Because this applet actually interacts with a browser and the Internet, you must have made your Internet connection before running the applet. Then, to run the applet, load its HTML document into a Java-compatible browser such as Netscape Navigator 2.0. When you do, you'll see a window similar to that shown in Figure 28.1. In this figure, the user has already entered the URL he wishes to visit. In Figure 28.2, the browser has made the requested connection. Figure 28.3 shows the browser when the user enters an invalid URL string.

> **Note:** You can load ConnectApplet's HTML file using Appletviewer, if you like. However, you will be unable to make a connection to the requested URL. You can, however, see what happens when you enter a badly constructed URL string.

Listing 28.3   ConnectApplet.java: An Applet That Connects to User-Requested URLs.

```java
import java.awt.*;
import java.applet.*;
import java.net.*;

public class ConnectApplet extends Applet
{
    TextField textField;
    boolean badURL;

    public void init()
    {
        textField = new TextField("", 40);
        Button button = new Button("Connect");

        add(textField);
        add(button);

        badURL = false;
    }
```

```
public void paint(Graphics g)
{
    Font font = new Font("TimesRoman", Font.PLAIN, 24);
    g.setFont(font);

    int height = font.getSize();

    if (badURL)
        g.drawString("Bad URL!", 60, 130);
    else
    {
        g.drawString("Type the URL to which", 25, 130);
        g.drawString("you want to connect,",
            25, 130+height);
        g.drawString("and then click the Connect",
            25, 130+height*2);
        g.drawString("button.", 25, 130 + height*3);
    }
}

public boolean action(Event evt, Object arg)
{
    String str = textField.getText();

    try
    {
        URL url = new URL(str);
        AppletContext context = getAppletContext();
        context.showDocument(url);
    }
    catch (MalformedURLException e)
    {
        badURL = true;
        repaint();
    }

    return true;
}
}
```

Tell Java that the applet uses the classes in the awt *package.*
Tell Java that the applet uses the classes in the applet *package.*
Tell Java that the applet uses the classes in the net *package.*
Derive the ConnectApplet *class from Java's* Applet *class.*
  Declare the class's data fields.
  Override the init() *method.*
    Create the TextField *and* Button *controls.*
    Add the controls to the applet's layout.
    Initialize the bad URL flag.
  Override the paint() *method.*
    Create and set the Graphics *object's font.*

> *Get the font's height.*
> *If the applet has a bad URL string...*
>> *Display an error message.*
> *Or, of the URL is OK...*
>> *Draw the applet's instructions.*
> *Override the `action()` method.*
>> *Get the URL string the user entered.*
>> *Start the try block.*
>>> *Attempt to create an URL object from the string.*
>>> *Get the `AppletContext` object.*
>>> *Make the connection.*
>> *Start the catch block.*
>>> *Set the bad URL flag to true.*
>>> *Repaint the applet in order to display the error message.*
>> *Tell Java that the applet handled the event message.*

Listing 28.4   CONNECTAPPLET.HTML: ConnectApplet's HTML Document.

```
<title>Applet Test Page</title>
<h1>Applet Test Page</h1>
<applet
    code="ConnectApplet.class"
    width=300
    height=250
    name="ConnectApplet">
</applet>
```

Figure 28.1

Here, the user is
ready to make a
connection.

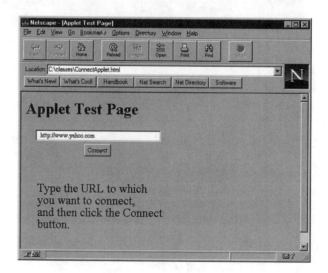

Figure 28.2

If the URL is OK,
the browser
connects.

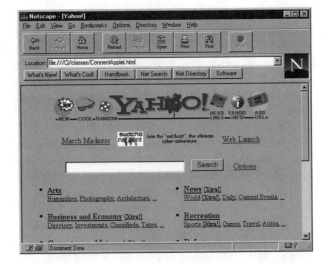

Figure 28.3

If the URL is
constructed
improperly, the
applet displays an
error message.

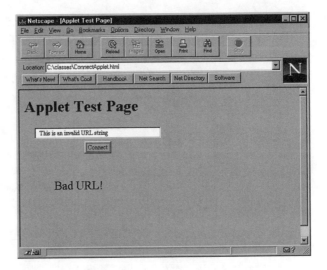

Creating a "Favorite URLs" Applet

Nothing, of course, says that the string from which you create an URL object must be typed in by the user at runtime. You can hard-code the URLs you want to use right in the applet's source code, which not only ensures that the URLs will always be correct (unless the associated server changes), but also makes it quick and easy to jump to whatever URL you want. Using this idea, you can put together an applet that gives you pushbutton control over your connections, selecting your URLs as easily as you'd select a radio station.

The ConnectApplet2 applet, shown in Listing 28.5, is just such an applet. In its current version, it provides four buttons that give you instant connection to the Web sites represented by the buttons. Want to jump to Microsoft's Web page? Give the Microsoft button a click. Want to check out the latest news at Macmillan Computer Publishing? Click the Macmillan button. Of course, just as with the original ConnectApplet, you must have your Internet connection established before you run the applet. And, you must run the applet from a Java-compatible browser.

When you run the applet from Netscape Navigator 2.0, you see the window shown in Figure 28.4. As you can see, the applet currently displays four buttons, one each for the Sun, Netscape, Microsoft, and Macmillan Web sites. Just click a button to jump to the associated site. (Figure 28.5 shows the browser after the user has clicked the Macmillan button.) When you're through with that site, use the browser's Back button to return to the ConnectApplet2 applet. Then, choose another site.

Sure, you can do the same sort of thing with an HTML document using Web links. But, let's face it, applets are way cooler.

Figure 28.4

ConnectApplet2
running under
Netscape
Navigator 2.0.

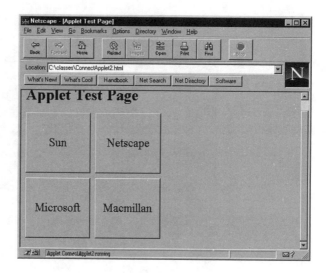

Figure 28.5

After clicking the
Macmillan button.

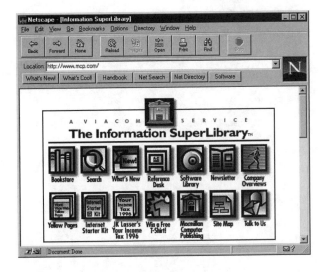

Listing 28.5   ConnectApplet2.java: A "Favorite URLs" Applet.

```java
import java.awt.*;
import java.applet.*;
import java.net.*;

public class ConnectApplet2 extends Applet
{
    boolean badURL;

    public void init()
    {
        GridLayout layout = new GridLayout(2, 2, 10, 10);
        setLayout(layout);

        Font font = new Font("TimesRoman", Font.PLAIN, 24);
        setFont(font);

        Button button = new Button("Sun");
        add(button);
        button = new Button("Netscape");
        add(button);
        button = new Button("Microsoft");
        add(button);
        button = new Button("Macmillan");
        add(button);

        badURL = false;
    }
```

continues

Listing 28.5 Continued

```java
public void paint(Graphics g)
{
    if (badURL)
        g.drawString("Bad URL!", 60, 130);
}

public boolean action(Event evt, Object arg)
{
    String str;

    if (arg == "Sun")
        str = "http://www.sun.com";
    else if (arg == "Netscape")
        str = "http://www.netscape.com";
    else if (arg == "Microsoft")
        str = "http://www.microsoft.com";
    else
        str = "http://www.mcp.com";

    try
    {
        URL url = new URL(str);
        AppletContext context = getAppletContext();
        context.showDocument(url);
    }
    catch (MalformedURLException e)
    {
        badURL = true;
        repaint();
    }

    return true;
}
}
```

Tell Java that the applet uses the classes in the awt *package.*
Tell Java that the applet uses the classes in the applet *package.*
Tell Java that the applet uses the classes in the net *package.*
Derive the ConnectApplet2 *class from Java's* Applet *class.*
  Declare the class's data field.
  Override the init() *method.*
    Create and set the applet's layout manager.
    Create and set the applet's font.
    Add four button controls to the layout.
    Initialize the bad URL flag.
  Override the paint() *method.*
    If the applet has a bad URL string...
      Display an error message.

Override the `action()` *method.*
  Declare a local string variable.
  Get the URL *string the user requested.*
  Start the try block.
    Create an URL *object from the string.*
    Get the `AppletContext` *object.*
    Make the connection.
  Start the catch block.
    Set the bad URL flag to true.
    Repaint the applet in order to display the error message.
  Tell Java that the applet handled the event message.

In Listing 28.5, notice how, even though the URLs are hard-coded into the program, the `action()` method still surrounds the call to the URL constructor with the `try` and `catch` program blocks. This is because Java insists that the applet handle the exception should the URL class throw it. If you remove the exception handling, the applet won't compile. Anyway, having a little extra protection never hurts. Handling the exception is a good way to test whether your hard-coded URLs are valid. I've never known a programmer yet who didn't need to be protected from himself!

Summary

Although a running applet has to deal with many security considerations, it can usually connect to other Web sites. To do this, the applet creates an URL object representing the site to which the applet should connect. The applet then instructs the browser containing the applet to make the connection, by calling the `AppletContext` object's `showDocument()` method. In spite of the telecommunications limitations inherent in applets, you can easily create Internet-aware applets.

Review Questions

1. What is the single argument accepted by the version of the URL constructor you studied in this chapter?

2. What is an AppletContext object?

3. How do you obtain a AppletContext object?

4. How can you be sure you have a valid URL object before trying to connect to the URL?

5. What are the two types of program blocks that handle exceptions?

6. How do you connect to the URL represented by an URL object?

7. What type of exception is thrown by the URL class?

Review Exercises

1. Write an applet that accepts URLs from the user and displays a message indicating whether the URL is valid or not.

2. Modify the ConnectApplet2 applet so that it features at least eight buttons that'll enable you to jump to your favorite Web sites. The final applet should look something like Figure 28.6 when it's running under Netscape Navigator. (You can find the solution for this exercise in the CHAP28 folder of this book's CD-ROM.)

Figure 28.6

The more Web-site buttons you add, the more places you can visit with a click of the mouse.

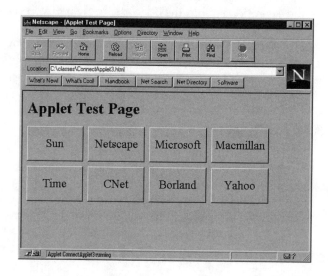

Part IV

Advanced Java

CHAPTER 29

Packages and Interfaces

As you write more and more Java source code, you're going to start having a hard time finding the snippets of code you need for your current project. You may, for example, have a number of classes that are related in some way, yet are scattered in separate files making it difficult to determine exactly what you have. One solution to this problem is *packages*, which enable you to organize your classes into logical groups.

You may also have a number of classes that contain capabilities that you'd like to use in a newly derived class. However, Java does not allow *multiple inheritance*, which is deriving a single class directly from two or more classes simultaneously. To get around this deliberate limitation, Java uses something called *interfaces*, which enable the programmer to define capabilities for classes without implementing those capabilities until the classes that use the interface are defined. In this chapter, you study both *packages* and *interfaces*.

Packages

You may not realize it, but you've been using Java packages since the first applet you created. That's because all of the Java Developer's Kit's classes are organized into packages. You've been importing those packages into your source code with code similar to this:

```
import java.awt.*;
import java.applet.*;
```

If you examine either of these lines, you'll see that each starts with the word java followed by a package name and an asterisk, each element being separated by a dot. The use of the different names separated by the dots illustrates the hierarchy that Java's creators used when they created the Java packages. This hierarchy is used not only as a way of referring to class names in source code, but also as a way to organize the .CLASS files that comprise a class library.

If you look in your JAVA\LIB folder, you'll find the JAVA folder, within which is the AWT and APPLET folders. In the AWT and APPLET folders are the .class files for the awt and applet packages. You can see that the import lines indicate the directory structure under which the package source-code files are stored. When Java's compiler runs into such import lines, it expects the directory structure to match the package's hierarchy.

In the preceding two sample import lines, the asterisks mean that Java should import all of the classes of the awt and applet packages into the applet you're writing. If you wanted to, you could streamline the import process by importing exactly the classes used in your source code. (When doing this, keep in mind that Java is case sensitive.) You would do this by replacing the asterisk with the name of the class you want to import. For example, to import only the Button class from the awt package, you use this line:

```
import java.awt.Button;
```

However, because you frequently need to access more than a single class in a package, it's often more convenient to import all of the classes at once.

Note: If you like, you can do without import statements at all. To do this, you need to use fully qualified package names when referring to a Java class. For example, to create a new button object, you could write java.awt.Button button = new java.awt.Button(label). As you can see, however, such program lines become unwieldy, which is why Java supports the import statement.

Creating Your Own Packages

As you write your own classes, you're going to want to organize the related classes into packages just as Java does. You do this by organizing your classes into the same sort of hierarchy. For example, you may want to start with a folder called MYPACKAGES into which you'll store the .class files that make up your class libraries. This folder should be in the folder in which your main source-code files are located. If you've been following the instructions given earlier in this book, you've been using a folder called CLASSES for this purpose.

To add a class to a package, you put the following line at the top of the class's source code:

```
package PackageName;
```

Here, the keyword `package` tells Java that you want to add this class to a package. The name of this package will be `PackageName`. The package line must be the first line in the class's source code (except for blank lines or comments).

Example: Creating a Simple Package

Suppose that you want to create a class called `DisplayClass` that returns a test string to be displayed in an applet. You want this class to be part of a package called DISPLAY. Listing 29.1 shows the source code for the `DisplayClass` class:

Listing 29.1   DisplayClass.java: The *DisplayClass* Class.

```
package MyPackages.Display;

public class DisplayClass
{
    public String GetDisplayText()
    {
        return "Display Text";
    }
}
```

Note: When you examine Listing 29.1, you may wonder how `DisplayClass` can reference Java's `String` class without including an `import` line at the top of the listing. The class gets away with this because Java automatically imports the java.lang package, where the `String` class is defined.

The first line of Listing 29.1 determines not only the name of the package, but also the way it must be stored on your hard drive. That is, the DisplayClass.class file must end up in a folder called Display, which itself must be in a folder called MYPACKAGES. To compile DisplayClass.java, follow these steps:

1. In your CLASSES folder, create a folder called MYPACKAGES. This is where you will create the folders needed by each of the packages you create.

2. In the MYPACKAGES folder, create a folder called DISPLAY. This folder will hold any of the classes that are part of the `Display` package.

3. Type in Listing 29.1 and save it in the DISPLAY folder, under the name DisplayClass.java. (If you don't want to type, you can copy the file from this book's CD-ROM.)

4. Select the MS-DOS Prompt command from the Start menu's Program group and switch to the CLASSES\MYPACKAGES\DISPLAY folder, as shown in Figure 29.1.

5. At the MS-DOS prompt, type `javac DisplayClass.java`. Java's compiler then compiles the DisplayClass.java file, creating the DisplayClass.class file in your DISPLAY folder.

Figure 29.1

To compile a package's class, you must switch to the folder in which the class's source code is stored.

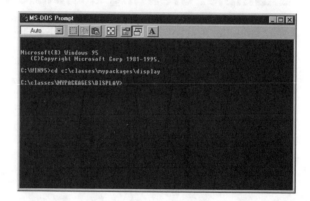

As you can see in Figure 29.2, if you now look in your DISPLAY folder, you'll have not only the original source code file for the `DisplayClass` class, but also the DisplayClass.class file, which is the class's byte-code representation that Java can understand. Congratulations! You've just created your first package.

Figure 29.2

After compiling, you will have the class's .CLASS file on your disk.

Example: Using the New Package

Now that you've created a package, you'd probably like to use it in an applet. To do this, you must first import the class into the applet's source code file. You can then use the class in exactly the same way you've been using Java's classes throughout this book. Listing 29.2 is an applet, called PackageApplet, that demonstrates how to use your new package. Listing 29.3 is the applet's HTML document.

Listing 29.2 PackageApplet.java: An Applet That Uses Your New Package.

```java
import java.awt.*;
import java.applet.*;
import MyPackages.Display.DisplayClass;

public class PackageApplet extends Applet
{
    public void paint(Graphics g)
    {
        Font font = new Font("TimesRoman", Font.PLAIN, 24);
        g.setFont(font);

        DisplayClass myClass = new DisplayClass();
        String s = myClass.GetDisplayText();

        g.drawString(s, 60, 80);
    }
}
```

Listing 29.3 PACKAGEAPPLET.HTML: PackageApplet's HTML Document.

```html
<title>Applet Test Page</title>
<h1>Applet Test Page</h1>
<applet
    code="PackageApplet.class"
    width=250
    height=250
    name="PackageApplet">
</applet>
```

Notice how the third line in Listing 29.2 imports the DisplayClass class from the Display package. You also could have used the line import MyPackages.Display.*, as you did with the Java packages in the first two lines of the listing. Because there is currently only one class in the package, using the asterisk achieves exactly the same results as specifying the class's name in the import line. However, when you add other classes to the package, the asterisk will tell Java to include those classes, as well.

To see how all this package stuff works with the PackageApplet applet, follow these steps:

1. Type in Listings 29.2 and 29.3 and save them in your CLASSES folder (the same folder that contains your new MYPACKAGES folder). If you prefer, you can copy the listings from this book's CD-ROM.

2. In your DOS window, switch to the CLASSES directory.

3. Type `javac PackageApplet.java` to compile the applet into a .class file.

4. Run the applet by typing appletviewer packageapplet.html.

When you run the PackageApplet applet, you see the window shown in Figure 29.3. The text that's displayed in the applet is acquired by the call to the `DisplayClass` class's `GetDisplayText()` method. This class is part of your new `Display` class. When you run the applet, Java knows where to find the `Display` class because of the hierarchy of folders you created to mirror the MYPACKAGES\DISPLAY \ DisplayClass.class hierarchy.

Figure 29.3

PackageApplet displays the text string obtained from a class defined in your new `Display` package.

Example: Extending the Package

Now that you've got the package started, you can extend it simply by creating new classes that have the line `package MyPackages.Display` at the top of the source code. Thanks to the folder hierarchy you've developed (and that Java insists upon), all the class files (both source and byte-code) in the `Display` package will end up in the DISPLAY folder. You could have one or a hundred.

You can add new packages to your growing library by creating folders inside the MYPACKAGES folder and storing the new classes there. Suppose, for example, that you want to start a new package called `Shapes`. The classes you want to add to this package are called `Star`, `Hexagon`, and `Triangle`. You'd then follow the steps given here:

1. Create a folder called SHAPES inside the MYPACKAGES folder. This is where you'll store all the files associated with the `Shapes` package.

2. Create the `Star`, `Hexagon`, and `Triangle` classes in separate source-code files, being sure to place the line `package MyPackages.Shapes;` at the top of each file.

3. Switch to the C:\CLASSES\MYPACKAGES\SHAPES folder and type `javac Star.java` to compile the `Star` class. Compile the `Hexagon` and `Triangle` classes in the same way.

4. Write the source code for the applet that uses your new `Shapes` package, storing the file in the C:\CLASSES directory. Remember to put the line `import MyPackages.Shapes.*;` at the top of the file. The asterisk ensures that all classes in the `Shapes` package are imported into the program.

Interfaces

Packages are fairly easy to understand, being little more than a way to organize related classes, whether supplied with Java or created by a programmer like yourself. Interfaces, on the other hand, are a concept that is a bit harder to grasp. To really understand Java's interfaces, you have to know about something called *multiple inheritance*, which is not allowed in Java, but which is often used in other object-oriented languages.

Multiple inheritance means creating a new class that inherits behavior directly from more than one superclass. To make this concept a little clearer, look at how you derive classes from superclasses in Java. For example, every applet you've created so far has been derived from Java's `Applet` class, like this:

```
public class AppletName extends Applet
```

The preceding line tells Java that you want to create a new class that inherits the data fields and methods of the `Applet` class. This is a sample of *single inheritance*. Now, suppose that you had a class of your own, called `MyClass`, that implemented some capabilities that you also want your new applet to inherit. In a language like C++, you simply add the class to a list of superclasses, like this:

```
public class AppletName extends Applet, MyClass
```

This would be an example of multiple inheritance if Java allowed such a thing. However, for many reasons, Java's designers decided that multiple inheritance was too cumbersome and unpredictable to be useful. They still liked the idea, though, of being able to declare a set of behaviors that can be inherited by one or more classes. So, they came up with *interfaces*.

The Basic Interface

An *interface* is very much like a class—with one important difference. None of the methods declared in an interface are implemented in the interface itself. Instead, these methods must be implemented in any class that uses the interface. In short, interfaces describe behaviors but do not detail how those behaviors will be carried out.

Interfaces are so much like classes, in fact, that they are declared in almost exactly the same way. You just replace the `class` keyword with the `interface` keyword, like this:

```
interface MyInterface
{
}
```

The preceding example is a complete interface, meaning that it can be compiled, after which other Java programs can reference it. You compile an interface exactly the same way you compile a class. First, you save the interface's source code in a file with the .java extension. Then you use the Java compiler, javac, to compile the source code into byte-code form. Just like a normal class, the byte-code file will have the .class extension.

Missing from the preceding sample interface are the methods that describe the interface's behaviors. In the sections that follow, you'll learn how to add this important element to an interface.

Example: Creating an Interface

Suppose that instead of creating a full-fledged class out of your Display package's DisplayClass class, you want to make it an interface. (Yes, just like classes, you can make interfaces part of a package.) Listing 29.4 shows how the source code would be modified.

Listing 29.4   DisplayInterface.java: Creating an Interface.

```
package MyPackages.Display;

public interface DisplayInterface
{
    public String GetDisplayText();
}
```

The first line in Listing 29.4 is exactly like the first line in Listing 29.1, which shows the original class. The first line specifies that this interface is to be part of the MyPackages.Display package. The second line declares the interface. The only difference here is the use of the interface keyword in place of class and the new name, DisplayInterface.

Now, the real difference between a class and an interface becomes evident. Although Listing 29.4 declares the GetDisplayText() method, it doesn't actually implement the method. That is, you can see from the interface that GetDisplayText() is supposed to return a String object, but there isn't a clue as to how that String object is created or what it contains. Those details are left up to any class that decides to implement the interface.

But before you worry about implementing the interface in a class, you have to compile the interface source code. To do that, follow these steps:

1. Type in Listing 29.3 and save it in the DISPLAY folder, under the name DisplayInterface.java. (If you don't want to type, you can copy the file from this book's CD-ROM.)

2. Select the MS-DOS Prompt command from the Start menu's Program group and switch to the CLASSES\MYPACKAGES\DISPLAY folder.

3. At the MS-DOS prompt, type `javac DisplayInterface.java`. Java's compiler then compiles the DisplayInterface.java file, creating the DisplayInterface.class file in your DISPLAY folder.

Implementing an Interface

Now that you have your new interface compiled, you can implement it in a class. This means not only telling Java that you'll be using the interface, but also implementing the interface within the new class. That is, every method that is listed in the interface's declaration must be defined in the class's source code. Listing 29.5 is a new applet, called InterfaceApplet, that shows how to implement the `DisplayInterface` interface. When you compile and run this applet, you see exactly the same display as that produced by the original version, PackageApplet. Notice how the listing uses the `implements` keyword to tell Java that the applet will be implementing the `DisplayInterface` interface.

Listing 29.5   InterfaceApplet.java: An Applet That Implements the *DisplayInterface* Interface.

```
import java.awt.*;
import java.applet.*;
import MyPackages.Display.DisplayInterface;

public class InterfaceApplet extends Applet
    implements DisplayInterface
{
    public void paint(Graphics g)
    {
        Font font = new Font("TimesRoman", Font.PLAIN, 24);
        g.setFont(font);

        String s = GetDisplayText();

        g.drawString(s, 60, 80);
    }

    public String GetDisplayText()
    {
        return "Display Text";
    }
}
```

Tell Java that the applet uses the classes in the awt *package.*
Tell Java that the applet uses the classes in the applet *package.*
Tell Java that the applet uses the Display *package's* DisplayInterface*.*
Derive InterfaceApplet *from* Applet *and implement* DisplayInterface*.*
   Override the paint() *method.*
     Create and set the Graphics *object's font.*
     Get the display string.
     Draw the display string.
   Define the interface's GetDisplayText() *method.*
     Return the display string.

Tip: A class can implement as many interfaces as it needs to. To implement multiple interfaces, just list the interfaces after the implements keyword, separating each interface name from the others with a comma. Remember, however, that you must implement in your new class all the methods declared in all the interfaces you implement.

Note: There's quite a lot to learn about interfaces. However, due to the skill level of this book and the fact that you probably won't have to worry about interfaces until you're an experienced Java programmer, only the basics have been presented here. Chances are good that you won't have to create interfaces at all. It's just good to know they're there in case you need them.

Summary

Packages are a great way to create and organize class libraries. The more Java code you write, the more you'll appreciate the ability to create your own packages. Although you won't need to use interfaces for some time to come (if at all), interfaces are a unique element of the Java programming language. Although other object-oriented languages such as C++ allow multiple inheritance, only Java supports the idea of interfaces, which can be powerful tools when they're needed.

Review Questions

1. What's a package?

2. How do you tell Java that a source-code file uses a particular package?

3. How do you add a class or interface to a package?

4. How do you tell Java that the class you're creating implements a particular interface?

5. What's the biggest difference between an interface and a class?

6. How are interfaces similar to classes?

7. How does the complete name of a package relate to the package's storage on your disk?

Review Exercises

1. Add a new class to the Display package. This class should return an integer representing the size of the font to use when drawing the display text.

2. Change the class you wrote in exercise 1 to an interface. Write an applet that implements the new interface.

CHAPTER 30

Exceptions

When you write applets or applications using Java, sooner or later you're going to run into exceptions. An *exception* is a special type of error object that is created when something goes wrong in a program. After Java creates the exception object, it sends it to your program, an action called *throwing an exception*. It's up to your program to *catch* the exception. You do this by writing the exception-handling code. In this chapter, you get the inside info on these important error-handling objects.

Java's Exceptions

In Chapter 28, "Communications," you got a quick look at exceptions and how they are handled in a program. Specifically, you had to be prepared to handle an exception when you created an URL object from a text string. This is because the text string may not use the proper syntax for an URL, making it impossible to create the URL object. In this case, the URL constructor throws an exception object called MalformedURLException. Listing 30.1 shows the code segment that handles this exception.

Listing 30.1   LST30_1.TXT: Handling an Exception.

```
try
{
    URL url = new URL(str);
    AppletContext context = getAppletContext();
    context.showDocument(url);
}
```

continues

Listing 30.1   Continued

```
catch (MalformedURLException e)
{
    badURL = true;
    repaint();
}
```

As you can see from the listing, you place the code that may cause the exception in a `try` program block, whereas the exception-handling code goes into a `catch` program block. In this case, the first line of the `try` block attempts to create an URL object from the string given in the variable `str`. If the string is not properly formatted for an URL, the URL constructor throws a `MalformedURLException`. When this happens, Java ignores the rest of the code in the `try` block and jumps to the `catch` block, where the program handles the exception. On the other hand, if the URL object gets created okay, Java executes all the code in the `try` block and skips the `catch` block.

> **Note:** The `catch` program block does more than direct program execution. It actually catches the exception object thrown by Java. For example, in Listing 30.1, you can see the exception object being caught inside the parentheses following the `catch` keyword. This is very similar to a parameter being received by a method. In this case, the type of the "parameter" is `MalformedURLException` and the name of the parameter is `e`. If you need to, you can access the exception object's methods through the `e` object.

Java defines many exception objects that may be thrown by the methods in Java's classes. How do you know which exceptions you have to handle? First, if you write an applet that calls a method that may throw an exception, Java insists that you handle the exception in one way or another. If you fail to do so, your applet will not compile. Instead, you'll receive an error message indicating where your program may generate the exception (see Figure 30.1).

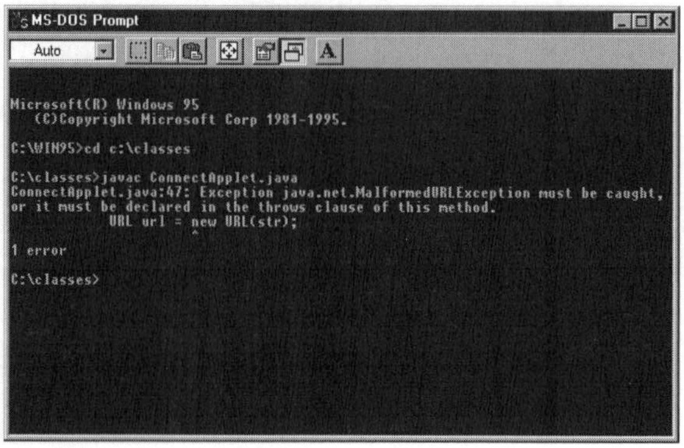

Figure 30.1

Java's compiler gives you an error message if you fail to handle an exception in your applet.

Although the compiler's error messages are a clue that something is amiss, the clever programmer will look up a method in Java's documentation before using the method. Then, the programmer will know in advance whether that method requires exception-handling code. If you're interested in seeing the exceptions that are defined by a package, find the package's section in Java's online documentation (see Figure 30.2), where the classes and exceptions are listed.

Figure 30.2

Java's online documentation lists the exception objects that may be thrown by methods in a class.

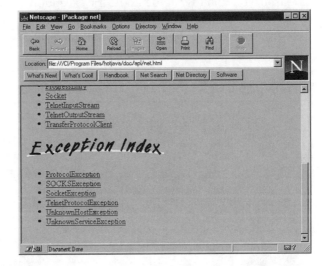

The online documentation also lists all the methods that comprise a particular package. By looking up the method in the documentation (see Figure 30.3), you can see what types of arguments the method expects, the type of value the method returns, and whether the method may throw an exception. If the method shows that it can throw an exception, your code must handle the right type of exception or the program will not compile.

Figure 30.3

The online documentation for a method shows the exception the method may throw.

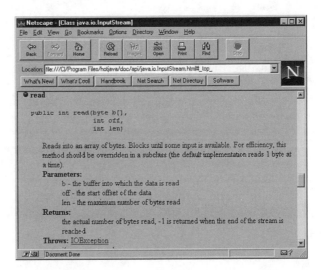

Throwing an Exception

One handy thing about exceptions is that you don't have to handle them in the same method in which the exception is generated. For example, in Listing 30.1, the applet tries to create an URL object. If the URL creation fails, the URL constructor throws an exception that the event() method handles in its catch block. But what if, for some reason, you don't want to handle the exception in the same method in which you call the URL constructor? You can simply pass the buck, so to speak, by throwing the exception on up the method hierarchy. Listing 30.2 shows one way you might do this with the MalformedURLException exception.

Listing 30.2 LST30_2.TXT: Throwing an Exception.

```
public boolean action(Event evt, Object arg)
{
    try
        GetURL();
    catch (MalformedURLException e)
    {
        badURL = true;
        repaint();
    }

    return true;
}

protected void GetURL() throws MalformedURLException
{
    String str = textField.getText();
    URL url = new URL(str);
    AppletContext context = getAppletContext();
    context.showDocument(url);
}
```

In this listing, the call to the URL class's constructor has been moved to a method called GetURL(). However, GetURL() does not directly handle the MalformedURLException exception. Instead, it passes the exception back to the action() method. Java knows that GetURL() wants to pass the exception, because GetURL() adds the phrase throws MalformedURLException to its signature. Throwing the exception, however, doesn't relieve you from handling it eventually. Notice that in Listing 30.2, the exception still gets handled in the action() method.

In short, you can handle an exception in two ways. The first way is to write try and catch program blocks exactly where you call the function that may generate the exception. The second way is to declare the method as throwing the exception, in which case you must write the try and catch program blocks in the method that calls the "throwing" method, as shown in Listing 30.2.

Types of Exceptions

Java defines many different exception objects. Some of these you must always handle in your code if you call a function that may throw the exception. Others are generated by the system when something like memory allocation fails, an expression tries to divide by zero, a null value is used inappropriately, and so on. You can choose to watch for this second kind of exception or let Java deal with them.

Just as with programming before exceptions existed, you should always be on the lookout for places in your program where an exception could be generated. These places are usually associated with user input, which can be infamously unpredictable. However, programmers, too, have been known to make mistakes in their programs that lead to exception throwing. Some common exceptions you may want to watch out for at appropriate places in your applet are listed in Table 30.1.

Table 30.1　Common Java Exceptions.

Exceptions	*Description*
ArithmeticException	Caused by math errors such as division by zero
ArrayIndexOutOfBounds Exception	Caused by bad array indexes
ArrayStoreException	Caused when a program tries to store the wrong type of data in an array
FileNotFoundException	Caused by an attempt to access a nonexistent file
IOException	Caused by general I/O failures, such as inability to read from a file
NullPointerException	Caused by referencing a null object
NumberFormatException	Caused when a conversion between strings and numbers fails
OutOfMemoryException	Caused when there's not enough memory to allocate a new object
SecurityException	Caused when an applet tries to perform an action not allowed by the browser's security setting
StackOverflowException	Caused when the system runs out of stack space
StringIndexOutOfBounds Exception	Caused when a program attempts to access a nonexistent character position in a string

> **Tip:** You can catch all types of exceptions by setting up your `catch` block for exceptions of type `Exception`, like this: `catch (Exception e)`. Call the exception's `getMessage()` method (inherited from the `Throwable` superclass) to get information about the specific exception that you've intercepted.

Determining the Exceptions to Handle

Experienced programmers usually know when their code may generate an exception of some sort. However, when you first start writing applets with exception-handling code, you may not be sure what type of exceptions to watch out for. One way to discover this information is to see what exceptions get generated as you test your applet. Listing 30.3, for example, is an applet called ExceptionApplet that divides two integer numbers obtained from the user and displays the integer result (dropping any remainder). Because the applet must deal with user input, the probability of disaster is high. ExceptionApplet, however, contains no exception-handling code.

Listing 30.3   ExceptionApplet.java: An Applet with No Exception Handling.

```
import java.awt.*;
import java.applet.*;

public class ExceptionApplet extends Applet
{
    TextField textField1, textField2;
    String answerStr;

    public void init()
    {
        textField1 = new TextField(15);
        add(textField1);
        textField2 = new TextField(15);
        add(textField2);
        answerStr = "Undefined";
    }

    public void paint(Graphics g)
    {
        Font font = new Font("TimesRoman", Font.PLAIN, 24);
        g.setFont(font);
```

```
int answer = int1 / int2;
        answerStr = String.valueOf(answer);
        repaint();
        return true;
    }
}
```

You'll use this applet as the starting point for a more robust applet. When you run the applet using Appletviewer, you'll see the window shown in Figure 30.4. Enter a number into each of the two text boxes and then press Enter. The program then divides the first number by the second number and displays the result (see Figure 30.5).

Figure 30.4

This is ExceptionApplet running under Appletviewer.

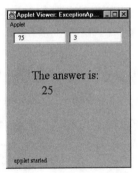

Figure 30.5

ExceptionApplet divides the first number by the second.

As long as the user enters valid numbers into the text boxes, the program runs perfectly. What happens, though, if the user presses Enter when either or both of the text boxes are empty? Java immediately throws a NumberFormatException when the action() method attempts to convert the contents of the text boxes to integer values. You can see this happening by watching the DOS window from which you ran Appletviewer, as shown in Figure 30.6. As you can see in the figure, Java has displayed quite a few lines that trace the exception. The first line (the one that starts with the word exception) tells you the type of exception you've encountered.

Figure 30.6

Here, Java reports a NumberFormat Exception exception.

Example: Catching a Runtime Exception

You now know that the user can cause a NumberFormatException if he or she leaves one or more text boxes blank or enters an invalid numerical value, like the string one. In order to ensure that your applet will not be caught by surprise, you now need to write the code that will handle this exception. Follow these steps to add this new code:

1. Load ExceptionApplet into your text editor.

2. Replace the action() method with the new version shown in Listing 30.4.

Listing 30.4   LST30_4.TXT: Handling the *NumberFormatException* Exception.

```
public boolean action(Event evt, Object arg)
{
    String str1 = textField1.getText();
    String str2 = textField2.getText();

    try
    {
        int int1 = Integer.parseInt(str1);
        int int2 = Integer.parseInt(str2);
        int answer = int1 / int2;
        answerStr = String.valueOf(answer);
    }
    catch (NumberFormatException e)
    {
```

continues

Listing 30.3   Continued

```
            answerStr = "Bad number!";
        }

        repaint();
        return true;
    }
```

3. In the class declaration line, change the name of the class to
ExceptionApplet2.

4. Save the new applet under the name ExceptionApplet2.java.

5. Load the EXCEPTIONAPPLET.HTML file.

6. Change all occurrences of ExceptionApplet to ExceptionApplet2.

7. Save the file as EXCEPTIONAPPLET2.HTML.

In Listing 30.4, the action() method now uses try and catch program blocks to
handle the NumberFormatException gracefully. Figure 30.7 shows what happens now
when the user leaves the text boxes blank. When the program gets to the first call
to String.valueOf(), Java generates the NumberFormatException exception, which
causes program execution to jump to the catch block. In the catch block, the program
sets the display string to Bad number! The call to repaint() ensures that this message
to the user gets displayed on the screen.

Figure 30.7

ExceptionApplet2
handles the
NumberFormat
Exception
exception
gracefully.

Example: Handling Multiple Exceptions

So, here you are, having a good time entering numbers into ExceptionApplet2's text
boxes and getting the results. Without thinking, you enter a zero into the second
box, Java tries to divide the first number by the zero, and *pow!* — you've got yourself
an ArithmeticException exception. What to do? You're already using your catch
block to grab NumberFormatException; now, you've got yet another exception to deal
with.

The good news is that you're not limited to only a single catch block. You can, in fact, create catch blocks for any exceptions you think the program may generate. To see how this works with your new applet, follow these steps:

1. Load ExceptionApplet2 into your text editor.

2. Replace the action() method with the new version shown in Listing 30.5.

Listing 30.5   LST30_5.TXT: Handling Multiple Exceptions.

```
public boolean action(Event evt, Object arg)
{
    String str1 = textField1.getText();
    String str2 = textField2.getText();

    try
    {
        int int1 = Integer.parseInt(str1);
        int int2 = Integer.parseInt(str2);
        int answer = int1 / int2;
        answerStr = String.valueOf(answer);
    }
    catch (NumberFormatException e)
    {
        answerStr = "Bad number!";
    }
    catch (ArithmeticException e)
    {
        answerStr = "Division by 0!";
    }

    repaint();
    return true;
}
```

3. In the class declaration line, change the name of the class to ExceptionApplet3.

4. Save the new applet under the name ExceptionApplet3.java.

5. Load the EXCEPTIONAPPLET.HTML file.

6. Change all occurrences of ExceptionApplet to ExceptionApplet3.

7. Save the file as EXCEPTIONAPPLET3.HTML.

If you examine Listing 30.5, you'll see that the action() method now defines two catch program blocks, one each for the NumberFormatException and ArithmeticException exceptions. In this way, the program can watch for both potential problems from within a single try block. If you discovered another exception that your program may cause, you can add yet another catch block.

Note: Although handling exceptions is a powerful tool for creating crash-proof programs, you should use them only in situations where you have little control over the cause of the exception, such as when dealing with user input. If your applet causes an exception because of a program bug, you should track down and fix the problem rather than try to catch the exception.

Tip: There may be times when you want to be sure that a specific block of code gets executed whether or not an exception is generated. You can do this by adding a `finally` program block after the last `catch`. The code in the `finally` block gets executed after the `try` block or `catch` block finishes its thing.

Summary

A good applet doesn't give the user nasty surprises. It's up to the programmer to check for potential problem spots in programs and guard against program failure. One tool the programmer can use is exceptions, which are objects created by Java when a program encounters a serious error. After Java creates an exception object, it throws the exception and expects some other part of the program to catch the exception.

The `try` and `catch` program blocks enable you to test for exceptions and respond to them as appropriate. Some types of exceptions must be handled in your program before the Java compiler will compile the program. Other exceptions—those that may be generated at runtime by more unpredictable problems like referencing a null pointer or dividing by zero—don't have to be handled in your program. However, a good programmer will design his or her applet so that common exceptions are handled where appropriate.

Review Questions

1. How do you use a `try` program block?

2. How do you use a `catch` program block?

3. Do you have to catch all types of exceptions that might be thrown by Java?

4. When a method you call is defined as potentially throwing an exception, do you have to handle that exception in your program?

5. How many exceptions can you associate with a single `try` block?

6. How do you pass an exception up from a called method to the calling method?

7. What are the two main types of exceptions that Java may throw?

Review Exercises

1. Write an applet that creates a button object. Set up exception-handling code for the OutOfMemoryException exception that could possibly occur when Java tries to allocate resources for the button.

2. Write an applet that catches all Exception objects and displays the string returned by the Exception object's getMessage() method. (Not all Exception objects return message strings. Test your program by generating a divide-by-zero error, which will cause Java to throw an ArithmeticException exception. This exception does generate a message string.) You can find the solution to this exercise in the CHAP30 folder of this book's CD-ROM. The applet is called ExceptionApplet4. Figure 30.8 shows what the applet looks like while running under Appletviewer.

Figure 30.8

ExceptionApplet4 displays the message string returned by an Exception object's getMessage() method.

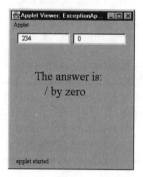

3. Write an applet that enables the user to enter values into an array. Use two TextField objects, the first being where the user should enter the index at which to place the value, and the second being the value to add to the array. Set up the applet so that it responds to ArrayIndexOutOfBoundsException and NumberFormatException exceptions. You can find the solution to this exercise in the CHAP30 folder of this book's CD-ROM. The applet is called ExceptionApplet5. Figure 30.9 shows what the applet looks like while running under Appletviewer.

Figure 30.9

This is
ExceptionApplet5
running under
Appletviewer.

CHAPTER 31

Threads

When using Windows 95 (and other modern operating systems), you know that you can run several programs simultaneously. This ability is called *multitasking*. What you may not know is that many of today's operating systems also allow threads, which are separate processes that are kind of a step down from a complete application. A thread is a lot like a subprogram. An applet can create several threads—several different flows of execution—and run them concurrently. This is a lot like having multitasking inside multitasking. The user knows that he or she can run several applications at a time. The programmer knows that each application can run several threads at a time. In this chapter, you'll learn how to create and manage threads in your own applets.

Two Kinds of Threads

In Java, you can create threads in a couple of ways. The simplest way is to take an existing class and turn it into a thread. You do this by modifying the class so that it implements the `Runnable` interface, which declares the `run()` method required by all types of threads. (The `run()` method contains the code to be executed by a thread.) In the previous chapter, you learned how interfaces in Java enable you to add capabilities to classes simply by implementing the interface in that class. Now, you get a chance to put that idea to work for real.

The second way to create a thread is to write a completely separate class derived from Java's `Thread` class. Because the `Thread` class itself implements the `Runnable` interface, it already contains a `run()` method. However, `Thread`'s `run()` method doesn't do anything. You usually have to override the method in your own class in order to create the type of thread you want.

Converting a Class to a Thread

As I mentioned in the preceding section, the first way to create a thread is to convert a class to a thread. To do this, you must perform several steps, as listed here:

1. Declare the class as implementing the Runnable interface.

2. Implement the run() method.

3. Declare a Thread object as a data field of the class.

4. Create the Thread object and call its start() method.

5. Call the thread's stop() method to destroy the thread.

The following sections look at each of these steps in detail.

Declaring the Class as Implementing the *Runnable* Interface

As you can see in step 1 in the preceding section, to create a thread from a regular class, the class must first be declared as implementing the Runnable interface. For example, if your class is declared as

```
public class MyApplet extends Applet
```

you must change that declaration to

```
public class MyApplet extends Applet
    implements Runnable
```

Implementing the *run()* Method

Now, because you've told Java you're about to implement an interface, you must implement every method in the interface. In the case of Runnable, that's easy because there's only one method, run(), the basic implementation of which looks like this:

```
public void run()
{
}
```

When you start your new thread, Java calls the thread's run() method, so it is in run() where all the action takes place. The preceding example of the run() method is the minimum you need to compile the new source code for the thread. However, in a real program, you'll add code to run() so that the thread does what you want it to do.

Declaring a *Thread* Object

The next step is to declare a Thread object as a data field of the class, like this:

```
Thread thread;
```

The thread object will hold a reference to the thread with which the applet is associated. You will be able to access the thread's methods through this object.

Creating and Starting the *Thread* Object

Now it's time to write the code that creates the thread and gets it going. Assuming that your new threaded class is an applet, you'll often want to create and start the thread in the applet's start() method, as shown in Listing 31.1.

Listing 31.1   LST31_1.TXT: Creating and Starting a *Thread* Object.

```
public void start()
{
    thread = new Thread(this);
    thread.start();
}
```

Note: Back in Chapter 15, "Writing a Simple Applet," you learned that start() is the method that represents the applet's second life-cycle stage. Java calls your applet's life-cycle methods in this order: init(), start(), paint(), stop(), and destroy(). Java calls the start() method whenever the applet needs to start running, usually when it's first loaded or when the user has switched back to the applet from another Web page.

Look at the call to the Thread constructor in Listing 31.1. Notice that the constructor's single argument is the applet's this reference. This is how Java knows with which class to associate the thread. Right after the call to the constructor, the applet calls the Thread object's start() method, which starts the thread running. When the thread starts running, Java calls the thread's run() method, where the thread's work gets done.

Stopping the Thread

When the thread's run() method ends, so does the thread. However, because threads tend to run for quite a while, controlling things like animation in the applet, the user is likely to switch away from your applet before the thread stops. In this case. it's up to your applet to stop the thread. Because Java calls an applet's stop() method whenever the user switches away from the applet, the stop() method is a good place to stop the thread, as shown in Listing 31.2.

Listing 31.2 LST31_2.TXT: Stopping a Thread.

```
public void stop()
{
    thread.stop();
}
```

Example: Using a Thread in an Applet

To understand about threads, you really have to dig in and use them. So in this section, you'll put together an applet that associates itself with a Thread object and runs the thread to control a very simple animated display. The animation in this case is not a bunch of space invaders landing to take over the earth, but rather only a changing number that proves that the thread is running. Listing 31.3 is the applet in question, which is called ThreadApplet. Figure 31.1 shows the applet running under Appletviewer.

Listing 31.3 ThreadApplet.java: Using a Thread in an Applet.

```
import java.awt.*;
import java.applet.*;

public class ThreadApplet extends Applet
  implements Runnable
{
    Thread thread;
    int count;
    String displayStr;
    Font font;

    public void start()
    {
        font = new Font("TimesRoman", Font.PLAIN, 72);
        setFont(font);

        count = 0;
        displayStr = "";

        thread = new Thread(this);
        thread.start();
    }

    public void stop()
    {
        thread.stop();
    }

    public void run()
    {
```

```
        while (count < 1000)
        {
            ++count;
            displayStr = String.valueOf(count);
            repaint();

            try
            {
                thread.sleep(100);
            }
            catch (InterruptedException e)
            {
            }
        }
    }

    public void paint(Graphics g)
    {
        g.drawString(displayStr, 50, 130);
    }
}
```

Figure 31.1

ThreadApplet uses
a thread to count
to 1,000.

Tell Java that the applet uses the classes in the awt *package.*
Tell Java that the applet uses the classes in the applet *package.*
Derive ThreadApplet *from* Applet *and implement* Runnable.
   Declare the class's data fields, including a Thread *object.*
   Override the start() *method.*
      Create and set the applet's display font.
      Initialize data fields.
      Create and start the thread.
   Override the stop() *method.*
      Stop the thread.
   Implement the run() *method*
      Loop one thousand times.

Increment the counter.
Create the display string from the counter.
Tell Java to repaint the applet.
Suspend the thread for one hundred milliseconds.
Override the `paint()` method.
Draw the display string.

There are a couple of interesting things in ThreadApplet of which you should be aware. First, notice that in `run()`, the thread loops one thousand times, after which the `while` loop ends. When the `while` loop ends, so does the `run()` method. This means that when you run ThreadApplet, if you let it count all the way to one thousand, the thread ends on its own. However, what if you switch to a different Web page before ThreadApplet has counted all the way to one thousand? Then, Java calls the applet's `stop()` method, which ends the thread by calling the thread's `stop()` method.

The next point of interest is what's going on inside `run()`. At the beginning of the loop, the program increments the counter, converts the counter's value to a string, and then repaints the applet so that the new count value appears in the window. That code should be as clear as glass to you by now. But what's all that malarkey after the call to `repaint()`? That's where the thread not only times the animation, but also relinquishes the computer so that other threads get a chance to run. Simply, the call to the thread's `sleep()` method suspends the thread for the number of milliseconds given as its single argument. In this case, the sleep time is 100 milliseconds, or one tenth of a second. If you want the animation to run faster, change the 100 to a smaller value. To count slower, change the 100 to a larger value.

> **Caution:** It's important that your threads not dominate the computer's processor for longer than necessary. This is because other threads and processes are almost certainly in competition for the processor at the same time. If your thread will be running for a while, you should call the `sleep()` or `yield()` methods in order to give other processes a chance to run. This is more important on some systems than on others, but since you can't know for sure which system your applet will be running on, be a considerate thread programmer.

Notice that the call to `sleep()` is enclosed in a `try` block and followed by a `catch` block that's watching for `InterruptedException` exceptions. You have to catch this exception because the `sleep()` method throws it. If you fail to catch the exception, your program will not compile.

Deriving a Class from *Thread*

The second way to create a thread is to derive a new class from `Thread`. Then, in your applet's class, you create and start a thread object of your thread class. This leaves you with two processes going simultaneously, the applet and the thread object created in the class. By giving the thread class access to data and methods in the applet, the thread can easily communicate with the applet in order to perform whatever tasks it was written for.

Example: Creating a Thread Class

Suppose that you want to write the same sort of applet as that shown in Listing 31.3, but now you want a separate thread to control the counting process. Listing 31.4 shows how you might write the new class for the thread. (Don't try to compile this code yet. You'll use it in the next example in this chapter.)

Listing 31.4   MyThread.java: A Class Derived from *Thread*.

```java
public class MyThread extends Thread
{
    ThreadApplet2 applet;
    int count;

    MyThread(ThreadApplet2 applet)
    {
        this.applet = applet;
    }

    public void run()
    {
        count = 0;
        while (count < 1000)
        {
            ++count;
            applet.displayStr = String.valueOf(count);
            applet.repaint();

            try
            {
                sleep(100);
            }
            catch (InterruptedException e)
            {
            }
        }
    }
}
```

Derive the MyThread class from Thread.
  Declare the class's data fields, including a Thread object.
  Declare the class's constructor.
    Store the constructor's single parameter.
  Override the run() method
    Loop one thousand times.
      Increment the counter.
      Create the display string from the counter.
      Tell Java to repaint the applet.
      Suspend the thread for one hundred milliseconds.

The first thing to notice in this thread class is that its constructor takes as a single argument a reference to a ThreadApplet2 object, which is the applet from which you'll be running this thread. The thread needs this reference so that it can communicate with the applet.

Next, look at run(). The thread still counts from zero to one thousand, but now it accesses the applet object in order to create the display string and repaint the applet. In the original version of the program, the thread was directly associated with the class, rather than a completely separate process.

Now that you have a new thread class, you'll want to call it up for active duty. You'll do that in the next example.

Example: Using a Separate Thread in an Applet

You'll now put that new thread class to work. To do this, you must have an applet that creates an object from the new thread class and calls that object's start() method to get the thread running. Listing 31.5 shows just such an applet, called ThreadApplet2. When you run the applet under Appletviewer, you'll see the same display that was created in the original version of the applet (ThreadApplet), but now the counting animation is being controlled by a separate thread class.

> **Note:** To compile Listing 31.5, make sure you have both the MyThread.java and ThreadApplet2.java files in your CLASSES folder. Java will then compile both files when you compile ThreadApplet2.java.

Listing 31.5   ThreadApplet2.JAVA: An Applet That Creates a Separate Thread.

```
import java.awt.*;
import java.applet.*;
import MyThread;

public class ThreadApplet2 extends Applet
{
```

```
    MyThread thread;
    String displayStr;
    Font font;

    public void start()
    {
        font = new Font("TimesRoman", Font.PLAIN, 72);
        setFont(font);

        displayStr = "";

        thread = new MyThread(this);
        thread.start();
    }

    public void stop()
    {
        thread.stop();
    }

    public void paint(Graphics g)
    {
        g.drawString(displayStr, 50, 150);
    }
}
```

Tell Java that the applet uses the classes in the awt *package.*
Tell Java that the applet uses the classes in the applet *package.*
Tell Java that the applet uses the MyThread *class.*
Derive the ThreadApplet2 *class from* Applet.
Declare the class's data fields, including a MyThread *object.*
Override the start() *method*
Create and set the applet's font.
Initialize the display string.
Create and start the thread.
Override the stop() *method.*
Stop the thread.
Override the paint() *method.*
Draw the applet's display string, which is the current count.

Synchronizing Multiple Threads

There may be times when you have several threads going, each competing for the same resources. This type of resource competition can be deadly for threads. For example, what if one thread tries to read from a string while another thread is still writing to that string? Depending on the situation, you'll get strange results. You can avoid these problems by telling Java where synchronization problems may occur so that Java can keep an eye out for unhealthy thread competition.

To put Java on guard, you use the synchronized keyword when you define a method (or even a code block). When you mark a method as synchronized, Java creates a monitor object for the class. The first time a thread calls the synchronized method, Java gives the monitor object to that thread. As long as the thread holds the monitor object, no other thread can enter the synchronized section of code. You can think of the monitor object as a key. Unless a thread is holding the key, it can't unlock the door to the synchronized method.

Example: Using a Synchronized Method

Using synchronized methods makes sense only when more than one thread is vying for an applet's resources. For that reason, to demonstrate thread synchronization, you need to create two threads. Listing 31.6 is a thread class, called MyThread2, that can count either forward or backward, depending upon the values you give to the class's constructor. By creating two thread objects from this class, you can experiment with thread synchronization.

> **Note:** To compile Listings 31.6 and 31.7, make sure you have both the MyThread2.java and ThreadApplet3.java files in your CLASSES folder. Java will then compile both files when you compile ThreadApplet3.java.

Listing 31.6   MyThread2.java: A Double-Duty Thread.

```
public class MyThread2 extends Thread
{
    ThreadApplet3 applet;
    boolean forward;
    int count;
    int increment;
    int end;
    int position;

    MyThread2(ThreadApplet3 applet, boolean forward)
    {
        this.applet = applet;
        this.forward = forward;
    }

    public void run()
    {
        InitCounter();
        DoCount();
    }

    protected void InitCounter()
    {
        if (forward)
        {
            count = 0;
            increment = 1;
            end = 1000;
            position = 120;
```

```
        }
        else
        {
            count = 1000;
            increment = -1;
            end = 0;
            position = 180;
        }
    }


    protected void DoCount()
    {

        while (count != end)
        {
            count = count + increment;
            String str = String.valueOf(count);
            applet.SetDisplayStr(str, position);

            try
                sleep(100);
            catch (InterruptedException e)
            {
            }
        }
    }
}
```

Derive the MyThread2 *class from* Thread.
  Declare the class's data fields.
  Declare the class's constructor.
    Store the constructor's parameters.
  Override the run() *method*
    Call the method that sets the values for this thread.
    Call the method that does the counting.
  Define the InitCounter() *method.*
    If the thread is to count forward...
      Set the data fields for forward counting.
    Else if the thread is to count backwards...
      Set the data fields for backwards counting.
  Define the DoCount() *method.*
    Loop until the counting is done.
      Increment the counter and set the display string.
      Go to sleep for one hundred milliseconds.

When you construct a MyThread2 thread object, you must pass two values as parameters: a reference to the applet and a boolean value indicating whether the thread should count forward or backward. The thread uses the boolean value in its InitCounter() method to set the values needed to accomplish the counting. These values are the starting count value (count), the counting increment (increment), the target count (end), and the position at which to display the count in the applet (position). Notice that the increment variable can be either 1 or -1. When the increment gets added to the count, a positive `increment` increases the count by one, whereas a negative `increment` decreases the count by one.

In its `run()` method, the thread calls the applet's `SetDisplayStr()` method, which, as you'll soon see, is the synchronized method. In other words, if the thread isn't holding the monitor object for `SetDisplayStr()`, it cannot enter the method. This prevents two running instances of the `MyThread2` thread from trying to change the display string at the same time.

Now it's time to look at the applet that's in charge of the threads. Listing 31.7 is the applet, which is called ThreadApplet3. This applet creates two objects of the `MyThread2` class: one that counts forward and one that counts backward. The applet's `SetDisplayStr()` method is where the synchronization comes into play because both threads will be trying to access this method.

When you run the applet, you'll see that when the first thread can display its count, the string will appear closer to the top of the display area. The second thread, however, displays its count below the first thread's. For this reason, when you get the applet going, you can sit back and watch the two threads battle over the `SetDisplayStr()` method.

Listing 31.7   ThreadApplet3.java: An Applet That Uses Thread Synchronization.

```
import java.awt.*;
import java.applet.*;
import MyThread2;

public class ThreadApplet3 extends Applet
{
    MyThread2 thread1;
    MyThread2 thread2;
    String displayStr;
    Font font;
    int position;

    public void init()
    {
        font = new Font("TimesRoman", Font.PLAIN, 72);
        setFont(font);

        displayStr = "";
        position = 120;

        thread1 = new MyThread2(this, true);
        thread2 = new MyThread2(this, false);
    }

    public void start()
    {
        if (thread1.isAlive())
            thread1.resume();
        else
            thread1.start();
```

```
            if (thread2.isAlive())
                thread2.resume();


        else
            thread2.start();
    }

    public void stop()
    {
        thread1.suspend();
        thread2.suspend();
    }

    public void destroy()
    {
        thread1.stop();
        thread2.stop();
    }

    public void paint(Graphics g)
    {
        g.drawString(displayStr, 50, position);
    }

    synchronized public void SetDisplayStr(String str, int pos)
    {
        displayStr = str;
        position = pos;
        repaint();
    }
}
```

Tell Java that the applet uses the classes in the awt *package.*
Tell Java that the applet uses the classes in the applet *package.*
Tell Java that the applet uses the MyThread2 *class.*
Derive the ThreadApplet3 *class from* Applet.
   Declare the class's data fields, including two MyThread2 *objects.*
   Override the init() *method.*
     Create and set the applet's font.
     Initialize the display string and display position.
     Create the applet's two threads.
   Override the start() *method*
     If the first thread is already started...
       Resume running the thread.
     Else if the first thread hasn't yet been started...
       Start the thread.
     If the second thread is already started...
       Resume running the thread.
     Else if the second thread hasn't yet been started...
       Start the thread.
   Override the stop() *method.*
     Suspend both threads.

Override the destroy() method.
  Stop both threads.
Override the paint() method.
  Draw the applet's display string, which is the current count.
Define the SetDisplayStr() method as synchronized.
  Copy the method's parameters into the class's data fields.
  Force Java to redraw the applet's display.

Understanding ThreadApplet3

The ThreadApplet3 applet is unique with regards to other applets in this book because it's the only applet that takes full advantage of the applet's life-cycle stages. In the init() method, the applet creates the two threads. The different boolean values given as the constructor's second argument cause the first thread to count forward and the second thread to count backward.

In the start() method, the applet calls each thread's isAlive() method to determine whether the thread has been started yet. The first time start() gets called, the threads have been created in init() but haven't been started. In this case, isAlive() returns false, and the applet calls each thread's start() method to get the threads rolling. If start() is not being called for the first time, it's because the user has switched back to the applet from another Web page. In this case, isAlive() returns true. The applet knows that it must call the threads' resume() method rather than start().

In the stop() method, which gets called when the user switches to another Web page, rather than stopping the threads, the applet suspends them. The threads remain suspended until the applet calls their resume() methods, which, as you now know, happens in the start() method.

Finally, when Java calls the destroy() method, the applet is going away for good. The threads, too, should follow suit, so the applet calls each thread's stop() method.

> **Caution:** When programming threads, you always have to watch out for a condition known as *deadlock*. Deadlock occurs when two or more threads are waiting to gain control of a resource, but for one reason or another, the threads rely on conditions that can't be met in order to get control of the resource.
> To understand this situation, imagine that you have a pencil in your hand, and someone else has a pen. Now, assume that you can't release the pencil until you have the pen, and the other person can't release the pen until she has the pencil. Deadlock! A more computer-oriented example would be when one thread must access Method1 before it can release its hold on Method2, but the second thread must access Method2 before it can release its hold on Method1. Because these are mutually exclusive conditions, the threads are deadlocked and cannot run.

Summary

Threads enable you to break an applet's tasks into separate flows of execution. These subprograms seem to run concurrently thanks to the task switching that occurs in multitasking systems. You can create a thread from a class by implementing the Runnable interface in the class. However, you can also create a separate class for your threads by deriving the class from Thread. Depending on how you want to use the threads, you can create and start your threads in the applet's start() method and stop the threads in the stop() method. If you want your threads to retain their state when the user switches to and from your Web page, you should create the threads in init(), start or resume the threads in start(), suspend the threads in stop(), and stop the threads in destroy(). Remember that if there's a chance that two or more threads may compete for a resource, you need to protect that resource using thread synchronization.

Review Questions

1. How are threads similar to multitasking?

2. What Java interface must be implemented by all threads?

3. What thread method do you call to start a thread?

4. What method does Java call to get a thread started?

5. What are the two applet methods in which you'll usually stop your threads?

6. What's the difference between suspending and stopping a thread?

7. How do you ensure that your threads share the computer's processor properly?

8. If you don't care about retaining a thread's state as the user switches between Web pages, where in your applet should you create and start your threads?

9. How can you take advantage of an applet's life cycle in order to retain a thread's state as the user switches between Web pages.

10. When would you use the synchronized keyword?

11. What's a monitor object?

Review Exercises

1. Modify the ThreadApplet applet so that the applet's state is retained when switching to and from the applet's Web page. Name the new version ThreadApplet4. (You can find the solution to this exercise in the CHAP31 folder of this book's CD-ROM.)

2. Modify the ThreadApplet2 applet so that the thread changes the color of three rectangles displayed in the applet (see Figure 31.2). The rectangles' colors should cycle between red, green, and blue. Repeat the color cycling until the user stops the applet. Name the applet ThreadApplet5, and name the new thread class ColorThread. (You can find the solution to this exercise in the CHAP31 folder of this book's CD-ROM.)

Figure 31.2

Your TheadApplet5 applet should look like this when running under Appletviewer.

3. Modify your ThreadApplet5 applet (naming the new applet ThreadApplet6) so that it runs two threads. One thread should change the rectangles' colors to red, green, and blue, and the second thread should change the rectangles to pink, orange, and yellow. Modify the ColorThread class from exercise 2, renaming it ColorThread2, and then create a new thread class called ColorThread3 for setting the second set of colors. Don't forget to use thread synchronization to prevent one thread from changing the rectangles' colors when another thread is already doing so. (You can find the solution for this exercise in the CHAP31 folder of this book's CD-ROM.)

CHAPTER 32

Writing Java Applications

The bulk of this book is dedicated to using Java to create applets for the Internet. However, Java is a full-fledged computer language that enables you to write complete, stand-alone applications. Although most Java users are interested in creating only applets (there are other, more powerful languages for creating applications), no introductory Java book would be complete without at least dabbling a little with Java applications. In this chapter, then, you learn the basics of creating standalone applications with Java.

About Java Applications

If you've run the HotJava browser, you've already had experience with Java applications. The HotJava browser was programmed entirely in Java and, although the browser is way out of date at the time of this writing, it demonstrates how much you can do with Java, even when dealing with sophisticated telecommunications applications.

Much of what you've learned about applets can be applied toward writing applications. After all, the language doesn't change, just the way you use it does. Of course, conversely, some of what you learned about applets doesn't apply to the writing of applications. For example, because Java applications aren't run "on the Web," they don't have to deal with all the security issues that come up when running applets. A Java application can access any files it needs to access, for example.

If you've ever programmed in C or C++, you'll discover that writing applications in Java is similar. If you haven't programmed in those languages, rest assured that, by this point in the book, you already have 95% of the knowledge you need in order to write standalone Java applications.

The Simplest Java Application

You can create a runnable Java application in only a few lines of code. In fact, an application requires only one method called `main()`. C and C++ programmers will recognize `main()` as being the place where applications begin their execution. The same is true for Java applications. Listing 32.1 shows the simplest Java application.

Listing 32.1   SimpleApp.java: The Simplest Java Application.

```
class SimpleApp
{
    public static void main(String args[])
    {
        System.out.println("My first Java app!");
    }
}
```

Declare the `SimpleApp` class.
   Declare the app's `main()` method.
      Print a line of text on the screen.

If you look a the first line of Listing 32.1, you'll see that even a Java standalone application starts off as a class. In this case, the class has no superclass—that is, the `SimpleApp` class is not derived from another class (although it could have been). The first line of the body of the class begins the `main()` method, which is where all Java applications begin execution. This method's single parameter is a `String` array containing the command line sent to the application when it was started.

Finally, the single line in `main()` prints a message on your computer's screen. Because this is not a Windows application, the class contains no `paint()` method. Instead, you display text by using the `println()` method of the `System.out` package.

To run the Java application, you must first compile it and then run the byte-code file using Java's interpreter. You compile the program exactly as you would an applet, using javac. The following example describes the entire process.

Example: Building an Application

Building a Java application isn't any more difficult that building an applet, although the steps are slightly different. Follow the steps below to compile and run the SimpleApp application.

1. Type Listing 32.1, and save it in your C:\CLASSES folder, under the file name SimpleApp.java. (If you don't want to type, you can copy the listing from the CHAP32 folder of this book's CD-ROM.)

2. Select the MS-DOS Prompt command from the Start menu's Program menu. The DOS window appears on your screen (Figure 32.1).

Figure 32.1

You must run SimpleApp from a DOS window.

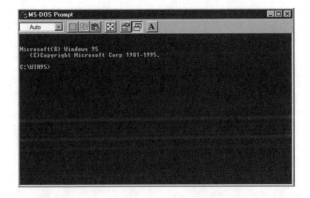

3. Type **cd c:\classes** to switch to your CLASSES folder.

4. Type **javac SimpleApp.java** to compile the application's source code. After compilation, you'll have the SimpleApp.class file in your CLASSES folder.

5. Type **java SimpleApp** to run the application. The message "My first Java app!" appears on the screen (Figure 32.2).

Figure 32.2

The SimpleApp applications prints a single line of text on the screen.

Example: Getting an Application's Arguments

You know that when you start a DOS program, you can sometimes append parameters to the command line in order to give the program information it needs to start. You can do the same thing with Java applications. For example, here's how you would start SimpleApp with two parameters:

```
java SimpleApp param1 param2
```

Of course, because SimpleApp ignores its parameters, the parameters in the command line don't mean anything. Suppose, however, you wanted to print a user-specified message a user-specified number of times. You might, then, write the Java application shown in Listing 32.2. When you run this application, add two parameters to the command line: the message to print (in quotes if the message is more than one word) and the number of times to print the message. You'll get output like that shown in Figure 32.3.

Listing 32.2   ArgApp.java: Using Command-Line Arguments.

```java
class ArgApp
{
    String message;
    int count;

    void GetArgs(String args[])
    {
        String s = args[1];
        count = Integer.parseInt(s);
        message = args[0];
    }

    void PrintMessage()
    {
        for (int x=0; x<count; ++x)
            System.out.println(message);
    }

    public static void main(String args[])
    {
        ArgApp app = new ArgApp();
        app.GetArgs(args);
        app.PrintMessage();
    }
}
```

Declare the ArgApp class.
  Declare the class's data fields.
  Define the GetArgs() method.

Extract the number of times to print the message.
Convert the count to an integer.
Extract the message to print.
Define the PrintMessage() method.
Loop for the requested number of times.
Display the message each time through the loop.
Define the app's main() method.
Create an ArgApp() object.
Call the method to extract the arguments.
Call the method to print the message.

Figure 32.3

The ArgApp application prints a message the number of times given in the command-line arguments.

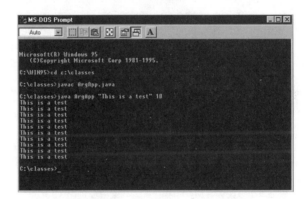

The ArgApp application not only shows you how to use command-line parameters, but also how to write a Java application that actually does something. The important thing to notice here is that you must first create an object of the ArgApp class before you can call its methods and access its data fields. This is because a class is just a template for an object; it doesn't actually become an object until you create an instance of the class with the new keyword.

One way to avoid having to create an object of the class is to declare all the class's data fields and methods as static. Such methods and data fields are accessible in memory, which is why the SimpleApp application in Listing 31.1 runs. Its main() method is declared as static. Of course, it's a heck of a lot easier to just go ahead and create an object of the class than it is to go through the source code and add static to everything.

Windowed Applications

You're probably thinking that it's pretty much a waste of time to write Java applications if you have to run them under the DOS or UNIX text-based operating system. All the action these days is in windowed applications. Yes, you can write windowed applications with Java, as the HotJava browser proves. But, if you've written conventional windowed applications, you're probably a little nervous about writing similar Java applications. After all, writing such applications with languages like C and C++ can be a nightmare.

The truth is, however, you already know almost everything you need to know to write your own standalone applications for GUI operating systems. You can take most any applet and convert it to a standalone application just by adding the `main()` method to the class. In `main()`, you have to perform some of the tasks that Java handles for you when running an applet. These tasks include creating, sizing, and displaying the application's window. The following example gives you the details.

Example: Changing an Applet to an Application

As I said in the previous paragraph, you can convert almost any applet to an application simply by adding a `main()` method that performs a few housekeeping tasks. Listing 32.3 is an applet from a previous chapter's exercises. The previous version drew a face image in the applet's display. The new version displays the face in its own standalone, frame window. When you run the application, you see the window shown in Figure 32.4.

Listing 32.3   FaceApp.java: Converting an Applet to an Application.

```java
import java.awt.*;
import java.applet.*;

public class FaceApp extends Applet
{
    public void init()
    {
        Button button = new Button("Close");
        add(button);
    }

    public void paint(Graphics g)
    {
        // Head.
        g.drawOval(40, 40, 120, 150);
```

```
        // Eyes.
        g.drawOval(57, 75, 30, 20);
        g.drawOval(110, 75, 30, 20);

        // Pupils.
        g.fillOval(68, 81, 10, 10);
        g.fillOval(121, 81, 10, 10);

        // Nose.
        g.drawOval(85, 100, 30, 30);

        // Mouth.
        g.fillArc(60, 130, 80, 40, 180, 180);

        // Ears.
        g.drawOval(25, 92, 15, 30);
        g.drawOval(160, 92, 15, 30);
    }

    public boolean action(Event evt, Object arg)
    {
        if (arg == "Close")
            System.exit(0);

        return true;
    }

    public static void main(String args[])
    {
        FaceApp app = new FaceApp();
        Frame frame = new Frame("Face Window");

        app.init();
        app.start();

        frame.add("Center", app);
        frame.resize(210, 300);
        frame.show();
    }
}
```

Tell Java that the class uses the awt *package.*
Tell Java that the class uses the applet *package.*
Declare the FaceApp *class.*
 Override the init() *method.*
  Create a button object and add it to the window.
 Override the paint() *method.*

Draw the face image using ovals and arcs.
Override the action() method.
   If the user clicks the close button...
     Shut down the application.
   Tell Java the message was handled.
Define the main() method.
   Create the FaceApp object and the frame window.
   Call the init() and start() methods.
   Add the "applet" to the window.
   Size and show the window.

Figure 32.4

The FaceApp application draws a face in a frame window.

Understanding the FaceApp Application

If you examine Listing 32.3, you'll see that most of the FaceApp application is written exactly like any other applet you've written throughout this book. The big difference is the addition of the main() method, where this program's execution starts. Because you're no longer running the program as an applet, you have to perform some of the start-up tasks that Java automatically performs for applets. The first step is to create an object of the class and a frame window to hold the object, like this:

```
FaceApp app = new FaceApp();
Frame frame = new Frame("Face Window");
```

Next, you have to call the methods that get the object going. These methods are init() and start(), which are usually called by Java:

```
app.init();
app.start();
```

Note that, although the FaceApp class doesn't show a start() method, it does inherit it from the Applet class. It's true that even the inherited start() method doesn't do anything, but you might as well be consistent and call it anyway. That way, you won't forget that some applets do override the start() method, without which they won't run properly.

Now, you can add the FaceApp object to the frame window, like this:

```
frame.add("Center", app);
```

Finally, you must be sure to resize and show the window, like this:

```
frame.resize(210, 300);
frame.show();
```

If you fail to resize the application's window, all you'll see is the title bar, forcing the user to resize the window by hand. More importantly, if you fail to call show(), the application's window won't even appear on the screen. That's sure to leave your application's user feeling abused.

Summary

Although Java is used almost exclusively for creating applets, it is possible to use Java to create standalone applications. These applications can be DOS-based (or UNIX, etc.) or be written for a windowed operating system such as Windows 95. The easiest way to create a windowed application is to write the program as if it were an applet and then add a main() method that creates the application object and the frame window that'll contain that object.

Review Questions

1. What method do you find in an application that you don't find in an applet?

2. How do you run a Java standalone application?

3. What is the single parameter received by the main() method?

4. How can you extract parameters from an application's command line?

5. What do you have to add to an applet to convert it to an application?

6. Why do you have to instantiate an object from a class before you can call its methods?

7. What do you have to do to create and display an application's window?

Review Exercises

1. Write a stand-alone application that accepts two numbers as parameters and prints out the numbers' sum.

2. Choose any applet from this book and convert it to a stand-alone application.

3. Convert the ThreadApplet5 applet from Chapter 31's exercises into a stand-alone application. (You can find the solution for this exercise in the CHAP32 folder of this book's CD-ROM.)

Part V

The Java Development Tools

CHAPTER 33

Development Tools Overview

Throughout this book, you've concentrated on building applets for use on Web pages. As you built these applets, you've learned only the very basics about Java's development tools, which include not only the compiler (javac) and the interpreter (java), but also several other useful tools that help you create more powerful applets and applications. Now that you have many hundreds of pages of Java experience behind you, you'll probably want to know more about the tools you've been using (and the tools you haven't been using!). In this chapter, you get a quick look at the Java tools that come with the JDK. Because the compiler and interpreter are the most important tools, they have their own chapters, which follow this chapter.

The Tools

The JDK comes with several development tools, a couple of which you must use frequently as you develop and run applets. Others, you may never use, but it's always good to know they're there should you need them. Table 33.1 lists the tools and their descriptions.

Table 33.1   Java Development Tools.

Tool	Description
appletviewer	This tool enables you to run Java applets without actually loading the applets into a Java-compatible browser.

continues

Table 33.1   Continued

Tool	Description
hotjava	This is the original Java-compatible Web browser.
java	This is the Java interpreter, which runs applets and applications by reading and interpreting byte-code .CLASS files.
javac	This is the Java compiler, which converts your Java source-code to byte-code files that the interpreter can understand.
javadoc	This tool creates HTML-format documentation from Java source code files.
javah	This tool produces header files for use with native methods.
javap	This tool is the Java disassembler, which enables you to convert byte-code files into a program description.
jdb	This is the Java debugger.

The two most important tools in Table 33.1 are the Java compiler, javac, and the Java interpreter, java. Because you will be using these tools a lot, they will be discussed in their own chapters. Specifically, for more information on javac and java, check out Chapter 34, "Using the Compiler," and Chapter 35, "Using the Interpreter."

Using Appletviewer

Outside of what you already know, there's not much to using the Appletviewer application. As you already know, to run an applet with Appletviewer, you type a command line like this:

```
appletviewer applet.html
```

The appletviewer portion of the command runs Appletviewer and the command line's parameter, applet.html, is the HTML document that loads the applet you want to view. One interesting thing about Appletviewer is that you can have more than one applet in the HTML file, in which case, Appletviewer loads each of the applets into its own window.

Example: Loading More Than One Applet at a Time

Suppose you've been working on the applets presented in Chapter 25, "Mouse and Keyboard Events," and you want to test KeyApplet, MouseApplet, and MouseApplet2 all at once. No problem! Listing 33.1 is an HTML file that loads and runs these three applets. To run the applets, you would type

```
appletviewer allapplets.html
```

at your command-line prompt. When you do, you'll see a screen something like Figure 33.1 as Appletviewer loads and runs the three applets referenced in the HTML document.

Listing 33.1   ALLAPPLETS.HTML: An HTML Document That Loads Three Applets.

```
<title>Applet Test Page</title>
<h1>Applet Test Page</h1>

<applet
    code="KeyApplet.class"
    width=250
    height=150
    name="KeyApplet">
</applet>

<applet
    code="MouseApplet.class"
    width=250
    height=150
    name="MouseApplet">
</applet>

<applet
    code="MouseApplet2.class"
    width=250
    height=150
    name="MouseApplet2">
</applet>
```

Running the Debugger from Appletviewer

In addition to being able to run several applets at once, Appletviewer can also start a debugging session with an applet. In fact, running the Java debugger, jdb, is the only parameter, besides the name of the HTML document, you can use with Appletviewer. To run an applet with the debugger, you would type a command like this:

```
appletviewer -debug applet.html
```

Figure 33.1

Appletviewer can
load and run
several applets at
once.

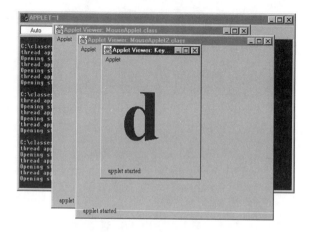

For more information about Java's debugger, refer to the section "Using the Debugger" later in this chapter.

Using HotJava

HotJava is a complete Web browser that was written using the Java language. Although it's a good example of how much mileage you can get out of the Java language, it hasn't been kept up to date. In fact, even though HotJava was the first Java-compatible browser, it can no longer load and run most current applets. This is because, as the Java language progressed from its beta versions to the version 1.0 release, the HotJava browser was not kept up to date. As a result, HotJava can load and run only applets that were created using the old version of Java. A set of these applets come with HotJava so that you can check them out. Figure 33.2, for example, shows HotJava running the Hang Duke applet.

Although you can still use HotJava to browse the World Wide Web, you're probably better off getting a copy of Netscape Navigator 2.0, which is available for download at http://www.netscape.com. Netscape Navigator 2.0 not only is a much more powerful Web browser, it can also load and run applets created with the latest version of Java. (It cannot, however, load the older applets, which are considered to be obsolete at this point.) Figure 33.3 shows Netscape Navigator 2.0 running the Fractal sample applet.

Figure 33.2

HotJava can only run applets that were created with the early beta version of Java.

Figure 33.3

Currently, Netscape Navigator 2.0 is the Java-compatible Web browser to use.

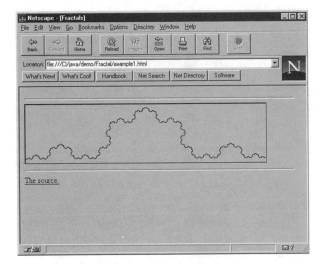

Using Java's Documentation Creator

The javadoc tool won't help you write better Java source code, but it'll sure go a long way towards helping other people use your code, not to mention help you remember six months from now what your code is doing. Basically, javadoc reads through your source-code files and creates HTML files that document your packages and classes, including methods and data fields. You can run javadoc on any old source code, but it works better if you document your code properly as you work.

For example, if you want javadoc to include descriptions of your methods in the HTML files it creates, you need to include a doc-comment block before each method. A doc-comment block begins with the characters /** and ends like a normal C comment. Listing 33.2 is an example of a simple doc-comment block:

Listing 33.2   LST33_2.TXT: A Simple Doc-Comment Block.

```
/**
 * Creates the applet's textfield controls and adds
 * the controls to the applet's display,
 */
```

When javadoc sees this comment block beginning with the characters /**, it'll know to include the text of the comment in the method's description.

Javadoc Tags

In order to simplify the documentation process even more, javadoc can understand special symbols called doc tags. Doc tags begin with the @ symbol. After the @ are the words see, version, param, return, exception, or author followed by the text associated with the symbol. The doc tag

```
@author Jeremy Bender
```

for example, creates an author entry in the class documentation files, whereas the doc tag

```
@version 1.0
```

adds a version entry to the class documentation.

Use the @param tag to decribe a method's parameters, like this:

```
@param paramName Description
```

Here, paramName is the parameter's name and Description is the text you want displayed as the parameter's description. The other tags are used like this:

```
@return Description
@exception exceptionName Description
```

The first line above describes the return value of the method, whereas the second line describes the exception that may be thrown by the method.

Example: Using Doc Tags

One of the most useful doc tags is @see, which enables you to create "See Also" hyperlinks in the HTML documents created by javac. By using @see tags in a method's doc-comment block, for example, you can add a convenient link in the documentation that can jump the user straight to a related method with a single mouse click. If you have complementary methods called `GetString()` and `PutString()`, for example, you might have a doc-comment block like the one shown in Listing 33.3.

Listing 33.3   LST33_3.TXT: Creating Hypertext Links in Doc-Comment Blocks.

```
/**
 * Retrieves a test string from the user.
 *
 * @param userNum The user's ID number
 * @return The string the user entered
 * @see #PutString()
 */
```

Example: Documenting an Applet

To give you a real-world example of documenting a class with javadoc, you'll now examine an applet from an earlier chapter in this book with doc-comment blocks added. Listing 33.4 shows the newly documented applet. To create the HTML documents for the class, copy the ArcApplet.java file to your CLASSES folder and type `javadoc arcapplet.java` to start the documentation process. After javadoc finishes, you'll have four new HTML files in your CLASSES folder: ARCAPPLET.HTML (Figure 33.4), ALLNAMES.HTML (Figure 33.5), TREE.HTML (Figure 33.6), and PACKAGES.HTML (which, in this case, contains nothing of value).

Listing 33.4   ArcApplet.java: An Applet Prepared for Javadoc.

```
import java.awt.*;
import java.applet.*;

/**
 * ArcApplet demonstrates drawing arcs by enabling the user
 * to input the arc's parameters.
 *
 * @version 1.0, 1/15/96
 * @author Clayton Walnum
 */
public class ArcApplet extends Applet
{
    TextField textField1, textField2;
```

continues

Listing 33.4 Continued

```
/**
 * Creates the applet's textfield controls and adds
 * the controls to the applet's display.
 *
 * @return None
 */
public void init()
{
    textField1 = new TextField(10);
    textField2 = new TextField(10);

    add(textField1);
    add(textField2);

    textField1.setText("0");
    textField2.setText("360");
}

/**
 * Retrieves the user-defined parameters from the text
 * boxes, converts them to integers, and uses them
 * to display an arc.
 *
 * @return None
 * @param g The applet's Graphics object
 * @see #action
 */
public void paint(Graphics g)
{
    String s = textField1.getText();
    int start = Integer.parseInt(s);

    s = textField2.getText();
    int sweep = Integer.parseInt(s);

    g.drawArc(35, 50, 125, 180, start, sweep);
}

/**
 * Responds when the user presses Enter from one of the
 * applet's text boxes. Calls repaint() to force the applet
 * to redraw its display with the new parameters.
 *
 * @return A boolean value indicating whether the
 *          event was handled.
 * @param event The action's event object
 * @param arg Event-dependent information
 */
public boolean action(Event event, Object arg)
{
    repaint();
    return true;
}
}
```

Figure 33.4

This is the
ARCAPPLET.HTML
file viewed in
Netscape
Navigator.

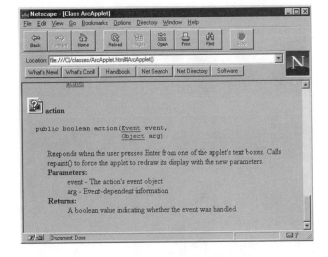

Figure 33.5

This is
ALLNAMES.HTML
viewed in
Netscape
Navigator.

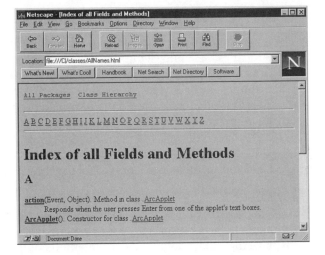

Javadoc Options

When you run javadoc, you can specify where your source-code files are located, where the generated HTML files should be stored, and how much information javadoc displays as it runs. The parameters associated with these options are -classpath, -d, and -verbose, respectively. Here's an example of using these options from the command line.

```
javadoc -classpath c:\classes -d c:\classes -verbose arcapplet.java
```

Figure 33.6

This is
TREE.HTML
viewed in
Netscape
Navigator.

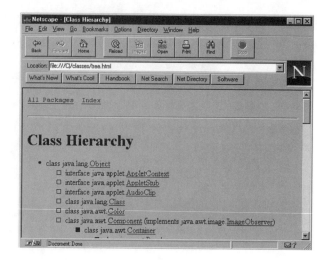

Using the Disassembler

The javap tool is Java's disassembler, which is a program that can take a byte-code (.CLASS) file and change it into a description of the original source code. However, if you've ever seen the output from javap, you know that I'm using the word "description" loosely. This is because there's only so much information that a disassembler can determine from a compiled program. The bottom line is that the output of javap doesn't look anything like a Java program, and unless you really understand the internals of the Java language, you won't be able to make heads or tails out of a fully disassembled file.

Still, if you're brave, you can give javap a try, using the following command line:

```
javap classFile.class
```

In the above, `classFile.class` is the name of the byte-code file you want to disassemble. When you use javap without specifying any options, the program displays the public data fields and methods of the class—not too hard to understand. The javap disassembler supports several command-line options that enable you to customize how javap does its disassembly. Those options are `-p`, which tells javap to display private and protected fields and methods along with the public ones; `-c`, which tells javap to display the byte-code instructions in the file; and `-classpath`, which gives the path javap uses to find class files.

Using the C Header Generator

Another tool that you probably won't use much is javah, which creates header and stub files for use with native methods. What's a native method? Well, because Java is an interpreted language, it tends to run a little slower than fully compiled languages like C. For this reason, Java's creators decided to enable programmers to write methods in C when they need some extra speed and then call those methods from within a Java program. The process of using native methods, however, is fairly complex, a process that even your humble author hasn't dug too deeply into. Because Java is fast enough for 99% of the applets you'll want to write, you're not likely to have to deal with native methods.

To put it simply, though, javah creates C source-code files that enable the programmer to reference a Java class's data fields from source code written in C. If the previous sentence didn't make sense to you then, believe me, you don't have to worry about javah at all. If you're interested in this stuff, however, you can find information on creating native methods in your Java online documentation. There was also a pretty decent tutorial at `http://java.sun.com/tutorial/index.html` on the World Wide Web at the time of this writing. If it's still there, you should check it out.

To give you a quick overview, though, you run javah against the class files created by the Java compiler. The javah command line looks like this:

```
javah className
```

As is the case with many of Java's tools, javah can accept a number of command-line options. When you specify these options in the command line, you place them before the class name. Table 33.2 lists the options and their descriptions.

Table 33.2   Options for javah.

Option	Description
-classpath path	Sets the path for finding classes.
-d directory	Sets the directory where the output files will be stored.
-o outputfile	Places all the output into the file specified by outputfile.
-stubs	Tells javah to generate C declarations from the input file.
-td directory	Sets the directory where temporary files will be stored.
-verbose	Tells javah to display status information as it works.

Using the Debugger

As I write this, the Java debugger, jdb, is still not complete. Good documentation on how to use the debugger is nonexistent, with only a very brief description of the debugger available online at Sun. Still, the dubugger does run, and—who knows?—by the time you read this, it may be fully functional.

To use the debugger, you run your Java program with the debugger rather than the interpreter. For example, if you were debugging this book's FaceApp application, you'd use a command line like this to start the application with the debugger:

```
jdb FaceApp
```

At this point, the debugger is running, and it has loaded the FaceApp application into memory. However, FaceApp is not yet running. Instead, the debugger is waiting for its first command, which you enter at the command prompt (Figure 33.7).

Figure 33.7

After you load a program into the debugger, it waits for a command.

To see the list of commands supported by the debugger (not all of which work yet), type **help** at the command prompt. Another command you're likely to use a lot is stop at, which sets a breakpoint at a specific line in a class. A *breakpoint* is a place where you want program execution to stop and wait for another command. For example, if you've loaded the FaceApp application into the debugger as described previously, you can now type the following command to set a breakpoint at the first line of executable code (the "4" is the line number):

```
stop at FaceApp:4
```

As you can see, the stop at command requires the class name and line number at which to stop, separated by a colon. When you enter the above command, jdb lets you know that the breakpoint was set okay (Figure 33.8).

Now, that you have a breakpoint set, when you tell the program to execute, it'll run until it hits the breakpoint, at which time the debugger suspends program execution and waits for another command. To set this string of events into motion, type **run** at the debugger's command prompt. When you do, the debugger informs you that it's running FaceApp, right after which it informs you that it has hit a breakpoint. The debugger shows the location of the breakpoint and waits for another command (Figure 33.9).

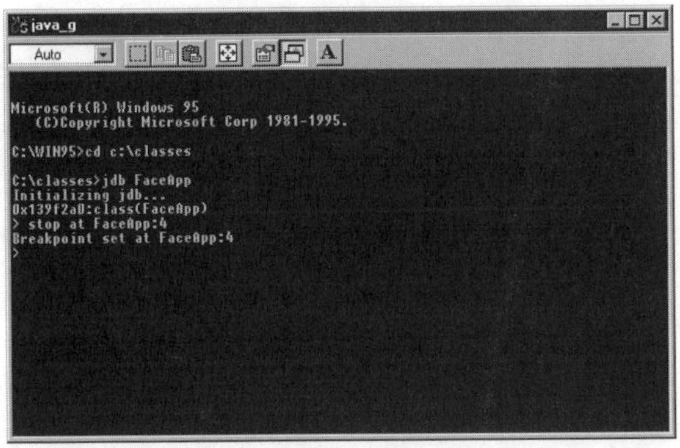

Figure 33.8

Setting breakpoints is something you do a lot with a debugger.

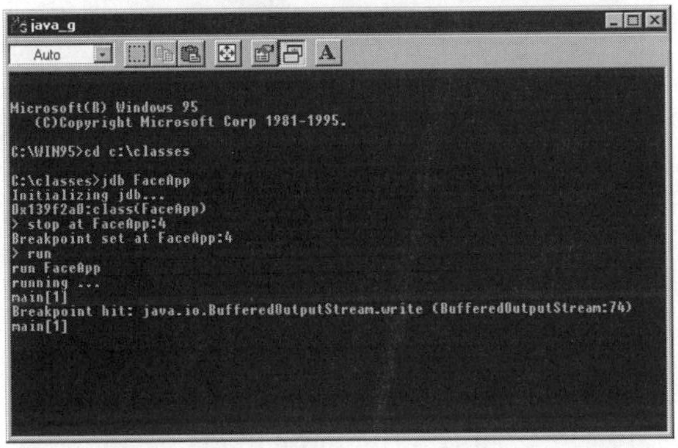

Figure 33.9

When the debugger hits a breakpoint, it stops and waits for your next command.

At this point, you'd probably want to do something called single-stepping through the program, which means telling the debugger to execute the next line of code and stop. In this way, you can trace through a program line-by-line in order to figure out where problems might be. Unfortunately, the debugger's step command is not yet functional, so you'll have to wait until the debugger's complete to try out single-stepping.

If you want to try something else with the debugger, type **memory** and press Enter. Now, the debugger tells you how much memory remains, as well as how much total memory there is in your system. If you type **threads**, the debugger lists all the Java threads in this system. Currently, there's only the main FaceApp thread, and, because you set a breakpoint, that thread is currently suspended. Typing **threadgroups**, on the other hand, gives you a list of all thread groups in the system. At this point, those groups would be system, main, and FaceApp.

If you want to see the methods for any class that's loaded, you can type `methods` followed by the class's name. To get the FaceApp application running again, type `cont`. To stop the debugger and get back to your regular operating system prompt, you can type `exit` or `quit`.

> **Caution:** As I tested the debugger for this chapter, my system kept locking up, and I wasn't always able to get the results I expected. If you decide to experiment with the debugger, make sure you don't have anything else running. Be especially sure that you don't have documents that need to be saved, because the debugger's unpredictability is liable to cost you any work you've done on those documents. Hopefully, though, by the time you read this chapter, the debugger will be in full working order.

Summary

The most important Java tools are javac (the compiler) and java (the interpreter). However, there are several other tools you can use when developing applets and applications with Java. Some of these tools, like Appletviewer and javadoc, are handy utilities that make writing Java programs easier. Others, like javah and javap, are used in only special circumstances. In fact, it's likely that you'll never need to use these tools. Because javac and java are the most important Java tools, they are covered in their own chapters, which immediately follow this one.

Review Questions

1. How can you run more than one applet at a time with Appletviewer?

2. Why will you have more luck with applets by using Netscape Navigator 2.0 rather than HotJava?

3. What's a doc-comment block?

4. What command starts a program that's loaded into the debugger?

5. How can you document a method's return value and parameters using a doc-comment block?

6. How do you start a debugging session with Appletviewer?

7. How can you create hypertext links in the HTML files created by javadoc?

8. How do you start a debugging session with jdb?

9. What does the javap tool do?

10. What are native methods?

11. How does javah help you use native methods?

12. How do you set a breakpoint with the debugger?

Review Exercises

1. Write an HTML document that loads and runs all the applets from Chapter 27. (You can find the applets in the CHAP27 folder of this book's CD-ROM.)

2. Start Appletviewer for a debugging session.

3. Add doc-comment blocks to ImageApplet.java from Chapter 27. Run javadoc on the new source-code file in order to create the HTML documentation.

4. Run the Java debugger on the ArgApp application from Chapter 32. (You'll find the files you need in the CHAP32 folder of this book's CD-ROM.) When the debugger is loaded, set a breakpoint and run the program.

CHAPTER 34

Using the Compiler

The one Java tool that you have to use constantly is the compiler, javac. This is because your Java source-code files are meaningful only to human readers. Your computer cannot understand them at all. The compiler's job is to take your program and convert it from human-readable form to machine-readable form. You've been using the Java compiler all throughout this book, but in this chapter, you'll learn some new tricks and tips that'll help you get the best results from the compiler.

What the Compiler Does

In languages such a C, a compiler converts source code (the stuff you write) to machine language, which your computer can execute directly. Because every type of computer uses a different form of machine code, programs that must run on different types of machines must be compiled specifically for each machine. For example, a C program compiled on a Windows machine cannot be run on a Macintosh, and vice versa. To run that Windows program on the Macintosh, the program would first have to be compiled by a Macintosh compiler (assuming that the source code was portable, meaning that the code contained no machine -specific instructions).

With Java, however, the compiler converts your source code into byte-code files, which are the same format on every machine. This means that a Java program compiled on a Windows machine will run equally as well on a Solaris or Macintosh machine. This feat of digital magic is possible because the Java byte-code files are not read directly by the machine. Instead, Java's interpreter reads the byte-code files and translates them into machine code for the specific machine on which the Java program is running.

The interpreter does this translation as the applet or application is running, meaning that the whole process is transparent to the user. The interpreter, of course, must be specially written and compiled for each type of machine that wants to run Java programs. Figure 34.1 illustrates this concept. From the user's point of view, though, this simply means that he must have Java installed on his system. The user doesn't need to know anything about the interpreter; it works automatically when the user views an applet in his Web browser.

Figure 34.1

Because Java programs are interpreted, they can be run on any machine that has a Java interpreter.

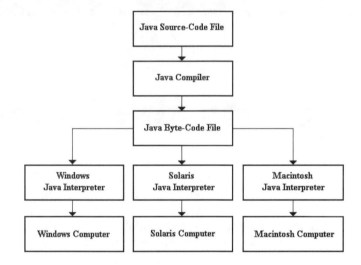

Running the Compiler

As you already know, you can run the Java compiler with a command line that consists of the compiler's name followed by the name of the file to compile, like this:

```
javac Applet.java
```

There are a couple of important things to remember about this command. First, the Java compiler is case-sensitive when it comes to comparing source-code file names with the names of the class contained in the file. For example, if your source-code file is named shapeapplet.java and the class it defines is ShapeApplet, the Java compiler will complain and not compile the file (Figure 34.2).

Second, the compiler requires that you include the source-code file's extension, which should always be .java. Notice that the extension is all lowercase. If you fail to include the extension when running the compiler, or if you fail to save your source-code file with the proper extension, you will get an "invalid argument" error (Figure 34.3). I'm not sure why Java's creators insist upon the file extension being present when you type the javac command line. Most compilers assume the proper file extension when the file name is typed without the extension. Not so with Java. Strange.

Figure 34.2

The source-code file name must match the name of the public class defined in the file.

Figure 34.3

A source code name without the proper .java extension is an invalid argument.

Like many of the tools included with java, the compiler recognizes some command options that you can add to the command line. Table 34.1 lists these command options and their meanings.

Table 34.1   Command Options for Javac.

Option	*Description*
`-classpath path`	Determines the path in which the compiler looks for classes.
`-d directory`	Determines the directory in which javac stores the output files.
`-g`	Tells javac to create debugging information, which is used by debugging tools.

continues

Table 34.1 Continued

Option	Description
-nowarn	Tells javac not to display warnings as it compiles a file.
-O	Tells java to optimize the compiled program.
-verbose	Tells javac to display status information as it works.

To use any of these options, place the options between the javac command and the source file name, like this:

```
javac options filename.java
```

In the following sections, you'll look at each of the compiler options in detail. In some cases, you'll even get some hands-on experience.

Setting the Class Path

In order to compile an applet, the compiler usually needs to draw upon other already compiled files. These files might be files that you've created for custom classes or they may be the class files that make up the class hierarchy of the class you're compiling. For example, when you derive your applet from Java's Applet class, the compiler needs to know about the Applet class in order to fully compile your applet. Moreover, because Java's Applet class itself is a subclass of yet other Java classes, the compiler needs to bring in many different class files. Obviously, before the compiler can access these class files, it has to know where they are.

Normally, when you compile a program, the compiler finds classes using the current setting of your system's CLASSPATH variable, whose default value is the folder that contains Java's classes. Java will also look in the active folder (the one you're in when you type the javac command line). However, you can change the setting of CLASSPATH temporarily for the current compilation by using the -classpath option, like this:

```
javac -classpath path FileName.java
```

In the above line, path is the path you want to include, each separated by a semicolon. For example, assuming that you installed Java in a folder called C:\JAVA and that your own classes are in the C:\CLASSES folder, the following line compiles your program using the same settings the compiler would use by default:

```
javac -classpath c:\java\lib\classes.zip;c:\classes FileName.java
```

Notice that Java's classes are in a file called CLASSES.ZIP. You must include this file name in the path in order for the compiler to find the classes it needs to successfully compile your applet.

Specifying the Target Directory

When you run javac by typing the `javac Applet.java` command line, the compiler reads the source-code file (or files), converts it to byte-code form, and stores the resultant .CLASS file in the directory from which the compiler was run. You can control this target directory by specifying the `-d` command option, like this:

```
-d directory
```

In this command, `directory` is the directory in which you want the output files (.CLASS files) stored.

Example: Setting the Target Directory

Suppose you have your Java source code files (the ones with the .java extension) in a folder called C:\CLASSES, as you have for the applets you've created in this book. Now you want to have the .CLASS files that are created by the Java compiler placed in a subdirectory of CLASSES called COMPILED. You'd first create the subdirectory with the command `md compiled`. Then you'd issue the following command:

```
javac -d c:\classes\compiled applet.java
```

Following the `javac` command are the `-d` option, the name of the directory in which to store the output files, and the Java source-code file to compile.

The directory name is either a full path or a path relative to your current directory. For example, if you're current directory is c:\CLASSES, when you type the above command, you can shorten the directory name, like this:

```
javac -d compiled applet.java
```

Creating Debugging Tables

To get the most out of a debugger, your programs need to be compiled in a special way, so that debugging information is included in the compiled byte-code files. The compiler switch that turns this option on is `-g`, and you use it like this:

```
javac -g applet.java
```

As you can see, the only thing extra here is the `-g` option itself, which requires no additional arguments.

You may decide that it would be cool to use the `-g` option all the time, so that your programs are always loaded with debugging information. Don't do it. This wouldn't be a good idea because programs with debugging information are not only a bit larger than programs without the debugging information, but also tend to run slower. The larger the program is, the more debugging information the `-g` option adds to the file.

Example: Adding Debugging Tables to an Applet

To test the -g option, copy the ShapeApplet.java file from the CHAP34 folder on this book's CD-ROM to your CLASSES directory. Then, compile the file with the following command:

```
javac ShapeApplet.java
```

Now, check the size of the ShapeApplet.class file. It should be 1,334 bytes. Next, compile the applet again, this time using the -g option, like this:

```
javac -g ShapeApplet.java
```

When you check the file size this time, you'll find it's 1,612 bytes, over 20% larger. The extra size is caused by the additional debugging information the compiler has stored in the .CLASS file.

Suppressing Warnings

Sometimes, when the Java compiler finds something questionable in your code, it issues a warning. Warnings represent the kind of errors that don't prevent a program from compiling properly, but that may generate a runtime error or just be bad programming practice. Because warnings are not critical to the compilation process, Java enables you to turn them off. You might do this, for example, when you already know about the problems that are creating the warnings. To turn off the warnings, you use the -nowarn option, like this:

```
javac -nowarn applet.java
```

Like the -g option, -nowarn requires no additional arguments.

> **Tip:** You can use more than one command-line option at a time. For example, you can both turn on debugging information and set the target directory with a command like this: javac -g -d c:\classes applet.java.

Optimizing a Program

When a compiler runs, it reads in source code and converts that source code to some other format, in Java's case, a byte-code file. As a programmer, though, you know that there are many ways to accomplish the same task in a program. A compiler doesn't normally take this sort of thing under consideration when it's working, though. It generates its output the same way for every source-code file.

However, the javac compiler knows how to perform certain types of optimization on your programs, but it only does so when asked. (And don't forget to say pretty please). To tell the Java compiler to optimize your program, you use the -O option, like this:

```
javac -O applet.java
```

The -O option requires no arguments.

Notice that the letter after the hyphen is an uppercase O. A lowercase o will not work. Also, be aware that compiling with the optimizing option may make the resulting .CLASS file incompatible with some other Java tools. For this reason, optimizing should be done only when compiling the program for the final time.

Switching On Verbose Output

When you run the Java compiler with no command-line option, the compiler runs and performs its task without displaying any sort of information on the screen (unless the program contains errors). With a large program that takes a while to compile, you may want to know what's going on behind your back, if for no other reason than to reassure yourself that everything is going okay. You can make the compiler report to you as it works by using the -verbose option, like this:

```
javac -verbose applet.java
```

When you add this command-line option, the compiler will tell you which files it's loading and compiling. It'll even tell you how long each step took to complete (Figure 34.4).

Figure 34.4

When you use the -verbose option, the compiler reports to you every step of the way.

Summary

The compiler is one of the most important of the Java tools, because without it you'd be unable to convert your source-code files into byte-code files, which are the only kind of files that Java's interpreter understands. Ordinarily, you can run the compiler simply by typing the command javac followed by the name of the file you want to compile. However, javac also recognizes a number of options that you can add to the command line. These include options to set directories, to optimize the program, to add debugging information, and to display status information as the compiler works. In the next chapter, you learn about the compiler's counterpart, the interpreter, which reads the files created by the compiler in order to run the program.

Review Questions

1. Why do you need to use a compiler?

2. What happens if you fail to include the .java extension when specifying your source-code file to the compiler?

3. When you use options with the javac command, where do you place them in the command line?

4. Can you specify more than one command-line option at a time?

5. How do you set a different target directory for the compiler's output files?

6. What does the -g command-line option do?

7. What does the -nowarn command-line option do?

8. How do you get the compiler to show you what it's doing as it works?

9. How do byte-code files enable Java to run the same programs on different types of computers?

Review Exercises

1. Compile an applet, instructing the compiler to include debugging information in the byte-code file.

2. Compile an applet with the verbose setting, and study the information the compiler displays on the screen.

3. Compile an applet, specifying no warnings, optimization, and an output directory of C:\CLASSES\MYCLASSES.

CHAPTER 35

Using the Interpreter

When you're running applets from within a Web browser, you don't have to be concerned with the Java interpreter and how it executes Java programs. However, the only way to run Java Standalone applications is by loading them directly into the interpreter. These means typing a command line in much the same way you did for compiling files. The command line not only tells the Java interpreter which program you want to run, but also the command-line options you want to use when running the program. In this chapter, you study the Java interpreter in detail.

What the Interpreter Does

As you learned in the previous chapter, the Java compiler converts your Java source code into a .CLASS file. Unlike the files created by a C compiler, which creates output files that are executable only on a specific type of computer, this .CLASS file is in a special format that is transportable between various computer systems. A .CLASS file contains byte-code information that represents the commands in your original source code.

The key to this intersystem transportability is the Java interpreter. Although a Java byte-code file can be run on any Java-compatible system, the Java interpreter must be created specifically for each system that needs to run Java programs. Therefore, the Java interpreter for the Macintosh will not run on a Windows system, even though both systems can execute the same byte-code file.

In the previous chapter, you saw a figure that illustrated the relationship between Java source-code files, compilers, byte-code files, and the different interpreters. Figure 35.1 reprints that figure for your convenience in this discussion.

Figure 35.1

The relationship between the various components of the Java system.

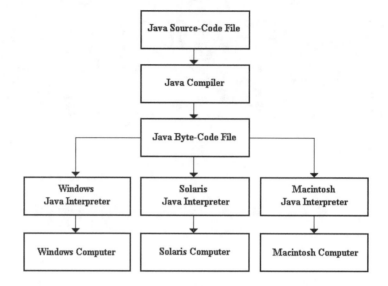

When the user installs Java on his system, he must install the correct version for that system. Once the installation is complete, the user can connect to the Internet and view any Java applets that may be contained in the Web pages he downloads. These applets are interpreted and executed automatically by Java, thanks to the connection between the Java-compatible browser and the Java system.

The only time the user must be concerned with the interpreter directly is when he wants to run a Java application, which is represented in the same kind of byte-code (.CLASS) file as an applet. The difference is that Java standalone applications cannot be executed from within a Web browser. Instead, the user runs them from his system's command line, invoking the interpreter "by hand," as it were.

Running the Interpreter

In Chapter 32, "Writing Java Applications," you got a brief look at the process of creating and running Java standalone applications. In that chapter, you learned that you can run a Java application with the following command:

```
java filename
```

In this command, `filename` is the name of the application's .CLASS file. For example, if you wanted to run an application called MyApp, your command line would look like this:

```
java MyApp
```

Notice that, unlike the compiler, the interpreter doesn't require the source file's extension. In fact, if you include the file extension, the interpreter generates an error

(Figure 35.2). This is because the interpreter is not able to tell the difference between a fully qualified class name (which uses dots) and a file name with an extension (which also uses a dot). Also, the interpreter expects upper- or lowercase letters in a file name. The file name MyApp, MYAPP, and myapp are all different to Java's interpreter.

Figure 35.2

Unlike the compiler, the Java interpreter will not accept file extensions.

Like the compiler, the Java interpreter recognizes a set of command-line options that you can use to tailor the how the interpreter runs. Those options are listed in Table 35.1.

Table 35.1 Command Options for the Java Interpreter.

Option	Description
-checksource	Instructs the interpreter to run the compiler on files that are not up to date.
-classpath path	Determines the path in which the compiler looks for classes.
-cs	Same as -checksource.
-D	Instructs the interpreter to set a property value.
-debug	Runs the debugger along with the application.
-help	Displays the commands you can use with the interpreter.
-ms x	Specifies the amount of memory allocated at startup.

continues

Table 35.1 Continued

Option	Description
-mx x	Specifies the maximum amount of memory that can be allocated for the session.
-noasyncgc	Tells Java not to use asynchronous garbage collection.
-noverify	Tells the interpreter not to verify code.
-oss x	Specifies the maximum stack size for Java code.
-ss x	Specifies the maximum stack size for C code.
-v	Specifies that the interpreter should display status information as it works.
-verbose	Same as -v.
-verbosegc	Specifies that the garbage collector should display status information as it works.
-verify	Tells the interpreter to verify all Java code.
-verifyremote	Tells the interpreter to verify code loaded by a classloader. This option is the default.

As you can see, the interpreter can accept quite a few command-line options. Of these options, though, only a few are used frequently. You'll get a look at those more useful options in the sections that follow.

Keeping Files Up to Date

When you're working on a new application, you'll make frequent changes to the source code. Whenever you change the source code, you must recompile the program before you run it. Otherwise, you'll be running an old version of the program. When you start writing larger applications, you'll have many files for the classes that are used in the program. As you change the contents of these files, you may lose track of which files need to be recompiled. This is where the interpreter's -checksource command-line option comes into play.

The -checksource option tells the interpreter to compare the dates and times of your source-code files with the dates and times of the matching .CLASS files. When a source-code file is newer than the matching .CLASS file, the interpreter automatically runs the compiler to bring the files up to date. You use the -checksource option like this:

```
java -checksource appname
```

Here, appname is the name of the class you want the interpreter to run.

> **Note:** When running a standalone application, any arguments that you place after the name of the file to execute are passed to the application's main() method. For more information on handling these application arguments, please refer to Chapter 32, "Writing Java Applications."

Setting the Class Path

In order to run a standalone application, the interpreter usually needs to load class files that are used by the program. These files might be files that you've created for custom classes or they may be the class files that make up the class hierarchy of the class you're executing. When you derive your applet from Java's Applet class, for example, the interpreter needs to load the Applet class, as well as Applet's super-classes, in order to run your application. Before the interpreter can access these class files, it has to know where they are.

Normally, when you run a program, the interpreter finds classes using the current setting of your system's CLASSPATH variable, whose default value is the folder that contains Java's classes. Java will also look in the active folder (the one you're in when you type the java command line). However, you can change the setting of CLASSPATH temporarily for the current program run by using the -classpath option, like this:

```
java -classpath path FileName
```

In the preceding line, path is the path you want to include, each separated by a semicolon. For example, assuming that you installed Java in a folder called C:\JAVA and that your own classes are in the C:\CLASSES folder, the following line runs your program using the same settings the interpreter would use by default:

```
java -classpath c:\java\lib\classes.zip;c:\classes FileName
```

Notice that Java's classes are in a file called CLASSES.ZIP. You must include this file name in the path in order for the interpreter to find the classes it needs to successfully run your applet.

Switching On Verbose Output

When you run the Java interpreter with no command-line option, the compiler runs and performs its task without displaying information on the screen. Sometimes, though, you may want to know what files the interpreter is loading and where those files are being loaded from. You can make the interpreter report to you as it works by using the -verbose option, like this:

```
java -verbose applet.java
```

Example: Running an Application with Verbose Output

To see what happens when you use the `-verbose` (or `-v`) command-line option, copy the SimpleApp.class file from the CHAP35 folder of this book's CD-ROM to your CLASSES folder. Then start an MS-DOS session and type the following command at the prompt:

```
java -verbose SimpleApp
```

When you press Enter, the interpreter runs, loading the application and displaying all the additional files it has to access in order to run the application. Figure 35.3 shows a portion of this output. Bet you didn't expect such a simple program could make the interpreter work so hard!

Figure 35.3

The -verbose option enables you to see what files are being loaded by the interpreter.

Tip: A special version of the Java interpreter can trace and display every command that's executed in your application. (You can find this tool in your JAVA\BIN folder, along with the other Java tools.) To invoke this special option, type `java_g -t AppName` at your system prompt. The `AppName` portion of the command is the name of the .CLASS file you want to run, without the file extension. Figure 35.4 shows a small portion of the output generated by this command. Even a small application results in many pages of trace information.

Figure 35.4

The *java_g -t* command displays every command executed in your application.

Getting Help

The Java interpreter has a long list of command, so you'll probably have a hard time remembering them all. Luckily, you can get a quick reminder of what the commands are and what they do. To get this information, type the following command:

```
java -help
```

When you do, you'll see the display shown in Figure 35.5. For more information than is displayed in the help listing, check this chapter or your online Java documentation.

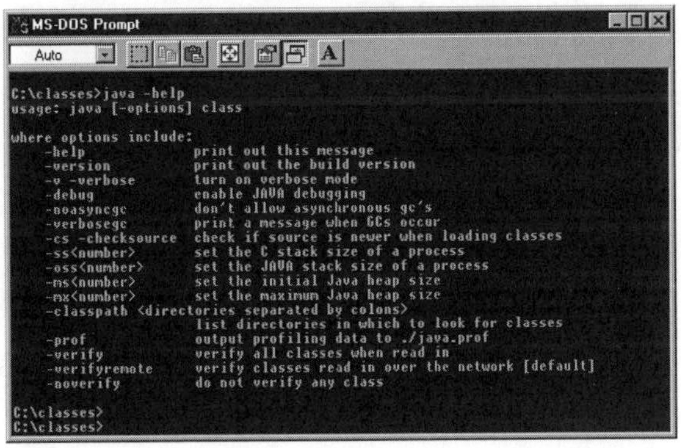

Figure 35.5

The Java interpreter features a built-in help display.

Summary

When you are using a Java-compatible Web browser to view applets, you don't need to be concerned with the Java interpreter. The browser displays the applets for you automatically. However, if you want to run a standalone Java application, you must invoke the interpreter from your system's command line. The interpreter accepts over a dozen different command-line options, although only a few are regularly useful to novice and intermediate Java programmers.

Review Questions

1. What happens if you fail to include the file extension when specifying your source-code file to the interpreter?

2. What extension do byte-code files—the files that the interpreter understands— have?

3. What are the two ways you can specify the verbose interpreter option?

4. When writing a Java application, what do you use first, the compiler or the interpreter?

5. How can you get a list of commands that the interpreter understands?

6. Why do you need to use an interpreter?

7. What does the `-checksource` command-line option do?

Review Exercises

1. Run one of the applications from Chapter 32, instructing the interpreter to check whether the .CLASS file is up to date with the .java file.

2. Run an application with the verbose setting, and study the information the interpreter displays on the screen.

CHAPTER 36

The Java Class Libraries

This book has given you a peek into the process of creating applets with Java. However, the key word is "peek" because Java is a huge development system that couldn't be fully covered in a book twice this size. For this reason, now that you have some Java programming experience under your belt, it's time to set off on your own to discover how much more you can do with Java. The first step in that journey is to explore the class libraries that come with Java. You'll discover all sorts of treasures there.

To give you a nudge in the right direction, this final chapter provides a brief overview of Java's most important class libraries. However, you should take it upon yourself to explore the latest documentation available from Sun at their Web site, as well as to peruse Java's source code. The language and its classes are changing constantly, so you have to make an effort to keep up.

The Packages

The Java class libraries are divided into two groups. The first group is the Java packages, which include the libraries for the Java programming language. These packages include the following:

♦ java.lang

♦ java.util

♦ java.io

The second group is called the HotJava packages and includes the libraries needed to create applets and to communicate over the Internet. The HotJava packages include the following:

- java.awt
- java.applet
- java.net

In this chapter, you'll get a brief look at some of these packages and the classes they contain.

The *java.lang* Package

Although you may not been aware of it, you've been using the lang package since the beginning of this book. That's because this is the one package that Java automatically imports into every program. Without the lang package, you wouldn't be able to write Java programs, because this package contains the libraries that make Java what it is. Table 36.1 is a list of the commonly used classes included in the lang package.

Table 36.1 Commonly Used Classes in the *java.lang* Package.

Class	Description
Boolean	Represents the boolean data type.
Character	Represents the char data type.
Double	Represents the double data type.
Float	Represents the float data type.
Integer	Represents the int data type.
Long	Represents the long data type.
Math	Contains methods that implement mathematical functions.
Number	The superclass for all number-related classes, such as Float and Integer.
Object	The root of the entire class library. All Java classes can trace their ancestry back to Object.
String	Represents text strings.

Class	Description
StringBuffer	Represents a string buffer that can grow dynamically.
System	Contains methods for performing system-level function calls.
Thread	The superclass from which thread objects are derived.

Of these classes, the ones that are most useful to you at this time are the data-type wrappers—Boolean, Character, Double, Float, Integer, Long—, as well as String, Math, System, and Thread. The following sections provide general descriptions and usage tips for these classes—except for Thread, which you learned about in Chapter 31, "Threads."

> **Note:** The java.lang package also includes the Runnable interface, which is used to convert classes into threads. For more information on this topic, see Chapter 31, "Threads."

Data-Type Wrappers

The data-type wrapper classes enable you to perform various operations on values in your programs. For example, in previous programs in this book, you've used the Integer.parseInt() method to convert strings containing digits to integer values, like this:

```
int value = Integer.parseInt(str);
```

Often, you can call static methods of the class, like parseInt(), to perform an operation on a value. But, you can also create objects of the class and operate directly on that object's value. To give you some idea of what you can do with the wrapper classes, table 36.2 lists the methods of the Integer class.

Table 36.2 Methods of the Integer Class.

Method	Description
Integer(int)	One of the class's constructors.
Integer(String)	One of the class's constructors.
doubleValue()	Returns the integer as a double value.

continues

Table 36.2   Continued

Method	Description
equals(Object)	Compares the integer to another object.
floatValue()	Returns the integer as a float value.
getInteger()	Gets a property of an integer.
hashCode()	Returns a hashcode for the integer.
intValue()	Returns the integer as an int value.
longValue()	Returns the integer as a long value.
parseInt(String, int)	Converts a string to an int value.
parseInt(String)	Converts a string to an int value.
toString(int, int)	Converts an integer to a string.
toString(int)	Converts an integer to a string.
toString()	Converts an integer to a string.
valueOf(String, int)	Creates an Integer object from a string.
valueOf(String)	Creates an Integer object from a string.

Example: Using the Data-Type Wrappers

Suppose that you need an integer data field in a class, but you want to be able to use all of the Integer class's methods in order to manipulate that value. First, you declare an object of the Integer class and then call the class's constructor. Then, you can access the class's methods, as shown in Listing 36.1. Figure 36.1 shows the applet running under Appletviewer.

Listing 36.1   IntApplet.java: Using the _Integer_ Class.

```
import java.awt.*;
import java.applet.*;

public class IntApplet extends Applet
{
    public void paint(Graphics g)
    {
        Integer value = new Integer(125);

        long longValue = value.longValue();
        float floatValue = value.floatValue();

        String str = value.toString() + "    " +
            String.valueOf(longValue) + "    " +
```

```
                String.valueOf(floatValue);
            g.drawString(str, 50, 75);
        }
    }
```

Tell Java that the applet uses the classes in the awt package.
Tell Java that the applet uses the classes in the applet package.
Derive the IntApplet class from Java's Applet.
    Override the paint() method.
        Create an Integer object with a value of 125.
        Convert the integer to long and float values.
        Create a display string and display it.

Figure 36.1

This is
IntApplet
running under
Appletviewer.

The *System* Class

The System class enables you to make system-level function calls to do things like perform simple I/O, get the current time, handle directories, copy arrays, get environment variables, get information about memory, and so on. You would use the class's I/O methods, for example, in a standalone applet in order to display text on the screen. Table 36.3 lists the more useful of the System class's methods and their descriptions.

Note: In addition to its many methods, the System class also defines standard input and output streams that you can use in your programs. For example, when you call the println() method, you're using an output stream.

Table 36.3   The Most Useful Methods of the *System* Class.

Method	Description
arraycopy()	Copies an array.
currentTimeMillis()	Gets the current time in milliseconds.
exit(int)	Ends the program.
getProperties()	Returns the current system properties.
getProperty()	Returns a specific property.
load()	Loads a dynamic library.
setProperties()	Set the system properties.

Example: Getting System Properties

Frequently, it's handy to know something about the system on which your application is running. That's why the System class makes it easy for you to find this information. Listing 36.2, for example, is a stand-alone application that displays Java's version, Java's class path, the OS name, and the OS version. Figure 36.2 shows the output from the program.

Listing 36.2   SystemApp.java: An Application That Displays System Information.

```
public class SystemApp
{
    public static void main(String args[])
    {
        System.out.println("");
        System.out.println("------------------------------");

        String str = "Java Version: " +
            System.getProperty("java.version");
        System.out.println(str);

        str = "Java Class Path: " +
            System.getProperty("java.class.path");
        System.out.println(str);

        str = "OS Name: " +
            System.getProperty("os.name");
        System.out.println(str);
```

```
        str = "OS Version: " +
            System.getProperty("os.version");
        System.out.println(str);

        System.out.println("-----------------------------");
    }
}
```

Declare the SystemApp.
  Define the main() method.
    Display blank and dashed lines.
    Get and display the Java version number.
    Get and display Java's class path setting.
    Get and display the OS name.
    Get and display the OS version number.
    Display an ending dashed line.

Figure 36.2

The SystemApp
application
displays system
properties

Note: The System class's getProperty() method accepts a string identifier for the property you want. The strings you can use are file.separator, java.class.path, java.class.version, java.home, java.vendor, java.vendor.url, java.version, line.separator, os.arch, os.name, os.version, path.separator, user.dir, user.home, and user.name.

The *Math* Class

If you need to do a lot of mathematical work in your applets and applications, you'll be glad to have the Math class at your disposal. Using the Math class, you can perform many types of calculations just by calling the appropriate methods. Table 36.4 lists the Math class's methods and their descriptions:

Table 36.4   Methods of the *Math* Class.

Method	Description
abs()	Returns the absolute value of a given number.
acos()	Returns the arc cosine of a value.
asin()	Returns the arc sine of a value.
atan()	Returns the arc tangent of a value.
atan2()	Converts rectangular coordinates to polar coordinates.
ceil()	Returns the smallest whole number greater than or equal to the given value.
cos()	Returns the cosine of an angle.
floor()	Returns the largest whole number less than or equal to the given value.
IEEEremainder()	Returns the remainder of a floating-point division.
log()	Returns the natural log of a value.
max()	Returns the greater of two values.
min()	Returns the smaller of two values.
random()	Returns a random number between 0.0 and 1.0.
round()	Rounds a floating-point or double number.
sin()	Returns the sine of an angle.
sqrt()	Returns the square root of a value.
tan()	Returns the tangent of an angle.

To call any of the math methods, reference them through the Math class, like this:

```
Math.Method()
```

For example, to get the square root of 10, you use this line:

```
double result = Math.sqrt(10);
```

The *String* Class

You're no stranger to the String class. You've used it in a number of programs in order to store and manipulate text strings. However, because this class is so useful to a programmer, you'll take a closer look at it here. As you'll see, the String class is powerful, enabling you to manipulate strings in more ways than you may have realized. Table 36.5 shows the most commonly used methods of the String class.

Table 36.5 Methods of the *String* Class.

Method	Description
charAt()	Returns the character at the given string index.
compareTo()	Compares a string to another string.
concat()	Joins two strings.
copyValueOf()	Copies a character array to a string.
endsWith()	Checks a string for the given suffix.
equals()	Compares a string to another object.
equalsIgnoreCase()	Compares a string to another object with no regard for upper- or lowercase.
getBytes()	Copies selected characters from a string to a byte array.
getChars()	Copies selected characters from a string to a character array.
hashCode()	Returns a string's hashcode.
indexOf()	Finds the index of the first occurrence of a given character or substring in a string.
lastIndexOf()	Finds the index of the last occurrence of a given character or substring in a string.
length()	Returns the length of a string.
regionMatches()	Compares a portion of a string to a portion of another string.

continues

Table 36.5 Continued

Method	Description
replace()	Replaces all occurrences of a given character with a new character.
startsWith()	Checks a string for the given prefix.
substring()	Returns a substring of a string.
toCharArray()	Converts a string to a character array.
toLowerCase()	Converts all characters in the string to lowercase.
toUpperCase()	Converts all characters in the string to uppercase.
trim()	Removes whitespace characters from the beginning and end of a string.
valueOf()	Returns a string representation of an object.

Example: Using the *String* Class

Listing 36.3 is an applet that shows you how a few of the String methods you haven't tried yet work. When you run the applet with Appletviewer, you see the window shown in Figure 36.3. The applet takes whatever text strings you type in the two text boxes, and compares them for equality without considering upper- or lowercase. It then concatenates the strings and displays the new concatenated string along with its length.

Listing 36.3 StringApplet.java: An Applet That Manipulates Strings.

```
import java.awt.*;
import java.applet.*;

public class StringApplet extends Applet
{
    TextField textField1;
    TextField textField2;

    public void init()
    {
        textField1 = new TextField(20);
        textField2 = new TextField(20);

        textField1.setText("STRING");
        textField2.setText("String");
```

```
        add(textField1);
        add(textField2);
    }

    public void paint(Graphics g)
    {
        String str1 = textField1.getText();
        String str2 = textField2.getText();

        boolean equal = str1.equalsIgnoreCase(str2);
        if (equal)
            g.drawString("The strings are equal.", 70, 100);
        else
            g.drawString("The strings are not equal.", 70, 100);

        String newStr = str1.concat(str2);

        g.drawString("JOINED STRINGS:", 70, 130);
        g.drawString(newStr, 80, 150);

        g.drawString("STRING LENGTH:", 70, 180);
        int length = newStr.length();
        String s = String.valueOf(length);
        g.drawString(s, 80, 200);
    }

    public boolean action(Event evt, Object arg)
    {
        repaint();
        return true;
    }
}
```

Tell Java that the application uses the awt *package.*
Tell Java that the application uses the applet *package.*
Derive the StringApp *class from* Applet.
   Declare the class's data fields.
   Override the init() *method.*
      Create two TextField *controls.*
      Set the controls' contents.
      Add the controls to the applet's layout.
   Override the paint() *method.*
      Get the contents of the two text boxes.

Compare the two strings.
Display the appropriate message about the strings' equality.
Concatenate the two strings.
Display the joined strings.
Get and display the new string's length.
Override the `action()` *method.*
    Force Java to repaint the applet.
    Tell Java that the action was handled okay.

Figure 36.3

This is
StringApplet
running under
Appletviewer.

The *io* Package

Although Java applets are extremely limited in their I/O abilities, Java applications are free to create, load, and save files just like any other application. All of Java's file-handling abilities are housed in the io package. This package includes many classes that enable you to handle files and other types of input and output streams. Table 33.6 lists the more commonly used of these classes and their descriptions:

Table 36.6 Commonly Used Classes in the *io* Package.

Class	Description
BufferedInputStream	An input stream that buffers data.
BufferedOutputStream	An output stream that buffers data.
DataInputStream	An input stream for reading primitive Java data types.
DataOutputStream	An output stream for writing primitive Java data types.

Class	Description
File	Represents a file.
FileInputStream	An input stream associated with a file.
FileOutputStream	An output stream associated with a file.
InputStream	The superclass from which input classes are derived.
OutputStream	The superclass from which output classes are derived.
PrintStream	An output stream that can be used for printing.
PushbackInputStream	An input stream that enables a program to return read values back into the stream.
RandomAccessFile	Represents random-access files.
StringBufferInputStream	An input stream whose data source is a string.

Example: Reading a File

There are many ways to read files using Java's I/O classes. The most basic, however, is to read a file byte-by-byte. Suppose, for example, you wanted to display on the screen the source code in the file test.java. Listing 33.4 shows such an application. Although this example is very basic, it demonstrates how to use one of Java's I/O classes, FileInputStream. Creating a file using an output stream isn't much different; you just need to create an output stream object and write, rather than read, data. Figure 36.4 shows FileApp's output.

Listing 36.4   FileApp.java: An Application That Reads a File.

```
import java.io.*;

public class FileApp
{
    public static void main(String args[])
    {
        System.out.println("");
        System.out.println("------------------------------");
        System.out.println("");
```

continues

Listing 36.4   Continued

```java
        try
        {
            FileInputStream inputStream =
                new FileInputStream("test.java");

            String str = "";
            int b = 0;

            while(b != -1)
            {
                b = inputStream.read();
                str += (char)b;
            }

            inputStream.close();
            System.out.println(str);
        }
        catch (FileNotFoundException e)
        {
            System.out.println("File not found!");
        }
        catch (IOException e)
        {
            System.out.println("I/O Error!");
        }

        System.out.println("-------------------------------");
    }
}
```

Tell Java that the application uses the io package.
Declare the FileApp *class*
   Define the main() *method.*
      Display blank and dashed lines.
      Create a FileInputStream *object.*
      Initialize the input variable and buffer.
      Loop until the last byte in the file is read.
         Read a byte from the input stream.
         Add the byte as a character to the string buffer.
      Close the input stream.
      Display the data read from the stream.
      Catch any exceptions and print error messages.
      Display the bottom dashed line.

Figure 36.4

The FileApp application reads and displays a text file.

The *awt* Package

You're already familiar with the awt package, which contains the classes you need to create and run applets in windowed environments. The awt package contain the Graphics class that you used to create displays for your applets, and all the control classes you used throughout the book to handle user interactions with applets. The awt package even has the classes for handling events and creating windows with menus. You've already explored much of the awt library, but for your reference table 36.7 lists the package's classes and their descriptions. Feel free to explore any of the classes with which you're not familiar.

Table 36.7   Classes of the *AWT* Package.

Class	*Description*
BorderLayout	One of Java's layout managers.
Button	Represents button controls.
Canvas	Represents a surface on which a program can draw.
CardLayout	One of Java's layout managers.
Checkbox	Represents a checkbox control.
CheckboxGroup	Represents a group of check boxes used as "radio buttons."
CheckboxMenuItem	A menu entry that can be checked.
Choice	A type of pop-up menu.

continues

479

Table 36.7 Continued

Class	Description
Color	Represents color values in Java programs.
Component	The superclass from which all Java components are derived.
Container	Represents an object that can hold Java components.
Dialog	A dialog-box type of window.
Dimension	Represents the width and height of an object.
Event	Represents various system and user events.
FileDialog	A dialog box for selecting files.
FlowLayout	One of Java's layout managers.
Font	Represents a character style.
FontMetrics	The attributes of a font.
Frame	A main window that can contain a menu and other window controls.
Graphics	Contains methods for drawing various shapes and controllong graphical attributes like color, fonts, clipping rectangles, etc.
GridBagConstraints	Used in conjunction with GridBagLayout managers.
GridBagLayout	One of Java's layout managers.
GridLayout	One of Java's layout managers.
Image	Represents graphical images, usually in GIF format.
Insets	Used as spacers for components in a container.
Label	Represents text labels.
LayoutManager	The superclass from which all layout managers are derived.
List	Represents a list box control.
MediaTracker	A class for organizing multiple images.

Class	Description
Menu	Represents menus in a menu bar.
MenuBar	Represents menu bars in frame windows.
MenuComponent	The superclass from which all menu components are derived.
MenuContainer	The superclass from which all menu containers are derived.
MenuItem	Represents an item in a pop-up menu.
Panel	A simple container class.
Point	Represents an X,Y coordinate.
Polygon	A list of coordinates for outlining a polygon.
Rectangle	An object the represents the X,Y coordinate and width and height of a rectangle.
Scrollbar	A scrollbar control.
TextArea	A simple text edit box.
TextComponent	A component for editing text.
TextField	A one-line text component.
Window	A general window class.

Summary

The Java Developers Kit is comprised of dozens of classes that do everything from define the basic language to enable programmers to create applets and applications for windowed environments. These classes are organized into six main packages: lang, util, io, awt, applet, and net. For the novice and intermediate Java programmer, the lang and awt packages, which define the Java language and supply classes for operating under a windowed environment, respectively, are by far the most important.

Although the io class enables the programmer to create various types of input and output streams, due to security considerations, Java applets are restricted on the types of I/O they can perform. For that reason, you'll probably use I/O methods mostly in Java standalone applications, if you are even interested in building applications rather than applets. Applets, of course, rely on the few classes that make up the applet package for the functionality that sets them apart from regular applications.

Finally, the `util` and `net` packages contain little of interest to any except advanced Java programmers. The `util` package contains classes that support the other Java classes by providing helper classes such as `Properties`, `Stack`, and `Vector`. Finally, the `net` package features the classes that enable programmers to include communication protocols for use with Internet connections in their applets and applications.

Review Questions

1. What are the six main packages of the Java classes?

2. Which package contains classes for operating in a windowed environment?

3. When would you use the `Math` class?

4. What's the advantage of using the `String` class to handle text?

5. How do you join two strings?

6. Do you need to instantiate an object of the `Math` class in order to call its methods?

7. What are data-type wrapper classes and how are they used?

8. How can you get information about the system on which your applet or application is currently running?

9. How can you write file-handling code for a standalone application?

Review Exercises

1. Write an applet that accepts a value from the user, and then displays the value's square root, logarithm, and absolute value.

2. Write an application called SystemApp2 that displays all system properties. Figure 36.5 shows what the program's output looks like. (You can find the solution for this exercise in the CHAP36 folder of this book's CD-ROM.)

Figure 36.5

The SystemApp2 application should display all of the system properties.

Part VI

Appendixes

Answers to Review Questions

Chapter 1

1. Probably the three most important reasons that Java is so suitable for Internet applications are the language's robustness, simplicity, and, most importantly, its security features.

2. A Java applet is a small program that is embedded in an HTML document and is run when the document is loaded. A Java standalone application doesn't need to be embedded in an HTML document and can be run just like any other application.

3. Java applets are compiled into byte-code files that can be executed by any computer that has a Java interpreter.

4. Applets are handled in an HTML document similarly to elements like images. The applet is referenced in the HTML document, which causes the HTML document to load and run the applet.

5. Java is platform-independent so that it can run on any system. Java is also multithreaded, which means it can handle multiple tasks concurrently and run fast.

Chapter 2

1. Use the Appletviewer tool included with the JDK.

2. The required attributes are code, width, and height.

3. The codebase attribute specifies the location of an applet's code (the .CLASS file). The given folder is relative to the folder of the HTML document that contains the reference to the applet.

4. Other optional attributes include alt, align, name, hspace, and vspace.

5. Applet parameters enable a user to configure an applet to fit his specific needs.

6. You can provide alternate content for non-Java browsers. You do this by placing standard HTML script commands for the alternate content right before the ending </applet> tag.

Chapter 3

1. A local applet is located on your computer system.

2. A remote applet is located on another computer system and must be downloaded onto your computer before it can be run.

3. The client is the computer that requests information (in this case, an applet) from another computer. The computer that supplies the information is the server.

4. Once applets can flow both from and to a remote computer, the client/ server relationship will become less important. This is because computers will keep switching from being a client and a server.

5. The Java interpreter validates every applet before the applet is run. This prevents applets that have been modified (maybe by having a virus attached) from affecting the destination system. The validation process also ensures that an applet cannot crash the system.

Chapter 4

1. When you use top-down programming, you divide a program up such that the detail goes from general to specific as you work your way down the program.

2. Top-down programming enables you to separate the general tasks that must be completed by a program from the details that implement those tasks, making a program easier to understand and organize.

3. OOP offers another organizational level to the programmer. Not only can the programmer divide tasks up into logical chunks in top-down, structured fashion, but he can also separate logical elements of the program into objects.

4. The two main elements of a class are data fields and the methods that operate on the data fields.

5. A class is like a template or blueprint for an object. An object is an instance of the class.

6. The three main OOP concepts are encapsulation, inheritance, and polymorphism.

7. Encapsulation is the act of enclosing both the data and the functions that act on the data within the object. Inheritance is the ability of a new object (a derived object) to inherit data and functions from a base object. Polymorphism is the ability of a derived object to implement a function of the base class in a different way.

Chapter 5

1. A constant is a value that can't be changed during a program's execution. Constants have symbolic names like `PI` or `NUMBEROFITEMS`.

2. A variable is a value that can be changed as much as needed during a program's execution. Like constants, variables have symbolic names. Examples of variable names are `count` and `area_of_circle`.

3. Constants and variables replace hard-to-understand values with English-like names. Moreover, variables enable you to name a value that must change many times during program execution.

4. Java's eight data types are `byte`, `short`, `int`, `long`, `float`, `double`, `char`, and `boolean`.

5. Variable scope determines where in a program a variable can be accessed. A variable goes into scope at the beginning of the program block in which the variable is declared and goes out of scope at the end of the block.

Chapter 6

1. Graphical text is text that must be drawn on the screen just like other shapes such as circles and squares, rather than printed using a built-in character set as is done under MS-DOS.

2. In a proportional font, each letter takes up only the amount of space it needs, whereas every letter in a non-proportional font takes up exactly the same amount of space.

3. Arguments are values that are sent to a method when the method is called.

4. The three arguments for the drawString() method are the text string to display, and the column and row at which to display the text.

5. The paint() method draws whatever needs to be displayed in the applet's display area. Java calls paint() whenever the applet needs to be redrawn.

6. One way to get user input is to add a TextField control to your applet.

7. Java calls the init() method almost immediately after an applet starts up in order to enable you to initialize objects needed by the applet.

8. Java calls the action() method whenever the user does something with the applet's controls. For example, when the user types text into a TextField control and presses Enter, Java calls action() so that the applet can respond to the user's input.

9. To convert a numerical value to a string, you call the String class's valueOf() method.

Chapter 7

1. The addition, subtraction, multiplication, and division operators are +, –, *, and /, respectively.

2. 5*3 equals 15.

3. 3 - 2 + 5 + 6 -1 equals 11.

4. The ++ operator increments the variable, so num ends up equal to 13.

5. 12 % 5 equals 2.

6. If num equals 25, the expression num += 5 makes num equal to 30.

7. You set the text is a TextField object by calling TextField's setText() method.

8. 12 + 3 * 6 / 2 equals 21.

9. You can change 3 / 5 from integer to floating-point division by changing one or both of the numbers to a floating-point value, like this: 3f / 5f.

10. You cast the result of 56 - 34.56f to integer like this: (int)(56 - 34.56f).

11. You convert digits in a string to an integer by calling the Integer class's parseInt() method.

12. (12 – 8) * 10 / 2 * 2 equals 40.

Chapter 8

1. An expression is a line of program code that can be reduced to a value or that assigns a value to a variable or constant.

2. The three types of expressions are numerical, assignment, and logical.

3. The expression (3 < 5) equals true.

4. The expression (3 < 5) && (5 == 4 + 1) equals true.

5. Expressions are recursive because they can contain other smaller expressions, which in turn may contain other expressions.

6. The six comparison operators are == (equals), != (not equal), < (less than), > (greater than), <= (less than or equals), and >= (greater than or equals).

7. The four logical operators are ! (NOT), && (AND), ¦¦ (OR), and ^ (exclusive OR).

8. The result of the expression (3 < 5) ¦¦ (6 == 5) ¦¦ (3 != 3) is true.

9. The result of the expression (5 != 10) && ((3 == 2 + 1) ¦¦ (4 < 2 + 5)) is true.

10. The result of the expression !(5 == 2 + 3) && !(5 + 2 != 7 - 5) is false.

Chapter 9

1. Program flow is the order in which program statements are executed.

2. Conditional branching occurs when a program branches to a new section based on the value of some data. Unconditional branching is when a computer instruction causes the program to branch regardless of any conditions.

3. Two ways to control program flow are if and switch statements.

4. No. The second line will execute only when choice equals 3.

5. You can write an if statement without opening and closing braces when only one program line will execute if the condition evaluates to true.

6. There is no difference between a logical and a Boolean expression. They are both expressions that evaluate to true or false.

7. The program skips over both the if and the else if.

8. The if and switch statements are similar in that they both enable the computer to choose a path of execution based on the value of a control variable. They are different in that a switch statement is more appropriate for situations in which there are many possible outcomes.

9. The variable num ends up with the value 3. If your answer was 2, you didn't notice that the second case has no break statement, causing program execution to drop through to the third case.

Chapter 10

1. You should use a loop when your program must perform some sort of repetitive task.

2. The body of the loop comprises the program lines that are executed each time the loop's conditional expression is true.

3. When the conditional expression evaluates to false, the loop ends.

4. There is no guarantee on how many times a while loop will execute. It could be any number of times from 0 on up. A do-while loop, on the other hand, always executes at least once.

5. You must properly initialize the loop control variable because the loop's conditional expression relies on the value of the variable to determine how many times to loop.

6. An infinite loop occurs when a loop's conditional expression can never result in false, causing the loop to repeat endlessly.

7. Both the while and do-while loops can be used to perform repetitive tasks in a program. However, the while loop may execute any number of times, including 0, whereas a do-while loop always executes at least once. This is because a do-while loop's conditional expression is at the end of the loop, whereas a while loop's conditional expression is at the beginning of the loop.

8. The loop will execute six times, and count will be equal to 16 at the end of the loop.

Chapter 11

1. You should use a `for` loop when you have a repetitive task that must be performed a specific number of times.

2. The three parts of a `for` loop are the initialization, condition, and increment sections.

3. A `for` loop stops looping when the condition section becomes false.

4. A `for` loop can count backward by decrementing the control variable in the increment section, rather than incrementing it.

5. A `for` loop can count by tens by adding 10 to the control variable in the increment section.

6. It's possible to create an infinite loop with a `for` loop, but it's unlikely because the loop control variable is handled by the loop itself.

7. The loop will execute five times, and x will be equal to 13 at the end of the loop.

Chapter 12

1. Top-down programming means organizing source code into levels that go from general functions to more detailed functions the further down the hierarchy you go.

2. Functions make top-down programming possible by enabling you to organize source code into well-defined tasks.

3. All functions have a return type, but the return type of `void` means that the function returns no actual value.

4. Arguments are values that you pass to a function when you call it. The receiving function can then access the values almost as if they were local to the function.

5. Defining a function is the act of writing the function's source code.

6. You return a value from a function by using the keyword `return` followed by the value to be returned. The returned value must be the same type as the function's defined return type.

7. The arguments in the function call must be in the same order and be of the same type as the arguments given in the function's definition.

8. The best way to break source code up into functions is to locate the groups of commands that perform a specific task and then replace those lines with a function call. The lines that are replaced become the body of the new function.

Chapter 13

1. An array is a data structure that enables you to store many related values under one variable name.

2. You can access the values of an array using loops, which greatly reduces the amount of source code needed to handle large numbers of related values.

3. An array subscript identifies a specific element of an array. The subscript is a number or variable enclosed in square brackets. A subscript and an index are exactly the same thing.

4. A two-dimensional array can store values in a table, with a specific number of columns and rows.

5. The largest subscript you can use with a fifty-element array is 49.

6. If you try to access a nonexistent array element, Java generates an exception.

7. A `for` loop is perfect for array access because you can use the loop control variable as an array subscript.

8. To initialize a two-dimensional array with `for` loops, you'd use nested loops. The outer loop counts through the columns and the inner loop counts through the rows.

Chapter 14

1. A class is a template from which you create an object. A class usually contains data fields and methods.

2. A class provides an additional level of program abstraction that enables you to organize data fields, and the methods that interact with those data fields, within a single structure.

3. The three parts of a simple, empty class are the keyword `class`, followed by the name of the class and the braces that mark off the body of the class.

4. The two program elements that you must add to the empty class in order to create a complete class are data fields and methods.

5. To create an object of a class, you use the new operator followed by a call to the class's constructor.

6. To use a class that's defined in a different file, you place the import keyword, followed by the class's name, at the top of the file that needs access to the class. You must also be sure that the compiler can find the class, usually by placing the class files all in the same directory.

7. Using inheritance, a new class (subclass) derived from a base class (superclass) inherits the data fields and methods defined in the base class. The programmer then only needs to add whatever additional functionality is required by the new class.

8. A subclass is a class that's been derived from another class using the extends keyword. A superclass is the class from which a subclass is derived. That is, the terms subclass and base class are equivalent.

9. You create a subclass by using the extends keyword like this:

```
class SubClass extends SuperClass
{
}
```

10. To override a method, you provide, in your subclass, a method with exactly the same name, return type, and arguments as the method of the superclass you want to override. Then, Java will call your class's version of the method rather than the superclass's version.

Chapter 15

1. All applets must be derived from Java's Applet class.

2. Applet classes must be public so that the system can run the applet. If you fail to declare an applet as public, it will compile fine, but it will not run.

3. The five life-cycle stages of an applet are initialization, start, paint, stop, and destroy.

4. The paint cycle isn't an "official" stage in the applet's life cycle. It isn't, in fact, even defined within the Applet class. Instead, the paint() method is inherited from Java's Component class.

5. The initialize cycle occurs only once in the applet's life cycle (when the applet is loaded and prepared to run), whereas start can occur numerous times (after initialization or whenever the applet is restarted).

6. The init(), start(), stop(), and destroy() methods as they are implemented in the Applet class do absolutely nothing. They are only placeholders that you can override in your applet class. The same is true of the `paint()` method.

Chapter 16

1. The area of an applet in which you can draw is called the canvas.

2. The origin of Java's graphical coordinate system is in the upper left corner with values of X increasing to the right and values of Y increasing downwards.

3. The `drawRect()` method draws a hollow rectangle, whereas the `fillRect()` method draws a filled (solid) rectangle.

4. The four arguments for the `drawRect()` method are the X,Y coordinates of the rectangle's upper left corner and the width and height of the rectangle.

5. The first four arguments for both `drawRect()` and `drawRoundRect()` are exactly the same, being the X,Y coordinates, width, and height of the rectangle. The `drawRoundRect()` method, however, has two additional arguments that are the width and height of a rectangle that determines the size of the rounded corners.

6. The `drawPolygon()` method uses arrays to store its coordinates because a polygon can have any number of sides, which means that the method call must have a way to pass differing numbers of points. The arrays enable you to define as many sides as you need while keeping the method's argument count consistent.

7. The six arguments required by the `drawArc()` method are the X,Y coordinates, width, and height of the bounding rectangle, as well as the starting drawing angle and the number of degrees around to draw.

8. The `Polygon` class provides several methods that enable you to manipulate a polygon in various ways.

Chapter 17

1. To get a reference to the currently active font object, you call the `Graphics` class's `getFont()` method.

2. To get a font's name, you can call the `Font` class's `getName()` method.

3. To get a font's height, you can call the `Font` class's `getHeight()` method.

4. You need to know a font's height so you can properly space lines of text.

5. You get a reference to a FontMetrics object by calling the Graphics class's getFontMetrics() method. The Font object for which you want the metrics is the method's single argument.

6. Use a FontMetrics object when you want to know more detailed information about a font. The Font class offers only general information about a font.

7. You can determine the width of a text string by calling the FontMetrics class's stringWidth(). The method's single argument is the string to measure.

8. A point is a unit of measurement of a font's height. A point equals 1/72 of an inch.

9. Leading is the amount of white space between lines of text. *Ascent* is the height of a character, from the baseline to the top of the character. *Descent* is the size of the area that accommodates the descending portions of letters, such as the tail on a lowercase "g."

10. A font's height is the sum of the font's leading, ascent, and descent.

11. Use the new operator to call the Font class's constructor. The constructor's three arguments are the font name, style, and size. Styles you can use are any combination of Font.PLAIN, Font.BOLD, and Font.ITALIC.

12. If the font you request is not available, Java substitutes a default font. This is one reason it's so important to get a font's size after you create the font.

Chapter 18

1. The two arguments required by the Label class's constructor are the text for the label and the label's alignment value.

2. When an applet containing labels is resized, the labels automatically reposition themselves as appropriate.

3. After creating controls, you add the controls to the applet with the add() method.

4. The single argument needed by the Button class's constructor is the text label for the button.

5. The values for setting a label's alignment are represented by the Label class's Label.LEFT, Label.CENTER, and Label.RIGHT fields.

6. The Label class provides methods for setting the label's text and alignment.

7. You can change a button's text label by calling the `Button` class's `setLabel()` method.

8. For a button click, the `action()` method receives a reference to the button object and the selected button's text label.

9. You can determine which button was selected by examining the text label passed as the `action()` method's second parameter.

10. Nothing happens when a user clicks a label object, because label objects do not generate events.

Chapter 19

1. The three arguments required by the `Checkbox` class's constructor are the text for the label, a reference to the `CheckboxGroup` object (or `null`), and checkbox's state (`true` or `false`).

2. Checkboxes that are set to exclusive mode are also called radio buttons.

3. The two arguments needed by the `TextField` class's constructor are the default text and the width (in characters) of the control.

4. To change the state of a checkbox control call the `Checkbox` class's `setState()` method.

5. When checkboxes are in nonexclusive mode, the user can select as many checkboxes at a time as he likes. In exclusive mode, the user can select only one checkbox at a time.

6. To create a group of checkbox controls (in exclusive mode), you must first create an object of the `CheckboxGroup` class.

7. You use echo characters whenever the information being entered into a textfield control should not be readable on the screen, such as when the user is entering a password.

8. You select an echo character for a textfield control by calling the `TextField` class's `setEchoCharacter()` method.

9. To determine which checkbox generated an event, you cast the first parameter sent to the `action()` method to an object of the `Checkbox` class. You can then call the checkbox object's `getLabel()` method to get the checkbox's label.

Chapter 20

1. The Choice class's constructor accepts no arguments.

2. You add items to a choice menu by calling the Choice class's addItem() method.

3. The two arguments needed by the List class's constructor are the number of visible rows in the box and a boolean value indicating whether the control will accept multiple selections.

4. You add items to a list by calling the List class's addItem() method.

5. You would use a TextArea control when you need to display, and enable the user to edit, more than one line of text. The TextField control can display only a single line.

6. To determine the selected item in a choice menu, examine the second parameter of the event() method. The selected item's text string gets passed to event() as that parameter.

7. You create a multiple-selection list exactly the same way you create a single-selection list, except that the value of the constructor's second argument should be true rather than false.

8. You retrieve the selected item from a list by calling the List class's getSelectedItem() method. If you want the index of the selected item, call getSelectedIndex().

9. To create a string containing multiple lines of text, add each line of the text to the string using the concatenation operator (+). Make sure each line of text ends with the newline character (\n).

10. To retrieve multiple selections from a scrolling list, call the List class's getSelectedItems() method. This method returns a string array containing the selected items.

11. Yes. You can delete items from a list by calling the List class's deleteItem() or deleteItems() methods.

Chapter 21

1. The Scrollbar constructor's five arguments are the scrollbar's orientation, value, page size, minimum value, and maximum value.

2. A canvas is a blank component on which you can draw graphics.

3. The Canvas class's constructor requires no arguments.

4. Use a page size of zero when you want the scroll box to be centered on the selected value and when you want the user to be able to select a value from anywhere within the entire range.

5. The easiest way to respond to a scrollbar change is to override the `handleEvent()` method. In the method, watch for a component target of `Scrollbar`. When you receive an event message from the scrollbar, call the scrollbar's `getValue()` method to determine its setting.

6. A scrollbar can generate `SCROLL_ABSOLUTE`, `SCROLL_LINE_DOWN`, `SCROLL_LINE_UP`, `SCROLL_PAGE_DOWN`, and `SCROLL_PAGE_UP` event messages.

7. To create a custom canvas component, derive a new class from Java's `Canvas` class.

8. To draw a canvas's display, override the class's `paint()` method.

Chapter 22

1. You can use multiple panels in order to organize sets of controls in a display. Each panel can have its own layout manager.

2. Java's five layout managers are `FlowLayout`, `GridLayout`, `BorderLayout`, `CardLayout`, and `GridBagLayout`.

3. The default layout manager is `FlowLayout`.

4. The `FlowLayout` manager positions components one after the other in rows. When a component won't fit on the current row, the layout manager starts the next row.

5. The `GridLayout` constructor's four arguments are the number of columns and rows in the grid, and the horizontal and vertical spacing of the cells in the grid.

6. The component positions you can use with the `BorderLayout` manager are North, South, East, West, and Center.

7. To add a component to an applet using the `BorderLayout` manager, you call a special version of the `add()` method that has the position string (North, South, etc.) and a reference to the component as arguments.

8. You can use `CardLayout` to simulate property sheets because the layout manager enables you to create "cards" that contains groups of controls. Each card can be displayed separately.

9. When using the CardLayout manager, you can switch from one card to another by calling the manager's first(), next(), last(), previous(), or show() method.

10. The constraints determine where in the layout a component will be placed.

11. GridBagConstraints.fill determines whether components will stretch vertically or horizontally to fill their cells.

12. To add a component when using the GridBagLayout manager, you first initialize and set the constraints. You then call add() as you normally would.

Chapter 23

1. To create a frame window, call the Frame class's constructor with the title of the window as the constructor's single argument.

2. To display a frame window, call the window's show() method.

3. To determine whether a frame window is visible, call the isShowing() method, which returns true if the window is currently visible and false otherwise.

4. You use MenuItem objects for regular items in a menu, whereas you use CheckboxMenuItem objects for items that can be checkmarked.

5. To create a custom frame-window class, you extend the Frame class, which itself extends the Window class.

6. To initialize a custom frame window's superclass (Frame), you call the super() method with the window's title string as the method's single argument.

7. You can draw in a frame window in exactly the same way you can draw in an applet's display area, by overriding the class's paint() method.

8. The six steps for creating a menu bar are create the MenuBar object, call setMenuBar(), create Menu objects, add the Menu objects to the MenuBar object, create MenuItem objects, and add the MenuItem objects to the menus.

9. To add components to a frame window, first create and set a layout manager for the window. Then create and add the components to the window as appropriate for the type of layout manager you chose.

10. You respond to selected menu items by watching for their strings in the `action()` method, which you must override in the window's class.

11. A menu separator is just a normal `MenuItem` object that has a single hyphen as its string.

Chapter 24

1. The `Dialog` constructor's three arguments are a reference to the dialog box's parent frame window, the dialog's title, and a `boolean` value indicating whether the dialog is modal.

2. You can display or hide a dialog box by calling the class's `show()` or `hide()` methods.

3. A dialog box must have a frame window as a parent window. The first argument in `Dialog`'s constructor is, in fact, a reference to this frame window.

4. Every dialog box should have at least an OK button that enables the user to dismiss the dialog box.

5. Modal dialog boxes must be dismissed before the user can continue with the program. Modeless dialog boxes do not need to be dismissed in order to continue using the program.

6. In order to add components to a dialog box, you must first create and set a layout manager for the dialog. Then, you create the controls you need and call the dialog box's `add()` method to add the controls to the layout.

Chapter 25

1. The most commonly used mouse event is `MOUSE_DOWN`, which indicates that the user pressed his mouse button.

2. An applet receives more `MOUSE_MOVE` event messages than any other type of mouse event. An applet receives hundreds of these messages as the user moves his mouse over the applet.

3. The six mouse event messages are `MOUSE_DOWN`, `MOUSE_UP`, `MOUSE_MOVE`, `MOUSE_DRAG`, `MOUSE_ENTER`, and `MOUSE_EXIT`.

4. The two most important keyboard events are `KEY_PRESS` and `KEY_RELEASE`.

5. To determine the type of object that generated a event, check the `Event` object's `target` data field.

6. To determine the event type, check the `event` object's `id` field.

7. The coordinates of the mouse event are passed as the second and third arguments of the specific mouse method. If you're overriding `handleEvent()`, you can get the mouse coordinates from the `Event` object's `x` and `y` data fields.

8. If the user single-clicked the mouse, the `Event` object's `clickCount` data field will be 1. With a double-click, `clickCount` will be 2.

9. The two methods associated with the `KEY_PRESS` and `KEY_RELEASE` event messages are `keyDown()` and `keyUp()`, respectively.

10. The `keyDown()` method receives as arguments an `Event` object and an integer holding the key's ASCII code.

11. The `mouseDown()` event receives as arguments an `Event` object and the X and Y coordinates of the mouse click.

12. You use the `SHIFT_MASK` and `CTRL_MASK` constants to determine whether the user had the Shift or Ctrl keys pressed.

13. To handle all events in a single method, you should override the `handleEvent()` method.

Chapter 26

1. Parameterized applets are easier for users who want to add the applets to their own Web pages. The parameters enable them to customize the applet to more closely fit their needs.

2. The `<PARAM>` tag's two parts are `NAME`, which specifies the parameter's name, and `VALUE`, which associates a value with the parameter.

3. To retrieve the value of a parameter, you call the `getParameter()` method, whose single argument is the name of the parameter you want.

4. You specify parameter values in the HTML document, as part of the applet's definition.

5. No. The whole point of parameters is that your applet can change the way it looks and acts without recompiling.

6. You can have as many applet parameters as you need.

7. The `getParameter()` method always returns the given parameter's value as a string. Therefore, you may need to convert the returned parameter to an integer or some other data type.

8. If you fail to define default values for all parameters, your applet may generate errors as it tries to use nonexistent or invalid parameter values.

Chapter 27

1. Java can load only GIF or JPEG files.

2. The two parameters required by many of the image and sound methods are the base URL and the relative location of the file to load.

3. Java recognizes only AU audio files.

4. To display an image after it's loaded, you call the `Graphics` object's `drawImage()` method.

5. No. You can store images and sounds in any directory relative to the base URL.

6. To scale an image, simply supply the `drawImage()` method with the width and height with which you want the image displayed.

7. To determine the normal width and height of an image, call the `Image` object's `getWidth()` and `getHeight()` methods.

8. The document base URL is the location of the HTML document, whereas the code base URL is the location of the applet's CLASS file.

9. You have more control over sounds with an `AudioClip` object because the `AudioClip` class provides the `play()`, `stop()`, and `loop()` methods, whereas the applet can only play an audio file from beginning to end.

Chapter 28

1. The single argument is a string containing the URL from which the URL object should be constructed.

2. An `AppletContext` object represents the application containing the applet. This application is usually a Web browser.

3. To obtain an `AppletContext` object, call the applet's `getAppletContext()` method.

4. To ensure that you have a valid URL object, you handle the exception that may be generated by the URL class.

5. To create an exception handler, you must create `try` and `catch` program blocks.

6. To connect to an URL, call the `AppletContext` object's `showDocument()` method.

7. The `URL` class throws a MalformedURLException exception if the URL's string is syntactically incorrect.

Chapter 29

1. A package is a group of related classes and interfaces.

2. To tell Java that a class uses a particular package, you use the `import` keyword followed by the full name of the package.

3. To add a class or interface to a package, place the `package` keyword at the top of the class's or interface's source code followed by the name of the package to which the class or interface will be added.

4. To tell Java that a class implements a particular interface, add the `implements` keyword to the class's declaration line, followed by the name of the interface.

5. The biggest difference between an interface and a class is that an interface declares, but never implements, its methods. An interface's methods must be defined in any class that implements the interface.

6. Interfaces and classes are similar in that they are declared in almost exactly the same way.

7. The complete name of a package mirrors the folder hierarchy on your hard disk into which the package files must be stored.

Chapter 30

1. You use a `try` block to hold the program statements that may generate the exceptions you want to handle.

2. You use a `catch` block to hold the program statements that should be executed when a particular exception is thrown.

3. You don't have to catch all types of exceptions in your applets, because Java has default handlers for many of them.

4. If you call a method that's declared with a `throw` phrase, you must handle the exception in your program.

5. You can have as many `catch` blocks as you need in order to respond to all appropriate exceptions.

6. To pass an exception on to a calling method, you declare the called method with the `throws` phrase. Java will then pass the exception to the calling function, where it must be handled or thrown again.

7. Java throws exceptions that must be handled in your program, as well as throws system, runtime exceptions that you may or may not decide to handle in your program.

Chapter 31

1. Threads are like small programs within the main program. Just as a multitasking system can run two or more applications simultaneously, so can an applet or application run more than one thread simultaneously.

2. All Java threads must implement the `Runnable` interface, which contains the `run()` method needed to start a thread.

3. To start a thread, you call the thread object's `start()` method.

4. When you start a thread, Java calls the thread object's `run()` method.

5. You'll usually stop your applet's threads in either the `stop()` or `destroy()` method.

6. When you suspend a thread, you put it to sleep so that it remains ready to run when you next need it. When you stop a thread, you kill the thread, meaning that you'll have to create a new thread object when you want to run the thread again.

7. To ensure that all threads get a chance to run, you should call, in any thread that takes a while to run, the `sleep()` or `yield()` method.

8. When retaining a thread's state is not an issue, you can both create and start the thread in the applet's `start()` method.

9. When you want to retain a thread's state while the user switches to and from the Web page containing your applet, you should create the threads in `init()`, start or resume the threads in `start()`, suspend the threads in `stop()`, and stop the threads in `destroy()`.

10. Use the `synchronized` keyword to mark a method or a block of code as a potential area of conflict for threads trying to access the same resources.

11. When a thread enters a synchronized area of code, Java gives the thread the class's monitor object. Until the thread releases the monitor object, no other thread can enter the synchronized area. In this way, a monitor object is much like a key that unlocks a synchronized method or block of code.

Chapter 32

1. The one method that you'll find in every application, but not in an applet, is main(), which is where a Java application's execution begins.

2. To run a Java application, you compile it using javac, and then run the byte-code .CLASS file with the Java interpreter, java.

3. The single parameter received by main() is the application's command-line parameters.

4. The parameters come into the main() method as an array of strings. Each parameter is in one element of the array, so you can access the elements by indexing the array.

5. To convert an applet to an application, you must add the main() method.

6. You must instantiate an object from a class before you can call its methods because a class is just a template for an object, much the same way a blueprint is a template for a manufactured object.

7. To create and display an application's window, you call the Frame class's constructor, and then call the Frame object's resize() and show() methods.

Chapter 33

1. To run more than one applet at a time with Appletviewer, create an HTML document that loads the applets you want to see. Appletviewer will load and run each applet in its own window.

2. Although HotJava is a good example of the type of programs you can create with Java, it hasn't been kept up to date with the Java programming language. For this reason, HotJava cannot run applets created with the latest version of Java. Netscape Navigator 2.0, on the other hand, can load and run these newer applets.

3. A doc-comment block, which is placed at the top of a class or right before a method, provides the information javadoc needs to create useful HTML documentation files.

4. To start a program that's been loaded into the Java debugger, type **run**.

5. To document a method's return value and parameters in a doc-comment, you use the @return and @param doc tags.

6. To start a debugging session with appletviewer, type `appletviewer -debug applet.html`, where `applet.html` is the HTML document that loads the applet.

7. To create hyperlinks in javadoc's HTML documents, add @see doc tags where appropriate in your doc-comment blocks.

8. To start a debugging session with jdb, type `jdb app.class`, where `app.class` is the .CLASS file of the application you want to debug.

9. The javap tool is a disassembler that converts byte-code .CLASS files into a description of the source code.

10. Native methods are methods written in a language other than Java.

11. The javah tool helps you implement native methods by creating the header files you need to gain access to data fields in Java classes from your C source code.

12. To set a breakpoint with the debugger, type `stop at class:line`, where `class:line` is the class's name and breakpoint line number separated by a colon.

Chapter 34

1. You must use the compiler to convert your source-code files into byte-code (.CLASS) files that Java's interpreter can read and run.

2. If you fail to include the .java extension when specifying a source-code file in the javac command line, the compiler will not compile the file and will instead generate an illegal argument error.

3. The options for the javac command line go between the `javac` command and the name of the source-code file.

4. Yes, you can specify multiple options in one command line. Just place them one after the other between the `javac` command and the name of the source-code file.

5. To set a target directory for the compiler's output files, use the `-d` option followed by the name of the directory.

6. The `-g` command-line option instructs the compiler to add debugging information to the byte-code files it generates.

7. The `-nowarn` command-line option instructs the compiler to suppress warning messages as it compiles a file. The compiler will still generate error messages.

8. To instruct the compiler to generate status information as it works, specify the `-verbose` command-line option.

9. Byte-code files are the same format on every computer system. Each type of computer has a Java interpreter specially written for it. The interpreter reads and executes the byte-code files.

Chapter 35

1. Everything will run fine if you leave off the file extension. In fact, the interpreter won't accept the file extension and will generate an error if you include it.

2. Byte-code files have the .CLASS file extension. These are the types of files that the interpreter can load and execute.

3. You can specify verbose output from the interpreter with the `-verbose` or `-v` command options. The second is just a short version of the first.

4. When writing a Java application, you must compile the source code before the interpreter can load and execute the program.

5. To get a list of options supported by the interpreter, type the command `javac -help`.

6. The interpreter is the only tool that can run a Java application. This is because the compiler produces Java byte-code files rather than regular executable files like most other compilers.

7. The `-checksource` (or `-cs`) command-line option instructs the interpreter to recompile any source-code files that have been changed since the last compilation.

Chapter 36

1. The six main Java packages are `lang`, `awt`, `applet`, `io`, `util`, and `net`.

2. The classes needed to write applications and applets that run in a windowed environment are found in the `awt` package.

3. You would use the `Math` class whenever you need to perform sophisticated mathematical calculations that require functions like sin, cosine, tangent, and so on.

4. By creating an object of the `String` class, you can use the class's many methods to manipulate the string.

5. To join (or concatenate) two strings, call the `String` class's `concat()` method.

6. No, you do not instantiate an object from the `Math` class. Because the class's methods are all static, you can call them like this: `Math.Method()`, where `Method` is the name of the method you want to call.

7. The data-type wrapper classes provide methods for manipulating Java's primitive data types, such as `int`, `float`, and `boolean`. To use the classes, you can either call static methods through the class's name (such as, `Integer.parseInt()`) or create an object of the class and call the methods through that object.

8. The `System` class provides two methods—`getProperty()` and `getProperties()`— that enable you to obtain information about the system.

9. The `io` package features many classes that you can use to perform various types of I/O operations using input and output streams. Usually, you create an object of the appropriate class and then manipulate the stream through the object's methods.

Glossary

applet   A small Java program that's embedded in an HTML document.

argument   A value that is sent to a method when the method is called.

array   A list of values of the same type. All values in an array have a common name.

ascent   The height of a character from the baseline to the top of the character.

ASCII   A standard set of values for representing text characters.

assembly language   The lowest-level, and most difficult, language you can use to program a computer.

assignment expression   Assigns a value to a variable.

base class   The class from which another class inherits functionality. In Java, a base class is often called a superclass.

bit   The smallest piece of data a computer understands. A bit can represent only two values, 0 or 1.

bitmap   A graphical image that's usually stored in a file. Windows bitmap files have a BMP extension. However, bitmap is sometimes used as a general term describing any graphical image stored in a file, including GIF and JPEG graphics files.

body of a loop   The program lines that are executed inside the loop.

Boolean   A value that can be either true or false.

Boolean expression   Same as a logical expression. That is, a Boolean expression evaluates to either `true` or `false`.

branching   When an execution of a computer program jumps forward or backward in the program.

breakpoint   A location in a program at which a debugger halts program execution and waits for a command.

byte   In Java, the `byte` data type, which is eight bits long, can hold a range of values from –127 to 128.

byte-code   The format of compiled Java programs. Byte-code files are similar to machine-code files, except that they can be executed on any operating system that has a Java interpreter. Byte-code files have the .class file extension.

canvas   A applet component that can display graphics and text.

casting   Telling Java's compiler that it's okay to convert one type of value to another.

character   A value used in text. For example, the letters A–Z, the digits 0–9 (when not used as mathematical values), spaces, and even tabs and carriage returns are all characters.

class   A template for an object. A class generally contains data fields and methods.

client   A program that relies on services provided by another program called a server.

code base   The directory from which an applet is loaded.

comparison operators   Operators like == (equals) and > (greater than) that compare two expressions, giving a result of `true` or `false`.

concatenate   Adding one text string to the end of another.

conditional branching   When a program jumps to a different part of a program based on a certain condition being met.

configurable applet   An applet that the user can customize by supplying different parameters when writing the applet's tag in an HTML document

constant   A value that never changes throughout the life of a program.

constructor   A special method that initializes an object when the object is created. In the class, a constructor has the same name as the class.

control variable   The variable that a program evaluates to determine whether or not to perform an action. Control variables are used in loops, `switch` statements, and other similar programming constructs.

data field   The data that's encapsulated in an object.

data type   The type of value represented by a constant, variable, or some other program object. Java data types include the integer types `byte`, `short`, `int`, and `long`; the floating-point types `float` and `double`; the character type `char`; and the Boolean type `boolean`.

deadlock   Deadlock occurs when two or more threads are waiting for resources that they can't get. An example would be when one thread must access Method1 before it can release its hold on Method2, but the second thread must access Method2 before it can release its hold on Method1. Because these are mutually exclusive conditions, the threads are deadlocked and cannot run.

decrement   Decrease the value of a variable.

derived class   A class that inherits from a base class.

descent   The height of the area that hold the descending portion of letters, such as the tail on a lowercase "g."

dialog box   A special pop-up window that can present important information to the user or that requests information from the user. A dialog box is an object of Java's `Dialog` class.

doc tags   Special symbols used by the javadoc tool to document Java packages and methods.

document base   The directory from which an HTML document is loaded.

double   In Java, the `double` data type, which is 62 bits in length, can hold values in the range -1.79769313486232 x 10^{308} to 1.79769313486232 x 10^{308}. This type of value in called a double-precision floating-point number.

dynamic linking   When functions called within a program are associated with the program at runtime rather than at compile time.

encapsulation   In object-oriented programming, this is the technique of enclosing data and the functions that act on that data all within an object.

exception   Exceptions inform a running program of serious errors and enable the program to manage the errors without risk of crashing the system.

exponentiation   Using exponents to raise a base number to a power, as in the expression 10^3.

expression   A line of program code that can be reduced to a value or that assigns a value.

field   A data object encapsulated in a class.

float   In Java, the `float` data type, which is thirty-two bits long, can hold values in the range of -3.402823 x 10^{38} to around 3.402823 x 10^{38}. This type of value is called a single-precision floating-point number.

floating point   A value with both whole number (including zero) and fractional parts. For example, the value 25.75 is a floating-point number.

font   A set of characters of the same style.

frame window   A special pop-up window that can be displayed from an applet. A frame window is an object of Java's `Frame` class.

GIF One type of data format for storing graphical images on disk.

GUI Stands for Graphical User Interface. It's pronounced like "gooey."

hard-coded When a literal value, such as 35, is written into a program. Values that are used often in a program are frequently better represented by symbolic constants rather than hard-coded values.

high-level language A computer language that isolates the programmer from the intricate details of programming a computer. Java is a high-level language. Assembly language, on the other hand, is a low-level language.

HTML Hypertext Markup Language. The scripting language used to create Web pages.

identifier A symbol that represents a program object. For example, an identifier for a variable might be `amountOfPurchase`, whereas an identifier for a function might be `CalcAverage`.

increment Increase the value of a variable.

index The same thing as a subscript. Used to identify a specific array element.

infinite loop A loop that cannot stop executing because its conditional expression can never be true.

inheritance In object-oriented programming, the ability of a new class to inherit the data fields and functions of another object.

initialize Set the starting state of a program object. For example, you should initialize variables to a value before you attempt to use them in comparisons and other operations.

int In Java, the `int` data type, which is 32 bits long, can hold values in the range –2,147,483,648 to 2,147,483,647.

integer A whole-number value. For example, the values 23 and –15 are both integers. (Notice that integers can often be negative.)

interface A special type of Java class that declares, but does not implement, a set of behaviors. Interfaces allow Java programs to take advantage of a special type of multiple inheritance.

Internet A huge world-spanning network of computers that can be used by anyone with a suitable connection.

I/O Stands for input/output and refers to a computer's ability to receive data (input) and send data (output).

java The Java interpreter.

javac The Java compiler.

javadoc A tool that automatically creates documentation from Java source-code files.

javah A java tool used to create header files for implementing native methods.

javap   The Java disassembler, which converts .CLASS files into a description of the original source code.

jdb   The Java debugger.

JPEG   Another type of graphical-image file format.

leading   The amount of white space between lines of text.

literals   Values, such as a number or text string, that are written literally as part of program code. The opposite of a literal is a variable.

local applet   An applet that's stored on your computer system, rather than somewhere else on the Internet.

logical expression   Results in a value of true or false.

logical operators   Operators like && (AND) and II (OR) that enable you to create logical expressions that yield `true` or `false` results.

long   In Java, the `long` data type is 64 bits in length and can hold truly immense numbers.

loop   A program construct that enables a program to perform repetitive tasks.

method   A method is a function that's encapsulated as part of an object.

modal dialog box   A dialog box that must be dismissed before the user can continue with the program.

modeless dialog box   A dialog box that allows the user to switch to another window while the dialog box is still on the screen. The opposite of a modal dialog box.

modular programming   Breaking a large program down into a number of functions, each of which performs a specific, well-defined task.

multidimensional array   An array that must be accessed using more than one subscript.

multiple inheritance   When a class simultaneously inherits methods and fields directly from more than one base class simultaneously.

multitasking   Running more than one computer program concurrently.

native methods   Functions that are written in a language other than Java, but are called from within a Java program. C++ is usually used to create native methods.

nesting   When one program block is placed within another program block.

numerical expression   Combines numbers, variables, or constants using operators.

Oak   The original name of the Java programming language.

object-oriented programming   A programming paradigm that treats program elements as objects that have data fields and functions that act on the data fields. The three main characteristics of OOP are encapsulation, inheritance, and polymorphism.

one-dimensional array An array that's set up like a list and requires only one subscript to identify a value contained in the array.

operator precedence Determines the order in which mathematical operations are performed.

order of operations Same as operator precedence.

override In object-oriented programming, this means replacing a method in a base class with a specific version in a derived class.

package A collection of related Java classes.

parameter A value that is passed to an applet or method. In the case of an applet, the parameters are defined in the HTML document, using the <PARAM> tag.

pass by reference When an argument is passed to a function by passing a reference to the actual value. In this case, if you change the argument in the function, you also change the original.

pass by value When an argument is passed into a function by passing a copy of the value. In this case, changing the copy doesn't affect the original value.

pixel The smallest dot that can appear on the screen.

platform-neutral language A programming language that can be used on any computer, regardless of the computer's operating system.

point A unit of measurement of a font's height. One point is equal to 1/72 of an inch.

polymorphism In object-oriented programming, this is the ability for a new object to implement the base functionality of a parent object in a new way.

program flow The order in which a program executes statements.

pseudocode Program code that uses a general type of syntax rather than being written using any specific programming language. Pseudocode is used to describe programming concepts in a non-language-specific way.

radio buttons A group of checkboxes in which only one checkbox can be selected at a time.

remote applet An applet that's stored on another computer and which must be downloaded to your computer over the Internet.

runtime exception An exception thrown by the system in response to unexpected problems when an applet is running. An example would be the exception generated when an applet attempts to perform a division by zero.

scope A variable's scope determines where in a program the variable can be accessed. In Java, a variable's scope is determined by the program block in which it first appears.

self-documenting code   This is program code that is written in such a way that someone reading the code can understand what the program is doing without having to read additional documentation. One of the best ways to create self-documenting code is to use carefully chosen constant, variable, and function names.

server   A computer system that supplies services to another computer called a client.

short   In Java, the `short` data type is sixteen bits in length and can hold values in the range of -32,768 to 32,767.

signature   A function or method's declaration that shows function's return type, name, and arguments.

signed   A value that can be either positive or negative. This is the opposite of unsigned.

single inheritance   When a class inherits methods and fields directly from only one base class.

spaghetti code   Program code that keeps jumping from one place to another in the program without any apparent organization.

standalone application   In the context of the Java language, an application that doesn't need to be embedded in an HTML document. The opposite of an applet.

stream   A flow of data between a source device and a destination device. Commonly, a stream transfers data between a disk file and memory.

structured programming   A style of programming in which the programmer divides his program's source code into logically structured chunks of code.

subclass   A class that inherits functionality from another class called the superclass (or base class).

subscript   A subscript is a number that identifies the element of an array in which a value is stored. A subscript is sometimes called an index.

superclass   A class from which another class inherits functionality. Also called a base class.

symbolic constant   A word that represents a value in a program. For example, the word PI could be used to represent the value 3.14 in a program.

tag   A command in an HTML document that identifies the type of document component you're defining. For example, you load and run an applet with an `<APPLET>` tag.

thread   A single path of execution that is a subprocess of the main process. All applications have at least one thread, which represents the main program. An application can create additional threads to handle multiple tasks concurrently.

top-down programming   A style of programming that divides tasks up into general modules. At the top level of the program are only the general tasks, whereas, as you work your way deeper into the program code, the programming becomes more and more detailed.

two-dimensional array   An array that's set up much like a table, with a specific number of columns and rows.

type cast   Tells Java's compiler that it's okay to convert one type of value to another.

unconditional branching   When program execution jumps to a new part of the program regardless of any conditions.

unicode   A new set of standard values for representing the symbols used in text. The unicode character set is much larger than the ASCII character set and allows for foreign-language symbols.

unsigned   A value that can only be positive. This is the opposite of signed. Unsigned numbers are not used in Java programming.

URL   Stands for Uniform Resource Locator, which is a fancy name for what is really little more than an Internet address.

variable   A value that can change as often as necessary during the execution of a program. Variables are always represented by symbolic names.

Web browser   An application used to access the Internet's World Wide Web.

World Wide Web   The graphical part of the Internet.

IDEs and Tools

by David Medinets

This book has shown you how to create simple Java programs. When you start to create larger programs with multiple classes you will need some tools to help you organize and compile your programming projects.

Fortunately there are IDEs, or Integrated Development Environments. An IDE is a program that lets you group a bunch of files into a project and thereby increase programmer productivity. Even though the Java language is still in its infancy the cutting-edge programmers of the world already have started to create the tools needed to bring Java into the world of corporate America and mainstream programming.

In addition to the basic IDE, a number of tools are becoming available to help you with programming tasks. For example, there is a program available that will let you design a dialog box in Visual Basic and have it automatically converting into Java using the AWT.

This appendix will take a quick look at the IDEs and tools that are available for downloading from the World Wide Web. Please remember that the state-of-the-art in Java development is changing so rapidly that the any details presented here are almost guaranteed to be obsolete when you read them. Therefore, only one IDE will be discussed in depth—to give you an idea what you can expect in an IDE.

There are two good ways to find more information about IDEs or Java tools:

♦ Internet Search Engines   These Web sites let you specify search criteria. Then, the engine will look at its database and display a list of Web pages that contain the text you specified. For example, you could search for "JAVA", "IDE", and "Win95" in order to find Java IDEs that run under the Windows 95 operating system. The JAVA.HTM file on the CD-ROM has links to some good search engines. If you are not already familiar with them, take the time to use them—they are a great resource.

◆ Java UseNet Newsgroup   This newsgroup (comp.lang.java) is where a lot of experienced Java developers hang out, help new programmers, and discuss the future. You will also see a lot of new programs being announced here. It should take no more than 10 minutes a day to monitor the newsgroup.

IDEs

I believe that the greatest advantage of an IDE is that it acts to isolate you from the command-line of a compiler. When a source file needs to be compiled, frequently you will only need to highlight the file and click a compile icon. The Java compiler will be called as a subprocess and all compiler messages will be captured into a window. Typically, you need only click an error message in order to see the offending source code.

You will also see gains in both productivity and organization because you will no longer need to type in the file name each time a compilation is needed. This will help organization—you will no longer be reluctant to give your classes (and hence, the source files) descriptive names because of the amount of typing needed for each compilation.

All IDEs work—more or less—in the same manner:

1. The IDE creates a project file. It is usually a good idea to isolate each project to its own directory. However, this is not a hard-and-fast rule. I frequently place small projects or example programs in the same directory.

2. The IDE changes project settings and preferences to reflect the requirements of the current project. For example, you might want all of your .class files to be placed into the same directory when the compiler creates them. Another example might be setting the command-line options for the compiler.

3. The IDE enables you to add source files to the project. Each project file holds a list of which .java files are used by the project. Some IDEs will also let you associate .htm or .html files with a project. This makes working with applets easier. When creating new source files, most IDEs will ask if you want to add the new file to the project.

4. A built-in editor allows you to change the source code as needed.

5. You can compile code by selecting a menu option or icon. Messages from the compiler are captured to a window.

6. You can run Appletviewer, Web browser, or Interpreter by selecting a menu option or icon. This allows you to test your code.

Note: In order for any IDE to compile your Java source code, Sun's Java Development Kit (JDK) must already be loaded. It will help if you place the BIN directory of the JDK into your path. This can usually be accomplished by added the following line to your AUTOEXEC.BAT file:

```
set PATH=%PATH%;C:\JDK\BIN;
```

Of course, you will need to replace the C:\JDK with the name of the directory in which you installed the JDK.

Let's take a close look at the Diva IDE. Diva will be used for the examples in this chapter for several reasons. The most important being that you can download it from the Net. The file JAVA.HTM on the CD has a link that you can use to download Diva. Once you have created a project in Diva, you will probably be able to adapt to any Java IDE with ease.

Diva

It is important to note that the version of Diva that is described here is an alpha version. The version that you download and use might look different.

Before you can follow along with the examples shown below, you will need to install both Sun's Java Developement Kit (JDK) and Diva. I'll assume that you already know how to install the JDK. Diva is installed by uncompressing the DIVA.ZIP. I'll use C:\DIVA as the base directory for the following examples, but you can use any directory you'd like.

An Example

In this example you will use Diva to create an application that displays a window—called a frame in Java—that responds to the user's clicking the Close button. Follow these steps:

1. Start Diva by double-clicking the DIVA.EXE file in the C:\DIVA directory.

2. Select the File, Create New Project menu option to display the Create New Javaside Project dialog box, as shown in Figure C.1

Figure C.1

The Create New
Project dialog box.

> **Note:** Diva was previously named Javaside. Some of the messages and dialog boxes in this alpha version still show the old name.

3. Enter myFrame into the file name field and click the Save button to close the dialog box. The Diva screen should now look like Figure C.2

Figure C.2

The Diva IDE.

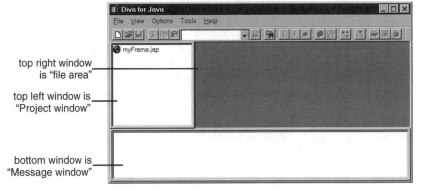

top right window
is "file area"

top left window is
"Project window"

bottom window is
"Message window"

4. Select <u>F</u>ile, <u>N</u>ew File to display the New dialog box. Then select Java in the choice list and click the OK button to close the dialog box. Diva will create another window to hold the contents of the new file as shown in Figure C.3. I added the text "Enter text here" to the new file so that you could easily see which window was added.

Figure C.3

An almost empty
Java File in the
Diva IDE.

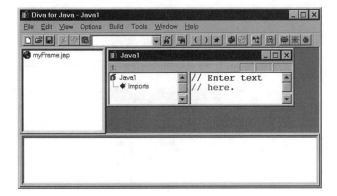

5. Enter Listing C.1 into the editor window.

Listing C.1   MYFRAME.JAVA: A Program To Display a Simple Frame.

```
import java.awt.*;

class myFrame extends Frame {

    public myFrame(String title) {
        super(title);
        resize(200, 350);
        show();
    }

    public boolean handleEvent(Event e) {
        if (e.id == Event.WINDOW_DESTROY) {
            dispose();
            return true;
        } else
            return super.handleEvent(e);
    }

    public static void main(String args[]) {
        myFrame app = new myFrame("myFrame");
    }
}
```

6. Enter Listing D.1 into the editor window. When done, select File, Save and
use myFrame.java as the file name. The file name and the class name must
be identical in order to compile. As you save, Diva will ask if you want to
add the file to the current project. Say yes. The saved file will be added to
the myFrame project, as shown in Figure D.4.

> **Note:** You'll notice that the color of various words change as you enter the listing into the Diva editor. This cool feature is called syntax highlighting.

Figure C.4

myFrame.java is now part of the myFrame project.

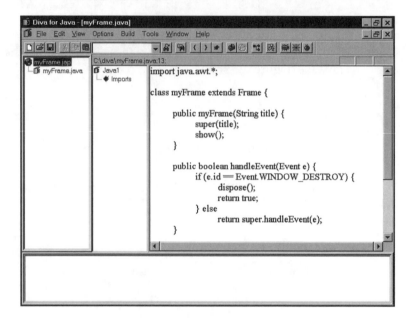

```
import java.awt.*;

class myFrame extends Frame {

        public myFrame(String title) {
                super(title);
                show();
        }

        public boolean handleEvent(Event e) {
                if (e.id == Event.WINDOW_DESTROY) {
                        dispose();
                        return true;
                } else
                        return super.handleEvent(e);
        }
```

7. Select Build, Compile Active Java File. This will start the javac compiler. Any messages produced by the compiler will be displayed in the window along the bottom of the IDE.

8. Right-click the myJava.java file in the project window, and then select Project Settings from the context menu. The Settings for the open project dialog box should appear with the Files tab displayed. If not, select the Files tab.

9. Click myFrame.java entry in the list and then click Mark as "main." This lets Diva know which Java file contains the main procedure. You'll notice that myFrame.java is now marked with a yellow star in the project window. You click OK to close the dialog box.

10. Click Build, Run Java to display the Run java dialog box. Then, click the Run button to actually start the Java interpreter. First, a DOS Window will appear entitled Java Console and then the myFrame application will appear.

11. Click the Close button to exit the myFrame application.

The Java console will continue running after the Java application is finished. Leave it running. It will be used for the next interpreted Java program that you run. After you close Diva, you can click the Close button of the DOS window to close it also. Be warned, however, that it may take a while to close.

The Hierarchy Window

The middle window in the top row of the Diva IDE shows the hierarchy of the open Java file. Figure C.5 shows the Hierarchy window for myFrame.java file.

Figure C.5

The Hierarchy window for myFrame.java.

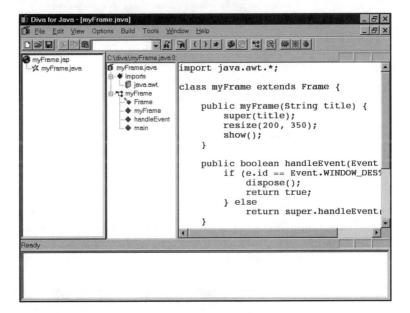

The Hierarchy window is very useful because you can collapse and expand sections of the file so that it's easy to see what a file contains—handy when looking at someone else's code. You'll also see that all of the procedures are shown. You can click any procedure name, and its corresponding code will be displayed.

Other Features

Diva has a primitive user interface design ability. You access this by creating a new file and selecting Diva Design Document as the new file type. However, very little documentation exists for this feature. You might be better off waiting for the beta version.

You can also use Diva to automatically generate skeleton code to handle a variety of common programming situations. Figure C.6 shows part of the list of code snippets that Diva has available. You access this list by selecting Edit, Insert Skeleton Code.

Figure C.6

Diva lets you insert code snippets by selecting from a list.

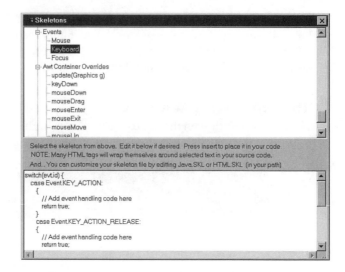

You can also add your own code to the list of snippets so that you can share code with other programmers or simply avoid retyping.

Java+

The Java+ IDE, shown in Figure C.7, seems to be designed to work with applets. You can compile your Java classes and the IDE will display any compiler messages in a separate window. This IDE does not use project files to group source files. Therefore, it is useful for only small development projects.

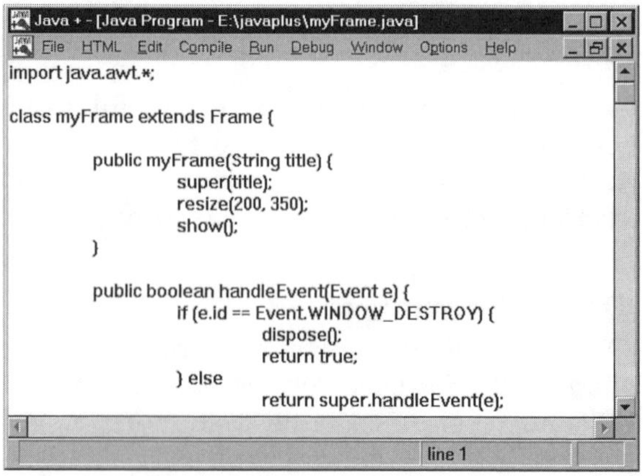

Figure C.7

The myFrame.java file inside the Java+ IDE.

JavaMaker

This is another IDE that automates the compilation process. It does have a nice Print Preview mode so that you can see how your Java code will print. Some people like to try to have only one procedure per page so that the code is more understandable. You can also launch the compiler and Appletviewer from inside the IDE. Figure C.8 shows what the myFrame.java file and the output of the compiler looks like inside the JavaMaker IDE.

Figure C.8

The myFrame.java file inside the JavaMaker IDE.

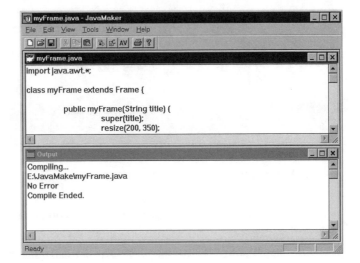

Tools

There are some programs out on the Net that are not directly related to compiling and running Java programs. Some programs will help you create a base program to start your project, and some will help with finding Java documentation.

This section describes a few of the tools that are available.

AppletGen

This extremely useful program is a source code generator. AppletGen creates a skeleton applet customized according to your needs. It has no provisions to help you compile or edit the code; it simply generates a text file. However, this ability might come in very handy. For example, it will free you from needing to remember how to add a menu to a frame. If you specify that your applet needs a menu, the basic menu code will be added to the text file.

When AppletGen is first started, you will see the window shown in Figure C.9.

Figure C.9

The AppletGen program.

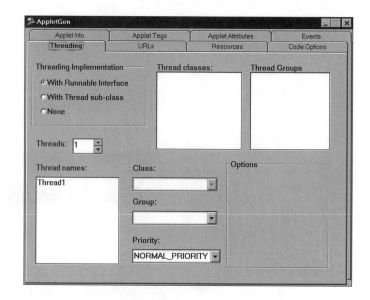

As you can see, AppletGen has eight tabs. Here is a summary of the tabs:

Applet Info—This tab lets you add some documentation to your applet. You can also specify which packages you need to import.

Applet Tab—This tab lets you specify the information that will be added to the <applet> HTML tag when AppletGen generates a HTML file. You can also list out the parameters needed for your applet.

Applet Attributes—This tab has two subtabs. One, called Options, lets you select the font, colors, and determine if menus, frames, or a stand-alone app is used. The other, called Constants, lets you enter a list of constants that your applet will be using.

Events—This tab lets you select which events your applet will respond to. Procedure stubs will be created for each events that you select.

Threading—Shown in Figure D.9 above, this tab will let you specify information about how you would like threads to be used in your application.

URLs—You can indicate which URLs your applet will be using as a resource.

Resources—This is a listing of the AU, GIF, or JPEG files that your applet will be using. If the files are not local, the resource names defined on the URLs tab will be used.

Code Options—This tab lets you determine which types of files AppletGen will create. You can choose to create HTML, Java Code, Documentation, Debug info, and an INI file. The INI file stores all of the choices that you made during the AppletGen session.

Code Window—This tab displays the Source code that AppletGen has created. You can also see the HTML and INI files. Each type of file has its own subtab. You need to click the button near the file name (top left of the tab) in order to save the files.

The AppletGen program is great if you are just learning Java. By changing the options on the various tabs and then looking at the source code that is generated, you will be able to see a lot of different situations. In addition, you can always recreate any given situation if you need a base of code to start developing from.

> **Note:** You can download this application—in beta form—from http://ugWeb.cs.ualberta.ca/~nelson/AppletGen/AppletGen1.html.

VbToJava

This application will let you design using Visual Basic and then convert the design into Java code. It has only one screen, shown in Figure C.10, which lets you specify which FRM file to convert. You will also need to specify the Java class name and .java file to create.

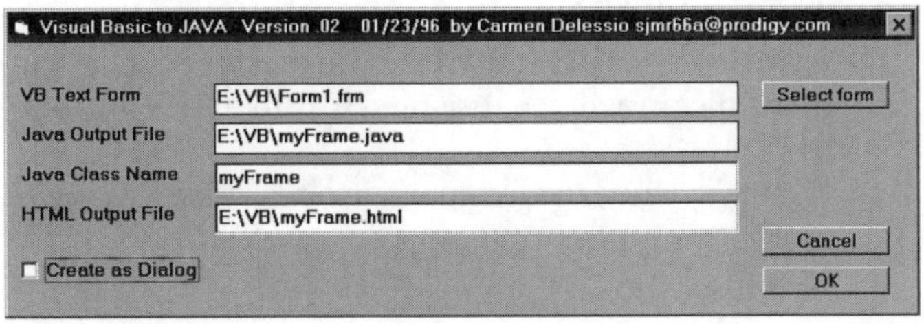

Figure C.10

The Visual Basic to Java Convertor.

PortaFilter

The Java documentation is a little difficult to search because it is in HTML format. Bill Bercik has converted the documentation into the Windows Help format and made the files available for you to download. You can download the 1.4M file by looking at this URL:

```
http://www.dippybird.com/download.html
```

The following documents have been converted into the Windows Help format:

Java× Language Specification

Java× White Paper

Java× API

Java× Man Pages

Java× Virtual Machine Specification

Java× FAQ's

Java× Tips and Tricks

Java× Resource Guide

The help file was last updated on March 3, 1996, so it is pretty up-to-date.

Summary

This has been a small sampling of the IDEs and tools available to you for download-ing from the net. By monitoring the comp.lang.java newsgroup, or searching the Alta Vista for Java + IDE, you can easily find others. Take a few moments to look at each tool to see if it will be useful to you. Every programmer uses a different set of utilities and it takes effort to find the set that is right for you.

One important determinate of which tools to use is the scope of your project. If you are just learning Java, your tools should be simple and easy to learn. If you are an accomplished programmer, using a complicated tool with many options might make more sense. Similarly, if you are developing a large program, a tool that tracks many files in a project-oriented way like Diva will be more useful than Java+, which does not.

Finally, the Java language itself is still evolving. It will change and so will the tools that support it. Java has a bright future ahead. Don't be blinded by it and don't wait for the perfect tool. Start coding today!

Index

CD-ROM License Agreement

Before using any of the software on this disc, you need to install the software you plan to use. If you have problems with this CD-ROM, please contact Macmillan Technical Support at (317) 581-3833. We can be reached by e-mail at support@mcp.com or by CompuServe at **GO QUEBOOKS**.

CD-ROM Instructions

The CD-ROM has an HTML interface to point you to the directories containing the software and sample code from the book. Start your favorite Web browser and open the file JBE-CD/JBEINDEX.HTM from the CD-ROM.

Read This Before Opening Software

By opening this package, you are agreeing to be bound by the following: